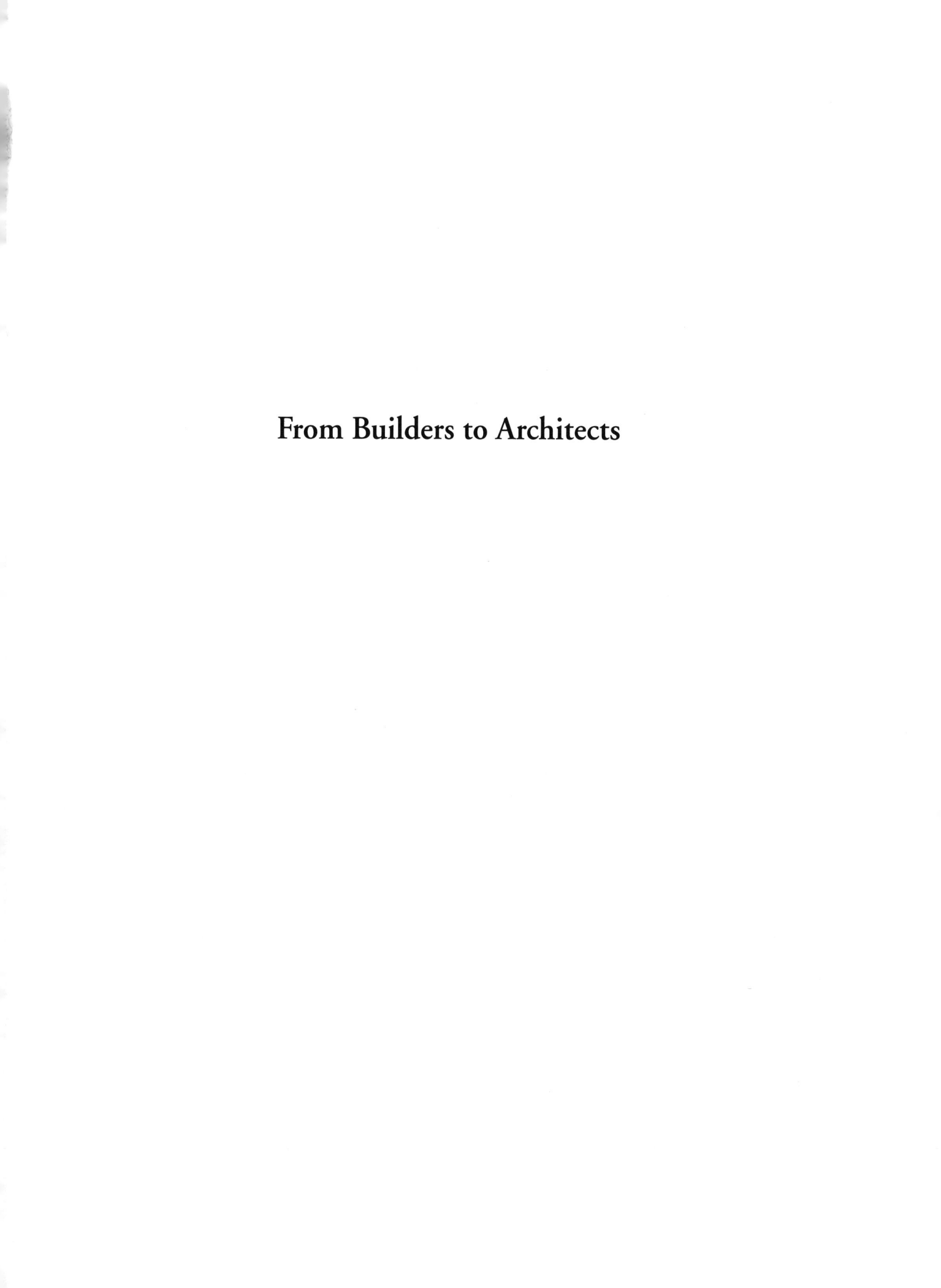

From Builders to Architects

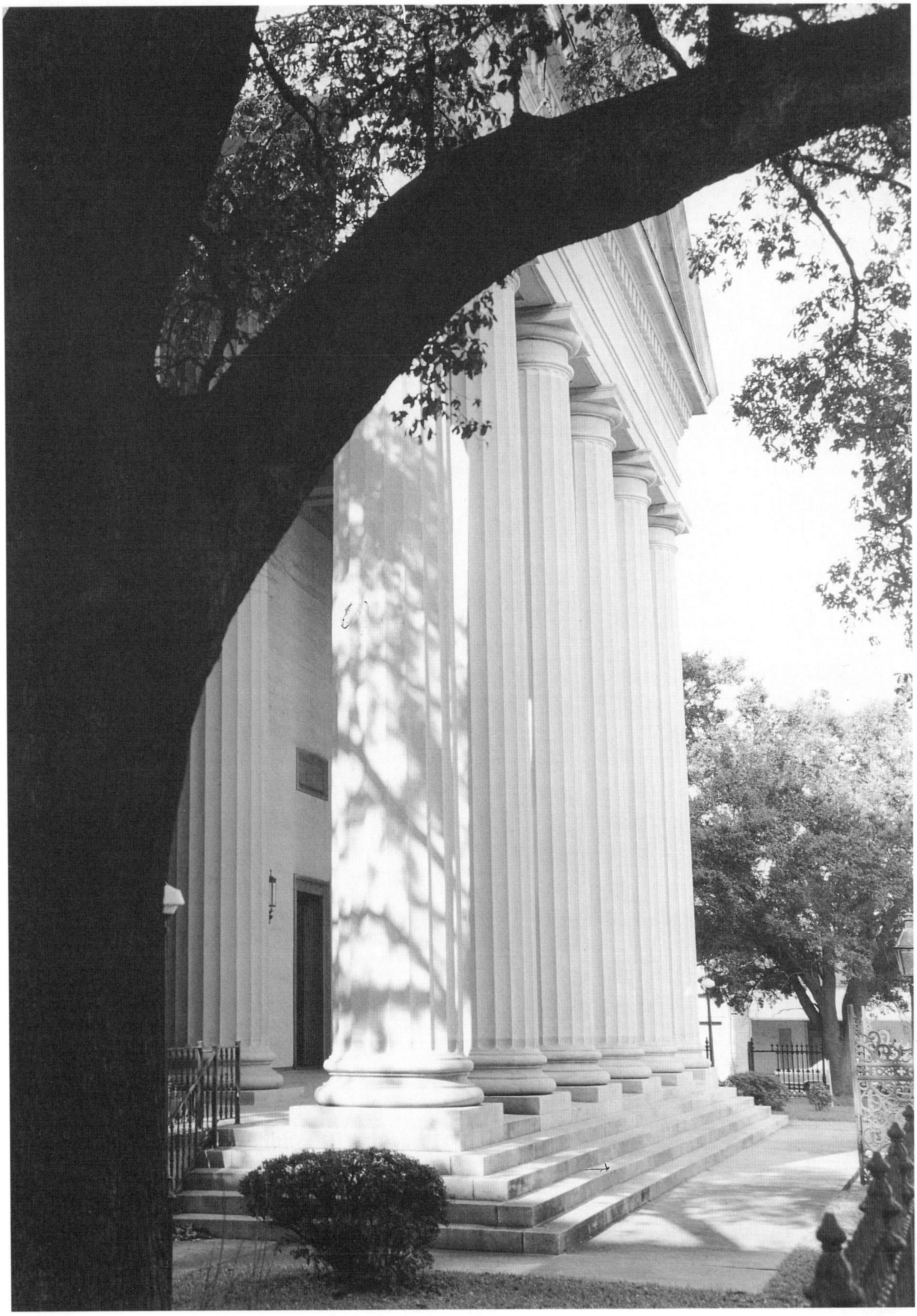

FROM BUILDERS TO ARCHITECTS

THE HOBART–HUTCHISSON SIX

By Elizabeth Barrett Gould

Introduction by Robert Gamble
Photographs by Paul Rossa Thompson

Devereaux Bemis, Consulting Editor

Black Belt Press
Montgomery

Black Belt Press
P.O. Box 551
Montgomery, Alabama 36101

Copyright © 1997 by Elizabeth Barrett Gould.
Photographs © 1997 by Paul R. Thompson.

Introduction © 1997 by Robert C. Gamble.
All rights reserved under International and Pan-American Copyright Conventions.
Published in the United States by Black Belt Press, an imprint of
Black Belt Publishers, L.L.C., Montgomery, Alabama.

Library of Congress Cataloging-in-Publication Data

Gould, Elizabeth Barrett, 1906-
From builders to architects : the Hobart-Hutchisson six / by
Elizabeth Barrett Gould : photographs by Paul Rossa Thompson.
p. cm.
Includes bibliographical references and index.
ISBN 1-881320-61-8 (hardcover)
1. Hobart, Peter House, 1776-1828. 2. Hutchisson family.
3. Architects—Alabama—Biography.
4. Architecture—Alabama—Mobile.
5. Mobile (Ala.)—Buildings, structures, etc. I. Title.
NA737.H53G68 1995
720'.92'276122—dc20.   95-39161
CIP

Editor and Proofreader: Devereaux Bemis

Printed in the United States of America

The Black Belt, defined by its dark, rich soil, stretches across central
Alabama. It was the heart of the cotton belt. It was and is a place of great
beauty, of extreme wealth and grinding poverty, of pain and joy. Here we take
our stand, listening to the past, looking to the future.

FRONTISPIECE, PLATE I
Portico of the Cathedral of the Immaculate Conception, 4 South Claiborne Street. The Cathedral, without the portico, was designed and built by Claude Beroujon between the years 1834 and 1849. The portico was designed by the architect, James H. Hutchisson, who supervised the construction from 1872 until his death in 1887. The portico was finished in 1890 under the direction of James F. Hutchisson II, who added the towers by 1895.

To A. BAILEY duMONT

*who made possible the acquisition of materials that created
the Hutchisson Research Library at the University of South Alabama*

Contents

Acknowledgments	ix
Preface	xi
Introduction	xii
Abbreviations	xiv
I Peter House Hobart (1776–1828)	3
II James Flandin Hutchisson I (1806-1856)	22
III James Henry Hutchisson (1830–1887)	39
IV James Flandin Hutchisson II (1856-1926)	85
V Clarence Lindon Hutchisson, Sr. (1872-1953)	103
VI Clarence L. Hutchisson, Jr. (1902-1993)	195
Appendix	217
Notes to the Text	234
Architectural Terms	241
Bibliography and Sources	245
Sources of Illustrations	248
Index	250
About the Author	258

Acknowledgments

WITHOUT the help of associates and friends who assisted in carrying out the initial research on the Hobart-Hutchisson family, this publication would not have been possible. I am indebted to the Mobile Historic Development Commission for sponsoring the initial project by which I was able to make a street-by-street survey of the standing buildings in Mobile that had been designed and built by this remarkable family. Assisting in this survey were Judy Allen-Leventhal and the staff of the Mobile Historic Development Commission. Special thanks to Mr. Clarence L. Hutchisson, Jr., with whose memory of family events, his identification of the buildings, and his release of the family archival material, this account was made possible; to Jay Higginbotham, city archivist and Richard Sommerville, formerly on his staff; to George Schroeter of the Special Collections Division of the Mobile Public Library; to Sister Anita of the Convent of the Visitation; to Mrs. E. Rehm, archivist for the Cathedral of the Immaculate Conception; to Michael Thomason and Elisa Baldwin of the University of South Alabama Archives; to Burney Crooks of Pensacola, Florida, who made available his extensive information on the military history of the Hutchisson family; and to the Mobile County Probate Court for allowing me access to the original Miscellaneous Books in the County Archives.

I am indebted to those owners who had the original drawings of their buildings and allowed them to be reproduced; to Bruce Knodel, AIA; Mr. and Mrs. Dent Boykin; V.B. and M.H. Blankenship; Mrs. Edwin Trigg; Dr. and Mrs. Edwin Mazey; Mr. and Mrs. Dennis Doan; The Dauphin Street Synagogue; Mr. and Mrs. Gordon Moulton and the Historic Mobile Preservation Society. Last and by no means least, is my appreciation to Devereaux Bemis, for his astute editing help in bringing this manuscript to publication, and to my daughter Betsey Hearne for her advice, encouragement, editing suggestions, and support throughout the preparation of this manuscript.

Sharing equally in this production is the photographic work of Paul R. Thompson of Mobile, who patiently took many views of the buildings erected by the Hutchissons, both in Mobile and in other locations in Alabama and Mississippi. All photographs, unless stated otherwise, are by Paul R. Thompson. All drawings, unless stated otherwise, are from the Family Archives.

Preface

HISTORY records the names of the many architects who played important roles in the development of American architecture. Well recognized are the masters of the eighteenth century, such as William Buckland of Annapolis and Richard Bundy of Newport, the first American architect Peter Harrison of Boston and the leaders of the Federal style, Hobart, Thornton and Latrobe. Yet, the builder-architects who constructed so many of the buildings in our cities, towns, and rural areas have not been remembered. These talented men learned the craft of construction by apprenticeship. They acquired their knowledge of composition by a diligent study of such publications as those by Asher Benjamin, John Haviland, Owen Biddle and Calvert Vaux. Added to this was their knowledge of local building materials, demands of climate, and vernacular traditions. They created buildings with such originality that even today, the difference in the ambience of a New England town from one in the deep South is easily seen.

Mobile, Alabama, is justly famous for its Barton Academy and Government Street Presbyterian Church, both by Gallier and Dakin. What is not known is the influence that one builder-architect family had on the architectural development of the city and the Gulf Coast area. From 1797 to 1967 a member of the Hobart-Hutchisson family worked in Mobile. From father to son, brother to brother, all put their stamp upon the city's architecture as it changed from decade to decade. The city today is not what is was when Peter Hobart arrived in 1797, nor will it be the same in the twenty-first century as it was when the last family member retired in 1967. But within their time span, the Hobart-Hutchisson Six played an important role, giving a visual record of the transformation in architectural styles and construction methods that appear within one community. In doing so, they not only reflected national trends but put their own interpretation on them.

Records of the buildings have survived in contracts, newspaper accounts, county and city records, and in the family archives in which many drawings of the last two Hutchissons are preserved. The author drew upon all of these sources [see Appendix] in compiling this history. Please note that the early contracts quoted in this book replicate the original spelling, punctuation and capitalization.

ONE THOUSAND and eighty-eight of the Hobart–Hutchisson buildings have been documented, of which 192 still stand. They can be found within the inner city and in each of the western suburbs as Mobile expanded during the years, from Spanish times to the present. Their work extended to other states and as far south as Panama. The buildings include residential, religious, government and civic structures. It is unique that one family of builder-architects can be traced within the history of a single city for such a long period of time.

Introduction

THE story of American architecture is usually told in terms of "hero" figures — the Frank Lloyd Wrights and H. H. Richardsons who blazed the trail for others in the building profession and established new visions of architectural taste and style. Only recently, in fact, have scholars begun to take a serious look at the contributions of that vast number of lesser-known architects who, after all, are responsible for most of the structures in and among which we live our everyday lives, and which we alternately revere and revile.

If these architects were, in general, followers rather than trend-setters and imitators rather than innovators, they are the ones who translated national building trends into the vocabulary of Main Street. As a new nation fanned westward from the Atlantic coast during the late 18th and 19th centuries, the countless courthouses and churches, commercial buildings and residences they designed symbolized to their contemporaries the inexhorable advance of "civilization."

The following study is a remarkable look at the architectural output of one extended family of such builder-architects in one American city: Mobile, Alabama. For over a hundred and seventy years, from 1798 until 1969, successive generations of the Hobart-Hutchisson clan designed scores of private homes, business houses, schools, religious edifices, and public buildings in Mobile and other locales throughout the Gulf region. Rarely does surviving documentation permit scrutiny of even a single generation's work. More rarely still is there an opportunity to trace the careers of an interconnected group of builders in one place, across the span of nearly two centuries.

Elizabeth Barrett Gould discovered the existence of the Hobart–Hutchisson papers — the raw material for this account — in the course of researching her monumental study of early Mobile architecture, *From Fort to Port,* published in 1988. Piecing together the story of the "Hobart–Hutchisson Six," as she dubs them, and their architectural output has been a labor of love, combining details from manuscript letters, diaries, old contracts, and newspapers with a painstaking assemblage of dozens of related illustrations.

Beginning with the earliest member of the clan, the shadowy Peter Hobart who made his way from Vermont to Spanish Mobile during the twilight of the colonial era, the story then picks up with the clan's co-founder, James Flandin Hutchisson, whose son married the granddaughter of Peter Hobart. Hutchisson arrived in Mobile during the building boom of the 1830s and became the first of four generations of Hutchissons to help sculpt Mobile's cityscape according to their particular architectural vision. During the early years of the American period, Peter Hobart produced what was probably Alabama's first fullbown neoclassical public building in his design for the 1825 Mobile County courthouse. Sixty-five years later Peter's great-grandson, James Flandin Hutchisson II, oversaw the completion of the city's mammoth Roman Catholic cathedral, with its monumental Doric portico and cupolaed towers. Between times there were cottages and suburban villas, warehouses and stores, a Reconstruction-era firestation and a foundry. Their stylistic frostings ranged from a muted Italianate to sober Gothic Revival to flamboyant Queen Anne — all dutifully reflecting passing national taste. Later, with the dawning automobile age, the Hutchissons added service stations to their repertoire — at least one such design exotically claiming to be "Chinese." And on the eve of World War II, C. L. Hutchisson, Jr., the last of the line, garnered the commission for Mobile's first municipal airport hangar. He also adroitly turned out single- and multifamily residential designs for the Federal Housing Administration during the New Deal era. And following the war, he graced Mobile's expanding suburbs with the classically flavored house designs for which conservative Mobilians have always shown a special affection.

In some respects, Betty Gould's story of the Hobart–Hutchisson clan is a study in microcosm of architecture and the building trade in America: a story not merely of shifting styles, but also of evolving architectural practice and training, and of technological advances as they were applied at the local level. If we come away perhaps wishing to know more about the "human" side of an unusual family of builders, we cannot help but be impressed by its sheer continuity and by the array of projects with which it was involved. Focusing on each of the "Six" in turn, Betty Gould details their work against the backdrop of Mobile's shifting economic, social and political fortunes.

Betty Gould was trained at Oberlin, Harvard, and Radcliffe, and was founder of the department of art history at the University of South Alabama. She has devoted more than twenty-five years to studying the architectural evolution of Mobile. Her diligent investigation of previously untapped municipal archives, both for the colonial and post-colonial periods, has illuminated the city's building history as never before. My most vivid impression of my first encounter with Betty in the 1970s was her infectious if academically tempered enthusiasm for her topic. I was pleased and honored when she contacted me several years later about the possibility of preparing an introduction for her proposed book on the Hobart-Hutchisson family. That Betty should conclude an illustrious career by revealing to us yet another aspect of the building history of an American city to which she has committed such energy and talent is fitting indeed. Her legacy is unique, and will be lasting.

ROBERT GAMBLE

Senior Architectural Historian
Alabama Historical Commission
Montgomery

Abbreviations

AIA	American Institute of Architects
ASP	American State Papers
CD	City of Mobile Directories
CPC	County Probate Court
DB	Deed Books
HABS	Historic American Building Survey
HMPS	Historic Mobile Preservation Society
LC	Library of Congress
MCPC	Mobile City Planning Commission
MHDC	Mobile Historic Development Commission
Misc. Bk.	Miscellaneous Books, Probate Court, Mobile County
MPL(SC)	Mobile Public Library, Special Collections Division
MR	*Mobile Register* (newspaper) For most of the nineteenth and early twentieth century it was known as the *Mobile Commercial Register* (*MCR*).
UAP	University of Alabama Press
USAA	University of South Alabama Archives
USTP	United States Territorial Papers

From Builders to Architects

Figure 1: Saucier Geneology of Ancestors of the Hobart-Hutchisson Family of Builders

Showing their relationship by the marriage of Peter Hobart's granddaughter
to James H. Hutchisson, the son of James F. Hutchisson I.

Jean Baptiste Saucier b. 1674, Dumay, Sillery, Quebec d. 1715 or 1716	*m. Sept. 4, 1704* *Mobile (6 children)* ▼	Marie Gabrielle Savary (Pelican Girl) b. Jan. 28, 1684, St. Denis, France d. c1725, New Orleans
Henri Saucier (2nd child) b. cAug. 1, 1706 d. 1761 or 1762	*m. Nov. 8, 1732* *Fort Condé (10 children)* ▼	Barbe La Croix (n. of Quebec) b. c1708?[1] d. 1778
Christian (Carlos) Saucier[2] b. April 25, 1745, New Orleans d. Nov. 24, 1800	*m. April 22, 1788* *Mobile (3 children)* ▼	Marguerite Baudin b. Feb. 1, 1763, Mobile d. ?
*Euphrosine Parmelia Saucier b. May 21, 1789, Mobile d. May 10, 1849, Mobile	*m. Oct. 29, 1806* *Mobile (9 children)* ▼	*Peter House Hobart b. Nov. 1776, Peachem, Vt. d. July 23, 1828, Bayou Serra
Euphrosine Parmelia Hobart b. Sept. 25, 1808, Baldwin Co. d. Dec. 25, 1888, Mobile	*m. Oct. 29, 1826* *(6 children)* ▼	Joseph Steele b. Oct. 8, 1803, Salem, Mass. d. July 18, 1839, Mobile
Martha Matilda Steele b. Sept. 25, 1834, Mobile d. Nov. 22, 1913, Mobile	*m. Jan. 31, 1855* *Mobile (8 children)* ▼	***James Henry Hutchisson** b. April 9, 1830, Hempsted, L.I. d. Aug. 26, 1887, Mobile

Hutchisson Family Geneology

James Flandin Hutchisson b. 1806, Hempsted, Long Island d. Dec. 26, 1856, Mobile	*m. 3 times[4]* *(1 child, by first wife)* ▼	Miss Brewster[3] b. Hempsted, Long Island d. Hempsted, L.I.
*James Henry Hutchisson b. April 9, 1830, Hempsted, L.I. d. Aug 26, 1887, Mobile	*m. Jan. 31, 1855* *Mobile (8 children)* ▼	Martha Matilda Steele b. Sept. 25, 1834, Mobile d. Nov. 22, 1913, Mobile
James Flandin, 2nd (eldest son) b. July 21, 1856, Mobile d. June 28, 1926, Chicago	Clarence Lindon Hutchisson (youngest son) b. Nov. 5, 1872, St. Elmo d. Jan. 4, 1953, Mobile	Henriette Elkin Homer *m April 7, 1901* *(2 children)*
		▼ Clarence L. Hutchisson, Jr. b. Feb. 19, 1902, Meridian, Miss. retired 1965, the last architect of the line d. Dec. 18, 1993

*Joining of family lines
[1]Not baptized until April 25, 1745, New Orleans
[2]In the geneology, called Christian; in the Catholic records, called Carlos, Fun. Rec. p10
[3]mother of James Henry Hutchisson
[4]married twice in Mobile: Ann Spenser, Sept. 19, 1836; d. 1837, no children: Amelia Graham, m. May 15, 1838, no children

Chapter 1

Peter House Hobart

(1776–1828)

THE cofounder of the Hobart-Hutchisson line of nineteenth and twentieth century builder-architects was Peter House Hobart (figure 1). As a young man of twenty-one, he left Peacham, Vermont, and traveled south to the Spanish-held Gulf Coast. In 1797, this journey would have been a hazardous one: long, uncomfortable and even dangerous. Not only were the modes of travel difficult, but in upper and central Alabama, the Creek Indians were hostile to the Americans.

The Gulf Coast to which Peter came had a very different culture from that of the Atlantic seaboard states (figure 2). At the time of Hobart's arrival, Spain controlled a band of land along the Gulf Coast extending from the Mississippi River east to the western border of Georgia. Known as West Florida, the area contained 1,658,880 acres, averaging about forty miles in width and effectively closing off all United States access to the Gulf waters. The long-disputed boundary between Spanish and United States lands was finally settled about the time that Peter took up his residency in Mobile. In 1798 Andrew Ellicott began his historic survey to establish the agreed upon boundary line at the 31st degree latitude.[1] He did not complete the survey until 1803. One of the markers on this line can still be seen about twenty-four miles north of Mobile. On the side facing north is the inscription, "U.S. Lat. 31, 1797." On the south side the inscription reads, "Dominios de S. M. Carlos IV, Lat. 31, 1797." The section that later became the coast of Alabama would include all of Baldwin County and most of Mobile County, while that of Mississippi would include George, Harrison, Hancock, Pearl River, Stone and Jackson counties.

At the time of Peter's arrival in 1797, the area was still largely uninhabited outside of the military centers. There were two main forts, Fort Condé at Mobile and the Bateria de San Antonio at Pensacola.[2] A small settlement was located by each of these forts. Pensacola also served as the capital of the Spanish colony. South of Pensacola was the post of San Marcos, located at the western terminus of a rough road connecting the Gulf Coast with St. Augustine on the Eastern seaboard. At the western end of West Florida near the Mississippi River was the settlement of Baton Rouge. Between these centers

FIGURE 2

Map of the Claims and Cessions of the Original 13 States, 1776–1802. The map shows the latitude line that separated the possessions of the United States from those of Spain. The boundary line was surveyed by Andrew Ellicott between 1798 and 1803. Peter Hobart arrived in Spanish-held Mobile in 1797.

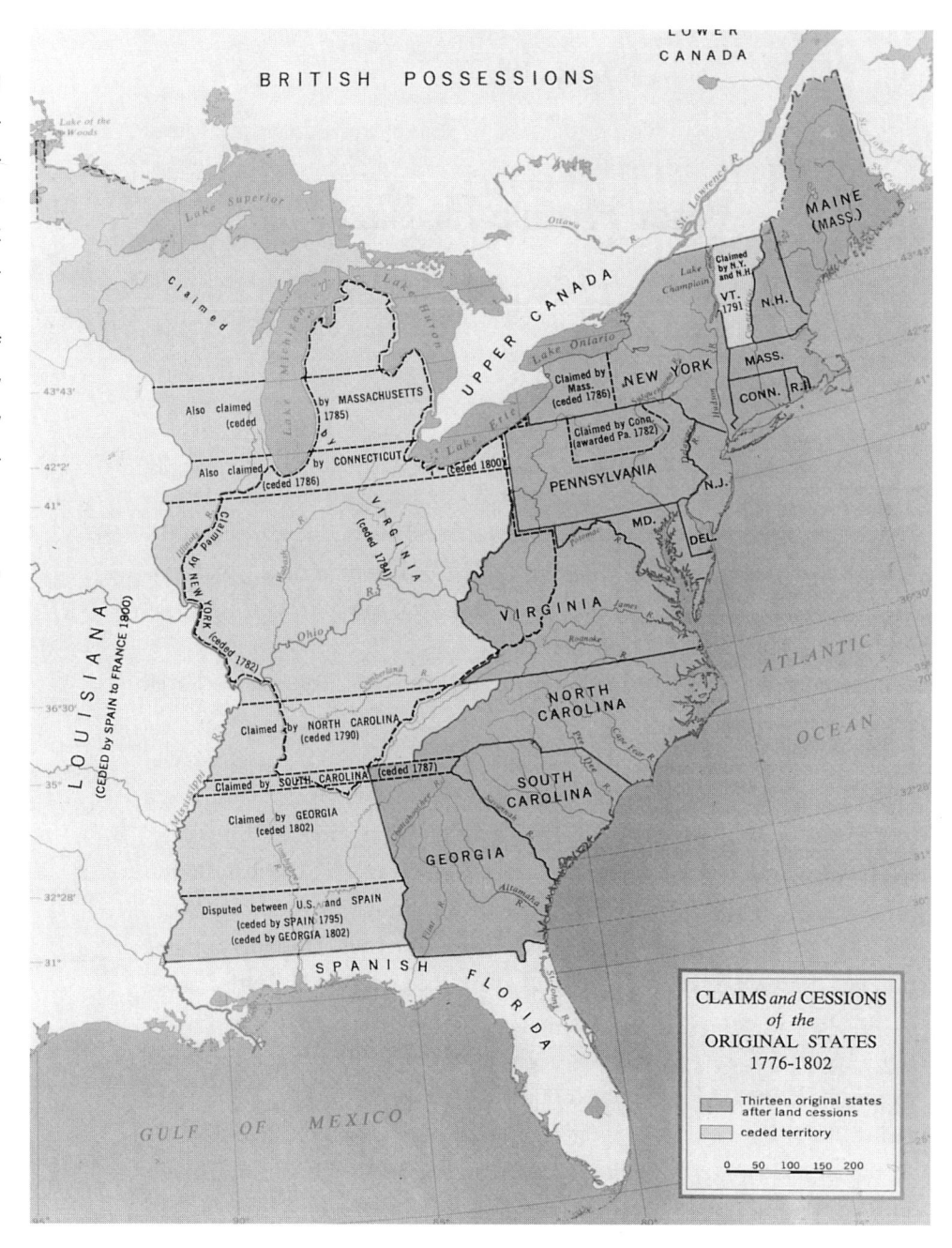

extended vast pine forests, swamps with cypress trees, rivers and bayous. Indian tribes claimed the uninhabited areas as their hunting grounds — the Choctaws in southern Mississippi and the Creeks in Alabama.

When the Spanish first took the territory from the English in 1780, they encouraged emigration into the settlements by offering free land, religious tolerance and some trade opportunities free from royal control. This policy changed after 1803 because too many Americans began pushing into their territory and upsetting the status quo. Americans were not accustomed to being under the control of a military form of government.[3] The Spanish commander of the fort was the dominant authority. He controlled all military

4 *From Builders to Architects: The Hobart–Hutchisson Six*

matters; he appointed the judges of civil court; and he, himself, served as the chief judge. He appointed all the notaries and custodians of the records and deeds.[4] But with the commercial concession made to individuals, trade with the Indians increased and a few Americans carried on successful businesses. John Forbes, whose company succeeded the Panton and Leslie Company of Pensacola and the Panton Company of Mobile, not only owned considerable business property, he was the first, in 1802, to build a wharf that was not owned by the Crown. James Mather, an Englishman, had two vessels that carried on Indian trade across the Atlantic, and the Panton and Leslie Company in Pensacola had fifteen such seagoing schooners at work.[5]

In addition to the Indian trade, an embryonic lumber business began. By 1802 a few sawmills had been established. One was the Durand Mill west of the Mandeville tract, southwest of Mobile.[6] Another was one built by Peter Hobart on Bayou Sara, north of town. The mill was located near the present town of Saraland. Nothing remains of the mill nor of Peter's home, but the foundations for the mill dam can still be seen off Highway 43 near Saraland. Old residents have told of finding the large stones that once served as the foundation for the mill.[7]

Peter owned other property. In 1797, his first year in Mobile, he purchased a lot from Gabriel Tixerrant and in 1798 a lot from Thomas Powell.[8] It is the dating of these properties that establishes the time of Peter's arrival (Appendix 1). Before his death he would have extensive properties including a section of Spring Hill.

In 1804 Peter Hobart married Martha Steele, a French descendent of Jean Baptiste Saucier, one of the first Canadians to settle on the Gulf Coast during the French times. It was through the family line of Jean Saucier that the talent for construction may have been passed to the Hutchisson family of builder-architects. While it is not known if Jean Baptiste was an engineer as well as a soldier, a later member of his family, François Saucier, was the engineer in charge of the strengthening and proposed enlargement of Fort Condé in the 1750s. Samuel Wilson, Jr., of New Orleans, referred to a François Saucier in his chapter, "Colonial Fortifications and Military Architecture in the Mississippi Valley," in *The French in the Mississippi Valley*, edited by John F. McDermott. To quote:

> Deverges designed the new buildings for Fort Tombeche in Alabama in 1751 and 1759, and the fort at Mobile was strengthened under the supervision of François Saucier, a surveyor and draftsman who had been in the colony since 1730 and who was assigned to the engineers in 1735.

Jean Saucier, who married Marie Gabrielle Savary from St. Denis, France, came from Dumay, Sillery, Quebec. He was recruited by Pierre Le Moyne d'Iberville and brought to Fort Maurapas at Biloxi on the Gulf Coast. When that fort closed in 1702, Saucier was transferred to Fort Louis de la Louisiane, at Twenty-seven Mile Bluff, north of the present site of Mobile. One year later he married Marie Gabrielle.[9] In 1711 Fort Louis de la Louisiane was abandoned and the French military personnel moved to the present site of Mobile to establish Fort Louis de la Mobile, later rebuilt as the brick Fort Condé. Thus the Saucier family began a residency in Mobile that continued uninterrupted throughout the eighteenth century. With this history one could trace the building skills of the Hobart-Hutchisson line back, through marriage, to the early French Period (1702-1763).

The plan of Mobile in 1809, when Peter had been there for twelve years, was still the same grid plan that had been established by the French (figure 3). The small community was still bounded by the Fort to the south, forests and swamps to the west, and bayous and swamps to the north. The shoreline was not the same as later developed. There were no Water or Commerce Streets. Where they were later located was a lagoon that extended from the shore to a shell bank that ran parallel to the land. In 1804, realizing that access to the navigable river was necessary to improve commerce, permission was given to Anthony Espejo to fill in the lagoon adjacent to his bakery. This gave him land to grow his grain for flour and lent him access to the river boats. The infilling of this lagoon would become an essential development when the area became part of the United States.

The Spanish also allowed construction in 1802 of the first wharf established for private investment. John Forbes's wharf was the first of many that would follow during the 1820 decade of early statehood.[10] In spite of the increase in the Indian trade, the populations of Mobile remained small. Josiah

FIGURE 3

The Map of Spanish Mobile of 1809. This plan shows the extent of Mobile as it existed during the early years of Hobart's residency. The blocks extend from about the present Government Street on the south to St. Louis Street on the north, Royal Street on the east to Joachim on the west.

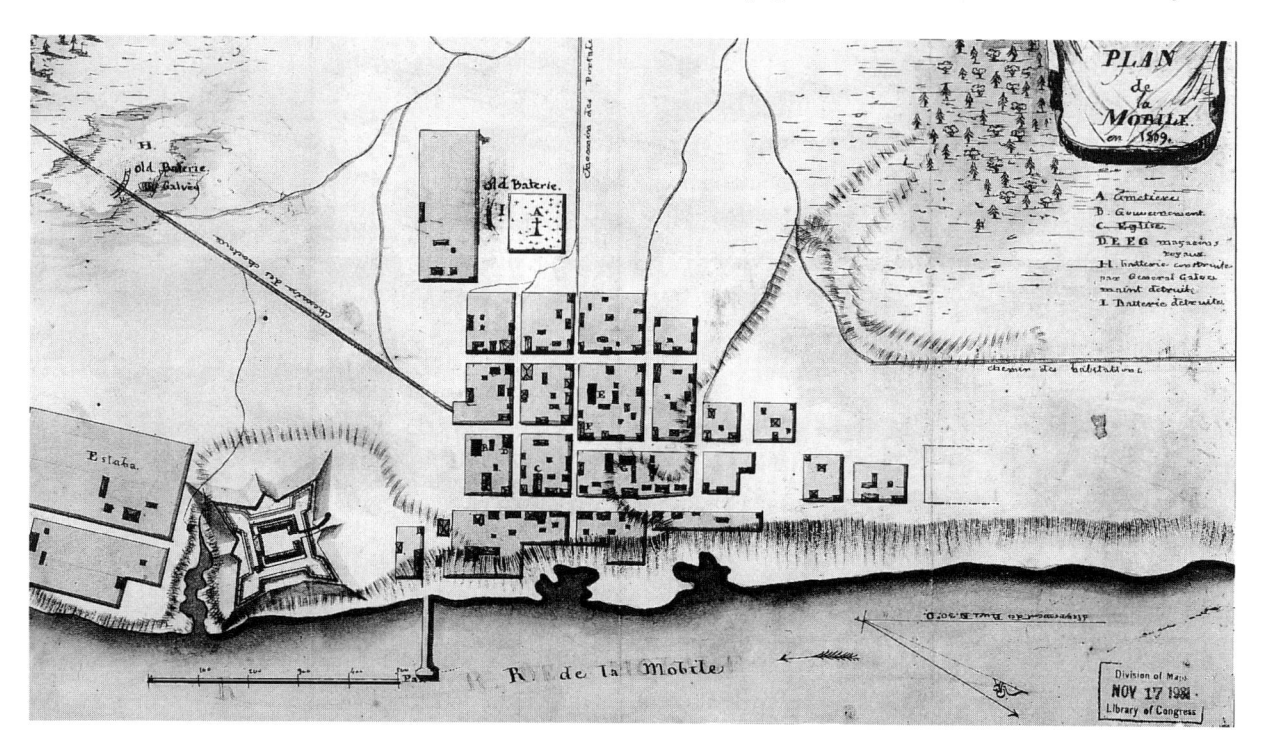

Blakely, a resident during Spanish times, wrote a letter to his niece on February 23, 1812, telling her that there were only "ninety homes, all wood and but one story high."[11] The brief description of Miguel Eslava's home verifies that the Creole cottage derived from the early French houses was still the most common form of Spanish homes. It was a frame dwelling of three rooms side-by-side, raised about five feet above ground level and surrounded by galleries.[12] This vernacular style of house was well established serving the 810 residents made up of Spanish, French, English, Blacks, Indians and a few Americans.

No style of folk housing was better adapted to the semitropical Gulf Coast than the Creole cottage. The plan with its single row of two or three rooms made openings possible on both the front and rear walls, providing for cross-ventilation that allowed any Gulf breeze to cool the rooms. The surrounding galleries under their wide overhanging roofs provided shade from the tropical sun and protection from the seasonal storms. Being raised above ground level protected the houses from the occasional flooding when the low-lying land did not drain fast enough. In addition to the climatic adaptability, the building materials were all easily obtainable: good pine and cypress close at hand; clay; shells; and bits of hair or Spanish moss for the nogging and thatch; or split shingles for the roofing.[13]

In 1887, one of these early cottages was still standing at the corner of Conti and Conception Streets (figure 4). It was one of several sketched by Roderick MacKenzie. It is not hard to visualize what Mobile looked like to Peter Hobart: unpaved streets, muddy when wet, dusty when dry, lined on either side with Creole cottages. The cottages' galleries served as outside working areas where the inhabitants chattered in French or Spanish, and wood smoke mingled with the odor of tropical flowers. Hobart's building skills would not be called upon until the area became part of the United States.

FIGURES 4 AND 5

An 1887 sketch by Roderick MacKenzie of the oldest style of Creole cottage, once on the corner of Conti and Conception streets. It is typical of the French Colonial influence in the wide overhang of the broken pitched roof, the galleries, and the ground-hugging form that was so well adapted to withstand the strong winds of the Gulf storms. Houses such as this once lined the streets of Hobart's Mobile. The right photo above shows widow Toulette's early 19th century cottage, now known as the Lavalle House, in Pensacola, Florida. The cottage originally stood at 111 West Government Street but was moved into the Historic District. The plan differs from the earlier cottages by having four rooms, two-behind-two, instead of a single row of two or three rooms side-by-side, but the construction was early French with its heavy timber framing and nogging in the walls.

FIGURES 6, 6B

W. T. Andrews Log Cabin, Monroe County, Limestone Creek between Monroeville and Peterson. In contrast with the old vernacular housing of the Spanish lands, the log cabin was the home of the pioneers in middle and upper Alabama. There were various ways of joining the ends of the logs, but the saddle notching was popular in Alabama as seen in the Andrews dwelling. Most of the log cabins that have survived have been altered by applied clapboarding enclosing the central breezeway or dog trot, and with added refinements to the entrances. The lower photo above is another example of a central Alabama log cabin, one that was moved from the country to a location by Bluff Hall, Demopolis, Alabama, 405 N. Commissioners Street.

Even in American times, as late as 1817, the old construction methods used in the cottages continued. A surviving contract between James Innerarity and a Mr. Kellog states that the framing was to be of heavy timbers with a nogging infill between the posts[14] (Appendix 2).

Pensacola was experiencing the same kind of development. In the Historic District is an early cottage, undated, now known to be the Lavalle House (figure 5). In plan it is larger than the earliest cottages. Instead of a single horizontal row of rooms, there are two in width and two in depth and each has access to a gallery. Originally all the walls had nogging, but when the cottage was moved, only the nogging in the north was retained.[15]

The Americans who entered the Spanish colony before 1804, such as Peter Hobart of Vermont, Joshua Kennedy of South Carolina, and Lewis Judson of Connecticut, did not disturb the Spanish way of life. Being greatly outnumbered, they were no threat to the Spanish government. But this situation was soon to change.

After 1804, local, regional, and national conflicts began and slowed any embryonic architectural development in the Spanish colony. However, the Mississippi Territory to the north continued to be colonized. North of the 31st degree latitude, Americans from Kentucky, Tennessee, and the Atlantic seaboard states entered the Territory to build their log cabins and establish communities. In contrast to the Creole cottage of the coast that derived from the French culture, the log cabin came with settlers influenced by former English colonies.[16] An early nineteenth century example of the latter has survived in the W. T. Andrews Home, located in Monroe County in the Monroeville vicinity (figure 6). Some cabins were only one room (figure 6b); others had two that were separated by an open passage or dogtrot. Some of these have survived where the dog trot has been covered with clapboarding making an enclosed central hallway.

Such primitive housing did not continue for very long,

for the pioneers in the Mississippi Territory came with a knowledge of the Federal style of architecture as it had been developed in their home states. While Mobile was struggling to survive, communities were growing in central and northern Alabama. Huntsville was founded in 1805 and successfully developed as both an agricultural area and as a trading center. By 1815, both frame and brick houses were under construction with Federal detailing and Adamesque refinements. The 1814 Colonel Leroy Pope brick home reflects this influence in its central hall plan, and its entrance with the transom embellished with a sunburst design.[17] Another example, the Weeden House, of 1819, (figure 7) has leaded glass in the fanlight above the entrance doorway (figure 7b). Interior mantels and interior trim have Federal refinements. Even the Flemish bonding of the brick walls is an outgrowth of the influence from such states as Virginia. These refinements would not appear in Mobile for another thirty years.

It was this development in the Mississippi Territory that started some of the local problems for the Spanish Colony. Americans began pouring over the Spanish boundary that separated the two national areas. This new emigration threatened the whole fabric

FIGURES 7, 7B

The Weeden House, Huntsville, Alabama, 1819, 300 Gates Street. Just as the pioneering dwellings differed in the two different nationally controlled areas so did the more developed architecture. In upper Alabama the Federal influence was introduced early in the century by settlers from the southern seaboard states, Tennessee and Kentucky. The Weeden House is a good example of the Federal style with its elliptical fan light over the entry and its interior detailing.

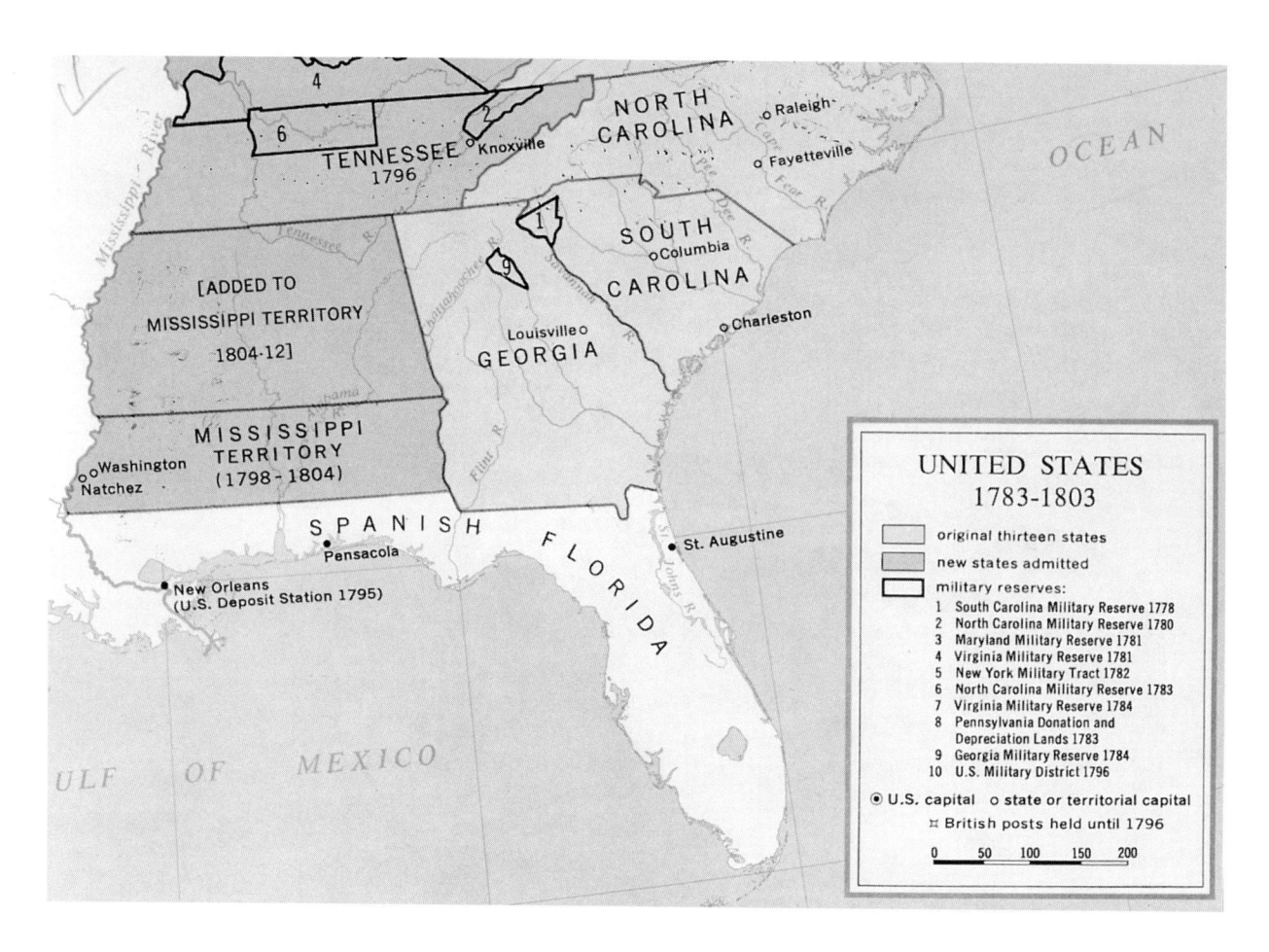

FIGURE 8

Detail of the United States Map of 1783-1803. The map defines the area that became the Mississippi Territory after the establishment of the boundary between the United States and Spain. The Territory included all the land from the Mississippi River to the Georgia line, north of West Florida. The new boundary opened up a vast wilderness for American settlers.

of Spanish control. In an attempt to stop the influx, the Spanish increased security at the borders, and passed a royal decree that no American could own land in its colony.[18] It was fortunate for Peter Hobart, and the other early settlers, that they already owned land and had established friendly relations with the local inhabitants. In spite of restrictions, the Americans continued to cross the border, which caused sporadic violence. As the new settlers took over more and more of their hunting grounds, the Creeks resented the growing American presence in both the Mississippi Territory and the Spanish-held land.

Alongside this local development, a regional conflict broke out that threatened the whole area. A movement, begun in Baton Rouge, declared the whole coast a free and independent country.[19] President Madison moved quickly to stop this by sending General Claiborne to annex the coast. Land from the Mississippi River to the Pearl River was taken in 1810, bringing the shores of the future state of Mississippi under American control (figure 8).

Still peace did not come to Mobile. As a result of the Spanish war with Napoleon's France and with England (Spain's former ally), both began to interfere with American shipping. England attacked and boarded United States trade vessels. France confiscated for sale any ships that were considered to disregard the trade restrictions imposed upon them. As a result, the War of 1812 began between the Americans and the British navy. In the spring of

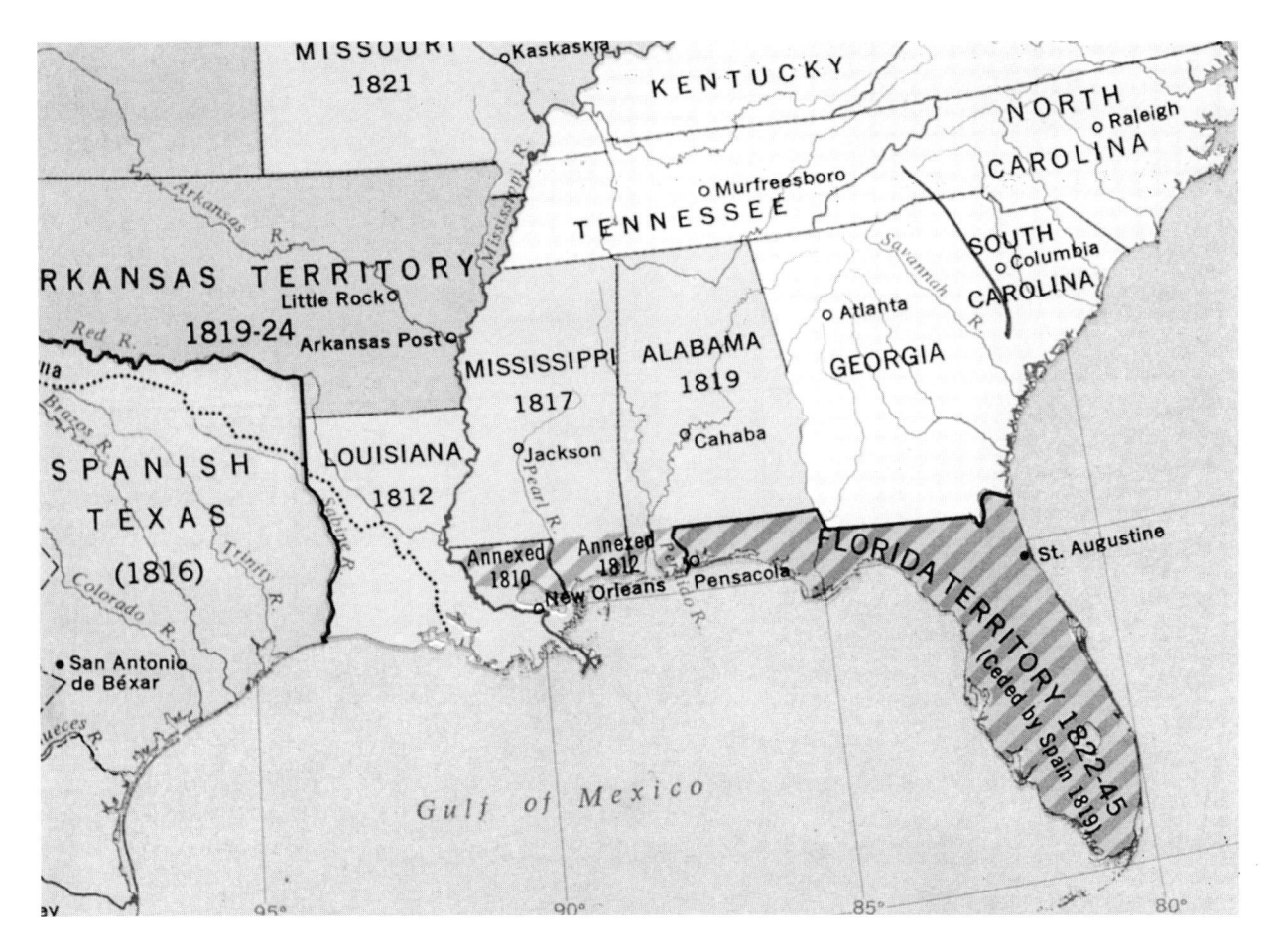

1813, General James Wilkinson was ordered to march on Mobile, take over the Spanish colony as far as Perdido Bay, and secure the defenses of Mobile. It was a bloodless coup, with the 6,000 man American army faced by only sixty Spanish soldiers left in the decaying old fort. As a result of an agreement made between Wilkinson and the Spanish Commander, Cayeton Perez, the Spanish were allowed to leave with their possessions and retire to Pensacola. On April 13, 1813, Mobile finally became part of the United States (figure 9).

While the threat from the British continued, trouble with the Creeks came to a head. For some time the Creeks had been harassing the settlers, but in 1813 they went into open war under the leadership of William Weatherford, who was half Creek and half Scotch. His warriors neither gave nor expected quarter. They fought to kill in protecting their rights to their land. Isolated settlers and forts alike became the object of their attempt to destroy the Americans. On August 30, 1813, they attacked Fort Mims killing men, women and children. Only a few of the 553 people who had sought shelter there were able to escape.

Settlers from the area and from other forts began to pour into Mobile. To control the Creeks, General Andrew Jackson was ordered to march into the territory and destroy their power (figure 10). The two armies met at several locations as shown on the map of the Indian Campaigns, but it was not until

FIGURE 9
Detail of the Map of the United States, 1812-1822. With Spanish control of her Gulf Colony crumbling, the local unrest erupting between American pioneers and the Spanish government, and the War of 1812, the Gulf Coast was gradually annexed by the United States. The area from the Mississippi River to the Pearl River was taken in 1810, from the Pearl River to Perdido Bay in 1812. Only a portion of old West Florida and the peninsula remained in Spanish hands by 1819, when a treaty was negotiated by Luis de Onis, the Spanish Minister in Washington, and John Quincy Adams, U.S. Secretary of State, by which Florida was purchased for $5,000,000.

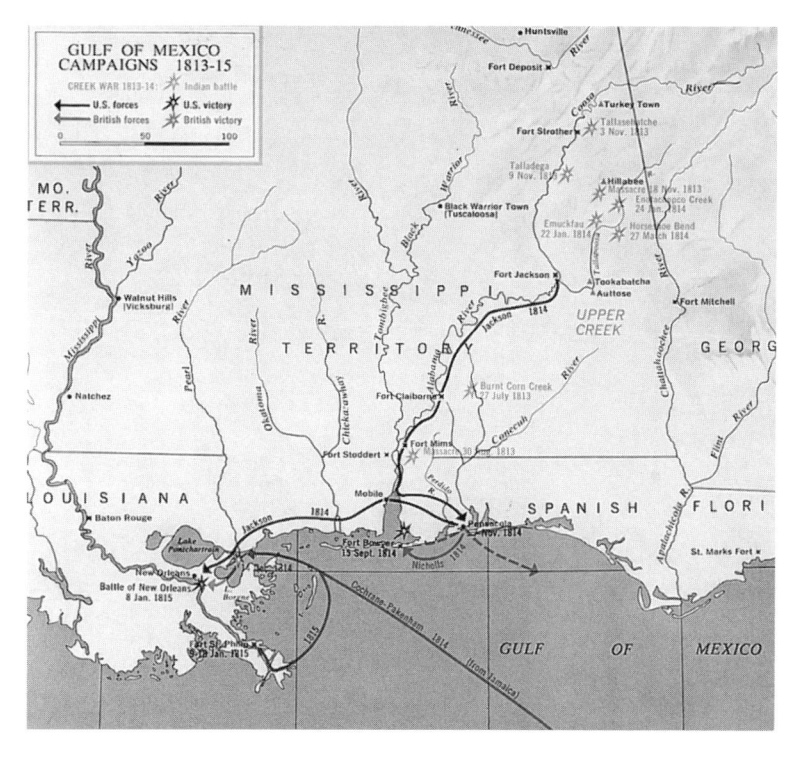

FIGURE 10

Gulf of Mexico Campaigns. Between 1812 and 1815, two wars were being fought, the War of 1812 with the British, the other with the combined Creek nation. General Andrew Jackson was the military commander for both in the Alabama area. After defeating the Creeks at the Battle of Horseshoe Bend, he marched through Mobile to liberate Pensacola from British Marines. He next defeated the British at the Battle of New Orleans on January 8, 1815. Throughout all these turbulent times, Peter Hobart remained in Mobile.

1814 that General Jackson was able to corner the Creeks at Horseshoe Bend on the Tallapoosa River. Here on March 27, the Creek warriors were wiped out with a loss of life of only forty-seven Americans and twenty-three Indian allies. With the Creek nation subdued, the Mississippi Territory was free to continue its development. But the Gulf Coast was still being threatened by the British. Pensacola had been captured by British Marines, and General Jackson was ordered to march to Mobile, secure its defenses, and retake Pensacola. After expelling the British, he returned Pensacola to the Spanish. General Jackson then sailed to the defense of New Orleans, leaving Major William Lawrence in charge of the defense of Mobile.

In 1815 the British attacked Dauphin Island. At first the battle went badly for the Americans and Mobile was prepared for invasion. But with Jackson's success at the Battle of New Orleans on January 15, 1815, the War on the Gulf was brought to a close. With the Treaty of Ghent, December 14, 1815, Mobile was at last free to begin a long-delayed progress. Six years later, when Spain ceded the whole peninsula for $5 million, Pensacola and Florida became part of the United States.

The Map of 1815 (figure 11) shows that the basic plan of Mobile had changed little since Spanish days (See figure 3, Map of 1809). The city blocks were essentially the same. A few new roads had been opened up and the old road to the Choctaw settlements leading to the southwest had been eliminated along with the "Baterie" of Galvez. A second wharf beside the old Kings Wharf had been built, but commercial development had not progressed to the point that it could be reflected on a map. There were several reasons for this. The coast was still under the threat of attack from the English until 1815. The population was a heterogeneous combination of the old colonial inhabitants, new Americans entering the territory, and the early settlers, like Peter Hobart, who formed the link between the two cultures. Perhaps the most formidable task that faced the residents was the transformation of the old autocratic colonial form of government into an American democracy. This process was undertaken almost immediately after 1813. No new city could develop until a sound economic base could be established that could finance building.

The immediate need, following the expulsion of the Spanish, was the establishment of an American form of government. Territorial laws were passed by the United States Congress, but local ordinances were also necessary. Even while Mobile was barely recovering from the threats of both the English and the Indians, the residents elected the city's first commission. Each of the seven commissioners served two years without pay. Hobart served two terms. The commission's first act was to determine the city's boundary. The line began at "Choctaw point and running in a straight direction to the western bank of the Bayou Chotage, at a point lying two hundred yards above the place on said island called the Portage; thence down the western bank of said Bayou to its mouth, thence in a straight line to the west bank of the island in front of Mobile; thence along the margin of said island to the south point of said island, and thence to a straight line to the place of the beginning."[20]

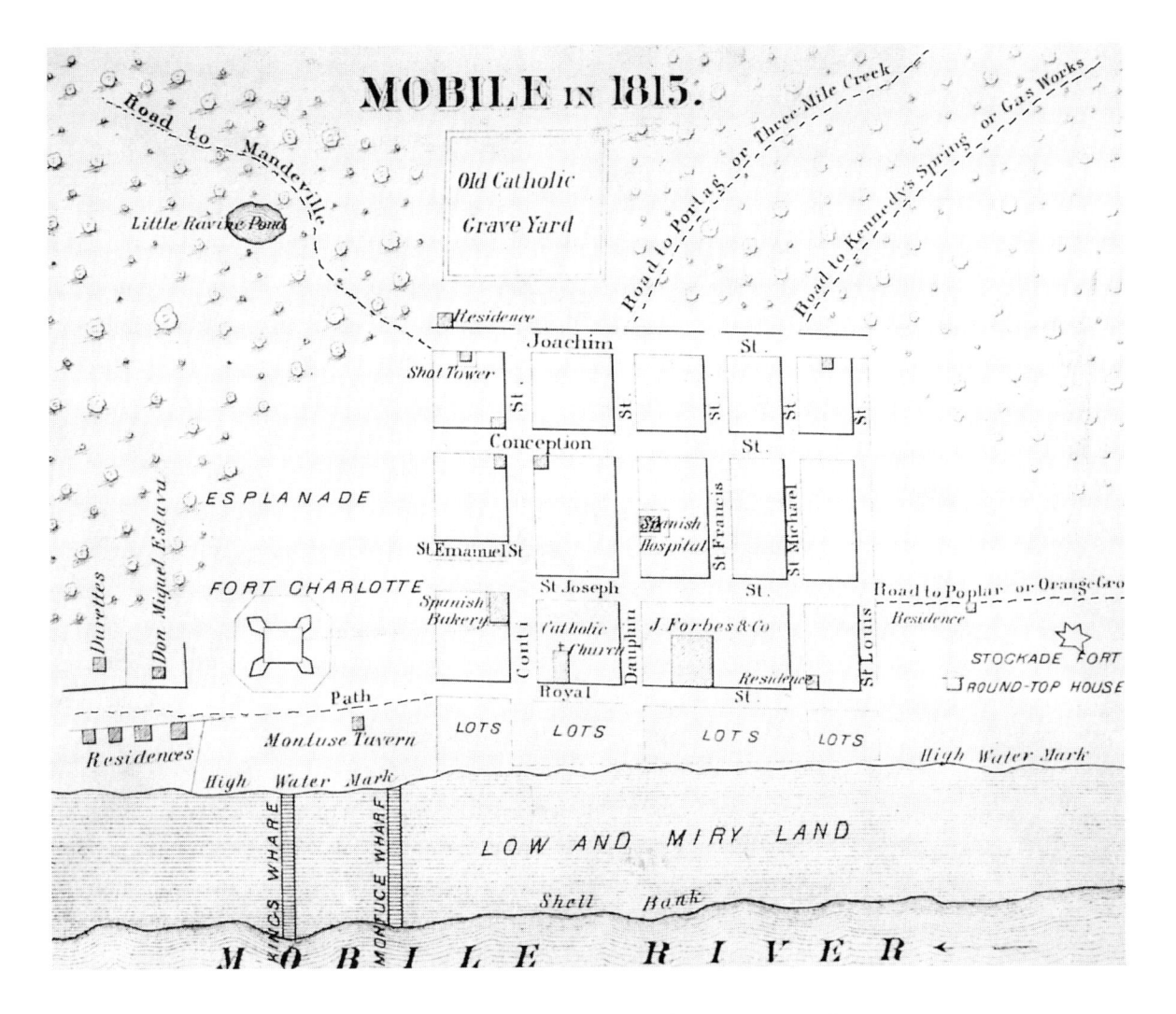

With the city limits established, the area within was divided into three wards with two police constables appointed for each ward and a police commissioner to oversee the whole city. A tax base was established of twelve and a half cents per $100 value of property, and license fees were set up for various commercial concerns, such as five dollars a year for grocery and general mer-

FIGURE 11

1815 Map of Mobile. The 1815 Map shows the plan of the city two years after the area had become part of the United States Territory. Except for the indication of some new roads, there is little change in the plan from that shown on the 1809 Spanish Map (figure 3). Before the embryonic city could develop, Peter Hobart and the other early American settlers had to transform the old autocratic Spanish colony into a democratic community with the laws, ordinances and taxes upon which sound commercial progress could be made.

chandise stores. Realizing the future importance of the port, a port warden was appointed and bond set for river pilots.

Some of the first ordinances are amusing but illustrate the undeveloped conditions of the time: goats and cows were prohibited from running at large; no digging was allowed in the streets; no shooting within the city limits was permitted except to kill dogs running wild. Other ordinances concerned such things as the inspection of chimneys, a constant source of fire in the city whose buildings were of wood, and the requirement that each house have a bucket of water ready to douse on any escaping flames from fireplaces.[21]

With the growing number of saw mills there was a threat to the cleanliness of the water that had to be brought into town in barrels. Laws were passed to protect these sources, such as the Portage on Three Mile Creek. Each barrel of water cost the householder fifty cents. As for the need for improving the streets and the creation of new ones, the president of the commission was given the right to have removed any building that stood in the public way.

Since the city was located almost at sea level, an early attempt at drainage was tried by creating ditches along the street edges. Later these were augmented by two canals, one near what are now Church and Canal Streets and the other near what is now St. Michael Street.[22]

The second city commission came to office in 1815, and Peter Hobart was reelected. It is from this term that several letters have survived written by Hobart to the Congress of the United States. In 1817 he wrote requesting Congress not to pass a bill that had been submitted by the governing body of the Mississippi Territory. The bill would have transferred an additional section of land that extended into Alabama "to Mobile and the Tombigbee River" to the Territory of Mississippi.[23]

During the same year, he wrote to Congress concerning Fort Condé (sometimes called by its English name, Fort Charlotte). The fort had not been maintained after the Spanish left, and further deterioration was caused by the paths cut across by the residents and free roaming cattle. In its ruinous state it held no future for the city, for it covered valuable land that could be developed and also prevented the planning for new streets leading to the southern section of ward three. The letter was couched in the polite terms of the day. It requested that:

> The same disposition be made of the mouldering fort, which was made of Fort St. Louis at New Orleans, or that a bountiful and indulgent Government will extend such Other relief as the Congress of the United States may see fit.[24]

As a result, Congress passed a bill on April 20, 1818, authorizing the sale of the fort, but it took several years for the fort to be demolished.

During these years, Hobart not only served on the commission, but also took his turn as night watchman — a civic responsibility required of all adult male residents.²⁵ While there are many records of his contribution to the city's development, there are no records of any buildings that he designed during the territorial years from 1813 to 1819. Even after statehood was established in 1819, he seems to have been still occupied with the governmental and commercial development of the city.²⁶ It was 1824 before there is a surviving contract for a building by him. His building would not be matched until the advent of the Greek Revival in the 1830s, when Gallier and Dakin brought to Mobile its two most famous buildings, the Barton Academy and the Government Street Presbyterian Church.

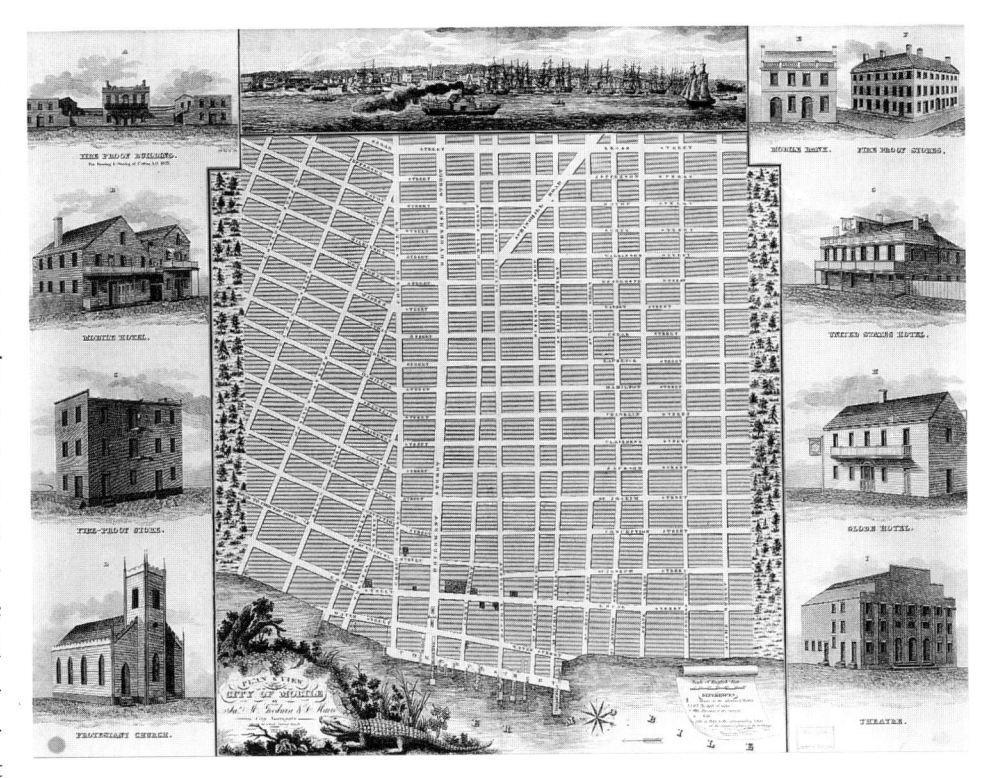

Though we have no records of Hobart's work during the first four years of the 1820s, building was ongoing. With many cottages burned in the fire of 1822 and the increase in residents from about 800 in 1820 to 2,800 in 1822, rapid housing construction was required. The local carpenters, trained in the old vernacular ways, performed the residential rebuilding. In 1828, a surviving contract finally called for walls with studs and lath, rather than heavy brace framing with nogging. A census, reported in the February 7, 1822, newspaper, listed among other buildings, 240 dwellings, 110 stores and warehouses, two churches, three "commodius" hotels and a building used as a courthouse.²⁷ The biggest change was the growing number of brick stores, though wood buildings still lined the streets and fueled the devastating fire of 1827.

An idea of the crudeness of most of the buildings can be ascertained by looking at the engravings on the Goodwin and Haire Map of 1824 (figure 12). The "commodius" hotels resemble pictures of some of the pioneering buildings out West during the great migrations at the time of the gold rush. Even the brick "fire-proof stores" shown on the map had few elements of any architectural merit. Only four buildings on the map are of architectural interest: the theatre in the lower right corner; the little frame Gothic Revival Protestant Church in the lower left corner; the cotton press in the upper left; and

Figure 12
Goodwin and Haire Map of Mobile, 1824. The buildings engraved on the edges of the map illustrate the architectural development of Mobile at the time that Peter Hobart was designing his Neoclassical county courthouse, the first Neoclassical building constructed in the Gulf Coast area of the old West Florida.

ELIZABETH BARRETT GOULD

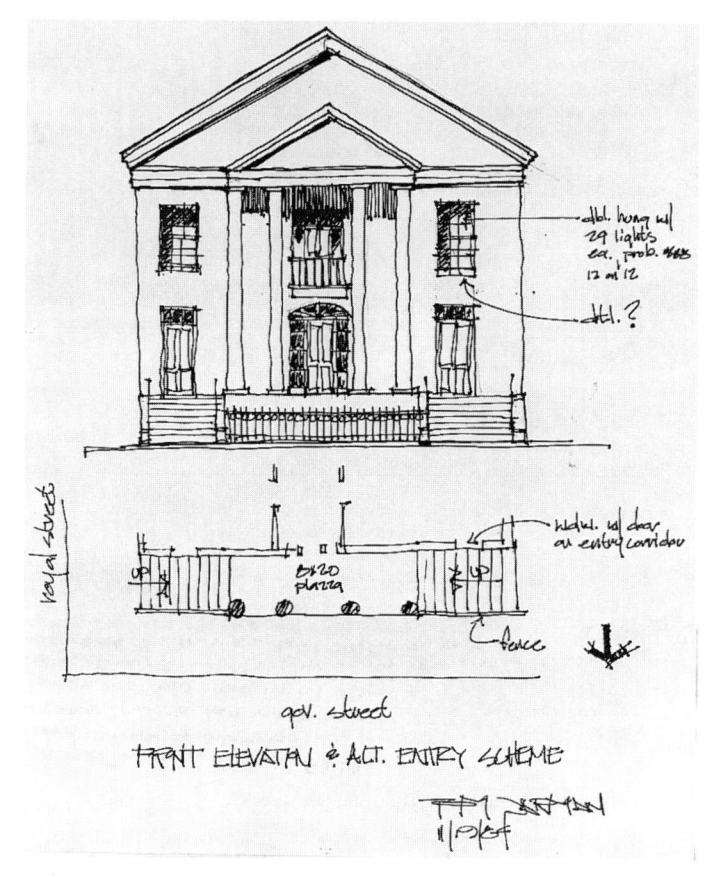

FIGURE 13

T.M. Jarman's sketch of the facade of the Mobile County Courthouse as it was described in the contract between the county and Hobart. The design illustrates a simplified interpretation of the Neoclassical phase of the Federal Style. Above a high basement, a two-story portico had four columns rising the full height to the cornice of the pedimented gable. It was the first time that the monumentally sized columns were used in Alabama, preceding those of the State Capitol at Tuscaloosa by two years.

the small bank at the left of the two buildings in the upper right.

Mention must be made of the theatre on the Goodwin and Haire Map, not because of any remarkable design, but because it is the first Mobile building on record to have been the work of a nationally-known architect, Isaiah Rogers.[28] He was in Mobile in 1823 as a young man, and the theatre has been attributed to him based on information in his diary.

It is not known who designed any of the other three buildings mentioned. Whoever built the little Gothic Church was familiar with the Gothic Revival vocabulary and also with the limits placed upon it by the availability of materials. It is very early for the style, particularly in Mobile. The cotton press was built for two New Orleans entrepreneurs, John Lapretre and Thomas Townsley. A local carpenter, John Ward, prepared the building with the necessary framing for the roof as stated in a surviving contract, but there is no mention of the mason or master builder of the entire structure. Presumably it was someone from New Orleans.

The small Bank of Mobile in the upper right corner of the map is the best brick construction in a modified Federal style that has survived in records. The semicircular-headed entrances, the string course marking the stories, and the balustrade at the eaves' edge show that the designer was very familiar with the Federal style as it developed in the Northeast. It was from that area that the founders of the bank had come: Hall from Philadelphia, H. B. Chamberlain from Massachusetts, A. W. Gordon and Lewis Judson from Connecticut.

Lewis Judson and Peter Hobart had been in Mobile during the Spanish occupancy and served together on the first two Alabama territorial city commissions. They signed as partners in the contract for the county courthouse, although only Hobart was named as responsible for the design and construction of the building. Judson's responsibilities were not mentioned, though we know he was a successful businessman even in Spanish times with a warehouse as early as 1811. So considering the other Mobile builders of the decade, Hobart would have been the only builder-designer who could have planned for the architectural style of the bank, though there is no documentary mention of that. The actual builder is thought to have been a local mason.

From the time of the founding of Alabama as a Territory, there are frequent references to the fact that Mobile needed a courthouse. Several times ordinances had been approved for one, but nothing materialized until 1822. Previously, court had been held in a cottage belonging to Catalina Mottus (rental receipts for which are in the Mobile County Probate Court). In February 1822, both a courthouse and a "Gaol" were approved, and a competition announced for the best design due to be submitted by April. Peter Hobart and Lewis Judson, as partners, won first place, though no record so far has been found of any of the other designs submitted.[29] (For a copy of the contract of 1825, see Appendix 3.)

Hobart must have been working on his plans during the years between the competition and the actual signing of the contract. Whether Hobart made drawings or not is not known as none have survived. He must have done some kind of sketches, for the classical proportions and elevation have been carefully worked out. The relations of the width of the facade, fifty feet, to the height of the rectangle, thirty-four feet, follows closely on the golden mean of the ratio of three to two. The entrance into the main room of the first story has a well-developed Federal framing with an elliptical transom that extends over the door and sidelights. Contrast in texture and color was planned in the white marble sills and lintels of windows, the first use of such material in any Mobile contract. It must have been customary to do drawings at that time, for in two contracts of the decade crude drawings were included: the sketch of the Government Street Market of 1823, built by John Ward and Turner Stark; and the simplified drawing of the elevation of a brick store of 1828, built by Samuel Garrow and Henry Center.[30]

The contract for the courthouse is sufficiently detailed that a tentative sketch can be made of its general appearance and plan; although without any original drawings or engravings, no accurate detailed representation can be made. The sketch of the facade (figure 13) exemplifies a different phase of the Federal style than was popular in middle and upper Alabama. In the Morgan County Courthouse at Somerville of 1837, the simple rectangular block, the strong horizontal line of the cornice, and the formal balancing of the windows place it in the first phase of the Federal as it emerged from the Georgian of the previous century (figure 14). The courthouse at Somerville is the oldest one still standing in Alabama. In sharp contrast to this Morgan County example, Hobart's courthouse has moved into a later phase of the Federal that was introduced by Charles Bulfinch (1763-1844) of Boston and Thomas Jefferson (1743-1826) of Virginia. These men, one a professional and the other a gentleman architect, turned to Palladio and the architecture of the Roman Republic

FIGURE 14

Morgan County Courthouse, Somerville, Alabama, 1837. In upper Alabama, the first phase of the Federal style dominated both residential and public buildings. Trained architects and builders already skillful in brick construction had entered from Virginia and the Carolinas. They were more advanced architecturally than those in Mobile. Still evolving from its colonial inheritance, buildings in Mobile were being constructed in the old vernacular ways. Only when the economy improved was it possible for Peter Hobart to bring his architectural knowledge to the city.

FIGURE 15

Charles Bulfinch (1763-1844), along with Thomas Jefferson (1743-1826), sought in the Neoclassical style a symbolism that expressed the newly established Republic. In so doing they turned architecture away from the Georgian and French past and inspired young builders. In Bulfinch's Federal Street Theatre, Boston, 1794, the architect formalized the three-part division of the elevation; the basement; the columnar portico; and the gabled roof.

FIGURE 16

Engraving of the State Capitol at Tuscaloosa, 1828-1830, William Nichols, architect. Following the example of the Capitol of North Carolina, Nichols built his Neoclassical style facade with engaged Ionic columns rising the full two stories of the large building. The building served as the Capitol until 1846, when the state government was permanently moved to Montgomery.

for their inspiration. To them the style was symbolic of the new republic of the thirteen states. It is buildings such as Bulfinch's Federal Street Theatre of 1794 that were a prototype for Hobart's adaptation of the Neoclassical style (figure 15). The projecting central pavilion with its engaged columns above the basement story is what most notably alters the elevations from that of the earlier Federal phase.[31] This new phase can be seen in the later and more monumental Tuscaloosa State Capitol of 1828, designed by State Architect William Nichols and based on a similar design for the State Capitol of North Carolina[32] (figure 16). Although the Tuscaloosa Courthouse has long been considered the first building in Alabama to use the giant classical columns, the discovery of Hobart's contract gives the honor to his building of 1825.

There is a double symbolism in the Hobart courthouse. First, it is the major building that stood between the closing of the city's Colonial Period and the coming of the mid-1830s. It was then that Gallier and Dakin introduced a refined Greek Revival into Mobile architectural history: the Barton Academy and the Government Street Presbyterian Church, both still standing. Moreover, as an architectural statement, Hobart's building established that the old French system of construction was gone and the new American way of building was in place. Mobile had become an American city.

Second, the site chosen for the location of the courthouse was auspicious. At the time the site was selected, Mobile had not yet developed very far to the south of the old French limits. The fort had stood in the way of development and was not even completely cleared when the courthouse was planned. New streets had been platted to the south of the old city as shown in the Goodwin and Haire Map (compare figures 3 and 12). A 100-foot-wide thoroughfare, Government Street, was laid. Running from the water's edge due west to the city limits, it was envisioned as the new central axis of the city. The old axis had been between Dauphin and St. Francis Streets, several blocks to the north. The Government and Royal Streets site was once the location for all the city and county government buildings, and Government Street remains the main thoroughfare through the heart of the city. Thus the Hobart courthouse on its site symbolized the new architecture and the new city.

The Mobile Courthouse was a rectangular building fifty feet wide by seventy-five feet long, not counting the projecting portico. That it possibly faced on Royal Street, rather than Government as did all subsequent courthouses, is suggested by a reference in the contract to three rooms on the "west end" of the second story (figure 18). The facade was a classically proportioned rectangle, fifty feet wide by thirty-four feet high to the cornice. The elevation was divided into a five-foot-high basement above which were two stories: the first floor was twelve feet in the clear and the second floor was fifteen feet in the clear. The gabled roof was covered with the best "Welsh slate."

The outstanding feature of the facade was the portico, called a "piazza" in the contract. It was twenty feet long and projected eight feet from the wall. Four brick, plastered columns "extended to the roof." Since there was no mention of the necessity of carving any capitals, it can be assumed that the capitals were either a simplified Doric or a plain block. No other known building in Mobile before the coming of the Greek Revival used this full-height columnar feature.

The contract called for "steps with railing up each side of it [the piazza, EBG] to the large door in the center a neat fence to extend from the foot of the railing to the end of the building." As the most difficult aspect of the contract to decipher, it is unclear whether the steps projected out from the portico, running parallel to the wall or whether they were located at right angles to the front of the two ends as indicated in the suggested sketch (figure 13). Based on the four subsequent courthouses, all following the Hobart general form, the steps would have been approached from the front. Until some engraving or photograph can be found this will be a moot question.

There is no question about the details of the doors and windows. The main central entrance was Federal in design, with an elliptical fan extending over both door and side lights. The two side doors that led into the two rooms on the east and west were both square headed with transoms. Windows were double hung with twenty-four lights each made up of panes of glass twelve by fifteen inches. All had marble sills and lintels, the windows of the lower story having paneled shutters.

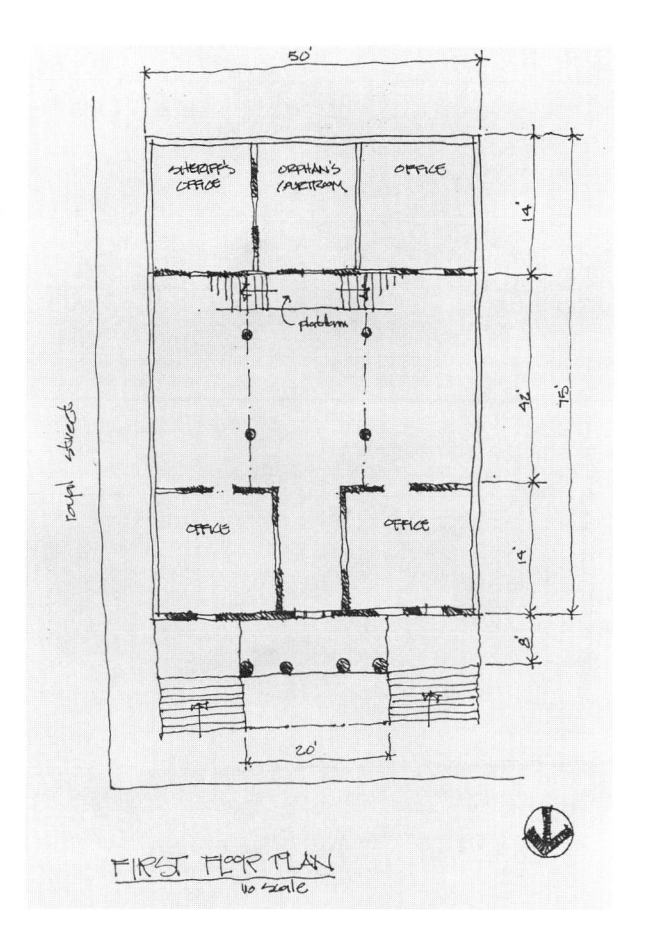

FIGURE 17

Jarman sketch for the plan of the Mobile Courthouse, Peter Hobart, architect. The first story above the basement was divided into six rooms, a large central area forty-two feet by fifty feet. Three small rooms were located at the west end, one of which served as the Orphans' Courtroom, and the two other rooms were located at the eastern end.

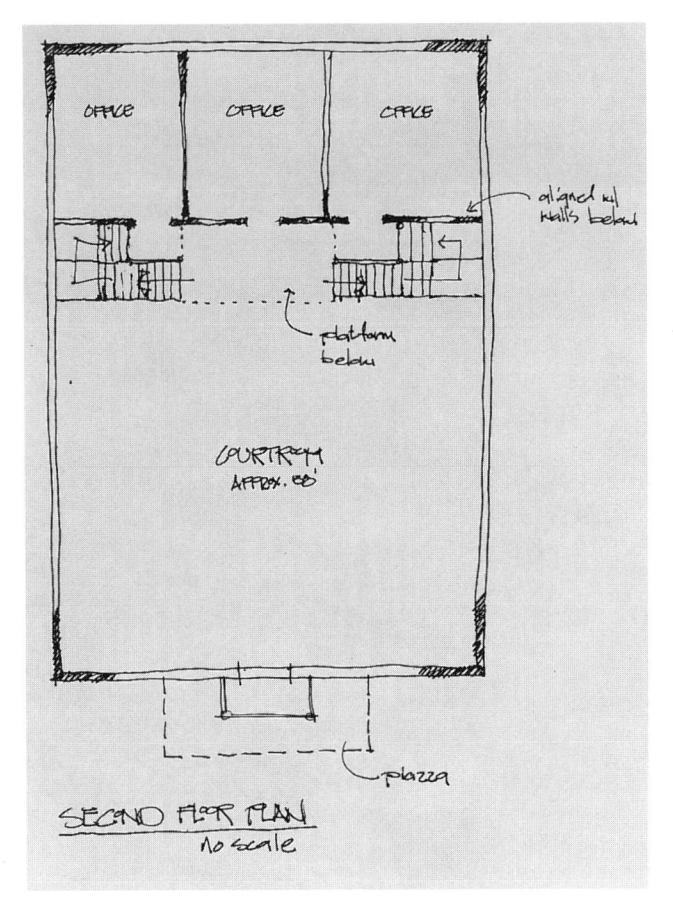

FIGURE 18

Jarman sketch for the plan of the Mobile Courthouse, Peter Hobart, architect. Jarman's sketch of the plan of the second story in which was located the main courtroom with three adjoining judges' chambers on the west.

As indicated in figure 17, the first story was divided with one large room the full width of the building, and forty-two feet deep. Five smaller rooms were arranged so that there were three at one end and two at the other. The smaller rooms served as various offices, one especially designated for the "Orphans' Courtroom." The only heat in the building was furnished by a fireplace in the Orphans' Courtroom and in the main courtroom on the second floor. Turned posts in the large first story room supported the floor above. At the rear of this room a platform was located with stairs "to run each way from it to the second story." The main courtroom, fifty-eight feet deep, occupied most of the second story (figure 18) with three equally sized rooms on the west end, these presumably for the judges' chambers. The contract stated that the courthouse was to be finished by 1826, but receipts for the final payment were made out to the widow after Peter Hobart's death in 1828.

Hobart's courthouse stood until early in 1851 when fire gutted the building. It was followed by four other courthouses, all continuing Hobart's original basic form. Only details differed as the changing styles required. The one designed by the Victorian architect, Rudolph Benz, still was a large rectangular building with a classically inspired portico, except for the addition of a complex roof line consisting of a central dome and multiple sculptures edging the pediments. It was not until 1956 that a different concept for a courthouse was developed and a modern building constructed.[33]

Reference in the records was made to one other structure with which Peter Hobart had input. A letter Ezekiel Webb, chairman of the Lafayette Committee, wrote to Hobart on March 18, 1825, requested that he cooperate with local builders in erecting the building for the upcoming ball and dinner.

Peter Hobart died in 1828 at the age of fifty-two. He had lived through some of the most dramatic changes in American history and in Mobile's history. He had helped forge a new American community, plan a future city, and lived long enough to build its first courthouse.

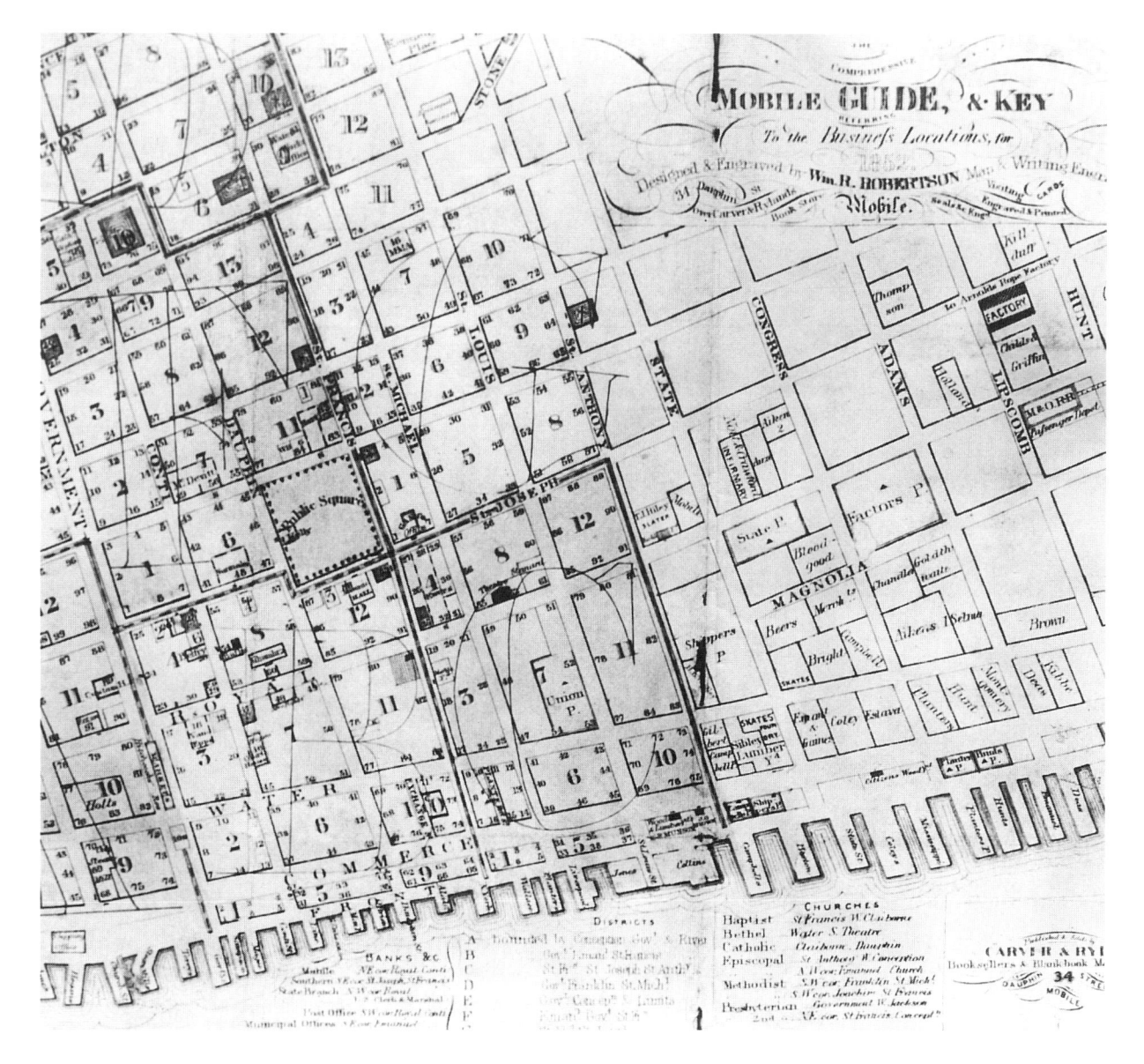

PLATE II

Detail of the 1852 Robertson Map of Mobile. The map shows the waterfront development during the 1840s and early 1850s. The map shows a large part of the city in which James Flandin Hutchisson made his contribution to the architectural history of Mobile. His skills added to the building of the river steamboats, housing for the inner city, and commercial buildings to meet the needs of the growing cotton trade.

ELIZABETH BARRETT GOULD

Chapter 2

James Flandin Hutchisson I

(1806-1856)

THE decade of the 1830s opened auspiciously for Mobile. The economy was booming. Following the fire of 1827, the streets of the inner city were being filled by brick buildings that rapidly were replacing the burned out areas. New housing for the growing middle class was in great demand. In the mid-1830s, the architects James Gallier and Charles Dakin introduced a refined Greek Revival style to the city with the construction of Barton Academy and the Government Street Presbyterian Church. Charles Dakin had begun the Government Street Hotel and together with his brother James had built the Planters and Merchants Bank. (See the engravings on the top of the La Tourrette Map, figure 19.)

Warehouses were increasing along the waterfront and long wharfs were stretching out in parallel lines along the river's edge. The development of the waterfront can be easily noted in a comparison of the five maps: 1809 (figure 3), 1815 (figure 11), 1824 (figure 12), 1838 (figure 19) and 1856 (figure 20). The last two maps cover the years when James Flandin Hutchisson was living and working in Mobile. The contrast in the city plan of 1809 and 1856 also illustrates the great change that had taken place between the time of the sleepy Spanish community and the developing American port. Like Peter Hobart who had taken part in the early transformation of the city, James Flandin Hutchisson, the cofounder of the Hobart-Hutchisson line of builder-architects, made his contribution during the first flush times of the cotton era when Mobile became the richest city on the Gulf Coast east of New Orleans.

From Hobart's time to the coming of the railroads in midcentury, the development of the river was interwoven with that of the city. Flowing into the river that formed the eastern boundary of Mobile was a network of tributaries webbing through the plantation counties of Alabama and upper Mississippi. Down these waterways came cotton, bringing seemingly boundless wealth. After the improvement in the cotton seed, developed by Rush Nutt,[1] plantations increased productivity and more bales were exported to the mills of New England and overseas. The fire of 1839 that destroyed so much of the town did not delay this lucrative trade for too long a time.

Because of the cotton trade, Mobilians saw little need to diversify. Manufacturing or industrial development might have saved the city when the Civil War cut off the production of the plantations. The few sawmills furnished lumber for local building, but lumber was imported as well. A door, sash and blind company was formed in 1837, but it was of minor importance. With this concentration on a single source of commerce, it was necessary to import most of the commodities and staples needed to support an active citizenry. The vessels leaving with cotton returned with cargoes to supply the city's needs as well as those "up river" at Selma, Tuscaloosa and Demopolis in Alabama, and Macon, Aberdeen and Columbus on the Tombigbee tributary in Mississippi. Old newspapers record the arrival of vessels with listings of their cargo:

> The Schooner Sophia, from Philadelphia: Beef, Oats, Flour, Whisky, Wine, Cloth.
> The Brig Fox: Shoes, Boots, Saddles, Bridles, Clothing.
> The Schooner Andea: Lumber, White Beans, Bricks, Soap, Candles.[2]

FIGURE 19

The La Tourrette Map of Mobile, 1838. Three years before the La Tourrette map was published, James Flandin Hutchisson arrived in Mobile. The city was experiencing its first Greek Revival buildings with the work of James Gallier and Charles Dakin.

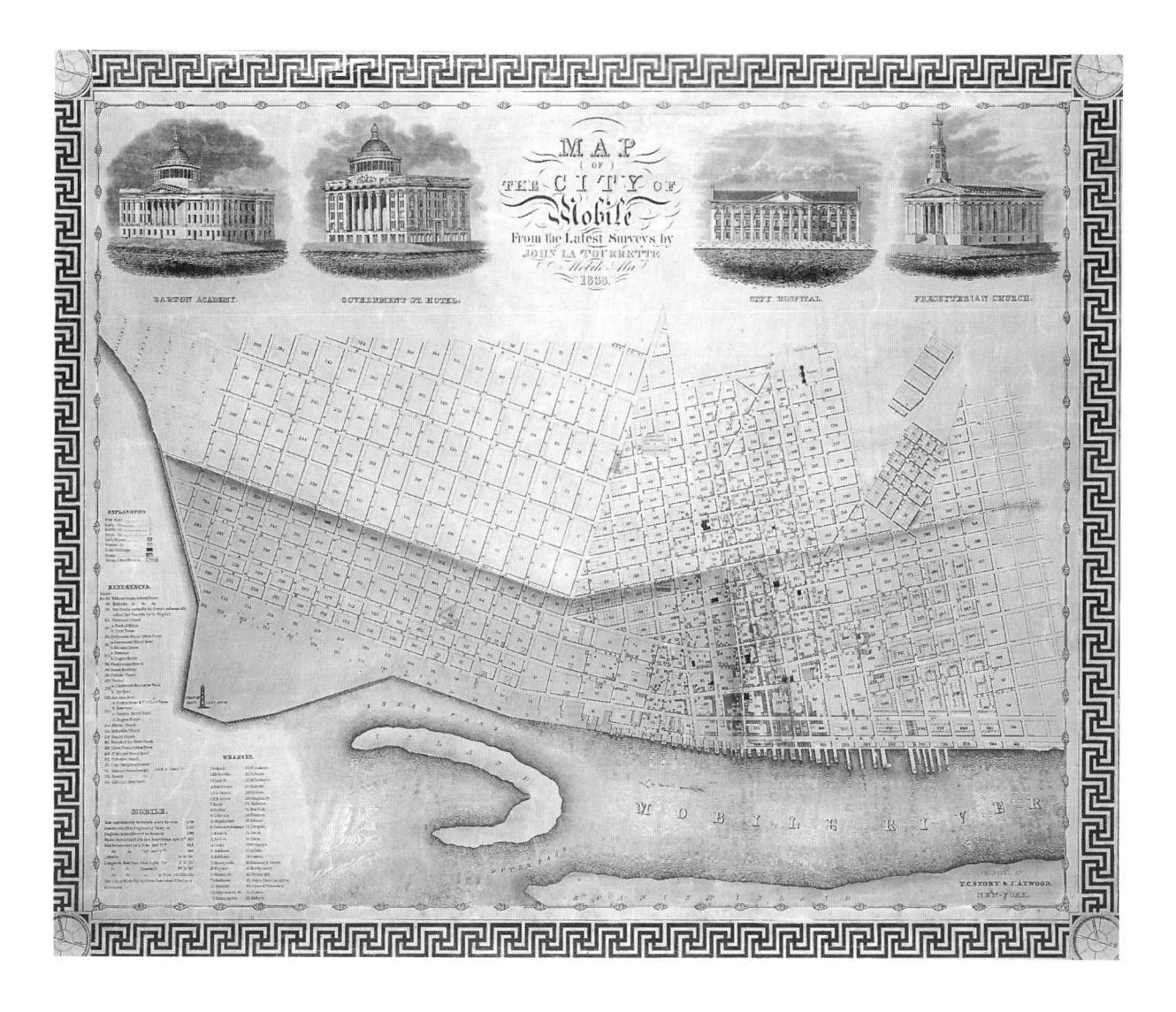

FIGURE 20

Detail of the Robertson Map of 1856 showing the waterfront from Madison Street on the south to Lipscomb on the north.

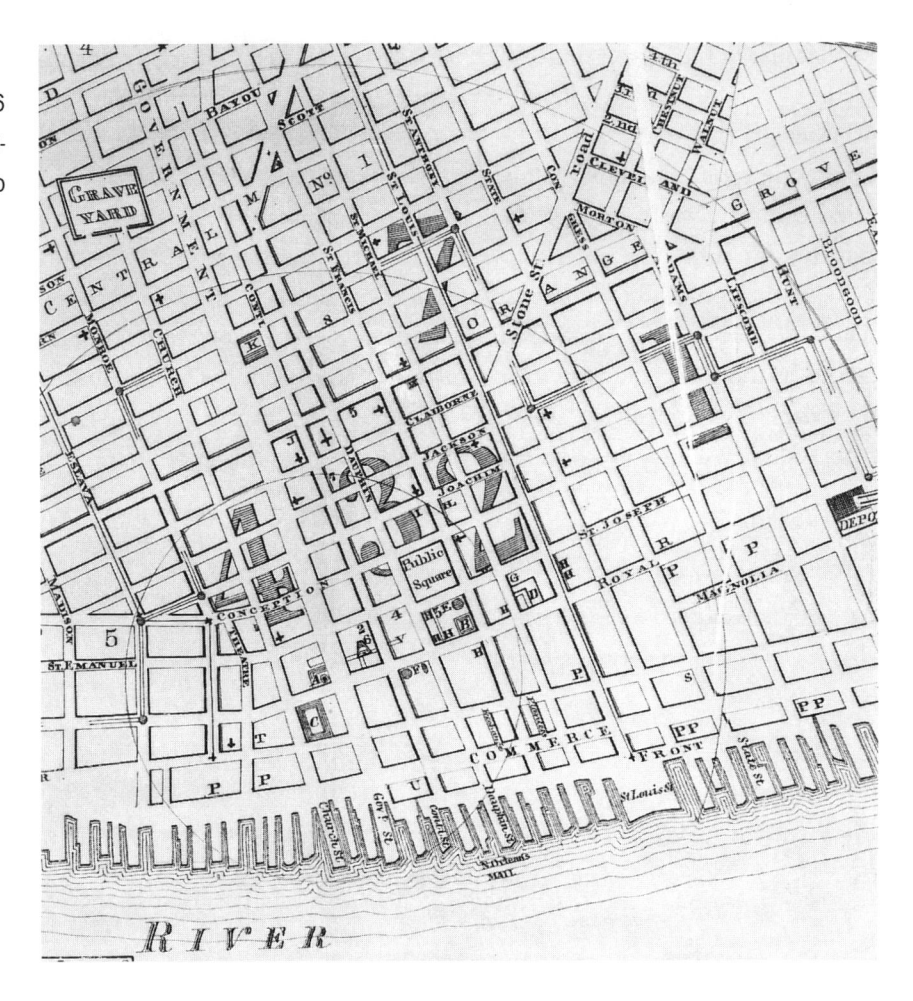

Stores to handle this merchandise lined the blocks from Commerce Street west along lower Government, Conti, Dauphin and St. Michael Streets. Only the streets formed an open space between the row buildings.

With the development of steam engines, the river traffic increased. Steamboat companies had been formed as early as 1818 when the Stephens Steamboat Company was chartered. John Fowler ran a line from Mobile to Blakeley, and the Mobile Steamboat Company was organized November 27, 1821.[3] But the "up river" trip was slow. In 1821 the *Harriet* made it from Mobile to Montgomery in ten days. The next year the *Tensaw* took twenty-three days to make it to Selma. The early steam vessels had trouble moving against the strong outward current of the river as it flowed to the Gulf, so that "up river" journeys had to be towed where the current was swiftest.[4]

As steamboats utilized more powerful engines, this problem was solved and traffic moved easily both ways. In 1839, 440,102 bales of cotton passed through the port of Mobile. By 1845, this number had been increased to 500,000 bales; and by 1856, the year of the death of James Flandin Hutchisson, there were 681,321 bales processed on the Mobile docks.[5]

To handle all this commerce, the population of Mobile increased proportionately. From 1839 to 1855, the number of residents rose from 13,621 to

29,744. Of the former number, 8,594 were whites, 4,470 were slaves, and 557 were free blacks. The 1855 census numbered whites at 20,287, slaves at 8,366 and free blacks at 1,041.[6] Forty percent of all the free blacks in Alabama were in Mobile.[7]

While there was a sizable but fairly constant number of cotton "kings," brokers, factors, and large warehouse and press owners, the major increase in the numbers of residents came in the merchant class. After 1840 another influx of Americans came and added to the middle and upper lower classes. Many were originally from Germany and Ireland and often reached the city by circuitous routes. While early Mobile had an open society of mixed cultural life styles, class distinctions now were based on economics rather than on race. At the top of the pyramid were the cotton brokers. Then came the professionals, the doctors and lawyers. The middle class was formed of merchants and skilled artisans. Just below them were the clerks, the semiskilled, the seamstresses, etc. The lowest class did the heavy unskilled labor, along with the slaves and the few remaining Choctaws and Chickasaws. These Indians lived on the edge of the town and came in only to sell small bundles of fatty pine and kindling. This was their sole source of income. Desperately poor, they never spoke or were spoken to, they were simply ignored.

Each class settled in its own area of the city. The rich occupied the fine houses in De Tonti Square and employed the most skilled of the builders and architects available. These men included Cary Butt who has been questionably credited with the Christ Episcopal Church of 1838 and served as a draftsman in the office of Charles Dakin, designer of the State Capitol of Florida.[8] They also include David Cumming, Jr., the architect for the 1859 Guesnard House, built by the master mason James Hill; James Barnes, the master builder who erected Christ Episcopal Church; Thomas James, the builder of both the Barton Academy and the Government Street Presbyterian Church; and John Collins, builder of the large City Hospital. Besides their city dwellings and business structures, the wealthy owned land in Spring Hill where summer homes, cottage type to Greek Revival villas, occupied five-acre lots.[9] These buildings have been well photographed and published. The builders for the merchant and working classes filled the blocks of the inner city from Water, west to Scott, south to Canal and north to the newly established Orange Grove area (figures 19 and 20). This area where James Flandin Hutchisson worked determined the character of the city from the mid-1830s to the Civil War. From his arrival in Mobile as ship and house carpenter to his status as master builder in the 1840s and early 1850s, he built structures from cottages to the largest warehouse of which we have record. Though his work was never photographed nor formally recognized in Mobile's architectural history, he made a lasting contribution to the development of the city.

James Flandin Hutchisson was born in 1806, and raised in Hempstead, Long Island, where he was trained as a ship's joiner and house builder. Very

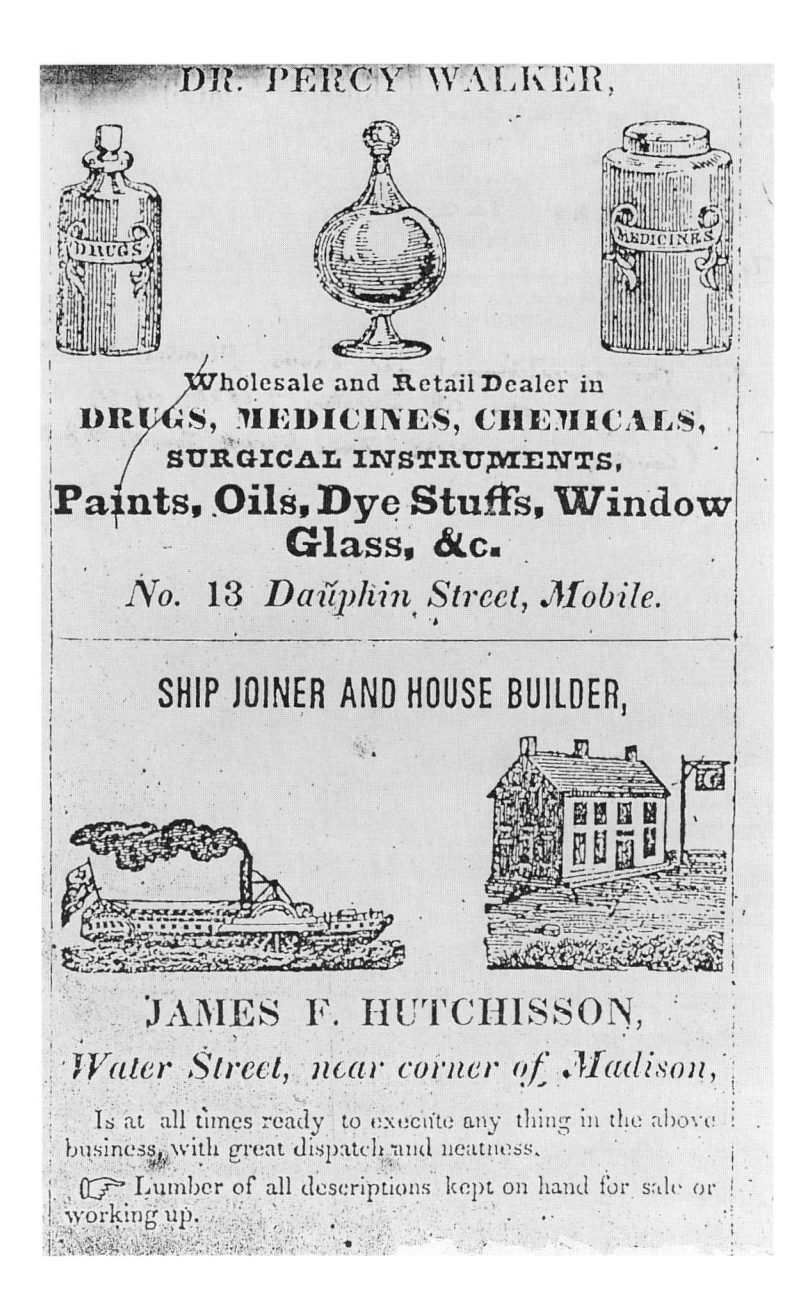

FIGURE 21
The advertisement for James Flandin Hutchisson as it appeared in the City Directory for 1838-9.

little has been discovered about his early life in New York except that he married a "Miss Brewster," the mother of his son, James Henry Hutchisson, who carried on the family building tradition. When James Flandin was twenty-seven years old, his wife died, and with young James Henry, he left the East for a new life on the Gulf Coast. He arrived in Mobile when the city was in the first flush of the cotton trade and two years before the financial panic of 1837.

Within four years of his arrival, the commercial section of the city was destroyed in the worst fire in its history. Three fires in quick succession swept up Royal Street, headed west up Dauphin and St. Francis Streets and was finally stopped just short of the Cathedral of the Immaculate Conception. Then as if to add a final death blow to the community, the second of the three major yellow fever epidemics to hit the city raged from 1837 to 1843.

These citywide tragedies also affected the private life of James Flandin. About a year after he had arrived in the city, he married Ann B. Spenser on September 19, 1836.[10] Before the year was out, the young bride died, presumably of the epidemic, though there was no cause of death listed on her death record. Records at the time must have been difficult to keep. Whole families were wiped out, children left orphans, one or both parents without children. Those with the means to do so, escaped to the high ground in Spring Hill where they were relatively safe from the infection. In 1838, Mr. Hutchisson married Amelia Graham who made a home for James Henry.[11]

In spite of the economic crisis of 1837, James Flandin was busily employed during 1838, proof of which is in the six contracts that have survived for that year. His skill as a ship's joiner was much needed as only two such trained men were listed in the City Directories of that time. His first advertisement (figure 21) appeared in the City Directory of 1838. In the advertisement he announced his profession as "Ship's Joiner and House Builder," located on Water Street near Madison, a part of the city now occupied by the

Bender Ship Building Company. Whether this was the site that burned in 1839 is not clear, but a request to the city to rebuild a new frame carpenter shop survives:

> To the Honorable Board of Mayar [sic] and Aldermen of the City of Mobile
> Gentlemen
> I wish to represent to your Honorable Board that on the night of the 28th of February my carpenter Shop and premises were destroyed by fire, which has proved a very heavy loss to me and I am not able to erect a Brick building in this Stead.

He went on to say that he would position the building in the middle of his lot to prevent a possible fire from spreading. He also promised to remove the building at any future time, when the development in that part of the city required it. Permission for him to rebuild was granted March 13, 1839.[12] He seems to have changed locations, for the 1839 Directory places him at 212 Dauphin Street where his business remains for the rest of his working years.

There is no accurate record of all the buildings that James Flandin Hutchisson constructed. Only seventeen contracts have survived, but there is evidence of other work that he carried out. There is a receipt for money paid to him for making a desk and platform for the court clerk.[13] One of his descendants has a silver pitcher given to him for constructing the cornice and roof of the Cathedral of the Immaculate Conception. On the pitcher is an inscription acknowledging his work. It is signed by Bishop Michael Portier. This important job indicates how highly regarded his work was in the community.

The seventeen surviving contracts include: two for ship's construction; six for one-story cottages; three for two-story store-residence combinations; one for a brick home; and one for a brick warehouse (the largest on record for that time). There are also two contracts for commissions to build an addition onto the existing Mansion House, one of the few hotels that survived the 1839 fire. (See Appendix 4 for the list of James Flandin Hutchisson's contracts.)

The first surviving contract dated January 17, 1838, is for a cabin to be added at the cost of $1,200 to the *Tallapoosa* owned by Aaron Livingston of Montgomery County.[14] The cost equals twice the price to build a single story cottage. A second contract, dated July 6, 1842, is for the housing on a steamboat owned by A. C. Wilson, costing $1,842.[15] The first contract included some specifications that give a good idea of the accommodations for travel on a river steamer in the 1840s. All the rooms were small, even those of the officers were only four by six feet. Aft on the vessel was the ladies' cabin, with a pantry on one side and a water closet on the other, both of the utilities being only three feet square. The berths were open and set end-to-end. Next came the gentlemen's cabin that was somewhat larger, with five berths set end-to-end ranging on both sides of the room. From this room the hall, three feet wide, led to the public rooms, three on each side. These rooms contained a bar, a pantry, offices and officers quarters. Forward of the vessel was the boiler and two wheel houses. Traveling in such cramped quarters certainly had its drawbacks, but it was still more comfortable than overland travel. Unfortunately, contracts dealing with the housing on the cargo vessels did not survive.

With the quadrupling of the population from 3,194 residents in 1830 to 13,621 in 1840, due largely to the increase in the working classes, inner city housing was a necessity. No accurate account can be made of the total number of new homes constructed, but enough evidence remains to suggest that the cottage was the most popular of the house types.[16] Only a total of nine contracts for cottages have survived, and of these James Flandin constructed six. Yet during the decade there were 120 carpenters and twenty-one builders listed in the City Directories. This does not count the bricklayers and masons, who did most of their work in the commercial area. The few photographs and contracts that have survived must be a mere token of the total number of homes built.

Two different plans for the cottage were employed. The smaller type, less expensive and better adapted to a narrow city lot, was a direct outgrowth of the early French cottage. It had no hall, and the usual four rooms were so placed that two rooms in front were backed by two in the rear. The front rooms were a living room and a bedroom, while the two back rooms were the owner's choice, either bedrooms or one bedroom and a dining room. The second plan allowed for a central hallway and usually had provisions for garret bedrooms. Both plans can be found in the Hutchisson contracts.

An example of the hall-less type is the cottage built for Oliver Pittfield, dated April 5, 1838. (See excerpt from contract in Appendix 5.)[17] The one-story cottage was located on South Conception Street, south of Canal in a part of the city that had only recently been opened up for development. Typically the cottage was twenty-four feet wide by twenty feet deep, with the long axis running parallel to the street. The gallery was six feet wide and supported by five "turned Collums, Rail and Bannisters, to have front and rear steps leading to yard."

The front and south side walls were covered with planed weatherboarding, also the "gallery overhead will be Ceiled with half inch weatherboarding, Planned Tongued and Groved." The north and rear walls called for unplaned weatherboarding, left "ruff." Obviously the cottage must have been exposed to the public on only two sides, and even in a cottage it was desirable to make a good appearance to one's neighbors.

The contract does not state whether the windows were double hung, but implies it since each window had twelve lights with glass panes ten by fourteen inches. During most of the early and mid-nineteenth century, the custom in Mobile was to have double hung windows with six lights in each sash. The exterior doors were paneled with the one leading to the living room having a three light transom. Interior room doors were "batten."

The interior plan details were quite specific. The two front rooms were a living room and a bedroom, both with doors opening up on the front gallery. The rear rooms were a dining room and a bedroom. A small room was partitioned off "on the opposite side of the rear bedroom for Pantrie or Closet as the said Pittfield may designate." All the ceilings were nine feet in the clear, such heights being necessary in the hot climate. The floor was laid of "good inch and a quarter plank Tongued and grooved" and the upper floor laid "of ruff inch boards as far as is necessary under the rafters." The interior doors and windows to be "Cased throughout." Though the cottage was small and the interior finish simple, it is amazing that it could have been constructed for $650 including the cost of the material.

The 1834 Dade Cottage that still stands at 503 St. Francis Street is one of the rare survivors of the 1839 fire (figure 22). It is not known to have been constructed by James Flandin, but it is typical of the early cottages that he built. The streets of the inner city were lined with these homes of the working classes. Although now some stand crowded in near to modern pavements, they once had small front green strips, or flowers, and usually a picket fence

FIGURE 22

The 1834 Dade Cottage at 503 St. Francis Street. The builder of the Dade Cottage has not been identified, but it is typical of the cottages that Hutchisson was building in the inner city during the 1830s.

ELIZABETH BARRETT GOULD

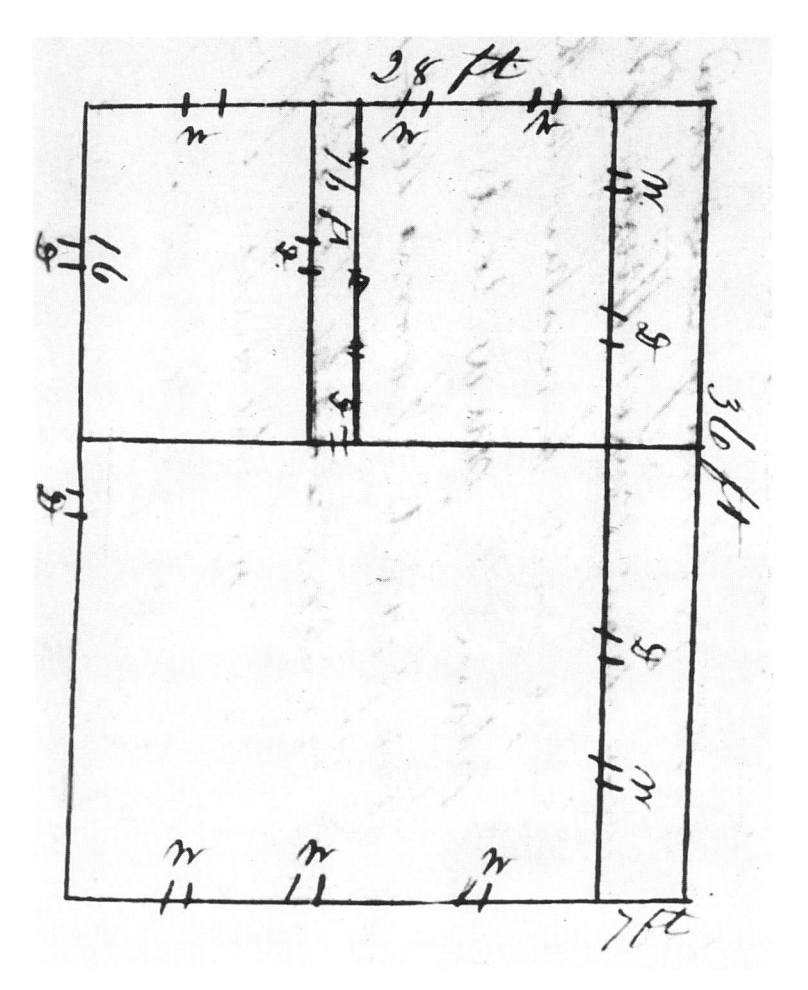

FIGURE 23

Sketch of a plan for a cottage for C. S. Hale, built by Hutchisson in 1838. The cottage originally stood on St. Francis Street, not far from the Dade Cottage. The contract was signed October 3, 1838. It is a typical plan without a central hall.

separated the lot from the narrow dirt-surfaced streets.

A larger cottage was constructed by Hutchisson for C. S. Hale (see excerpt from contract in Appendix 6 and a sample page). It was located on St. Francis Street, not far from the Dade House. It was built in October 1838 and cost twice as much as the Pittfield cottage. Twenty-two brick piers raised the cottage three and one-half feet above ground level, about half as high as some of the other dwellings built in areas of frequent flooding. A crudely drawn ground plan was included with the contract (figure 23).

The rectangular building was thirty-six feet long by twenty-eight feet deep, and, as in all the cottages, the long axis faced the street. The plan was unusual in that only three rooms were indicated. The largest room was twenty feet wide and extended the full twenty-eight-foot depth of the building. From the lack of any details concerning this room, it seems that it remained unfinished. Adjoining this room on the side were two rooms, the front being sixteen feet square and the back room twelve by thirteen feet.[18] There is an interesting correction made on the drawing of the partition between these two rooms. Originally, Hutchisson had divided the space equally between the two rooms and then decided to make the front room larger, so he crossed out the original partition wall and drew in the correct location. However, the rear room was specified in the contract to be only thirteen feet long, and this left the three feet of the full sixteen-foot length of half of the house unaccounted for in the drawing. He may have planned a closet there as he did in the Pittfield House but did not specify this in the drawing.

The seven-foot-wide front gallery was divided into five bays by six "pillars," ten inches thick with "a suitable flight of steps descending said gallery." The interior specifications called for ceilings eleven feet in the clear. The two outside doors, one leading into each of the rooms, were to be paneled and finished with transoms.

The interiors of the two rooms were to be finished in "Good style with wash boards painted and plastered with two coats." The fact that the large

From Builders to Architects: The Hobart–Hutchisson Six

room may have been left unfinished is suggested in the statement that there was an additional "back door leading from the unfinished part of the house." One double chimney provided for two fireplaces in the first story rooms and two in the garret that was also left unfinished.

The closing paragraphs of the contract recorded one of the customary stipulations made for the protection of the owner. It stated that if "Hutchisson did not have the cottage finished by the seventh day of November next, he would forfeit payment at the rate of two hundred dollars per month according to the time of work delayed."

At the same time that the Creole cottages with their three and four room plans were continuing in popularity, a larger version with a central hall was developed. In Mobile, at the same time, the late Federal and early Greek Revival styles were introduced by the settlers coming in from the Atlantic seaboard states. An early hall type was recorded in a contract between the trustees of the Catholic Diocese and the builder, George Hilliard, May 23, 1825.[19] Developing simultaneously with the appearance of the central hall was a change in the columniation of the galleries, the old posts or small squared supports

FIGURE 24

The Roberts-Staples Cottage (mid-century) at 1614 Old Shell Road. The builder of the Roberts-Staples Cottage is not known, but it is an excellent example of the fully developed Gulf Coast cottage with central hall, four large rooms on the first floor, and modified Greek Revival influence in the square gallery columns. It is similar in style to the O'Conner Cottage built by Hutchisson that once stood on Dauphin Street outside the city limits.

were being supplanted by variations of the Greek Doric order, both of semi-circular and squared section. With these developments, the cottage changed from the Creole form to the mature Gulf Coast cottage. An example of this is the Staples dwelling on Old Shell Road (figure 24). In this plan, four rooms of approximately equal size were separated by a central hall that extended the full depth of the house with large doors opening onto both the front and rear galleries. Windows were either the usual double hung of six lights in each sash, or a double hung window with the bottom sash nine lights that could slide by the upper one into a slot in the wall, making a large open passageway allowing for a free flow of air throughout the house.

A dwelling out in the country, similar to the Staples home, was built by James Flandin Hutchisson for Edward O'Conner.[20] The O'Conner home was located west of the city limits on Dauphin Road, a single dirt lane extension of the inner city Dauphin Street. The contract was dated June 7, 1839, and called for outbuildings as well as the main structure and costing $3,350. The cottage was a typical hall plan with the addition of a rear two-story wing fifteen feet wide by twenty feet long, with galleries on both levels. The home was a story and a half in height with the rear gallery divided into three sections. Each end was partitioned off for small rooms but the central area was open, and in this space, the stairway was built to the upper level. The stairway gave access to both the upper gallery of the wing and the central hall of the upper story.

The single family dwelling was not the only residential form that James Flandin Hutchisson built. In the commercial district there was the storehouse combination in which the first story was used for commercial purposes and the second for housing. These were all of brick construction and of two different types. The one was a row building attached to other stores. The second type was a double building with a passageway separating the two first floor stores. The former is typified by a contract for a row store for John Marshall, located on Jackson Street and costing $3,350.[21] The other type was recorded in two contracts, one for the partners James Burns and John Riley on Dauphin Street and the other for the partners Miguel Eslava and A. D. Dumée that occupied most of a block between Monroe, Eslava, Commerce and Water Streets.[22] Both of these contracts have detailed specifications. As shown in the contracts, James Flandin Hutchisson had developed into a master builder, employing a number of masons, carpenters, plasterers, slaters and other workmen necessary to carry out such complex designs — several under construction at the same time. No longer was he the ship's joiner and house carpenter of the 1830s.

The contract with Burns and Riley was signed February 20, 1841. The brick building was seventy-four feet eight inches long with the first story divided into four stores, each sixteen feet five inches wide by thirty-eight feet deep. Each had "2 sash doors in front one window and one pannel door in rear." Each had a chimney with a mantelpiece, and all had two coats of plaster and two coats of white lead paint.

An unusual feature of the building was the presence of a cellar under one of the stores. It was the same width as the store and six feet six inches deep with steps leading to the rear yard. The stairway was covered by two batten doors. With Mobile's water table so high, the presence of a cellar was not often attempted. At the rear of the building a gallery extended the full width of the second story. Two pairs of steps led from the "yard underneath to the gallery floor." Supporting the gallery roof were square columns connected by railings and bannisters.

The second story seemed to have been one single large residence with a six-foot hall leading from the gallery to a cross hallway that divided the front from the rear rooms. The hall, dining room and "setting" room were all finished with a "single architrave and brick moulding." The bedrooms were finished with plain casings and plain bases. Each bedroom was provided with a paneled door with locks. Each room had one window of twelve lights except the "setting room" that had two windows.

All doors were paneled and those leading from the hallway had transoms adding a much needed cross-circulation of air in a downtown building in the hot climate. Folding doors were called for between the dining room and "setting room."

The contract continued with specifications for the structural members, the required thicknesses for the brick walls, the sizes for wooden framing, flooring and casings. For all this Burns and Riley promised to pay James Flandin Hutchisson $5,000 in installments commensurate with the stage of construction. The last payment was to be on August 5, 1842, presumably when the building would be finished.

The most complex of all the surviving contracts is one for the store-residence for Eslava and Dumée. Because of its value to anyone interested in the details of construction in the early 1840s, the contract has been copied in its entirety in Appendix 7. The complex was located on the west side of Water Street, across from a warehouse built for the same partners by Mr. Hutchisson. The contract, dated March 3, 1841, points out the fact that Mr. Hutchisson was designing and supervising the construction of the Burns-Riley and Eslava-Dumée buildings at the same time.

The Eslava-Dumée building had a fifty-two-foot front and was fifty feet deep. The first story was divided into two stores, each thirteen feet high in the clear. They were separated by a nine-foot "corridor." The second story was divided into two "tenements," the one on the south to have four rooms and the one on the north to have three. Both living quarters had twelve-foot ceilings.

In addition to the main building, there were two kitchens divided by the continuation of the wall that separated the two apartments. This double kitchen formed a two-story wing with an eight-foot open space between it and the main building. Unusual for its details were the specifications for a double privy eight by eight feet in size with double compartments that had doors "neatly finished and painted." There was even a ventilator specified for the roof.

The details of the foundation of the main building give an idea of how the large brick buildings were supported in the sandy soil of Mobile. With no bedrock to reach, pilings were of little use. Two feet below the level of the floor, the foundation was laid to be "footed four courwes [of brick, sic] on two thickness of the best plank." In another building, not by Hutchisson, the contract stated cypress was used and laid in alternate courses, forming a type of raft floating on the sandy soil. (It preceded by some years the development of the floating slab by the Chicago School of Architects.) With cypress being so easily available in the nearby swamps and since it did not rot, it was so commonly used that Mr. Hutchisson may not have thought it necessary to mention the type of wood used in this foundation.

Flooring in the stores was laid by planks seven by one-fourth inches, "plained and jointed." The kitchen floor was paved with "good hard brick" and the flooring of the second story of the main building was seven inches wide by one and one-fourth inches thick planed and "tongue and grooved."

Two details of the refinements are especially interesting. Among the directions given for the various doors and their locks is the statement that the front doors of the residences "were to be painted two coats grained imitation of sap wood and varnished." The inside trim and outside bannisters were to be painted with two coats of "pure white lead except the mantel which was painted black." The caps on the railings of the first story were bevelled and those of the second story were given a three-fourth inch "bead" and all upstairs "Casings to have one-half inch bead." A garret above the second story was described and instructions for covering a "well hole" with a single piece of zinc extended "so that no rain could enter" the building.

One other building by Hutchisson must be mentioned in some detail. It is the warehouse built for M. D. Eslava and A. D. Dumée.[23] As noted on the 1856 Robertson Map, (figure 20) the length of the waterfront was being filled with wharfs and warehouses. Some of the warehouses were small, some even occupying sites on the wharfs. Some were large, occupying whole blocks along Front, Commerce and Water Streets. The largest that has a surviving contract was the warehouse for Eslava and Dumée. It had a frontage of fifty-four feet on both Water and Commerce Streets and extended in depth 228 feet, being located between Monroe and Eslava.

Unfortunately no drawings were included in the contract such as were preserved in two contracts for smaller warehouses built by the master mason James Deas.[24] Since the warehouses had similar interior arrangements, the Deas's drawings give a quick visual impression of the large open spaces divided by the supporting columns for the upper levels. The Hutchisson contract has specific notations for all details of the Eslava-Dumée building, from foundation to roofing. The foundation of the warehouse was more complex than that for the store-residence built for the same owners. It called for two rows of piles:

> well driven, close, and topped with flat boat 'gunnels' not less than 24 inches wide and the brick work to begin one foot below the present surface of the ground to be footed four courses and diminished gradually until it makes the size of the wall which is to be two and a half bricks thick as far as the second floor and the balance two bricks.

The first story was to have a height of fifteen feet between the floor and tie beams. To support the floor of the second story were two rows of twelve-by-twelve-inch square posts placed "not more than ten feet apart with a 'trimmer' 8 x 12 inches." To add to the strength of the support, each post was set on an additional block of three piles with a piece of cypress separating the piles from the posts.

Both the Water and Commerce Street fronts had four large doorways, each door five feet six inches by nine feet with "head lights besides two feet high 'grauted' with round Inch Iron five inches apart and cross Bars of Flat iron half inch thick by Three inches wide Screwed in each end to the door frame." Adding to the security of the building, openings were also covered with heavy shutters, those on the Water Street side were made of iron as were the shutters over the side windows. The sills of the doorways were made of pieces of granite eight by twelve inches and extending for ten inches beyond the actual openings. The flooring of the first story was doubled with wood planking "clear of sap and not over ten inches wide" laid over a solid brick pavement.

Slate covered the roof with copper gutters and tin "conductors" that were painted. The contract mentions two chimneys, one at each end, that "rose from the second story." Access to this second story was by two sets of stairs and "two skuttle holes" were cut into the floor of the second story.

The general appearance of the building must have been like a jail with its gratings, grilles and iron shutters. Some concession was made to a less austere effect by painting the doors on the Commerce Street side a dark green. These were set in frames painted a lead color.

Other types of buildings were going up in the city as well. At best, the hotels of Mobile during this part of the century were inadequate. After the fire of 1839 destroyed most of the commercial city, hotel space was critical. One of the few hotels still available was the Mansion House that stood on the corner of Royal and Conti Streets. In 1849 Mr. Charles Cullum engaged J. F. Hutchisson to construct a large addition.[25] The addition had a three-story

FIGURE 25

An engraving of the old Mansion House, a hotel to which Hutchisson constructed an addition in 1849.

elevation along Royal Street for fifty-eight feet, ten inches. It extended along Conti Street as a two-story building for 119 feet. Since the specifications called for a continuation of the same elevation details as present in the older building, Hutchisson had no opportunity to do any planning of his own (figure 25).

Mention has been made of Hutchisson's work on the cornice and roof of the Cathedral of the Immaculate Conception. There is no surviving contract for this work but the silver pitcher that was presented to him is evidence of his contribution to the Cathedral construction.[26] It also establishes the high regard with which he was held — from all the builders available at the time including Cary Butt and James Barnes, he was chosen to finish the most prestigious building in the city. The inscription on the pitcher (figure 26) reads:

> To James F. Hutchisson, Esq., from the Managers of the M.C. B. So.
> In Testimony of
> Their Esteem and entire Satisfaction with the fulfillment of his
> contract for
> Erecting the Roof and the Cornice
> of the
> Cathedral
> M. Portier, D.D.
> Bishop of Mobile

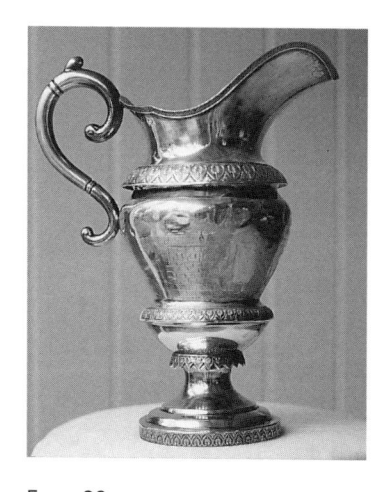

FIGURE 26

The silver pitcher that was presented to James Flandin Hutchisson for constructing the cornice and the roof of the Cathedral of the Immaculate Conception.

The Cathedral cornerstone had been laid in 1834, but it was not until 1842 that Claude Beroujon had the contract to proceed with the construction of the main body. His contract specifically stated that he was not to construct the portico or the towers. James Flandin Hutchisson completed the main body of the Cathedral by adding the cornice and the roof (figure 26b). It would be his son, James Henry, who (in 1872) began the great Classical portico, and James Flandin II, who finished the portico on his father's death and later added the towers. (See chapters three and four.)

James Flandin Hutchisson I continued working into the early 1850s for there are several contracts surviving from that period. One was especially interesting for it establishes the time of the development of the Orange Grove community, north of the original city limits. There he was employed by J. Bloodgood to construct three kitchen houses.[27] The last contract found in the Probate Court records was for a brick home for Matthew Anderson, located on the northwest corner of Church and South Lawrence Streets, another new section opened up for homes, and now included within the Church Street Historic District.[28]

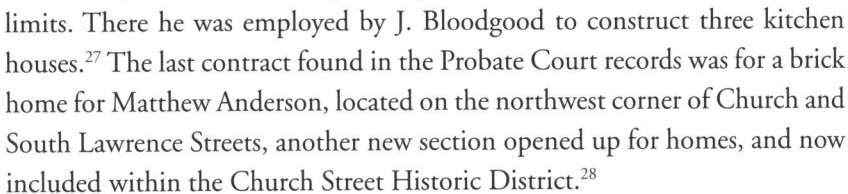

With the death of James Flandin Hutchisson, December 26, 1856, his building skills were passed on to his son James Henry. There was no record of the years of training that James Henry had in his father's office. Nor was there any known record of buildings that they may have done together, but James Henry was well prepared to pick up his father's mantle, becoming the outstanding builder-architect of the post-Civil War period.

James Flandin Hutchisson had arrived in Mobile during the early years of the city's development as a major port. He made his first contribution to the city by his skill as a ship's carpenter and house builder. In the 1830s, he constructed simple wood frame cottages to house the growing numbers of the working classes. By the 1840s, he was a master builder; erecting important brick commercial and residential buildings in the inner city, and employing many of the masons, carpenters, and slaters whose names are listed in the City Directories. He made his civic contribution by membership in the Torrent Fire Company and served his time as sheriff. He gave his name to the four members of the family who followed in his footsteps. He never introduced any historic architectural styles in his work as had Peter Hobart, the cofounder of the family. He never achieved the status of being an architect as would his son. But by his sense of design, his engineering skill, and his knowledge of construction, he made an indelible impact on the development of the architectural history of the inner city of Mobile.

FIGURE 26B

Detail of the cornice and roof lines of the Cathedral of the Immaculate Conception, showing the work of the first member of the family to work on the Cathedral.

PLATE III

The East facade of the Cathedral of the Immaculate Conception, 1872-1895, 4 South Clairborne. From 1872-1887, James H. Hutchisson, architect. From 1887-1895, James Flandin Hutchisson II, architect. From the building of the cornice and roof of the Cathedral in 1849 to the finishing of the towers in 1895, four generations of the Hutchisson family contributed their skills to the final completion of the building.

Chapter 3

James Henry Hutchisson

(1830–1887)

JAMES Henry Hutchisson was born in Hampstead, Long Island, and came to Mobile as a boy of about five. His life and work spanned the years of the Civil War and Reconstruction. These years brought profound changes in the social order and economic conditions to the deep South. It was a period ranging from the demands of war to the deep melancholy and despair of defeat. The postwar and reconstruction years that followed (1865 to 1879) were desperate for both races. The white race was filled with fear and deeply divided between the conservative Democrats and radical elements of the Republican Party. The black race was disappointed and disillusioned. The greater freedom they sought was not forthcoming. Former slaves expected the government to take care of them, and former free blacks found the world of democracy an unequal place. The attitude of the former was expressed by a former slave of Anne Quigley who, in her diary quoted: "Massa Lincoln gwine take care o'dem — White folks take care of dey selves—gegroe grwine rest now some."[1] Racial tensions between conservative whites and a group formed from radical whites and the black community led to belligerency and finally to violent riots. As the decade passed, Mobile slowly began to face the realities of its economic problems, to seek a solution, and to evolve a kind of peace. The result was much like a semidormant volcano concealing the smoldering eruptive power within.

That any kind of building program could be undertaken from the years 1865 to 1870 was amazing. With the war and its resulting loss of all personal and public wealth, and the 1865 catastrophic explosion of the Ordnance Depot that destroyed eight blocks of the commercial district, it speaks to the tenacity of Mobilians that they attempted any building programs.

The contrast between the architectural activity of the 1850s with the following decade dramatically points out the paucity of Reconstruction when James Henry Hutchisson began his career. The 1850s were indeed a "Golden Age" socially, economically and architecturally for Mobile.[2] There seemed no limit to the wealth and importance that cotton would bring to the port city. The port and the city grew to accommodate the increase in activity (figure

FIGURE 27

The Robertson Map of 1856 shows the plan of the city of Mobile when only a limited area west of Broad Street was opening up. When James H. Hutchisson was twenty-six years old, the residential and commercial development of the city was concentrated between Broad Street on the west and the river on the east, and between Church Street on the south and St. Louis Street on the north with warehouses and wharves extending north to Beauregard.

27). Ships left port to return with all the material delights of the world as well as the needed staples. Architecturally, the decade attracted architects from the national scene as well as granted commissions to local architects and builders. Ammi Burnham Young designed the United States Custom House (constructed 1852-1856), though his right to that attribution was challenged by the Mobilian, Thomas James.[3] Isaiah Rogers (1800-1869) designed the first Battle House in 1851-52. Frank Willis (1822-1856) and Henry Dudley (1813-1894) of New York designed the 1853 Gothic Revival Trinity Episcopal Church that once stood on the corner of St. Anthony and Jackson Streets but was moved to 1900 Dauphin Street.

Besides these nationally known architects, there were nine locally listed in the City Directories for the 1850s. Among them were William S. Alderson, who was the architect for the 1853 second County Courthouse built after the destruction of the Courthouse of Peter Hobart. David Cumming, Jr., designed the 1853 St. John's Episcopal Church, among other buildings. Philip Daughtery was the architect for some fine Italianate homes of the decade. Besides the decade's architects there were five master builders of which two master masons were from England, and many carpenters, bricklayers, plasterers and others needed in the building trade.[4]

Greek Revival style remained prominent in the plantation counties of Alabama in the 1850s with such homes as architect Thomas Helm Lee's 1853 Sturdivant Hall in Selma, but the Italianate dominated in the commercial city of Mobile. The Italianate expressed the jubilant spirit of Mobile society more than the dignified and formal Greek Revival. While cottages still incorporated the elements of the classical orders, the more informal Italianate house with its decorative cornices, cast iron columns, and decorative friezes on the galleries expressed the age. The 1857 City Hall incorporated many Italianate characteristics that were found in residential examples. The Tuscan Villa phase of the Italianate was rare in Mobile though it appears in other parts of the state.

Public and private records identified a number of James Henry Hutchisson's buildings. In all, 195 have been listed of which 18 still stand in various parts of the city, largely east of Monterey Street, at the Monastery of the Visitation and at Spring Hill College.[5] Two also remain standing in other Alabama cities. His body of work includes buildings for all economic classes, whites and blacks, residences, commercial buildings, churches and civic structures. (For a list of the standing buildings see Appendix 8.)

During his early years he was under the tutelage of his father. The custom of that day for any young man aspiring to be a builder or an architect, was to work in the office or private "atelier" of some established master. Education in an architectural school did not become common practice in the United States until the first quarter of the twentieth century. In 1898 of the only 362 students enrolled in United States' architectural education programs, 309 were in private "ateliers." As late as 1930, a total of only 507 degrees had been granted, and of this number only 10 in Alabama.[6]

The well-known architects of the eighteenth and nineteenth centuries, such as John Haviland and Henry Latrobe, were trained in Europe and emigrated to America. Robert Mills (1781-1855) was the first American-born architect of note. He graduated from Charleston College as a Classics major and then studied under Latrobe. For both the students in the private "ateliers" and the "gentlemen builders," who had no private tutelage, the builder's guides and pattern books were the main source of education. Publications such as John Haviland's *The Builder's Assistant* (1818-1820) and numerous works by Asher Benjamin were widely studied. One such book, *The Rudiments of Architecture*, was advertised in the Mobile newspaper of October 22, 1823. Books such as these furthered James Henry Hutchisson's education.[7] Some builders guides and pattern books from James Henry's time are contained in the Hutchisson family library. These include:

1. Benjamin, Asher, *The Builder's Guide, or Complete System of Architecture* (Boston: Mussey and Co., 1850).
2. Gould's *House Carpenter Assistant*, Newark, 1853, May.

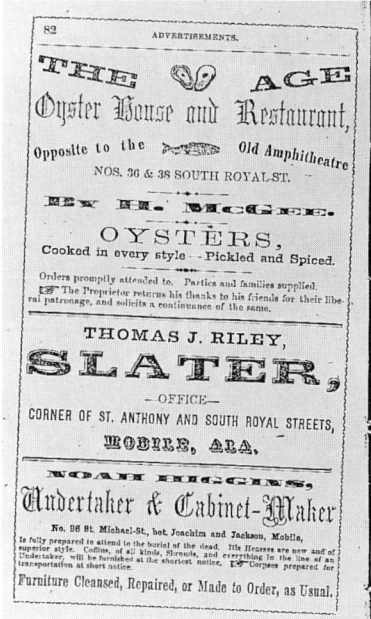

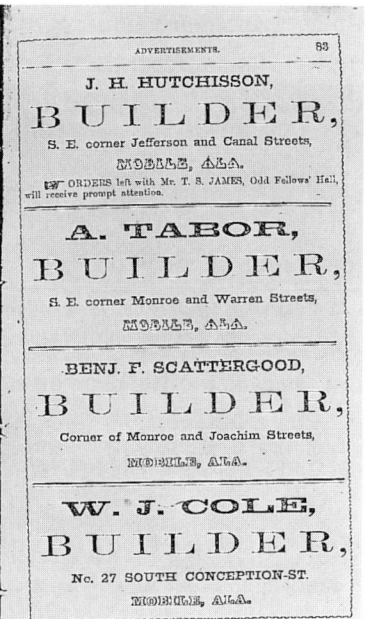

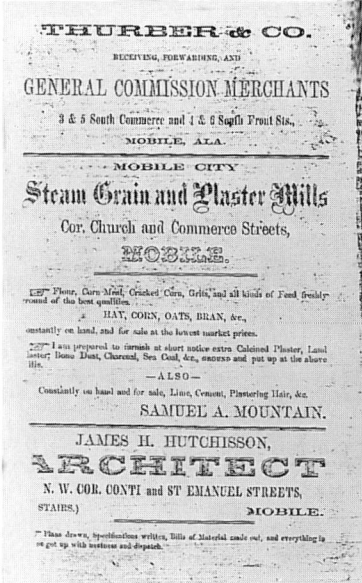

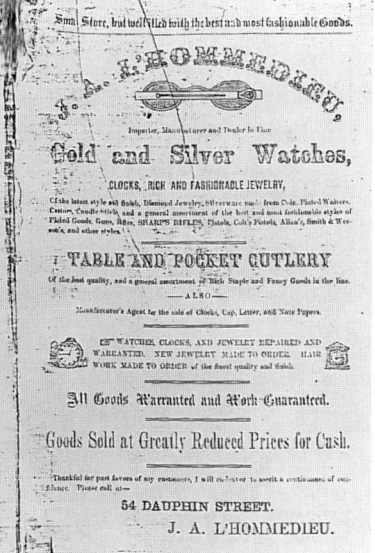

FIGURE 28
The 1859 advertisement of James Henry Hutchisson as builder, published in the City Directory, 1859, pg. 83.

FIGURE 28B
The 1861 pre-Civil War advertisement for James H. Hutchisson, architect. Published in the City Directory of 1861.

3. Le Roy, M., *Architects, Ancien Pensionnaire du Roi a Roma de l'Institut de bologna. Les Ruines des plus beaux Monuments de la Greece: ouvrage divise en deux parties: dans la premiere ces Monuments du cote de ilisoirs; et dans la seconde, du cote de l'Architecture*, MDCCLVIII (1758).

4. Lefever, Minard, *Builder's Guide*. New York, 1833, Sept.

5. *Nicholson's Dictionary of the Science and Practice of Architecture, Building, etc.*, Edited by Edward Lomax, Esq., C.E. and Thomas Gunyon, Esq., Arch. and Peter Jackson, Late Fisher, Sons and Co. London-The Caxton Press, Angel St., St. Martin's Le Grand.

6. A. Pugin and A.W. Pugin, architects. *Gothic Architecture Selected from Various Ancient Edifices in England*, Vols. I, II, III. London, Henry G. Bohn, 1850.

7. Ricke, August, *Wohn-Gebaude fur Stadt und Land in Facaden, Grundrifsen, Durchshnitten, und Details*. Berlin, August, 1853.

8. *Robinson's Rural Architecture or Designs for Ornamental Cottages*. London, Henry G. Bohn, 1850.

9. Sloan, Samuel, *The Model Architect, a series of Original Designs for Cottages, Villas, Suburban Residences, etc.* Philadelphia, E.S. Jones and Co., 1852.

10. Sloan, Samuel, *The Architectural Review and American Builders' Journal*, Vol. I, Philadelphia, Claxton, Remsen and Haffelfinger, 1839.

11. Vignole, *Classique D'Architecture Apres Jacques Barozzio. de Vignole. de Lannoy Architecte, lithographie par E'Gillet*. Paris: Monroco Freres Imprimeurs-Editeurs R. Suger P. Stmichel, Plates, no date.

With the formalization of architectural education in America, there soon came a split between the training of an architect and an architectural engineer. The former concentrated on design and the latter on construction. This division of responsibility appeared even outside of the professional programs, as the builder gradually elevated himself to the status of architect. This is well exemplified in the life of James H. Hutchisson. During his training period under his father, he is still listed in the City Directory of 1856 as a carpenter. By 1859, his advertisement reads, "Builder" (figure 28). In 1861 he has become an architect (figure 28b), contracting out his designs to various builders. Along with his name as architect appeared the names of masons, carpenters, plasterers, painters, etc., who erected his buildings. James H. Hutchisson always maintained a close "hands on" supervision. He recorded many visits to the construction sites in his diaries. The 1869 City Directory has the advertisement for James H. Hutchisson as it appeared in its final form (figure 28c). The same Directory lists his residence as being on the west side of Lafayette, between Government and Dauphin Way.

As yet it has not been possible to document any of the buildings Hutchisson erected before the Civil War. From January 7, 1861, when the seven southern states seceded to form the Confederate States of America, the Port of Mobile was a major point of contention (figure 30, Map of Western Campaign of the Civil War). Both sides recognized the strategic position of Mobile with its river access to the interior of the southern states and its open access to the sea. Governor A.B. Moore of Alabama immediately called out the Alabama militia to take and hold Fort Morgan and Fort Gaines, key defense positions for the harbor of Mobile. On April 19, 1862, the North ordered a blockade of all southern ports and Mobile became an armed camp. The North hoped the blockade would bottle up the cotton trade, the revenues from which financed the South's forces. This blockade lasted until Admiral David Farragut finally captured Forts Morgan and Gaines in July 1864.

All able-bodied men in the city were in the war. The youth that were left plus some militia and older men, who could still carry on some work, built three strong defences around the city, as well as further fortifications on the eastern shore of the river. All ele-

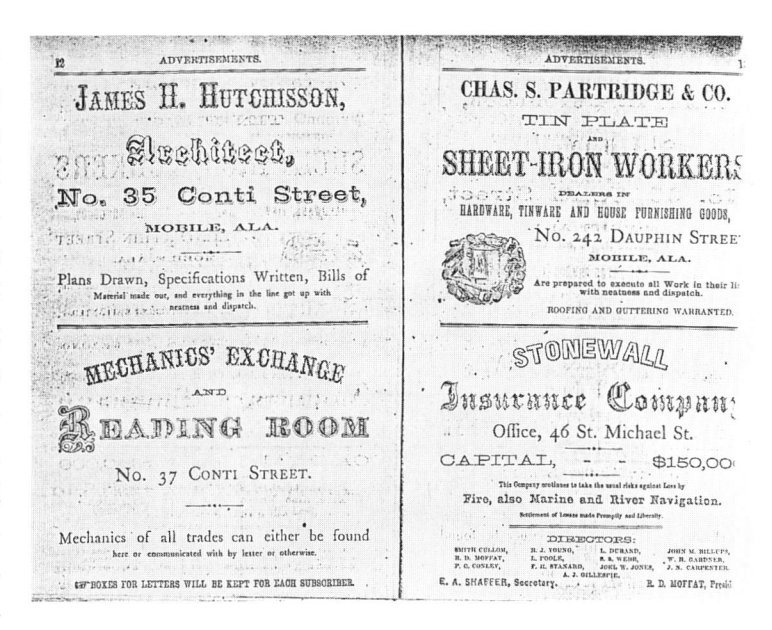

FIGURE 28c

In the 1869 post-Civil War edition of the City Directory, James H. Hutchisson's name appears as architect designated with elaborate script commensurate with his growing status.

FIGURE 29

Portrait of James H. Hutchisson in his early adult years.

FIGURE 30

An 1862 Map of the Western Theatre of the Civil War showing the campaigns fought between January and June of that year. The events listed along the line of the map from Shiloh, Tennessee, to Mobile, Alabama, depict those in which James H. Hutchisson as a member of Company E, Second Battalion, Alabama Light Artillery, participated.

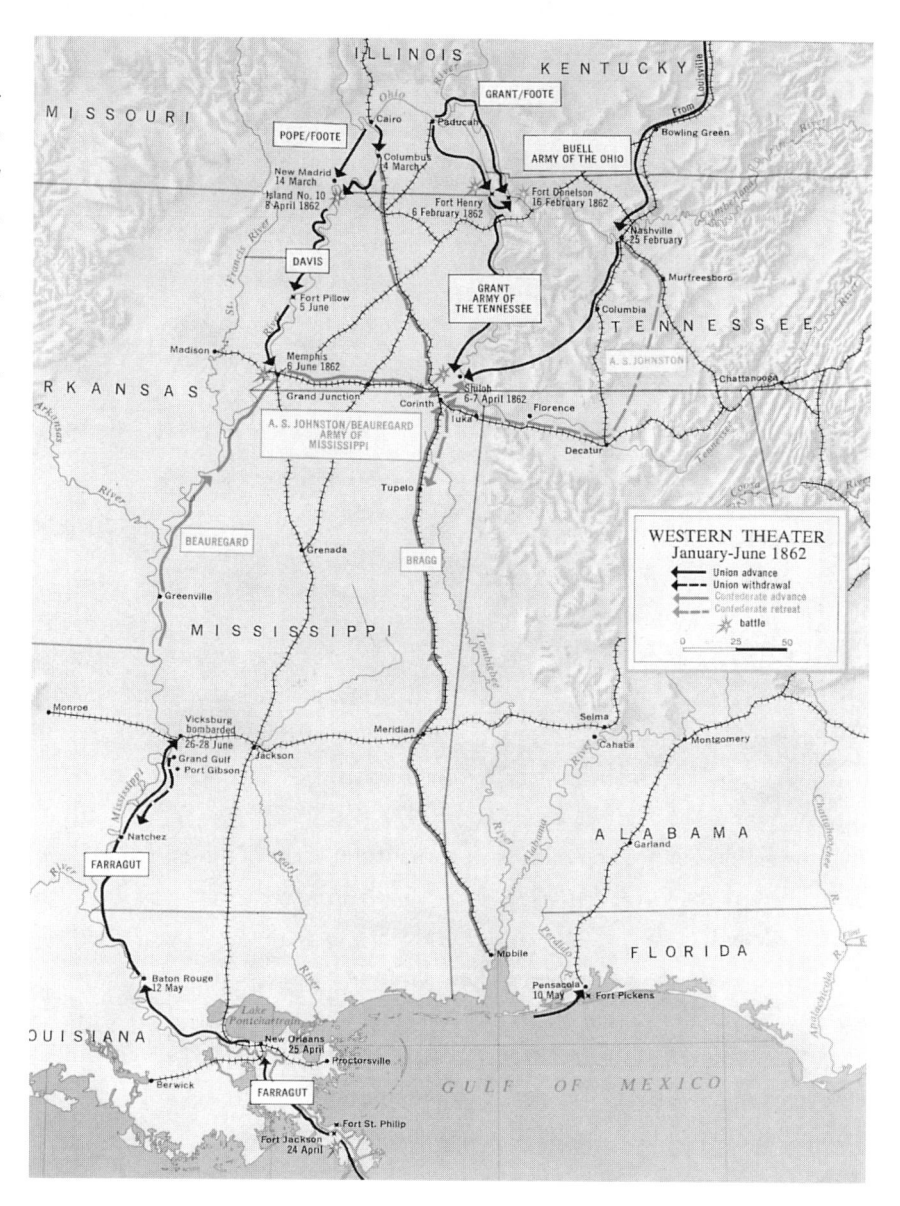

ments of the city were utilized in the war effort. With the blockade, staples and commodities in Mobile became more and more scarce, and what was available skyrocketed in price. In Ann Quigley's diary, she lists the costs of staples. Between 1861 and 1865:

> Butter rose from 50 cents/lb to $16.00/lb.
> Coffee rose from 75 cents/lb to $60.00/lb.
> Tea rose from $2.00/lb to $100.00/lb.
> Flour rose from $62.00/barrel to $225.00/barrel.[8]

When New Orleans fell in 1862, Mobile was the only Gulf Coast port left through which blockade runners could continue. Adding to the confusion after the closing of New Orleans, Mobile became a training center for the troops of Louisiana and Mississippi, further depleting the scarce supply of food. In 1863 a riot broke out in which the citizens demanded bread or peace. Meanwhile, on the war front, it was not going well for the South. City after city fell. (Map, figure 30).

Mr. Burney Crooks of Pensacola, Florida, has compiled Mr. Hutchisson's Civil War records from the National Archives as well as collected his portrait, pistol and other memorabilia. Early in the War years, James H. Hutchisson enlisted in Company E of the Second Battalion Alabama Light Artillery, serving as sergeant major at the Battle of Shiloh on April 6, 1862. Some idea of his personality can be gained from his portrait (figure 29) and from a newspaper account of his action in battle at Shiloh recorded by a fellow soldier:

> Sergeant Hutchisson, who was the chief of Caissons that day, was remarkably self possessed. A bullet passed close to his head in the fourth engagement. A remark was made to him that this bullet was very close. "There's a good many of them of the same sort," was his reply, and he sat on his horse as impassive as a statue.[9]

The Battle of Shiloh was one of the bloodiest battles of the Civil War. General Ulysses Grant, with his Federal troops, engaged with General Albert Johnston in a two-day battle that took 13,647 Northern and 10,694 Southern lives including General Johnston's.[10] After the war, one of James Henry Hutchisson's men mailed him a sketchbook he made with scenes of the battle.

FIGURE 31

A page reproduced from a sketch book of the Battle of Shiloh, drawn by one of the soldiers under Hutchisson. The soldier mailed it to him after the war.

ELIZABETH BARRETT GOULD

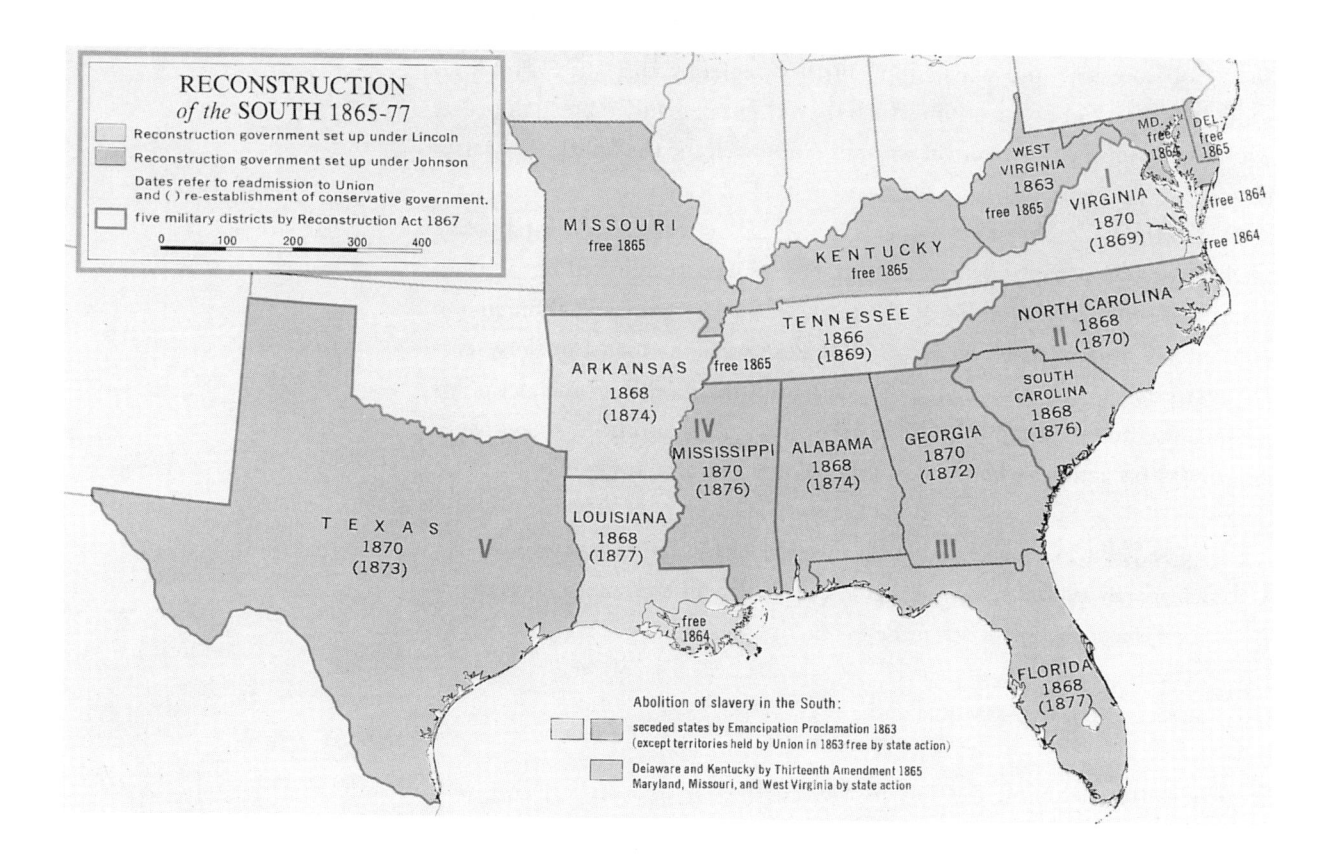

FIGURE 32

Map of the Reconstruction of the South, 1865-1877, in which Alabama is shown as one of the five states with a military district established by the 1867 Reconstruction Act. It was under this controlled governmental rule that James H. Hutchisson began his mature architectural years.

The drawings were crude but captured the spirit of terrible slaughter. The sketchbook is now in the possession of a collector in Pascagoula, Mississippi. A page of it was reproduced in the Mobile newspapers (figure 31).

After the Battle of Shiloh, James H. Hutchisson returned to Mobile to assist in the defense of the city. In quick succession he was promoted to lieutenant in May of 1862 and then to captain on February 16, 1863. Being recognized as an architect and a builder, he was sent to various defense locations. In May he was sent to Fort Gaines, the next month to Fort Morgan and to other assignments at the sand battery. Following the fall of Mobile, his battalion boarded steamers to travel up the Tombigbee intending to join General Lee, not having yet been informed that Lee had already surrendered. While on the river at Demopolis, he wrote his last war letter to his wife, dated April 14, 1865. The letter explained where he had hidden some food — ham, flour, etc. and where she might go to collect some money. Elements of the battalion surrendered to General Taylor G. Canby, allowing James H. Hutchisson to return home to begin a new life in a very troubled Mobile.

As Federal troops accompanied by some Negro soldiers marched the city streets, Mobile surrendered to a decade filled with bitterness and upheaval. Hatred and fear by the white population was commonplace. The event is vividly described in Ann Quigley's diary. To add to the situation, eight blocks of the inner city were destroyed by the 1865 explosion of the Ordnance Depot, in which not only buildings were leveled but hundreds of people and animals were killed. Four-fifths of the city's warehouse and storage facilities were destroyed.[11]

The depression and hopelessness was increased by the Reconstruction Acts incorporating the 13th and 14th Amendments to the Constitution (figure 32, Map of the Reconstruction of the South). In the former, slavery was abolished by law and in the latter the Civil Rights Act stated that no citizen could be deprived of life, liberty or property without due process of law. With these two Acts, a traditional way of life was wiped out, leaving the white population unsure of any way to form a new future. As a result, the next decades found Mobile and the South locked in a struggle between conservative and radical whites, the latter joined by the black community.

Physically, Mobile's commercial life lines were in ruins. Because of destroyed bridges and ruined tracks, the railroads were useless. The river and harbor were clogged with war debris and with mines. With the economy at a standstill, and no money either privately or publicly available, no jobs existed for the hundreds of ex-slaves that poured into the city. As a result, many former slaves became entangled in the city's long established vagrancy laws, by which idlers were either jailed or put to forced labor. Many blacks found themselves in a situation as bad or worse as before the war when they at least had a bed and food. The conditions resulted in the development of Mobile's first real shanty town.

Frequent confrontations, sometimes violent, occurred. Usually the conflicts were resolved, until the fatal day in May of 1867 when the Pennsylvania Congressman William D. Kelley came to Mobile for a political speech. The crowd was mixed, made up of radical whites, blacks, and conservatives. What started as heckling ended as a bloody riot with two people killed, at least ten wounded, and tempers completely out of control. The result was a military takeover of the city with martial law declared and all local government officials dismissed. A military mayor was installed until the next election could take place in which the blacks would have the right to vote.

In this environment James Henry Hutchisson began his building career. Although already classified as an architect, with the lack of community incentive and even less capital, his scant record during the early Reconstruction years is no surprise.

The Architectural Career of James H. Hutchisson

Records exist for four buildings Hutchisson built between the years 1866 and 1870. Of these, only one is still standing. Among those destroyed was a three-story, brick commercial building that he designed for Mr. C. P. Gage in 1866. Located on the north side of Government Street and facing Commerce and Front Streets, the building had a width of ninety feet on Front Street, eighty feet on Government, and was constructed of the best quality of "home-made brick."[12] The first story was fourteen feet high and contained stores. The second story, thirteen feet high, was used as offices, and the top story, twelve feet high, was planned for apartments and storage. The building was one of the first of many in which James H. Hutchisson, as architect and supervisor of construction, also contracted with builders to carry out his plans. The brick work and plastering for the Gage building was under contract to B. S. Scattergood and the carpentry to A. M. Swasey. Old photographs of the last decades of the nineteenth and early twentieth centuries show the solid rows of buildings along Front and Commerce Streets. All were of brick, connected by party walls, but differing in cornice and fenestration. They varied from two to three stories, but collectively they made a homogeneous street scene. Some were still standing as late as the 1970s. Their large warehouse doors formed a continuous pattern of vertical and horizontal lines along the street. If they had not been destroyed, the buildings would have had the same possibility for development as those in Factor's Walk along the river in Savannah.

In 1866 James H. Hutchisson also designed a commercial building for the Messrs. Forcheimer, wholesale grocers. It was a two-story brick building on Commerce and St. Michael Streets. The building did not last long, for on January 8, 1886, a fire swept the whole waterfront, destroying the Forcheimer building along with many others. The grocers immediately made plans for a new and larger warehouse. As the newspaper account of September 1, 1886, said, "The walls had hardly got through crumbling when estimates were already made for the erection of another structure." This new building, reported in the September trade journal of the newspaper, was also designed by James H. Hutchisson (See figure 46).

That brick buildings could be completely devastated by fire is hard to understand unless one recognizes that the interior partitions, floor joists, ceilings, and roof supporting members were wooden. In spite of building codes passed to regulate the thickness of party walls and the height of fire walls above the roof level, fires plagued the city throughout the nineteenth century. Once a fire got started and reached a certain temperature, nothing including the valiant attempts of the volunteer fire companies could control the flames. It was not until 1888 that a fire department was established as an official department of city government.

Before 1888, fire control had been provided by independent companies made up of young business and professional men who bought their own equipment and constructed their own fire stations. These early companies also served as clubs where members donated their time to fire control for a community and, at the same time, participated in social activities, such as balls and annual parades. In addition to the considerable social prestige of being in a company, members were excused from compulsory night patrol and from paying poll tax.

Among these early fire company members was James H. Hutchisson. In his death notice in the *Mobile Register* of August 26, 1887, is a brief survey of his life, including a paragraph dealing with his contribution to the fire companies (See Appendix 9):

> The deceased was a prominent fireman. He signed as a member of Fire Company #3 on the 5th of February, 1853, and was afterwards foreman of that company. In 1855 he was elected second assistant chief under A.M. Quigley. In 1856 he was chosen first assistant under J.F. Jewett, and in 1857 he was elected Chief. ——Capt. Hutchisson was one of the original organizers of Fire Company #9 on the 2nd of April, 1866.

In spite of the fire companies' dedication, they were not always successful in stopping a blaze once it got started. An adequate water supply was not always available before the 1886 Bienville Water Works was established. With twentieth century fire protection, it is hard to realize how primitive was the service in the nineteenth century. Some idea of this can be gained when checking on the building codes of the last century. All party walls had to have a thickness of no less than one and one-half bricks.[13] The placement of timbers had to be further protected by eight inches of solid masonry between their ends and by three inches from the party walls. Fire walls had to rise two feet above the roof. Every house had to have a fire bucket ready for instant use, while three buckets were required for warehouses and hotels.

The first of ten companies was the Creole Fire Company, Number 1, founded in April of 1819 by John McCluskey[14]. At first located on North Joachim Street, in 1869 it obtained property at what is now 15-17 North Dearborn and employed Mr. Hutchisson to design its new building, which is still standing (figure 33). Mr. Hutchisson's building is typical of all the fire stations, being a two-story, brick building with a stable for the horses used to draw the pumping engines and other equipment. At the street level, large double doors opened to allow for the passage of pumping engines that required sixteen men to operate.

The facade of the fire station is divided into three bays, the central bay wider than those of the sides. All the openings of the facade have segmentally curved heads. The two side bay doors are slightly recessed, giving the impression of a panel, with both the inner and outer orders segmen-

FIGURE 33

The Old Creole Fire Station, Number 1, 1869. 15-17 North Dearborn Street. James H. Hutchisson, architect. The building is the earliest extant example of the architect's post-Civil War years. The building served the city from 1869 to 1960, first as a station of the independent Creole Fire Company, and then after 1888 as part of the city fire department.

FIGURE 33B

Detail of the second story parapet and cornice of the Creole Fire Station. Hutchisson became a master at designing buildings in brick. His material was both structurally sound and decorative. Various bricks were shaped and sized to form the multiple moldings, corbels, keystones and other details as seen in the stepped parapet framing of the station's name.

tally curved. The original door in the north bay has been replaced by a window, but the outline of the door is still visible and the sill is still in place below the infill. The second story of the station was occupied by offices, social rooms, and the men on duty awaiting calls. There was usually some attempt to give the social room elements of architectural refinement. The second story exterior brick work is most remarkable. The three bays are separated by narrow, twin pilasters rising from a multimolded string course to corbelled brackets that divide the cornice into three parts. Each section of that cornice forms a panel framed by a molding of shaped bricks. Above the cornice, a solid, stepped balustrade repeats the three-part division. The center section of the parapet is framed by short piers forming a brick recessed niche that has the number "1" engraved in its surface. The word "Creole" in high relief is surrounded by a frame of molded bricks.

The long windows of the second story have hood moldings resting on corbels and accented with a central keystone (figure 33b). The details of the bricks of the hood molds and the cornice illustrate the interest the architect had in making his building material decorative. The same attention to the laying of the bricks is continued in the triple corbels at the sides of the building that support the horizontal cornice. These corner corbels serve the double purpose of capitals for the twin corner pilasters and supports for the projecting cornice of the parapet above. The parapet is crowned by a double molding of bricks that step up to the central panel in which the name of the fire hall is placed. In each case, the bricks have been especially sized and shaped for their location as is easily seen in the keystones of the segmental arches over the windows and the main doorway of the first story. Decorative iron grills that once formed a balcony now cover the lower sash of the second story windows. The window on the north wall of the second story has a jack arch without elaboration. The north wall was badly damaged in the 1979 hurricane and has been restored.

In 1867 Hutchisson began work at the Convent of the Visitation. Just what he did at that time has not been documented; but throughout the 1870s and 1880s, he continued an active program of building at the Convent, which will be discussed along with buildings of the next decade.

The 1870s

Politically, the early 1870s were a continuation of the 1860s. The radical Republicans dominated the local government and held political power until the middle of the decade when, because of their growing dishonesty and double dealing, the Democrats gained a foothold in the political scene. Economically, while the situation was still bad, there was some hope of improvement with the first attempts to establish new sources of income. When the merchants realized that the cotton trade was not going to revive because what little cotton existed was being shipped to Memphis, not Mobile, they organized a Board of Trade in 1868. The first important substitute for the cotton was found in shipping lumber. In 1869 there was a small beginning in industry by the formation of the Magnolia Sugar Refining Company and the Mobile Fertilizer Manufacturing Company.[15] In July 1871, the foundry industry was revived by the chartering of the Phoenix Foundry and in January 1872, came the Mobile Wooden Ware Company.[16] James H. Hutchisson was appointed to the Manufacturing Committee of the Board of Trade in 1872 and served two terms.[17]

This early attempt at restoration of the economy was abruptly stopped by the panic of 1873 in which capital for investment was gone. With the collapse of the Bank of Mobile in 1874, bankruptcies replaced investments.[18] In the Miscellaneous Books I and J in the probate court, notices of forced sales and bankruptcies fill page after page. The La Clede Hotel that had opened so hopefully in 1861 was closed with the sale of much of its contents.

With such conditions, very little building was possible. A few structures were built before the panic such as the third county court building, designed by W. O. Pond and built by Charles Fricke. It was not until 1877 that building activity began to emerge again.[19] Only the Catholic Diocese was able to engage in any major architectural undertaking. Not only did the number of new buildings decline drastically, but so did the number of architects and builders. In the City Directory for mid-decade only three architects were listed, James H. Hutchisson, W. O. Pond, and Louis Monin, a contrast from the nine listed in the pre-Civil War days of 1860. By the end of the decade, there were four architects listed: James H. Hutchisson, W. O. Pond, Ferdinand Meyer and Rudolph Benz, the last erecting his first known building in 1877.

Based on the work of James H. Hutchisson and the few other buildings of the decade, the architectural styles continued from those of prewar years: a simplified Italianate, Gothic Revival and neoclassical. Toward the end of the decade, a variation of the Italianate, locally named Bracketed, can be seen in the residential buildings.

Had it not been for the Catholic Diocese, there would be little surviving

FIGURE 34

The Cathedral of the Immaculate Conception, 1834 to 1895. 4 South Claiborne Street. From 1834 to mid-century, Claude Beroujon, architect. Cornice and roof, 1849, James Flandin Hutchisson I, architect. Portico, from 1872 to his death in 1887, James H. Hutchisson, architect. Willard Hutchisson, son of James H., draftsman for many of the classically detailed drawings. James Flandin Hutchisson II, son of James H., finished the portico in 1890 and built the towers, 1890-1895, at a cost of $12,800. Portico stone and stuccoing by Pat Houston, $6,000.

evidence of structures from the depression period of 1873 and 1874. During this time, James H. Hutchisson built three religious structures that still stand. In 1873 he was actively engaged in beginning the monumental portico on the Cathedral of the Immaculate Conception. It occupied his attention until his death in 1887, and finally was finished in 1890 by his son James Flandin Hutchisson II (figure 34). The final design of the portico was quite different from that originally proposed by the first builder, Claude Beroujon. At the time of Beroujon's contract of 1843,[20] it was specifically agreed that he would not erect the portico, but his idea for it was reported in the *Mobile Register* of August 22, 1849. "There will be four columns in front, — the steeples when completed will have an altitude of one hundred and fifty feet."

Due to the lack of funds, the Diocese was not able to carry out any plans for a portico until the time of Bishop Quinlan in the 1870s. James H. Hutchisson built a hexastyle portico with two additional columns in antis instead of Beroujon's plan for four. The high ceiling of the portico is deeply coffered. The entablature and pediments follow the Greek Classic tradition. The destroyed preparatory drawings for the classical moldings were drawn by Willard Hutchisson, second son of James H. Hutchisson. Willard died quite young, before his career as a builder-architect had a chance to develop. Thus the portico of the Cathedral is the work of four members of the family. The roof and cornice follow the plan of James Flandin I in 1849; the portico designed by James H. Hutchisson, with Willard making many of the drawings; and James Flandin II continued the work of his father and finished the towers in 1895 at a cost of $12,000.[21] The final documentary record of the portico program was recorded with the payment of $6,000 for the stucco work to Pat Houston and for the stone to McDonald, March and Company.[22]

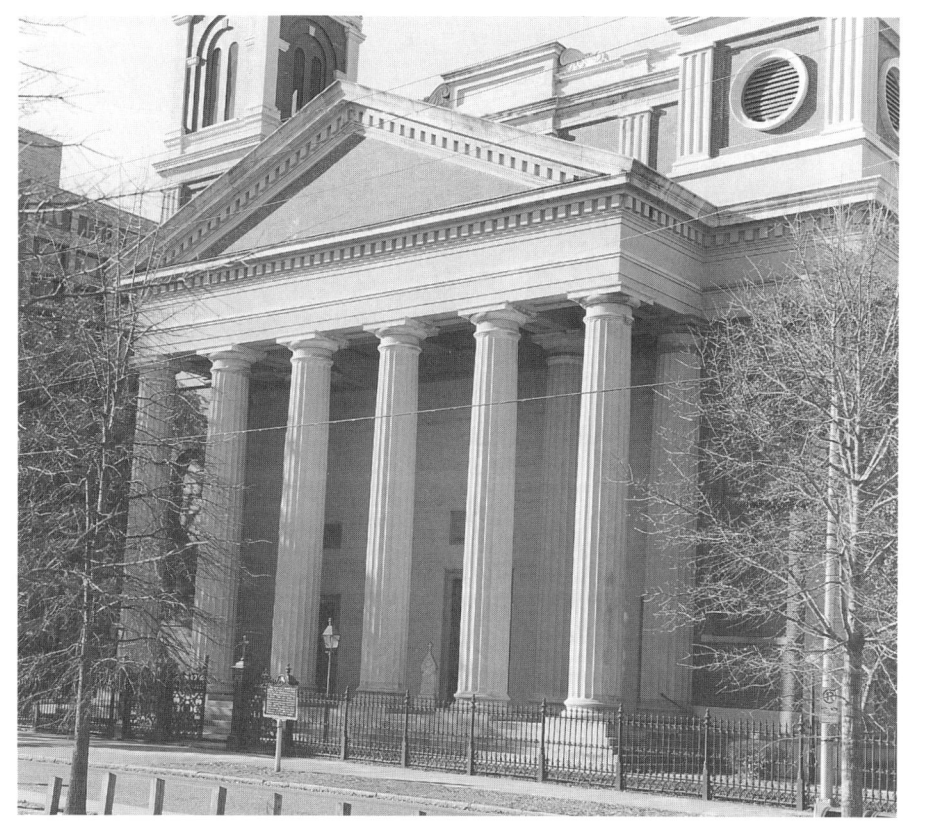

In 1874 Hutchisson designed the Gothic Revival Church of St. Vincent de Paul, (figure 35) now renamed the Church of the Prince of Peace. The Gothic Revival first appeared in Mobile in 1822 as shown in the engraved 1824

52 From Builders to Architects: The Hobart–Hutchisson Six

Goodwin and Haire Map (figure 12). It was a popular style in the 1850s with several fine churches erected during the prewar era. Among these was the 1853 Trinity Episcopal Church, designed by Willis and Dudley of New York. The building was torn down and rebuilt on its present site in 1945-46 by C.L. Hutchisson, Jr. (See Chapter 6). St. Vincent de Paul still stands at 454 Charleston Street.

While the postwar Gothic Revival differed considerably from that of antebellum days, it is interesting to compare Hutchisson's design with an engraving found in a book from his library, Samuel Sloan's *The Model Architect*. In that volume of plates is an engraving for a Gothic Church in which the proportions and the details differ, but there are enough similarities to suggest James H. might well have gotten his basic idea from the Sloan engraving. Both are long rectangular buildings with the facade dominated by an axial tower flanked on either side by the sloping roofs of the side aisles. Both buildings have corbel tables running along beneath the roof of the side aisles, lancet windows, and applied buttresses. The differences between the two buildings show that Hutchisson's design was conceived in the beginning stages of the Victorian Gothic Revival, rather than the earlier phase.

Originally, the Church of St. Vincent de Paul had no spire. Mr. Hutchisson's tower terminated with a square crown embellished with small turrets at the corners in the late English Gothic fashion. During Hurricane Frederick in 1979, the top was badly broken up and rebuilt with a new upper level and a spire that considerably altered the appearance of the building.

With the original tower, the facade was wider in relation to its height than that of the Sloan engraving, a characteristic that places the style in a later period. The same tendency can be seen in other churches in Alabama and Mississippi, such as the postwar First Presbyterian Church in Eufaula (1869), the late Grace Episcopal Church in Anniston (1882-1885), the First Presbyterian Church of Jacksonville (1858-1865), all in Alabama (See figure 36); and the First Presbyterian Church in Holly Springs (1860-1869), and the First Methodist Church in Columbus, both in Mississippi.[23] None of these have the taut verticality of the Sloan design. The post-Civil War Gothic Revival also had more complex surfaces accented by contrasts in the use of color, as

FIGURE 35

St. Vincent de Paul (renamed the Prince of Peace), 1874. 454 Charleston Street at corner of Lawrence. James H. Hutchisson, architect. J. Coyles and M. Smith, builders. $40,000. The original church, designed by Hutchisson, did not have a spire. The 1870s were still lean years for the economy of Mobile, which remained under military occupation, but St. Vincent stands as proof that designers and craftsmen were still available after the Civil War.

FIGURE 35B

Detail of the first level of the central bay of St. Vincent de Paul. Incorporated within the brick construction are decorative details created by shaped and sized bricks. These form the stepped back arches of the entrance framing the outer crowned key stones; the recessed cross-shaped niches in the base of the applied buttresses; and the delicate double molding on the brackets beneath the upper window brick work, around the entrance, and the base of the tower.

FIGURE 35C

The south transept entrance of St. Vincent de Paul. Color contrasts are made by the red brick and the white stone caps of the stepped buttresses, and by the wide white molding of the raking cornices of the gable end, repeated in the narrow molding just below. A brick corbel table further accents the line of the rake.

Hutchisson used in the white stone capping of the steps of the buttresses and the coping seen against the red of the brick. While both the Sloan engraving and the Hutchisson building have corbel tables running beneath the pitch of the side aisle roofs, Sloan's were more lancet in shape. In the Hutchisson and other late Gothic Revival examples, the corbelled brackets supporting each of the arches are as important an element as the connecting arches (figure 35d).

The three circular windows on St. Vincent de Paul (figure 35) and the Jacksonville church also add to the wider effect of the facade, and place them at a date in the early Victorian period of the Gothic Revival. The side elevation further documents this attribution (figure 35d). In the Sloan example, the buttresses rise to the full height of the wall and extend upward into pinnacles. In St. Vincent de Paul, they rise to just below the peak of the lancet window and are connected with the corbel table above by narrow flat pilasters.

The facade best illustrates the Hutchisson sensitivity to brick, (figure 35b), using it both as a decoration and a structural material. Seen in the beautifully sized and placed voussoirs of the triple ordered arches that frame the entrance, their keystones are like a crown. Minor details add much, such as the placing of a narrow white stone slab forming a capital halfway up the outer arched order, while allowing the two inner orders to rise unbroken to the crown. The two leaf wooden doorway has a cutout motif of the cross. This motif is repeated in the brick work of the front of the buttress piers by indenting the brick to form a recessed panel (figure 35b).

Color adds interest to the whole design in the contrast between red brick and white Alabama stone trim. Stone caps the steps of the buttresses as they rise and form the brackets for the hood moldings, the belt courses, and the coping along the pitch of the roof. Hutchisson's use of brick as a decorative element incorporated in the structure is characteristic of his designs. This is especially notable in the framing of the oculus window above the triple stained-glass window of the facade.

The cornerstone of the church was laid in 1874, but it was not finished until 1877, when, on January 21, the building was dedicated by Bishop Quinlan.[24] The workmen were P. Houston, John Coyle, and Michael Smith. McDonald, March and Company furnished the stone. The brick masons deserve a great deal of credit for being able to carry out the complex brick work that Mr. Hutchisson designed. The cost of the construction was estimated at $40,000, a sizeable sum for a time when a large brick store might cost $15,000.

St. Bridget's is another Catholic Church with which Hutchisson was associated, though there is a question about its construction date (figure 37). An

FIGURE 35D

Detail of the north side elevation of St. Vincent de Paul. Rising from a stone drip molding, the buttresses are stepped back into a flat pilaster that divides the corbel table into separate bays. The white stones at strategic changes in the contours of the building foreshadow the coming Victorian elaborations which move the design away from the pre-Civil War Gothic Revival.

FIGURE 36

The First Presbyterian Church, Jacksonville (Calhoun County), Alabama, 1858-1865. Northeast corner of East Clinton and North Chinabee Streets. The mid-nineteenth-century church of Jacksonville, differs from St. Vincent de Paul in the shape of the windows, the former being semicircular and the latter being lancet. The Jacksonville church also illustrates the changed massing from the earlier verticality of the models following such examples as Sloan's Gothic Revival designs, to a broader, more horizontal rectangle with wide side aisles and lower-pitched roof lines. Before its reconstruction, St. Vincent de Paul would have appeared similar.

earlier church, built in 1867, was destroyed in a storm in 1874, and it is generally believed that the present church was begun immediately. This assumption is based on the fact that there were baptisms being carried out in the St. Bridget's Parish in that year. There has been no documentation found so far to prove that these baptisms were performed in the existing church. There is documentation for the erection of the spire. In Mr. Hutchisson's diary for 1885, he wrote that he was drawing the plans for the spire for Father O'Reilly in the town of Whistler, Alabama. Father O'Reilly was the resident priest at St. Bridget's in 1885. Several other entries also were related to the Whistler construction, including payment for the plans. Without question, the spire was erected by Hutchisson in 1885. An examination of the church does not disclose any break in the construction between the main body of the church and the tower supporting the spire. Unfortunately, no 1874 or 1884 Hutchisson diary exists that might settle the question of when the church was actually built. Oral history in the Hutchisson family claims James H. Hutchisson as the architect of the entire structure.

The stylistic qualities certainly suggest his work. The proportions and detailing of the classically styled entrance are characteristic of his other classical designs. There is a subtle upward movement to the spire by way of the pediment and the oculus above it. Two small churches of the pre-Civil War period make an interesting contrast with Hutchisson's St. Bridget's of 1885. While all three buildings have the same basic shape, a simple rectangle with a front axial tower, their differences point out the changing styles of the pre- and postwar periods. The Gothic Revival First Presbyterian Church of Wetumpka, Alabama (1857), is an excellent example of the style as it was popularized at that time (figure 38). There is little in the design that does not derive from the earlier Gothic Revival movement. The simple, small First Baptist Church of Orion, Alabama, (figure 39) has a modified origin in the Greek Revival, without any embellishments of that style. In contrast, Hutchisson's 1885 design has harmoniously combined elements of the Greek Revival, the Renaissance and the Italianate movements, creating one of Mobile's first Neoclassical style designs, a style that will dominate during the first decade of the next century.

St. Bridget's sequence of arches leading back to the recessed door are framed by pilasters that support a two-part frieze. A string course, serving as a taenia molding, forms both the base of the pediment above and a connection with the horizontal cornice of the main gable. The transition of the sections of the

FIGURE 37

St. Bridget's Church, Whistler, Alabama, spire 1885, date of church is not verified. 3625 West Main Street. James H. Hutchisson, architect. The little frame Church of St. Bridget's illustrates a more broadly horizontal shape to the body of the church with an even less steeply pitched roof than noted in St. Vincent de Paul. Here the architect has incorporated classical and renaissance detailing that foreshadows the coming Neoclassical movement that will dominate in the first years of the twentieth century.

FIGURE 38

The First Presbyterian Church of Wetumpka (Elmore County), Alabama, 1857. Northwest corner of West Bridge and North Bridge Streets. As noted in the contrast of the brick churches of Jacksonville and St. Vincent de Paul, the two frame churches of St. Bridget's and Wetumpka differ in style but are similar in the general massing that is typical of the third quarter of the century.

FIGURE 39

The Little Baptist Church of Orion (Pike County), Alabama, 1858. This is a stripped down version of the basic rectangular shape that Hutchisson used at St. Bridget's Church in Whistler to which he added the classical features that embellish the facade.

ELIZABETH BARRETT GOULD

FIGURE 40

Bernstein House (now the Museum of the City of Mobile), 1872. 355 Government Street. James H. Hutchisson, architect. Charles Fricke, builder. $15,200. There were very few two-story brick homes built during the depressed years of the military occupation. In design, the Bernstein Home was one of the last to incorporate the pre-Civil War Italianate style as it developed in Mobile. With the coming of better times in the 1880s, the Victorian style influenced architectural development.

tower from the pediment above the door to the cross that crowns the concave sided pyramidal roof could have been designed at that time only by Hutchisson. None of the other three architects in residence in the 1880s were as familiar as Hutchisson was with the Neoclassical motif.

The semicircular-headed windows look back to the Renaissance rather than forward to a Romanesque influence. In spite of the tower's details, there is a simplicity about the whole that has the clean-cut, uncluttered quality of the Greek Revival. In spirit, though, it certainly belongs to post-Civil War developments. If it were not for the priest's belief that the building was erected in 1874, it logically should belong to the 1880s. The spire resembles the cupola Hutchisson was designing for the south building at the Convent of the Visitation in 1885. The interior of the church is without any superficial decoration; the simple lines and open space contribute to the beauty of the design. The nave is separated from the high side aisles by tall octagonal columns that support a shallow barrel vault, an unusual feature for a small parish church. It may have been inspired by the vault on the Cathedral nave, the portico of which Hutchisson was working on at the time. While no record states that Hutchisson was responsible for the church's body as well as the spire, all elements point to that assumption.

During this same decade, Hutchisson designed the male orphanage that once stood on Wilkinson Street, renamed Washington Street. The building was mentioned in the *Mobile Commercial Register* of September 1, 1877, but no detail was given, merely that the contractor was M. Smith.

Fortunately one of the 1870 houses that Hutchisson designed has survived. A contract for the construction was dated January 16, 1872, between the builder Charles Fricke and the owner, Henry Bernstein. Charles Fricke was the contractor for several other important Mobile buildings, among them the administration building at Spring Hill College, designed by James Freret of New Orleans, and the 1872 Mobile County Courthouse by W. O. Pond. In the contract, Mr. Fricke agreed to "erect and build for the said Henry Bernstein a building according to the Plans and Specifications made and drawn by James H. Hutchisson, Architect" — and under the direct supervision of the said Jas. H. Hutchisson, Architect." The contract further states that the building was to be finished by October 18th and that the building would cost $15,250[25] (figure 40).

The home is one of the last large brick houses designed in the Italianate style in Mobile. Characteristics are the off-center entrance, the recessed bay to the west of the entrance that forms the first story of the right wing, the overhanging low-pitched roof with decorative scrolled brackets, panels between the brackets on both soffit and fascia, and the east porch bay. The slender twisted iron columns and thinly cast members of the porch frieze and balustrade are typical of the cast iron designs of galleries of the 1870s and 1880s (figure 40b). The rope motif that wraps around the enframement of the front entrance is an unusual feature in Mobile architecture.

The building remained in the Bernstein family until February 9, 1891, when it was sold to J. Curtis Bush.[26] Some modifications were made to the original Hutchisson plan sometime during the early years of the twentieth century. Whether the changes were made during the Bush ownership or when the house was adapted as the Roche Funeral Home in 1922 has not been determined. The west side bay window does not appear on any of the plans in the Sanborn maps of 1885, 1891, or 1915.[27] It appears on the overlay of the 1950 Sanborn map, and present residents of the city can recall some work being done on this side. But no record exists of the bay being added, and as it seems to be an integral part of the facade, it probably belongs to the Hutchisson design. In 1972 the City of Mobile acquired the property through the Urban Renewal Program, and with a generous gift from the Chandler Foundation combined with a government grant, renovated the building as the Museum of the City. At this time major changes were made on the rear by infilling the open spaces and by attaching the old carriage house, which was adapted as a large exhibition space.

Very little information about Hutchisson's smaller homes has been preserved. In the local newspaper for September 9, 1877, there is a brief reference

FIGURE 40B

Detail of the rope-designed molding that surrounds the door framing of the Bernstein House. This motif is unusual for Mobile. The design of the cast iron balustrade and the slender, twisted columns are very different from the flowing organic iron patterns of the 1850s.

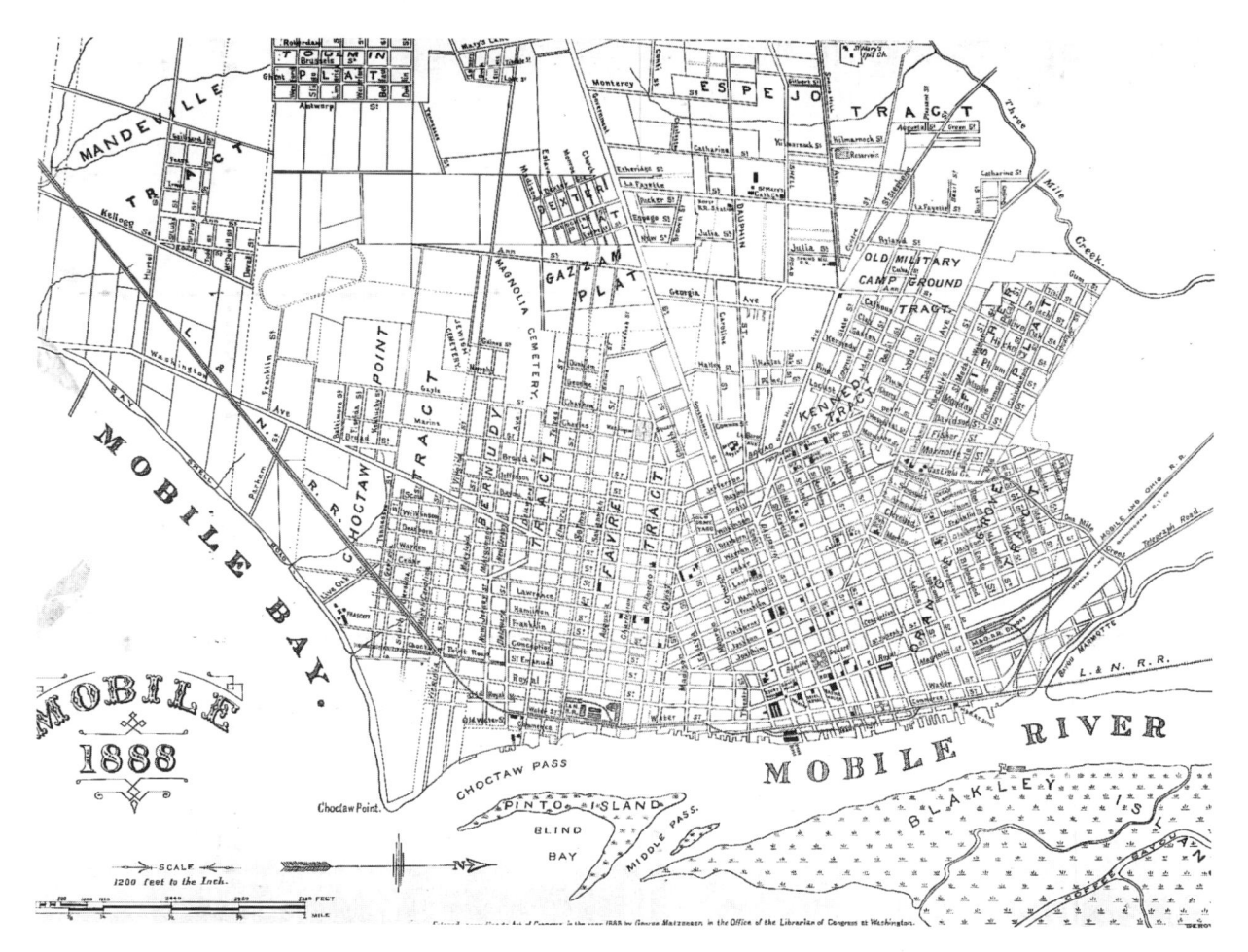

FIGURE 41

The Matzenger Map of Mobile, 1888. By 1888 the westward expansion of the city had extended to Ann Street with a spotting of isolated platted areas beyond Monterey. This was the city in which James H. Hutchisson contributed his major works and in which his son James Flandin II, began his career.

to a cottage built for J. H. Raulston located on Dauphin Way near the car stables. The contractor is given as A.L. Linden, the brick mason and plasterer as P. Houston, and the plumbers as the Young Brothers. This reference to plumbing indicates progress being made in bathroom facilities. No longer did water have to be hauled into the house from a well or cistern, and the outdoor privy or "necessary" was being abolished.[28]

As in the case of the small houses, little is known about Hutchisson's commercial buildings of the 1870s. Judging from his extensive work in the 1880s, he must have built a considerable number of the stores that were springing up after the ordnance explosion. The only information about these can be found in the newspapers. One such account was for a commercial building for the Phelan and Delamare Company located on Dauphin Street. Added to the announcement was the tantalizing notation, "it is one of the finest structures of its kind in the city."[29]

The 1880s

In the 1880s the economy began to recover. Mobile grew as an international port. Lumber export expanded to include white oak, yellow pine and cypress. Other commodities such as coffee and bananas became significant as imports. The influx of new residents changed the make up of the population. By 1880 only 14 percent of the population was Mobile born, and only 46.5 percent were of southern birth.[30] Socially, this polarized the residents into separate groups expressed by the numerous limited membership clubs that were established during that time.

A comparison of the 1856 map (figure 27) and the Matzenger Map of 1888 (figure 41) shows the changes that had taken place between the years when James H. built his first large buildings, and when he reached the height of his career just before his death in 1887. By the mid-1880s and 1890s, the city had developed toward the west. The once fashionable area for well-to-do homes in de Tonti Square was relocated to sites on Government Street as far west as Georgia Avenue and the Oakleigh Garden District. The workmen's homes spread out on the north into the Orange Grove community and on the south to the streets between Canal and Brookley Field.

With the 1880s came various phases of the High Victorian style that began to dominate the Mobile architectural scene. Victorianism varied from the exuberant complexity of Rudolph Benz's designs to the understated use of Victorian elements by James H. Hutchisson. Unlike the Benz buildings that were a sharp contrast with Mobile's past, the Hutchisson structures harmoniously combined the new with the older established forms. Benz either added a profusion of decorative details to an otherwise classical building as in his fourth county courthouse of 1888, or he built complexly combined elements of towers, bays, dormers, and broken roof lines as in his houses of the 1890s.[31] Hutchisson used Victorian motifs sparingly and usually as part of the structure, rather than as a decorative addition. As conditions improved in Mobile, other architects began to return to the city. One such was George Watkins of New York, who introduced into Mobile new ideas foreshadowing the twentieth century.

The records of the work that Hutchisson did during the 1880s are much more complete than those of the 1870s. The last seven years of his life were very productive ones, as noted in his work diaries of 1885-86. (For a sample page from the 1885 diary see Appendix 10.) The diary information, combined with the yearly account of buildings reported in the trade journal of the newspaper, annually published after Labor Day, gives an idea of his extensive influence on a variety of buildings. Of these there are sixty commercial buildings, fifty-four cottages, forty-one two-story residences, eleven religious buildings and ten miscellaneous structures such as schools or civic buildings, all designed between the years 1880 and 1887. This does not include the major repair jobs he undertook. From each of these categories, the following examples have been selected to illustrate the scope of his work and the characteristics of his personal style.

FIGURE 42

Junger's Drug Store (now used as offices for the Mobile Housing Board), 1887. 809 Government Street. James H. Hutchisson, architect; T. B. Smith, builder. The tall, narrow proportions of the Junger Building are typical of the many stores that formed block-long rows along the inner city streets. Unfortunately the original first story and portions of the second were altered in the early twentieth century. Upon restoration for use by the Housing Board, a typical 1880 store front was constructed to replace the "modernized" show case windows. The cornices and the parapet are original to Hutchisson's design.

Commercial Buildings of the 1880s

One of the stores built for individual owners is the Junger Building, standing at 809 Government Street, on the southeast corner of Government and Jefferson. While Hutchisson carried out a $600 repair job on a building that stood on the same site in 1884, it was not until 1887 that he designed the drugstore for Charles and Anna Junger (figure 42). The narrow and deep two-story brick building had the usual massing for the commercial row buildings of that time. The unusual brick work of the cornice and the parapet, where the architect skillfully combines the bricks both as structure and decoration, distinguishes this building. This quality has already been noted in his Creole Fire Hall and the Church of St. Vincent de Paul. The Junger Building has the detailing in the cornice and parapet. A double string course made of double moldings forms the transition from the flat wall to the frieze of the cornice entablature. The cornice on the side elevations differs from that of the facade. On the sides, a dentillated molding is divided into three parts by an elongated motif that has a small recessed panel. On the facade, the dentil course is doubled and broken at the central bay by a projecting panel that is framed by small capped piers, each with recessed panels, and all in brick work. These piers are connected by multiple moldings. All these elements are carried out skillfully, shaped, and laid in special coursing.

The original segmentally arched windows of the side elevation are not repeated on the facade, for the front was altered sometime in the early twentieth century to make it more "modern looking." When the building was restored for use by the Mobile Housing Board just after the midtwentieth century, an effort was made to reestablish what might have been the original first story. The present first story was designed in a fashion typical of the early 1880s, based on what is known of other examples of that date. The second story windows also seem to have been altered.

In 1886 Hutchisson designed a two-story brick store for Mr. M. Turner, one of several done for the same client. It was originally numbered 116 Dauphin Street but is now 209 (figure 43), forming the central building in a block-long row of attached stores. As in most cases along Dauphin Street, the first stories of the nineteenth-century stores have been altered by the introduction of modern showcase windows. In the case of the Turner building, it has been greatly disfigured by changing a three-bay division into two store fronts that differ in design. The second story and the parapet still retain their original configuration. The three tall, slender, segmentally arched windows have hood molds resting on panels. Large keystones accent the center of each arch. Flanking the windows, in a line below the hood molds, are two widely spaced square panels that seem to be anchors for tie rods. At the outer edges of the second story wall are painted metal pilasters. These are embellished with square, embossed panels of a stylized flower motif. The dark metal parapet makes a striking contrast with the white stucco of the facade. It is formed of alternating bands of plain and embossed moldings. The central section of the parapet forms a raised rectangle, crowned by a wide string course and a small gable. It is the parapet that distinguished the Turner building from its attached stores. This use of a metal parapet can be seen in other areas of Alabama. In Selma there is a row of nineteenth-century buildings along Water Street. The large corner store, dated 1869, has a metal cornice of which the pagoda-like parapet crown differs in style from the rest of the facade, suggesting it might have been a later addition.

None of the large commercial buildings designed by Hutchisson have sur-

FIGURE 43

The Turner Building, 1886. 209 Dauphin Street. James H. Hutchisson, architect. Mike Smith, builder. $1,800. As in all the nineteenth-century row stores along Dauphin Street, the first stories have been altered, but the second stories retain their original configuration. The architect's use of a metal cornice and parapet was a popular device at the time.

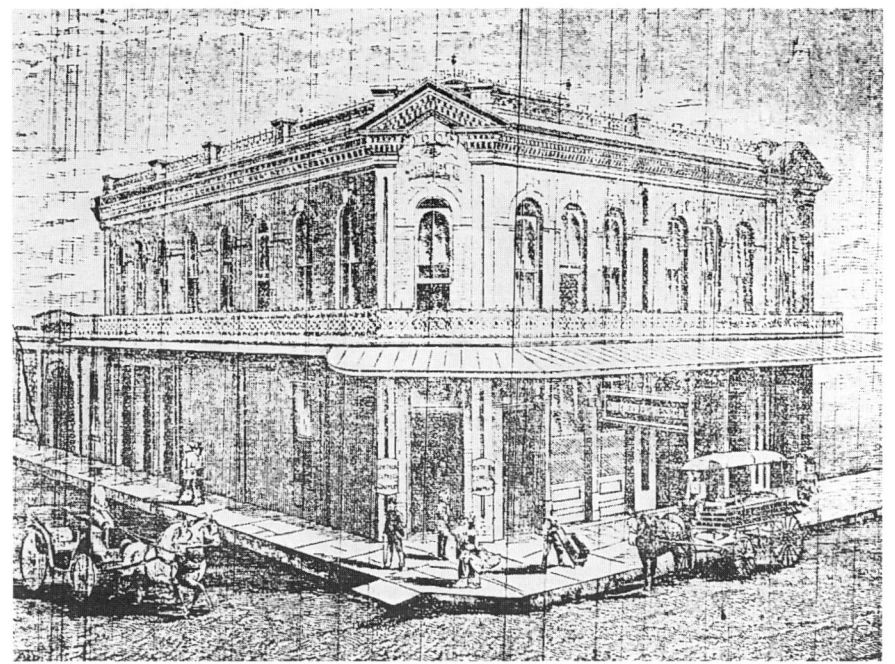

FIGURE 44

The Southern Express Building with the Odd Fellows Hall on the second story, 1886. Formerly located on the corner of Royal and St. Michael Streets. James H. Hutchisson, architect. W. O. Pond, builder. $16,000. Only this drawing survives to give an idea of the complex form of The Southern Express Building with its public rooms, storage, shipping and receiving areas, stables and wagon rooms, and even washing spaces for both horses and wagons. The second story rooms with a pleasing atmosphere were designed for the private and public gatherings of the Odd Fellows.

vived, but the drawings for two have been preserved in an article in the September trade journal in the *Mobile Register* for 1886. The large, two-story brick building that once stood on the corner of Royal and St. Michael Streets served two purposes. The first story was occupied by the Southern Express Company and the upper floor by the Odd Fellows Lodge. Reports of the building first appeared in the 1885 newspaper and in Hutchisson's 1885 diary. The client for the building was Mr. Lavretta, who paid $16,000 for its construction (figure 44).

The Italianate-style red brick building faced on Royal Street for fifty-six feet, seven inches, and extended on St. Michael for seventy feet plus a forty-foot-wide stable. The building was well planned. Facing the street corner, the right angle of the building was clipped off to form a flat bay that contained the main entrance to the express office. The story-high openings of the first level were all straight-headed. The windows of the second story had semicircular heads and were double hung with two-over-two lights, making an interesting contrast with the first story fenestration. Each window that filled a bay was framed by brick pilasters, the capitals of which formed a base for the springing of the arch. A sidewalk-wide canopy extended from above the first story along the Royal Street side. Above this, a cast iron balcony surrounded the two facades, one facing on Royal Street and the other on St. Michael Street. The second level windows could be opened for access to the balcony, a valuable addition for social events. Crowning the building was a buff-colored, two-course brick cornice that was broken with short returns over the entrance bay. The entrance bay was given importance by a pediment whose raking cornice repeated the design of the horizontal cornice and the last bay on the Royal Street side. Above the cornice was a crested parapet that extended between low, capped piers. A secondary crest further elaborated the importance of the entrance bay.

The interior of the Express Company was designed to meet a variety of business needs: offices, freight rooms, provisions for the horses, wagons, and rooms for other equipment. The main office was finished with pine, cypress, and black walnut, and the floor covered with black and buff German tile. The floor of the freight room was raised twenty inches in order to make it easier to load and unload the merchandise from the wagons. To the north of the freight room were rooms used for storing the company records, washing the wagons, and keeping the lamps.

The stable was entered from the St. Michael Street side, through an ingeniously designed recoiling iron door, bought from the New York firm of J. Wilson. The stable had two box stalls and open stalls for six horses, a room for the hostler and for coal storage with watering troughs for the horses, and a room for the wagons plus plenty of space for storage of harness and other needed supplies. All the feed troughs and partitions were made of iron. Water was supplied from a large iron tank on the second story. The tank was situated to catch any rainfall and supplied with city water by two pumps. The stable was eighty-five feet deep, with the rear portion raised to two stories. In this second level were feed rooms and sleeping accommodations for the company employees.

The second story of the main building was occupied by the Odd Fellows. Four main rooms served their purposes: anteroom; main lodge room; property room; and large reception hall. The rooms were light and airy. All had large windows that opened to the gallery. In addition to the main rooms, there were lockers and storage rooms for coal and other necessities. The entrance was by means of a staircase on the Royal Street side. To carry out this complicated commission, Hutchisson employed William Pond and Son as contractors, Fincher and Rosette as masons, and J. Fermier as plumber.

It is interesting to contrast the Express Building with a High Victorian building such as the English Block designed by Rudolph Benz (figure 45). Benz was a contemporary of Hutchisson who worked in a highly decorative style.[32] Hutchisson always used great restraint in decoration, regardless of what style he employed. He preferred to have the decoration as an integral part of the structure. In the Express Building, the projecting flat roofed cornice with its complex double dentillated molding and the stepped back balustraded deck above suggest an Italianate imprint on the Victorian mode. On the other hand, Benz with his use of steep roofs, broken by high dormers of which the gables

FIGURE 45

The English Block, 1886. Formerly on the southwest corner of Dauphin and Water Streets. Rudolph Benz, architect. The two 1886 buildings, the Southern Express Building and the English Block, are examples of the contrast in personal style of the two leading architects of the city in the 1880s, the reserve with which Hutchisson used decorative elements and the exuberance of the Victorian detailing in the work of Rudolph Benz.

FIGURE 46

The Forcheimer Building, 1886. Formerly occupying the block bounded by Commerce, St. Michael, Front and St. Louis Streets. James H. Hutchisson, architect. In this warehouse, the architect used intensive construction methods to provide for large, open storage areas without partition walls or multiple iron columns that usually broke up spaces.

FIGURE 46B

A photograph of the Forcheimer Building taken from the publication Mobile, Its Port and Industry, 1896. Regardless of the style that Hutchisson adopted in his designs, one of his major interests was that his building would fit harmoniously with its surroundings, in height, proportions, and architectural features.

are crowned by finials of various designs, and corners accented by small turrets, definitely belongs in the early High Victorian style. Hutchisson's fenestrations do not destroy the two-dimensionality of the wall, but Benz with his windowed bays produces the contrast in light and shadow that is found in the national Victorian trends. Hutchisson's building, while it belongs to the 1880s, still has ties with Mobile's past.

The second large commercial building for which we have illustrations is the wholesale grocery warehouse of the M. Forcheimer and Company (figure 46 and 46b). It occupied the corner lot on Commerce and St. Michael Streets and extended east to Front Street. The 108-foot-long, main facade faced on Commerce Street. The first warehouse of the Forcheimer Company burned in

January 1886, and plans were immediately made to rebuild it. In order to enlarge his building, Forcheimer bought additional footage on Commerce Street. The building was only two stories in height, but due to the tall ceilings, it rose above the height of the nearby stores.[33]

The first story was eighteen feet high and the second story was seventeen feet high. An interior feature was so unusual for Mobile at that time that it received special comment in the newspaper of September 1, 1886. "A peculiarity of the new building is the absence of dividing walls; the whole floor of the three stores Nos. 38, 40, 42 and 44 North Commerce Street being in one room connected by a large archway." The description suggests that Hutchisson employed some kind of a truss or arch to support the weight of the second floor storage area, since there were no partition walls, columns, or piers. If so, it is the first so far found in the history of Mobile architecture, and reflects the structural changes taking place in the development of American architecture. Another unusual feature was the installation of an elevator operated by two gas engines of fifteen horsepower. The elevator was from New Orleans and was installed along with the two gas engines by John F. Brown.

The building was constructed of Mobile brick with the belt course, the pilasters, and window arches composed of pressed Zanesville brick, giving an interesting contrast in texture. The corner of the second story was accented by two pilasters. The pilaster pattern was repeated between each of the bays of the second story, thus establishing a relationship important in uniting the elements of the long facade. The architect varied these upper bays, changing the fenestration by alternating three with four windows on the Commerce Street side. On the St. Michael Street facade there were three bays, the central one with three windows and the side bays with only two. At the first story, the facades on both Commerce and St. Michael Streets had an unbroken series of windows and doors: those on the Commerce Street side were straight; those on the St. Michael street side had segmental arches connected by a narrow string course. All these variations in the fenestration relieved the long facades of the monotony often created by a series of repetitive windows. The second-story windows were semicircular headed, with the arches connected by a decorative string course.

The whole building was crowned by a galvanized iron cornice and crest in the center of which were eighteen-inch-high, gilt letters with the company name. The frequent use of metal cornices on a brick building was typical of the Victorian movement in Mobile in the 1880s as noted before in the Turner Building (figure 43). On the Commerce Street side a canopy covered the sidewalk, supported by slender iron posts. Above this an iron gallery extended the length of the Commerce Street side. For a Mobile building not to have had a balcony would have been atypical.

The main office of the interior was forty feet long by seventeen feet wide and closed off by large windows. The total cost of the building was $25,000.

FIGURE 47

The Home Industry Foundry (The Kling Foundry), 1884. Formerly at 250 North Water Street. James H. Hutchisson, architect. Farley and Lyndall, builders. $6,400. This strictly functional building was planned in close cooperation with Mr. Kling, the owner. The building contained three separate operations, each requiring space for different mechanical equipment to serve the different functions.

The contractor was William S. Foster, who built many Hutchisson designs. The masonry work was by Charles Farley, the slate work and cornice by C. S. Partridge and Son, and painting by Adams, Harris and Dore.

These few examples of Hutchisson's commercial architecture in no way do justice to the large number of other store, warehouse, and entertainment buildings that he designed. A better appreciation of his contribution can be gained from his diaries and from the trade journal reports published in the local newspapers. A few other examples of his work include: in 1883 he carried out extensive alterations of the Battle House, costing $23,000, and a $9,000 store for Mr. Spotswood; in 1885, a $12,000 addition to the Grand Hotel on the Eastern Shore, the covered grandstands at the Bascomb Race Track, and buildings at the Arlington Fairgrounds; in 1886, the Gulf City Oil Company Building, the Lowenstein Bank, the Factors and Traders Company Building and a building for the Mobile Life Insurance Company, plus a $6,000 hotel at Spring Hill. He also designed in 1886 the Adams Glass Warehouse and the surgical room addition to the old City Hospital. Space prevents the listing of the various stores and shops that he built on Dauphin and other streets in the inner city. It must be remembered that his commercial buildings were a small part of his total work, which included residential and religious structures as well.

None of Hutchisson's industrial buildings has survived, but photographs and engravings of two give an idea of his work in that category. Of these two, the more impressive is the Kling Foundry that once stood at 250 North Water Street (figure 47). Over the years it became known as the Hunley Building, an incorrect title, for it was mistakenly believed that the *Hunley*, the first submarine to sink an enemy ship in battle, was fabricated in the Kling shop. Research has proven that the little iron vessel was built in the Spear and Lyons machine shop on Water Street at the foot of Church Street. The submarine was named after the man who financed its construction. That the *Hunley* submarine was not fabricated in the Kling shop in no way diminishes the importance of the Kling contribution to Mobile's architectural need for structural as well as decorative iron.

The simple blocky mass of the building does not suggest the complexity of the interior, which was subdivided into three shops: the foundry, a machine shop, and a blacksmith shop. The equipment needed for all three, the presses, the boilers, the forges, the furnaces, the cranes and more, required a close collaboration between designer and craftsmen. The building stood until highway progress demanded its removal. An interesting account of the building was given in the *Mobile Register* of August 31, 1884. To quote a short passage:

> The building is 180 feet by 112 feet and faces both on Water and State Streets. —The central of the three divisions is the machine shop and is two stories high. It contains two cupolas of a melting capacity of five tons per hour, with the necessary cranes, core ovens, fan blowers and other fixtures. In the blacksmith shop is the largest steam hammer in this part of the country, being an eight-hundred weight Massey hammer of the best English make and manufactured by Massey & Co., of Manchester, England.

In contrast to the Kling Foundry, Hutchisson designed for Mr. J.G. Lauber a house-shop that once stood in the middle of the block where Rousso's restaurant now stands at 150 South Royal. In the Tax Records for 1864, Mr. Lauber is listed as having a shed located at 5 Theatre Street, 3 east of St. Emanuel. This record continued until 1885, when he is listed as having two lots and a shed at the same site. Hutchisson's diary entry for January 13, 1885, is the first reference to the drawing up of plans for a Mr. Lauber. In 1886 the Tax Record shows a house and two lots, 3 and 4, west of Royal on Theatre Street.[34] From this information it can be established that the house-shop was constructed in 1885-1886, not 1863 as previously believed. The brick home, costing $1,300, was designed with a wide carriage entrance in the eastern bay. Large double-leaf doors, under a semicircular relieving arch, opened up to a passageway leading back to the blacksmith shop. Oral tradition also states that the shop served as a carriage repair or small factory.

Mr. Lauber's two-story

FIGURE 48

The Lauber Home and Carriage Shop, 1885-86. Formerly at 107 Theatre Street. James H. Hutchisson, architect; W. O. Pond, builder. $1,300. All the visual evidence that remains of this small home industry is a sketch made by Marian Acker for the 1935 publication, *Where Time Bears Witness to Sound Building*. The large, semicircular-headed door at the left bay of the house opened into a passageway leading back to the shop.

ELIZABETH BARRETT GOULD

FIGURE 49

The 1880s street scene of the block on Royal Street between numbers 200 and 206. Of these four homes, two were designed by Hutchisson and one by Rudoph Benz. These small one-story homes replaced the Creole cottages of the 1830s as the most common form of dwelling for the working class.

FIGURE 49B

Compare the Benz cottage at 204 with the cottage designed by Hutchisson in figures 49 and 50.

brick home (figure 48) rises directly from the sidewalk and has a canopy that extends out to the street curbing supported on iron posts. Above this covered walkway a cast iron decorative gallery covers the four bays of the house, leaving the shop's passageway bay without either canopy or gallery. The flat roof above the gallery partially conceals the paneled parapet.

The building, a simple rectangular form with shallow brick panels in the low parapet, is in a style familiar to Mobile and New Orleans. The double hung windows, six lights over six with their flat arched lintels, the balcony with its cast iron columns, balustrade, and frieze might have been seen on any residential street during the midnineteenth century as well as in the 1880s. The only drawing of the building that has survived can be found in the little publication, *Where Time Bears Witness to Sound Building*. The dating in the publication legend is incorrect based on the research evidence stated above. Unfortunately the artist's drawing leaves some architectural questions unanswered.[35]

The 1880s residential buildings designed by Mr. Hutchisson cover a wide variety of styles. From cottages to mansions, he built homes for both the white and black residents of Mobile. Of the many recorded, only four cottages remain (along with one impressive house on Dauphin Street): an 1883 one-story cottage for P. J. Hanlon; an 1886 Victorian crested cottage at 907 Dauphin Street for Whiting Ames; an 1885 one-and-a-half-story cottage at 552 Eslava Street for Anne Williams; and an 1886 simple cottage at 206 Royal for John Dunn. Of these four, the Hanlon cottage best represents the group.

The Patrick J. Hanlon Cottage stands at 202 South Royal Street, the second in a group of four that forms a harmonious street scene of the 1880 decade. The four differ in style, from the classical influence expressed in the house at 200 South Royal to the decorative Queen Anne of Rudolph Benz at

204 South Royal (figure 49, figure 49B) Between these two extremes are Mr. Hutchisson's two cottages at numbers 202 and 206. Hutchisson's designs have elements of both the classical and the Victorian (figure 50, Hanlon cottage). Coming from the classical tradition is the axial balance achieved by the centrally located entrance and porch with equally spaced windows on either side. It makes an interesting contrast with the porch in Rudolph Benz's design next door. The two interior chimneys, one at the south end and the other on the north, add to this sense of classical balance.

Hutchisson's Victorian features are low keyed and confined to decorative elements of the porch frieze and the gable of the porch roof. The pediment of the porch gable is divided into sections by a central pendant and diagonal cross beams. A jigsaw-cut frame surrounds the attic vent. Turned Victorian columns support the porch roof. One of these at the left front has been replaced by a square, chamfered post. Between each column capital, a slender, spindle frieze extends above open-cut brackets. The balustrade has turned balusters, a simple molded top rail, and a reeded bottom rail. The balustrade continues down the stairway to terminate in round-topped newels. The double sash windows (of the side elevation) are all six lights over six, a traditional Mobile characteristic of the nineteenth century. On each side of the central entrance is a slide-by window with six lights over nine. This latter style of window was commonly found in the Greek Revival Period, since it was so well adapted to the climate, providing for direct access to the porches and increasing the movement of air through the interior. All four of the cottages, from 200 to 206 South Royal, are sited about equally distant from the sidewalk, which helps to unify them into a pleasing street scene.

An example of a large house designed by Hutchisson still stands at 1000 Dauphin Street. It is not only an imposing mansion but also an ingenious structure, incorporating the rear part of a former home that burned down. Except for portions of the rear and rear west wing, the older 1856 house of Daniel C. Aldrich was destroyed. In 1884 Mr. Hutchisson designed the Perryman renovation.[36] The Doric Neoclassical portico and front rooms were

FIGURE 50

The Hanlon Cottage, 1883. 202 Royal Street. James H. Hutchisson, architect; G. Discher, builder. Though the four houses on the block differ in style from the classical detailing at 200 to the Victorian of Rudolph Benz at 204, they are all sited at equal distances from the sidewalk, with harmonious proportions and green strips so that they create a pleasing street scene. Hutchisson's design at 202 has qualities that blend with the classical elements of 200 and the Victorian elements of 204.

FIGURE 51

The Perryman House, 1884. 1000 Dauphin Street. James H. Hutchisson, architect; G. J. Lyndall, builder. $2,500. When all but the rear wing of the 1856 Daniel Aldrich Home was destroyed by fire, Hutchisson designed a large two-story home incorporating the original earlier wing. The facade design combines the influence of the Greek Revival columnar portico, the bracketed Italianate overhanging cornices, and developments of the 1880s.

added to the still-standing rear elements of the old Aldrich home. The junction is skillfully carried out but can be traced in the middle west room by the changes in the flooring.

The two-story, three-bay house is built of black cypress that was recently exposed during the removal of all the old paint. The tall, fluted portico columns are beautifully proportioned (figure 51). A second-story balcony extends out to the plane of the columns. The balustrade that connects the columns is made up of unusual, delicately designed members in a geometric pattern of verticals, horizontals, and diagonals. The gable roof, with pediment facing the street, is given a touch of the Italianate in the scrolled twin brackets that accent the raking cornice near the midpoint of the pitch and under the horizontal cornice.

The main entrance is located in the west, first bay. The framing is simple, but with a two-course transom of three lights each. The French doors in the middle and east bays are unusual and have four light transoms. On the east is an offset, one-bay, two-story wing with a one-bay portico that repeats the design of the main facade.

The design of the Perryman house reflects the changes made in a late revival of the Greek Revival of the 1830s. A comparison of the Perryman house with examples of the earlier form such as Rosalie in Natchez,[37] begun in 1820 by Peter Little from designs by his brother-in-law, James S. Griffin, or the portico in the 1840 Kenan house near Selma, Alabama,[38] (figure 52) shows both similarities and differences. Basically, both have tetrastyle columniation with modified Doric capitals. Both have a full-length balustraded balcony at the second-story level, the width of which extends out to the line of the columnar shafts. Both have a low-pitched gable with simply molded horizontal and raking cornices.

The differences are even more noticeable and show the changing times in which the buildings were constructed. The balustrade of the 1840 house has simple vertical balusters, the 1884 house has a balustrade formed of panels with crow's-foot patterning, made up of vertical, horizontal, and diagonal members. These panels alternate between square and rectangular shapes. The Kenan house has no brackets beneath the cornices, but the Perryman house has twin scrolled brackets below the overhanging and raking cornices. The Kenan house has a symmetrical plan with central hall and axial entrance. The later building has a side hall and entrance into it through the west bay of the facade. The windows of the first story are traditional double sash in the 1840 structure; whereas in the Perryman House, French doors are employed. If it were not for the transoms above them that continue the line of the door transom, one might question if the French doors were not a late nineteenth or early twentieth century alteration. Since Hutchisson had both the Asher Benjamin *Builders' Guide* and the Minard Lefever *Builders' Guide*, he may have started with one of their plates and modified it to meet both the changing times and the desires of the owners. Before designing, the custom of the Hutchisson family, according to the last survivor, was to consult the owners for their requirements. Then they would inspect the planned site, noting the neighborhood. The Hutchissons would try to design buildings that would harmonize with their surroundings as well as satisfy the requirements of the owners. This harmonious relationship of a building with its location has already been noted in the commercial buildings of Hutchisson. The narrow lot on which the Perryman house was rebuilt and the limits set by the surviving rear portions that the owners wanted to incorporate certainly limited

FIGURE 52

The Kenan House, 1840. Selma vicinity (Dallas County), Alabama. West side of County 37 (Summerfield Road) about two miles north of the intersection with U.S. 80. The Kenan House illustrates the more pure Greek Revival characteristics of the pre-Civil War years as opposed to the eclectic adaptation of the 1880s.

FIGURE 53

The Kitchen-McMillan Country Home, 1885, enlargement and renovation. Stockton (Baldwin County), Alabama. East side of County 26, about one-tenth mile north of the intersection with Alabama 59. James H. Hutchisson, architect. The McMillan alterations to the older house represent one of the few, still-standing houses for which Hutchisson was responsible in areas other than in Mobile.

FIGURE 53B

The 1844 Kitchen House, as it originally was built, was a four room country home with unattached dining room and kitchen as well as other dependencies. Visible from the front elevation, it can be seen that the dependency on the left was brought forward and attached to the house. The open shed on the right beneath the overhanging roof was filled in with board and batten siding to make interior rooms. Other additions and changes were made at the rear of the house.

Hutchisson's choice of what to do with designing the front half. Because of the crowding by the next door sites, the building does not have the monumental quality that it could have had, had it been on more open ground.

Hutchisson's diaries of 1885 and 1886 recorded his work extending beyond the Mobile neighborhoods. Unfortunately the ink of the 1886 diary has so faded that many of the pages are unreadable, depriving a researcher of a great deal of valuable information. His two diaries have interesting records of traveling upriver to various locations to construct homes for other Alabamians (See Appendix 10). In the 1885 diary, plans are listed for Mr. McMillan at Stockton (figure 53), the Keys family at Sheffield (figure 54), and the Raulstons at Portersville. Two of these homes are still extant. In Stockton, Baldwin County, Alabama, is the 1884-1885 Kitchen-McMillan House. In 1885 the Kitchen family sold the property to the McMillan family of Mobile for a country home. The McMillan city house was a beautiful Greek Revival villa that still stands in Spring Hill. Whether the McMillans were friends of James H. Hutchisson is not known. In the architect's diary, Hutchisson writes that he had a call from Mr. McMillan about making plans for his house in Stockton. The Kitchen house had been a small four-room building, with unattached dining room and kitchen, along with other dependencies (figure 53b, photograph of original house).

Following the diary notation of June 11, there are daily references to making plans for the McMillan house until June 22, when he wrote, "Mailed plans to McMillan." In the *Alabama Catalog* by Robert Gamble is a statement that the original house was "frame, rectangular, one story — consisting of four rooms clustered around a central chimney, porch across the front with shed rooms at one end — later greatly altered and enlarged."[39] By comparing the photograph of the original with the alterations by Hutchisson (figures 53 and 53b), one can see the detached building on the left side of the dwelling was brought forward and attached at the left side of the house with its roof intersecting the main gable.

The proportions of the original gallery have been altered; the rake of the roof made less steep to provide for a high clearance. The porch has been screened and a narrow frieze of lattice work inserted beneath the eaves of the porch roof. Both the right and left side additions have been covered with board and batten. According to the present owner, related by marriage to the McMillan family, he found the original drawings for enlargement of the house, but they were so badly deteriorated as to be almost illegible. He could make out the name of Hutchisson. It is most unfortunate that they were not salvable as they are the only known drawings by James H. Hutchisson discovered. They do prove, however, that the midnineteenth-century architect was preparing drawings for commissions. There is structural evidence in the attic that shows how the architect changed the four-room house into a five-bedroom, three-bath dwelling with parlor, dining room, kitchen, pantry and closets. Of special interest to the owner is the large broom closet off the pantry. Hutchisson was ahead of his time in planning for three bathrooms for a country home of 1885. The home is still a simple country dwelling without stylistic elements or outstanding architectural features but as such is an excellent example of a nineteenth-century country home.

The same year that Hutchisson worked on the Stockton house, he received a request for plans from Major George Presley Keyes (1829-1906) of Sheffield, Alabama (Colbert County).[40] Mr. Keyes had been a newspaper editor in Athens, Montgomery, and Florence, Alabama, and moved to Sheffield when that community was founded in 1885. In Hutchisson's diary for September 3, he stated that he took a steamer for the trip north to Sheffield. The journey lasted nine days with the information of his return on September 12. Thereafter a daily record was kept of his work on the Keyes plans until October 10, when he mailed the plans to Sheffield. He did not make any trips north for supervision of the

FIGURE 54

The Keyes House, 1885. Sheffield (Colbert County), Alabama. James H. Hutchisson, architect. Regarded as the oldest house in Sheffield, its eighteen-inch-thick walls still stand as evidence of the sturdy design Hutchisson planned for the newly formed river bluff town. While some modification of the original house has been made over the years, the essential Hutchisson building remains intact. In the Hutchisson diary is a record of the nine-day trip he took by boat to visit the site before beginning his drawings.

construction as there was no note of such trips in his diary. In Sheffield, *City on the Bluff*, published by Friends of Sheffield in 1985 to commemorate the town's centennial, is the statement that the Keyes house is the oldest dwelling in the city. This statement may seem to conflict with the recording of the three houses in Sheffield that are dated earlier in the *Alabama Catalog*. But two of those are located in the vicinity of the town and the third is a surviving, altered log cabin that is located on the bluff in the original plantation acreage on which the city of Sheffield was founded. The Keyes house as it now stands (figure 54) has been altered from its Hutchisson plan by a porch inserted at the left front bays, and a dormer added in the right side elevation when the house was enlarged by finishing the attic as a second story. The original chimney that rose through the roof on the left side elevation has been removed. The present owner had lattice infilling added to the porch. But in spite of these alterations, the original brick home with its eighteen-inch-thick walls and fourteen-foot four-inch high ceilings is still intact. There is an unusual decorative treatment of the gable ends of the front dormer and the roof of the projecting right wing. The solid panel inset of the gable end has a series of rows of coffered panels; the panel of the dormer has pierced designs along its outer edge and an open semicircular cutout midpoint at the base of the triangle.

The religious buildings that Hutchisson designed in the 1880s were as important as those of the 1870s. Of those documented, four are still standing. In 1884 he was employed by the African Methodist Episcopal Church, located on State Street, to replace their earlier 1854 frame structure. From the records, it is known that the facade and first bay of the foyer with two vestry rooms belong to the 1884 Hutchisson building period (figure 55). Whether he also designed a new auditorium and sanctuary at the same time is not known as the present main body of the church was built in 1896 by the architects Watson and Johnson.[41] Since the work of Mr. Hutchisson came to only $4,000, it is likely that the facade was simply attached to the first wooden building and left that way until the auditorium replacement by Watson and Johnson some fifteen years later. Unlike the interior, which is in a Gothic Revival style, the facade of Hutchisson is an adaptation in massing of the earlier forms, with its dominating axial front tower.

However, the brick moldings, string courses, and corbelled capitals of the pilaster-like flat buttresses are of a later style. The eclectic combination of the sharply pointed recessed panels of the tower's flat buttresses, the semicircular arching of doors and windows, and the complex coursing of corbels and hood moldings certainly belong to the Victorian era. At the same time, there is an underlying similarity to earlier forms in the triple division of the facade with its central tower creating a balance and harmonious relationship of the parts. It is difficult to say whether the arched openings are an outgrowth of an earlier Renaissance Revival or an early expression of a coming Romanesque Revival.[42] The heavy enframent of the central oculus in the tower and the four rather

FIGURE 55

The State Street A.M.E. Zion Church. Facade, 1884, James H. Hutchisson. $4,000. Auditorium, 1896, Watkins and Johnson, architects. Jackson and Company, builders. The original wood frame church was altered in 1884 by a foyer and brick facade designed by Hutchisson. Here, as in St. Bridget's, the wider, lower shape of the building is utilized with semicircular-headed openings that may either reflect a dying influence of the Italianate or a foreshadowing of the Romanesque Revival to come. The low, pedimented, overhanging cornice beneath the spire is accented by twin brackets and a quatrefoil pierced frieze.

deeply inset, cross-shaped panels in the entablature, between the twin brackets that support the cornice and pediment above each side of the tower cornice, create a heaviness not found in the Renaissance Revival. Since he owned two volumes by Samuel Sloan, he may have adapted a plate from those and given it Victorian qualities. Certainly the design of the State Street A.M.E. Zion Church is very different in totality from the facade of St. Bridget's Church at Whistler, (figure 37) even though the latter had a spire designed in 1885. Much of the brick coursing's complexity in the State Street example is lost because the white color blends the light with the thin shadows cast from varied surfaces. It is especially difficult to see in a photograph.

The front central tower of the State Street Church projects from the plane of the side bays. The outer angles of the tower are strengthened by twin, flat, paneled buttresses that step back as they rise to the second story. At sidewalk level, a central, two-leaf, solid, paneled doorway leads into the foyer; its inner walls help to support the weight of the spire above. The central window of the

FIGURE 56

South Building of the Convent of the Visitation Cloister, 1885. 2300 Springhill Avenue. James H. Hutchisson, architect. In the last two years of Hutchisson's life, he was deeply involved in building programs for the Catholic Diocese, the Portico of the Cathedral of the Immaculate Conception, the Convent of the Visitation, and Spring Hill College. An older, small school building that once formed the south building of the Convent was transformed by Hutchisson into the long, three-story brick building standing today. The two facades, south and north are very different. The facade on the north, facing the private cloister is severely plain; while the one facing the south, now open to the public, has beautifully designed semicircular-headed openings and transoms deeply shaded by the cast iron galleries at all stories. The central bays are accented by a low pediment and well-designed clock tower.

second story is taller than those in the side bays and is crowned by a hood mold on corbelled brackets formed of beautifully shaped bricks. Above this central stained-glass window is an oculus framed by brick moldings, accented by keystones placed at the ends of the major axes. A multiple string course extends across the plane of the side bays, separating the second story from the half triangle formed by the side aisle and gallery roof.

The African Methodist Episcopal Congregation became affiliated with the Zion Churches and is now known as the A. M. E. Zion Church. It is still a very active congregation, and the building is one of the three surviving large, nineteenth-century church buildings that served the black community.

At 2300 Springhill Avenue stands the Convent of the Visitation, whose buildings range in date from 1854 to 1895 (figure 56). The heart of the Convent is the cloister, which is bounded on three sides by buildings (figure 56b). Originally, a school enclosed the cloister on the west, but the building was destroyed after the school was closed in 1953. The buildings on the north and east are occupied by the Order, while the south building was originally an academy run by lay sisters. In 1885 Hutchisson was retained to design two buildings for the Order, a chapel and the south building as it now stands. From January 10 to February 6, he was busy with the plans for a chapel. On February 6 he had an interview with Bishop Manucy concerning some interior details and the next day turned the plans over to the Bishop.[43] The chapel, however, was never built. The *Triennial Book* for 1882-1885 states the Bishop did not approve of the plans. Instead, it was decided to spend the funds on the academy building. An old chapel continued to serve the nuns until 1894, when Harrod and Andry, New Orleans architects, were employed to construct the present stone Romanesque Revival, semipublic Oratory that is attached to the east building of the Convent.

As soon as Hutchisson had finished the chapel plans, he turned his attention to the south academy building (figures 56 and 56b). From February 24 to October 30, there is a day-by-day account of the work done. From the placing of the second story joists to the design for the bookcases, the diary documents both the planning and the construction.[44] In addition to the main body of the building, he was responsible for the three-story cast iron gallery on the south facade and for the charming, little gazebo that stands on the shady south lawn. (See Appendix 11). While his diary contains several references to payments made to him, the final cost is given in the *Mobile Register* for September 1, 1885, as $10,000.

The north facade on the building, facing on the cloister, differs from that

FIGURE 56B
Aerial view of the Convent of the Visitation with the cloister on the upper western side, and the semipublic chapel at the center right, with the former clergy building further east.

FIGURE 56C
The South Building showing its north facade from the private cloister area.

ELIZABETH BARRETT GOULD

FIGURE 56D

A detail of the South Building as seen from the public south side through the late nineteenth-century gazebo.

of the south (figure 56c). At the first story on the north side, an arcaded passageway continues across all the buildings, forming a covered walkway around the cloister. Above this arcade, the academy building is severely plain, with a row of double hung windows, six-over-six lights, repeated across the length of the building at the second and third story. On the south, the facade (figure 56d) is heavily shaded by deep galleries that are supported by slender, fluted iron columns with waterleaf capitals. Thin, delicate iron members in a leafy design form a frieze that connects the capitals of the upper story. At the ground level, double leaf doors are glazed above with blind molded panels below. Transoms admit additional light to the classrooms within, as do the round-headed windows with four panes of glass over four. The shutters are solid and paneled. The windows of the upper stories are smaller, six-over-six, and have louvered shutters. A beautifully shaped clock centers above the roof (figures 56,b,c).

The wide lawn with its many trees is enclosed by a high brick wall that surrounds the whole complex. There is a quiet withdrawal from the busy world that passes by on Springhill Avenue just beyond the wall. This old academy building has now been adapted for retreats, a suitable setting to withdraw from daily pressures for contemplation.

While busy at the Convent, Hutchisson was also designing two buildings at Spring Hill College. The college had been founded in 1830 by Bishop Portier as an institution of higher learning and was the first such educational center in the State of Alabama. Over the years, fire had destroyed all the early buildings, but they were gradually replaced. Today, the quadrangle, the heart of the institution, is enclosed by four buildings. The one on the west, originally planned as a refectory with a chapel on the second story, was designed by J. H.

Hutchisson. On April 29, Hutchisson received the order to design a two-story brick refectory that would be 43 feet wide by 113 feet long[45] (figure 57). He worked on the plans through the next month and a half and on May 11, turned them over to the college. On that same day, he received a further request to design a one-story brick kitchen. The kitchen has not survived, but the refectory is still standing and has been adapted for use by the finance and fine arts departments of the college. Unlike the Convent account, where he recorded the step-by-step construction process, there is no further mention in his diary of work on the Spring Hill College buildings. It would seem he simply turned the plans over to the authorities to contract for the construction. There is one more reference to Spring Hill College in his diary for the next year, 1886. On February 21 is the statement that he was making plans for the college, but the following days' records are impossible to read due to fading ink and his increasingly erratic writing.

Along the length of the first story of the old refectory (figure 57), a pointed, arched arcade continues the covered walkway surrounding the quadrangle. Partially hidden by the arcade, the first story of the east wall of the building must be examined closely to appreciate the fine brick work that forms its details. Each of the ten bays is framed by rusticated pilasters that rise to a belt course marking the division between the first and second stories. The textured brick pilasters continue up through the second story to be crowned by twin-scrolled brackets under the projecting eaves. Between the pilasters of the third and seventh bays are single-leaf, six-paneled, solid-core doors with an unusual double transom above. The lower section of the transom is rectangular in shape with six glass panes. The upper section is semicircular-headed, hooded, and divided into two sections of glass.

FIGURE 57

The west building of the quadrangle at Spring Hill College campus, 1885. 4307 Old Shell Road. $13,000. The 1885 building was designed originally by James H. Hutchisson as a refectory on the first story and a chapel on the second. The building has now been adapted for other college uses. The four buildings that enclose the quadrangle extend in time from the 1866 Moore Hall on the east, the James Freret 1869 Administration Building on the south, Hutchisson's 1885 building on the west, to the 1909 Gothic Revival chapel by Downey and Denham on the north.

FIGURE 58

Hygeia Sanitarium, 1885. Citronnelle, Alabama. Destroyed. Whether James H. Hutchisson designed the whole complex of the sanitarium is not known. His diary records commissions from Dr. Jacob Michael to enlarge the main building and to construct several other structures in the complex at a cost of $20,359. The rare illustration of one of the buildings is from James F. Sulsby, *Historic Alabama Hotels and Resorts*.

The north and south ends of the building have three bays divided by the same style textured pilasters. The same rusticated pilasters form quoins at the corners of the building. Once again, Hutchisson used variations in brick texture as the decorative element in his designs.

There seems to be no limit to the variety of work in which this mid-nineteenth-century architect was involved. Besides his contribution to residential, commercial, industrial, and religious architecture, he was also in demand by the medical community. In the busy years of 1885, 1886, and 1887, he designed offices for Drs. James F. Heustis, D.E. Smith, and William Mastin.[46] Of these three, only the last has survived. The two-story brick building, number 9-13 S. Joachim at the northeast corner of Joachim and Conti, has little distinctive architectural features having been altered over the years.

In 1887, on a larger scale, Hutchisson did the plans for the surgical wing of the Old City Hospital, an addition that no longer stands. During 1885 he consulted with Dr. Landers on plans for the Medical College, but the building is credited to Rudolph Benz. In the same year, he began extensive additions to the Hygeia Hotel in Citronelle, a tuberculosis sanitarium retreat (figure 58). In 1882, the location was chosen by Dr. Jacob Michael because it was far enough away from Mobile winter fogs and yet close enough for "guests" to enjoy an occasional trip to the city.[47] The original building, constructed in 1882 at the same time that a railroad was established from Mobile to Citronelle, soon proved too small to accommodate all the guests, many of whom were not suffering from the disease but simply enjoyed the various recreational facilities provided by the center. Whether Hutchisson planned the first building cannot be established, but in 1885 he designed the annex that consisted of three two-bedroom cottages and a two-story, eight-bedroom addition to the main building. The drawing of the complex that has survived and is reproduced in James Sulsby's book, *Historic Alabama Hotels and Resorts*, is not clear enough to give an accurate idea of the architecture. The book does give a lively account of the retreat and its various activities. A small cottage has been moved and restored by the Citronelle Historical Society.

The architectural contribution that James H. Hutchisson made to Mobile and its vicinity is astonishing in its variety and quality. It is even more amazing considering that it was during the Reconstruction years that many of his major works were erected. It was largely due to his influence that good design and construction methods survived during the chaos of the 1870s and 1880s, when there was a loss of architects, master builders, and workmen after the Civil War. With the creation of the shanty towns from the influx of the black population, Hutchisson began to design simple cottages for the new working classes, both white and black. At the same time, his influence was important in the revitalization of the city's commercial sections destroyed by the destructive explosion of the Ordnance Depot. He helped in planning a more varied source of commercial development to replace the South's former economic dependence upon cotton. When cotton presses and their warehouses were no longer the main buildings constructed along waterfronts, he designed new types of warehouses to store the changing commodities.

The styles employed in his work included all those national movements of the third quarter of the nineteenth century, but he adapted them according to his own vision and to fit into the traditions of the Mobile in which he had been raised. He passed on to his son and future descendents a belief that sound construction was basic and that aesthetic qualities were inherent in the building material, not in applied decoration. This has been shown in the many ways he used bricks in different sizes, shapes and textures to form corbels, hood molds, moldings and details of cornices and parapets.

Between the "Golden Years" of the 1850s and the last decade of the nineteenth century, when his son carried on the family tradition, James H. Hutchisson kept alive the knowledge that a building, however small, deserved as much careful consideration as more important structures. His buildings that still stand are as sound as when first built and are still sought after and appreciated by their successive owners. Good design may change in style but it does not go out of style, and it is still an important part of the architectural scene long past the age in which a particular structure was built. James H. Hutchisson's 1872 Bernstein House is now the actively visited City of Mobile Museum, and his St. Vincent de Paul, renamed the Prince of Peace, serves a large and active congregation. The Convent of the Visitation south building opens its doors for weekend retreats as hospitably as it once sheltered a school. His cottages and houses still are a haven for families though the original owners have long since gone. His academic buildings at Spring Hill College have been adapted to meet the changes of a modern university. While present owners may not know who designed the buildings that they occupy, the work of James H. Hutchisson has stood the test of time.

PLATE IV

The J.W. Little House, 1892-93. 1312 Dauphin Street, Mobile, Alabama. James Flandin, architect. Detail of the recessed porch with spindled Queen Anne balustrade and frieze contrasting with the heavier Victorian brackets.

Chapter 4

James Flandin Hutchisson II

(1856-1926)

WHEN James Flandin Hutchisson II began his independent architectural career after the death of his father, Mobile was entering the last decade of the nineteenth century. The Pauli 1891 Bird's Eye View of Mobile, Alabama, (figure 59) shows the city's expansion to the west, north, and south. It was not until the 1890s that Mobile began a sporadic recovery that would continue in varying degrees into the twentieth century. The events that made this improvement possible had taken place in the 1880s with the opening of river traffic, made possible by the 1881 Rivers and Harbors Act. The Alabama, Coosa, Tombigee and Warrior Rivers were cleared of their debris. The railroads were once again operable and the channel and bay deepened and widened for larger vessels.[1]

The changing condition of the city and its decline is exemplified by the contrast in its relative size as compared with other southern urban areas. In 1860, before the Civil War, Mobile had been the fourth in size in the South. By 1880, it had dropped to eighth place and by 1910 was down to fifteenth position.[2] It was during the depressed years of the 1870s and 1880s that other cities, such as Memphis and centers on the Tennessee and Mississippi Rivers, took over the river traffic of the expanding trade developing from mineral rich sections of northern Alabama. Yet even when the Southern Railway system was established in 1893 by J. P. Morgan and Mobile began to traffic in coal as well as some of the products coming from Birmingham, the commercial improvement was slow. There were psychological and social reasons that prevented the possible leap forward. Despite the slow recovery, the developing suburbs to the west of Broad Street were where the fourth member of the Hutchisson family made his major architectural contribution to the city's development.

Mobile was a city divided, split along racial lines and within the white community itself. In place of leadership, there was a dichotomy between the nostalgia of the upper class who had controlled the cotton economy and the entrepreneurship of the new arrivals who sought a different direction. An example of the latter was Albert C. Dannar from Virginia, who with very little

FIGURE 59

The Pauli 1891 Bird's Eye View of Mobile, Alabama, showing the extent of the city's development during the years of James Flandin Hutchisson II's professional career.

capital began a thriving lumber business. He lost the business in 1884 but regained it in the 1890s and continued successfully into the next century.[3] While some of the former cotton factors hoped to reestablish the cotton trade, others looked to the exporting of coal to Cuba.[4] Different products became important as imports, such as the fruits and bananas that brought a colorful scene to the docks at the foot of Government Street.

There were other signs of Mobile's potential for growth. The tentative manufacturing attempts of the 1880s were continuing, largely developed by newcomers. In the 1890 City Directory, there is a list of fifteen cigar manufacturing companies, as well as their outlet stores.[5] Ship building was an active business by 1890 when sixty-two vessels were constructed in the Mobile dry docks. This led to the 1904 establishment of the Ollinger-Bruce dry docks that played an increasingly important role in the city's economy.[6] In the publication *New Men, New Cities, New South,* is a chart showing that between 1880 and 1900, local industry increased from 91 to 222 concerns.[7]

Why then, with all this development, was Mobile still struggling to work its way out of the aftermath of the Reconstruction years? Within the divided city, positions of power were still held by the "white elite." They determined the social divisions of the community. The blacks were segregated with their own living areas, schools and commercial districts developing along Davis Avenue and in the Orange Grove area. There were local, strictly observed rules about where blacks could drink from public fountains. What before the Civil War had been a more relaxed atmosphere, even with the slaves, by the end of the century this changed to fear and hostility in both the white and black communities.

Nor did the restrictions stop with race; the chasm extended to other groups based on religion and economic level. Each group had its own social clubs. The "elites" had the Manassas and the Athelstan Clubs that controlled the entré into high society.[8] Even the military had its division with a nostalgic group forming the 1890 Raphael Semmes Company of Southern Confederate Veterans. Besides these groups were the Masons, the Odd Fellows, the Knights of Columbus, and the many secret societies that grew around Mardi Gras. The upper class women met in literary groups and garden clubs.

Mardi Gras, with its frivolity and unrestricted exuberance, was a sugar coating over the underlying frustrations of all classes and the apathy of the upper levels of society. Don Doyle, in his *New Men, New Cities, New South*, wrote that "a defeated people in a depressed state"[9] lack the ability to come to grips with the realities of the present or with a vision to look forward to a different future.

During the last ten years of the nineteenth century, Mobile's building activities were also at times up and down. The *Mobile Register* published a trade journal in September 1889 that summarized the construction of the previous twelve months. The report opened with the statement that most of the work that year had been of "moderate circumstances," consisting largely of repairs and renovations. The article went on to say that there was very little money available for construction purposes. Out of the $300,000 spent that year for the whole city, most of it went to mechanics and laborers "Thereby tending to make them prosperous." The only two architects listed during the last of the 1880s were James F. Hutchisson II and Rudolph Benz.

With the 1890s, construction took an upward trend. Benz began the Pincus Building and Hutchisson finished the facade of the Cathedral of the Immaculate Conception and began the towers. An out-of-town architect, B. D. Price, designed the Gothic Revival Methodist Church on the corner of Government and Broad, a building that was later altered by George Rogers to the Spanish Revival style. But the record shows most of the construction that was carried out was by builders and carpenters.

The 1890 City Directory listed twenty-six builders and carpenters, up from the nineteen in the 1885-86 edition. The upward trend continued in 1892 and 1893. Throughout this time, many cottages were constructed along with a few new manufacturing buildings. Some new stores appeared on Dauphin and Royal Streets. For the first time, the name of George Watkins appeared in print.[10] Watkins was a New York-trained architect who brought a new concept of store front design to the city. He, along with a partner, V. Johnson, built some of the most impressive of the late nineteenth-century public buildings in Mobile. In 1903 Watkins asked C. L. Hutchisson, Sr., to become his partner.

The construction activity continued up through 1895 with some variation in quantity though not in quality. In 1893 the *Mobile Register* reported that there had been a falling off of the building industry "as far as the quantity of the work done is concerned, but the quality shows no backward trend." The article went on to state that the cause was due to a "general financial depression."

The best and last year of the construction developments of the decade was 1895. In that year new building projects were undertaken and many extensive renovations done due to the new developments in plumbing and lighting. So frequent were these later improvements made that companies, such as the Simmons and Young Plumbing Company, listed their contracts in the press.

In 1896 a downward trend began that continued for the rest of the century. In 1898, the year of the Spanish American War, only 400 building permits were granted for the entire twelve months. It is during these years that the name of James Flandin Hutchisson II disappeared from the published architectural records, though it is known that he remained in the city until 1901. A possible explanation is the *Mobile Register* no longer published the names of architects in their list of buildings in the trade journal. Another reason was that simply no work was available, as was the case in the 1927-1930 Great Depression. From the city records of the last part of the century, it is known that Hutchisson was involved in various other occupations besides architecture. In 1899 and 1900 he was a field deputy for the United States marshal. In 1901 he was the engineer for the newly constructed Bienville Hotel (now destroyed) designed by G. L. Norrman of Atlanta. It must have been during that year that he left Mobile, because in 1902 his name appeared in the Chicago City Directory as architect for the Carnation Milk Company. Contact with the Carnation Milk Company confirmed Hutchisson's employment, but the company's records did not designate which buildings Hutchisson designed.[11] He continued living in Chicago up to the time of his death in 1926.

It is unfortunate that so few buildings that were erected during the 1880s and 1890s have survived to give a record of Mobile's Victorian period. All the turreted mansions by Rudolph Benz are gone. Only two of J. F. Hutchisson's thirty-six large, two-story mansions are still standing, and these have been so altered that they no longer have their original configurations. Not only the Victorian residences are gone but so too are the public buildings. The elaborate courthouse by Benz was replaced and only one of his major commercial buildings still exists, the Pincus Building.[12] A few of the large Queen Anne homes of the turn of the century bear witness to the major developments of the times.[13] It is the cottage and the one-and-one-half-story homes that remain as an architectural record of the variety of designs that prevailed during the last years of the nineteenth century. This was the city and the uncertain times in which James Flandin Hutchisson II made his contribution to the architectural history of Mobile.

James Flandin Hutchisson, the eldest son of James Henry Hutchisson, was born in Mobile in 1856. He was named for his grandfather, the first James Flandin, but was known in his family as Jim. He served a long apprenticeship under his father. He also had his father's library plus the books that he added to it. Most of his purchases were concerned with the new methods of construction. Two such volumes were written by William H. Berkmire, published by John Wiley and Sons of New York. They were *Skeletal Construction in Buildings*, 1894 and *The Planning and Construction of High Office Buildings*, 1898. From Collier Engineering Company, he had volume II of *A Treatise of Architecture and Building Construction*, first edition, 1899 and volume VI, first edition, 1899. Also his library included a book by Clarence H. Martin, *Details of Building Construction*, published by Bates and Gould of Boston, 1899. Perhaps the most interesting, considering his later life, was a volume, *Architectural Engineering with Special Reference to High Buildings including Many Examples of Chicago Office Buildings*, written by Joseph Kendall Freitag, published by John Wiley and Sons, New York, 1895. Whether he was familiar with the work of William Le Baron Jenney or Adler and Sullivan is not known but his selection of books seems to indicate that he was.

For most of James Flandin's young adult life, he remained in his father's office, subject to his father's domination. This is verified by a statement in his father's diary of 1885 that Jim was paid fifty cents a day for his work, not much compensation for a young man who was twenty-nine years old at the time. In December of that same year is recorded the information that Jim was making some plans for a Mr. Irving (whose last name was undecipherable). In February 1886, he was allowed to design a home for Mr. Pond. In 1887, the year of his father's death, he was still listed in the Mobile City Directory as a clerk in his father's office. It was not until the early 1890s that the name of James Flandin Hutchisson appears as an architect with his office upstairs at 60 North Royal Street.

It speaks well of J. F. Hutchisson's natural ability that at the age of thirty-one he stepped away from the influence of his father, and from 1887 to 1897, when building activity was curtailed, completed his father's commissions and established his own career. For those ten years, we know that James Flandin Hutchisson II designed 118 buildings in Mobile. Of these there were nine churches, twelve commercial buildings, fifty-four one-story cottages, thirty-six two-story houses and seven miscellaneous commissions that included a brick stable and major alterations exceeding $1,000 in value. None of the commercial buildings has survived, and only six of the two-story houses and seven of his fifty-four cottages remain.

Of the seven one- and one-and-one-half-story homes designed by James F.

FIGURE 60

Charles Scott shotgun, 1889. 209 South Cedar, moved from 105 Jefferson Street. James Flandin Hutchisson II, architect; G. Overton, builder. $800. One of the earlier cottages designed by J. F. Hutchisson II, after the death of his father in 1887. The Victorian detailing is limited to the porch of the otherwise simple design.

FIGURE 61

Standing side-by-side are the Herman shotgun, 1898, 307 Chatham and the Frank White shotgun, 1899, 309 Chatham, Mobile, Alabama. The two homes are the same in plan and form but differ in decorative detailing of the porches. Architect and builders unknown.

Hutchisson II still standing, four have been selected to represent the group. They illustrate the architect's variety while still using a limited number of motifs. The earliest of the four is a small two-bay shotgun built in 1889 for Charles Scott. The shotgun developed as the need for low-income housing increased with the growing laboring class. They lived on the outskirts of the commercial district to be near their places of employment. Before the Civil War, the cottages for this purpose were on lots wide enough to accommodate the cottage form with its long axis parallel to the street. Toward the end of the century, the land per front footage increased in value and lots were narrowed, providing space only for the shotgun. Along the streets near the inner city, rows of shotguns were erected such as those that still stand along Caroline Street and in some areas of the Orange Grove Community. Standing close together, sited at equal distance from the street, these narrow homes were lined up like a string of beads.[14] The shotgun first appeared in Mobile during the end of the 1880s and early 1890s and did not reach its greatest numbers until well into the 1920s.

Hutchisson's Scott shotgun was one of the earliest in Mobile (figure 60). Originally it stood on Jefferson Street next to a two-story house built for the same client in the same year. Both buildings were moved to Cedar Street during a Community Development Revitalization program for the inner city. The Scott shot-

From Builders to Architects: The Hobart–Hutchisson Six

gun was an inexpensive little house costing only $800. Yet within its budget, the builder, V. G. Overton, succeeded in carrying out the details of the architect's design. In plan, it is a simple rectangle with an offset wing on the north at the rear of the building. The rooms, placed one behind the other in tandem, are entered from a doorway in the left bay of the porch. The most interesting element in the facade is the detailing of the porch with its three turned and tapered columns with their Victorian bulb-shaped bases. The connecting balustrade has balusters of the same design as the columns, except for the addition of a narrow band of incised lines at intervals around the baluster shaft. Delicately cut jigsaw-shaped brackets connect the column capitals with the porch architrave. A small pendant drops at the center of each bay. The gable end of the roof, facing into the street, has a centered, pointed, louvered vent. When the building was moved to its present location and restored, the entrance stair was changed from a position leading up to the side of the porch to its present location on the front. In the inner city of Mobile, it was quite common to have the porch entered from the side as many houses had their galleries rising directly from the sidewalk.

All shotguns were the same in plan and form, but the porch decoration varied with changing styles and the money invested. Rare indeed was the little house designed by an architect, as most were built by local carpenters. They could be perfectly plain with simple corner posts or could be elaborated by Queen Anne detailing. Hutchisson used simplified Victorian motifs in designing his columns and brackets. Two shotguns that still stand on Chatham Street in Mobile, builders not known, illustrate other types of porch embellishments. The 1898 Frank White shotgun at 309 Chatham has only turned columns without other details. The 1899 Herman shotgun at 307 Chatham has plainer columns but with added brackets connected by a narrow, decorative molding (figure 61). While Mobile has examples of porches with Queen Anne detailing, it is in New Orleans that the best of these can be found, such as on the single shotgun at 5309 Dauphine (figure 62) and the double shotgun at 721-723 Marigny (figure 63). With prefabricated spindles, brackets and moldings available from local sources or catalogues, the simple shotguns were transformed into attractive fairy book houses.

Since the shotgun was too small for the lower middle class, the cottage form survived and received its final alteration during the 1890s. The simple Creole cottages of the 1820s and 1830s had been transformed in the 1850s by

FIGURE 62

A single shotgun at 5309 Dauphine Street, circa 1890, in New Orleans. The two-bay house has porch detailing from both the Victorian and Queen Anne styles. Builder unknown.

FIGURE 63

A double shotgun of four bays, standing at 721-23 Marigny Street, New Orleans. A spindled frieze extends across the porch above the turned columns. In the gable is a typical Queen Anne window with central glass panel surrounded by small square panes of colored glass. Builder unknown.

FIGURE 64

Mitchell Cottage, 1895. 107 South Dearborn Street, Mobile, Alabama. Larger than the shotgun and more expensive to build, the cottage continued to be the dwelling of choice for many Mobilians. The Mitchell cottage with its slender Queen Anne brackets is an excellent example of the decor popular in Mobile during the mid-1890s. Builder not recorded.

the Greek Revival with classically styled columns, moldings and interior refinements. After the mid-1880s, the Victorian and the Queen Anne styles replaced the former classical influence. In Mobile, the 1895 Mitchell cottage at 107 South Dearborn is a good example with its delicately formed brackets that cast their shadows on the wall behind (figure 64). In Biloxi, Mississippi, is a cottage at 121 Oak Street that uses different motifs derived from the Queen Anne style (figure 65). To create this pleasing facade, the builder combined turned columns with brackets and a spindled frieze. The unusual balustrade is formed of designs cut from a solid board. As was the case with the shotguns, most of these cottages were constructed by local builders and carpenters.

It was the middle economic class and the wealthy who employed architects. Some of these suburban homes were designed by James Flandin Hutchisson II. The homes could be one-, one-and-one-half-story, or large two-story mansions. During the 1890s, they were built in the Victorian or Queen Anne styles.

The Hutchisson homes were all built in the 1890s in, what was at that time, the western suburbs of the city. It included areas that are now in the

Oakleigh Garden and the Old Dauphin Way Historic Districts. In 1891 James Flandin Hutchisson II designed a home for the Kilduff family at 200 George Street, now in the Oakleigh Garden area (figure 66). It does not seem possible that the home could have been built for $1,800, even considering the monetary values of that decade. The Sossaman Brothers Company were the contractors, as they were for many other buildings of the 1890s. While the Kilduff home is only one-story in height, it has comfortable large rooms; with a two-bay offset wing on the north (right) and an extension to the rear, it has as much space as a two-story structure. A rather high gable roof covers the front porch and front parlor, with a similar gable crossing at right angles covering the central block and the offset wing.

The three-bay porch has entrance steps at the right side bay. It is the detailing of the porch that gives the house its charm. The porch extends the full

Figure 65

121 Oak Street (formerly numbered 207), circa 1890, Biloxi, Mississippi. The late Victorian and Queen Anne cottages were popular all along the Gulf Coast. The Biloxi example is an especially pleasing one with its slender spindles, and pierced brackets and balustrade cut from a flat board. The detailing is more delicate than any detailing seen in Mobile.

Figure 66

The Kilduff House, 1891, 200 George Street. James F. Hutchisson II, architect; Sossaman Brothers, builders, $1,800. During the 1890s, the architect developed a more elaborate use of Victorian detailing as seen in this and the following example.

Elizabeth Barrett Gould

FIGURE 67

The Louis Brown House, 1891, 51 South Georgia Avenue. James F. Hutchisson II, architect; J. Bride, builder, $1,500. The elaborations of the porch brackets and detailing of the gable end have a skillful combination of various Victorian motifs. While the individual elements are complex, the general design remains one of a simple, single story house.

width of the facade. Twin, slender, chamfered columns share a common abacus block and base. Above the abacus, twin pilasters continue the lines of the columns. The space between the pilasters is filled by a panel decorated with incised lines forming a diagonal pattern centered by a circle. Triangular-shaped brackets, cut from a thin board, taper to a pendent at the center of each bay. Incised lines in a foliate pattern lighten the solidity of the bracket's surface. The solidity or "heaviness" in the brackets and other decor places the influence as Victorian, rather than Queen Anne.

The bay-wide balustrade has balusters cut from flat boards in a lozenge whose lines harmonize with those of the interpilaster panels. The use of the balusters shaped from flat boards rather than being turned first appeared in Mobile in some houses of the so-called Bracket style of the 1870s. The overhanging porch cornice forms a firm base for the large triangle of the gable roof above. The pediment has a smooth tongue and groove siding infill in which the boards are laid in a diagonal line. At the center is an oculus that has a frame embellished at the diagonal corners by curved cusps. A barge board formed of alternating cusps and pendants extends along the slope of the gable and continues along the side of the house and across the eaves of the offset right wing.

A wide, two-leaf door has beautifully etched glass panels. The framing of both the door and windows is kept plain so as not to distract from the porch detailing. The windows are all double hung, two-over-two lights pointing to the fact that large panes of glass were commonly used by the 1890s.

Mary Kilduff bought her lot in 1890 and then in the following years took out a mortgage for $1,000 to pay for construction of the house. Little did she realize that her home would become one of the important buildings in the Oakleigh Garden Historic District, a showpiece on its historic homes tours.

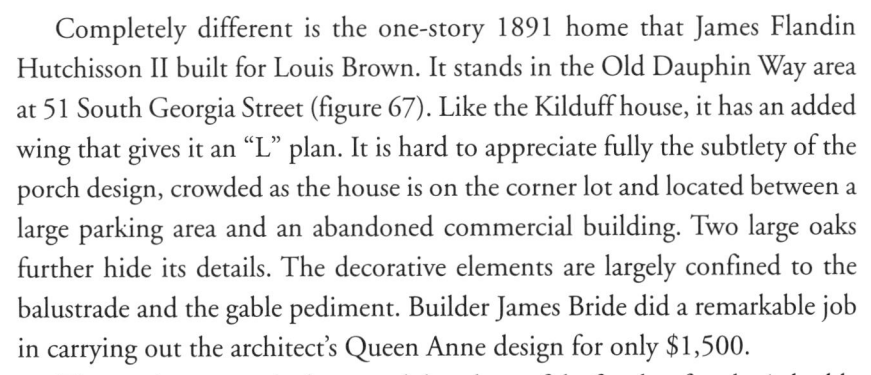

Completely different is the one-story 1891 home that James Flandin Hutchisson II built for Louis Brown. It stands in the Old Dauphin Way area at 51 South Georgia Street (figure 67). Like the Kilduff house, it has an added wing that gives it an "L" plan. It is hard to appreciate fully the subtlety of the porch design, crowded as the house is on the corner lot and located between a large parking area and an abandoned commercial building. Two large oaks further hide its details. The decorative elements are largely confined to the balustrade and the gable pediment. Builder James Bride did a remarkable job in carrying out the architect's Queen Anne design for only $1,500.

The porch covers only the central three bays of the five-bay facade. A double hung window is placed in the bays on either side of the porch. The columns are turned and tapered with incised rings located to the top and bottom of the shafts and at intervals in between. At one time, corner brackets pierced by radiating lines met at a pendant in the center of each bay.

The balustrade is unusual in that each bay section is divided into three parts. The two side panels are subdivided into two bands, the upper one open and the lower one screened with spindles that repeat the scored lines of the columns. The central panel is filled with a circle inscribing a star.

The detailing of the gable end is complex, using a variety of motifs (figure 67b). The major portion of the surface forms a screen that projects a few inches in front of the pediment surface. The top of this screen has a wheel design in which the spokes are formed of spindles that converge to a decorative hub. On either side of the wheel, the spaces are filled with acanthus and other foliate designs. Below the wheel, a band consisting of three sections extends across the pediment. The outer two panels of this band are formed by knobbed spindles in which the knobs alternate above and below the center of the spindle shafts. The central panel is again divided into three parts, the outer two being formed of blocks pierced by diagonal lines emanating from a circle. Small brackets in the same design as those of the porch form the central panel. It takes time to note all these motifs, yet the architect has so skillfully com-

FIGURE 67B
Detail of the gable end of the Louis Brown House with its pierced designs and central wheel.

FIGURE 68

The J.W. Little House, 1892-93, 1312 Dauphin Street. James F. Hutchisson II, architect; Sossaman Brothers, builders. $2,500. In the Little house, the architect has broken with the cottage facade elevation and recessed the porch by the addition of the right, projecting bay. The spindles of the balustrade and gable decor reflect the slenderizing of the elements of the Queen Anne style.

bined them that they do not distract from the harmony of the whole.

In the Brown home, the door framing was given decorative detailing that was not found in the Kilduff example. Bull's-eye blocks form the upper and lower corners of the frame, with an additional block midpoint of the jambs. The window framing, however, was left quite plain. Double hung windows with two-over-two lights extend to the floor on the porch but are of standard size over the rest of the house.

The last one-story cottage selected to represent the designs of James Flandin Hutchisson II is the J. W. Little home at 1312 Dauphin Street. It was begun in 1892 and finished the following year by the building company of Sossaman Brothers. The construction cost $2,200 (figure 68).

Some of the one-story homes were sometimes enlarged by the addition of a projecting front bay whose roof intersected the main roof at right angles. This plan resulted in two different porch treatments. One was a recessed porch as in the Little house. Another solution was to have a small projecting porch with axis parallel to the projecting bay. In the Little house and in the William Gordon home at 210 State Street, Hutchisson employed the recessed porch.

The Little House breaks with the strict symmetry found in the Brown House. A five-sided bay projects from the east side of the facade, a stepped back porch extends across the three western bays. The turned columns use large, incised cubic blocks, an unusual design for Mobile. The brackets are cut from a solid board and pierced by a linear pattern. Above the capitals is a spindled frieze that extends the width of the porch.

FIGURE 68B

Detail of the gable end of the bay of the Little House. The decorative details of the gable along with the columns and spindled frieze of the porch (Plate IV) are the most elaborate of any of J.F. Hutchisson's designs.

The design of the balustrade is formed by three panels in each bay. While all sections are spindled, the outer two have the spindles set vertically, and in the center panel, spindles are horizontal (Plate IV, page 84). The designs of the balustrades of different homes show the variety achieved by the architect using a limited number of motifs.

Typically, the bay has the corner clipped off, forming a recessed area in which a decorative element is hung from the extended cornice above (figure 68b). The gable above the bay is quite elaborate. A jigsaw cut panel is recessed behind a panel of turned decorations giving an appearance of two horizontal divisions. The various design elements complement the rest of the decoration on the house.

The Queen Anne style as employed by Hutchisson was different from that found in other cities such as New Orleans or Biloxi, Mississippi. The Mobile architect limited his use of spindles and combined them with designs cut from flat boards creating a heaviness that harmonized with the popular Victorian style. In contrast to Hutchisson's use of Queen Anne motifs, the use of spindles reached its finest expression in Biloxi (figure 69). Technically, the Biloxi house is not a true bayed type for the front projection is a room, joined by two at the rear and forming a "T" plan. A Mr. Brielmaier bought the house from his sister soon after the building was finished. Much of the detailing may have come from the T. J. Rosell Blind Sash and Door Company of which Mr. Brielmaier was the superintendent and foreman. While spindles were a common motif in Mobile's late nineteenth-century houses, none have survived that can compare with the Biloxi example.

Of the thirty-six large, two-story homes designed by James Flandin Hutchisson II, only six have survived, and, except for one, none of the five have enough of the original fabric left to give an idea of their original design. Nor are there surviving photographs of the Hutchisson mansions as is the case with some of the Benz 1890 houses.[15] As the classical revivals of the early twentieth century took over, the great Victorian homes were modified or torn down. Some, as with those designed by Hutchisson, were divided up into

FIGURE 69

The Brielmaier House, formerly at 436 Main Street, now on Highway 90 and adapted as the Visitor's Center, Biloxi, Mississippi, circa 1895. This beautifully designed and restored one-story Queen Anne home still stands as an example of others that may have, at one time, graced the streets of Gulf Coast cities. These types of homes have been destroyed throughout the twentieth century.

cheap multi-unit dwellings. At 550 St. Michael Street in the inner city, a large house still stands from which all original details have been removed, the siding altered, and the spaces broken up into small apartments. Recently it was vacated and is now boarded up. At 1202 Dauphin, in the Old Dauphin Way Historic District was the 1894 Tunstall Home, which has been destroyed. The Trinity Episcopalian Rectory that was built in 1893 at 263 North Joachim and was in poor condition has been restored. When the Church was moved out to Dauphin Street, the rectory passed through several owners and is now only a shell of its former design. It is one of the few buildings known to have been designed by the two brothers, James Flandin and C. L. Hutchisson, Sr.

The only two-story home by James Flandin that still has its original form is his earliest, built in 1889, just two years after his father's death (figure 70). It was built for the same Scott family for which he designed the little Victorian shotgun. It is a narrow building and looks like one cottage placed on top of another to achieve the two-story elevation. The house is narrow, only about twenty-seven feet wide, but extends back some fifty-three feet. An inset porch cuts into the middle of the north side of the rectangle. A two-bay-wide porch extends the width of the facade at both stories. As in the shotgun next door, the turned columns are of Victorian style with winged, pierced brackets and a pendant at the center of each bay. The balustrade is quite simple, with round balusters incised with a double line of rings. The gable end has the usual pierced-wood detailing with one unusual addition. The date of construction, 1889, is inscribed in a circle at the apex of the pediment. The upper section of the gable end projects beyond the lower portion; however, it does not form a screen, but rather a solid surface that is supported by three small brackets.

98 *From Builders to Architects: The Hobart–Hutchisson Six*

Only five small holes are pierced through within the carved foliate designs. The lower segment of the gable has a centered, louvered opening with fish-scale shingles covering the rest of the surface, adding textural variation in the Queen Anne fashion.

The two-leaf door in the left bay has glass panels and is covered by a transom. The windows on the porches of both stories extend to the floor and have two-over-two lights. The windows of the second story on the south side of the house are also floor length and open onto narrow balconies. By the time the house was rescued from its deteriorating condition, the balconies had been destroyed, but their foundation supports were still present in the wall. Their presence was also specified in the Sanborn maps. In designing their replacement, Thomas Karwinski, AIA, adapted the detailing of the porch brackets to form the balcony supports. After removal of the house to its new location, it was beautifully restored as a private residence.

It would be unfair to the record of James Flandin Hutchisson II not to mention one of his best large homes, even though it is no longer standing. In the *Mobile Register* for Sunday, September 1, 1889, there is a half column devoted to the description of his home for Mr. Boykin Boone. The forty-eight-foot-wide house was located on the north side of Government Street, the fourth lot west of Charles Street. The builder, C. C. Griffin, constructed it at a cost of $6,500.00. The article states, "The front and sides are ornamented with immense bays and mullioned windows, each sash having a single light of plate glass. A broad gallery occupies the western half of the front of the lower story and also runs along the eastern side of the house." The reference to a single pane of plate glass is one of the early documentations for the use of that material in a private home. Plate glass was just beginning to be popular in commercial buildings.

The article goes on to say:

> The roof is highly ornamented by a succession of turreted gables, with dormer windows, the apex being surmounted by an elaborate galvanized iron cresting with numerous grotesque finials, the highest point being crowned with a handsome weathervane.—The front entrance doors are ornamented with elaborate art glass panels with transoms to correspond.

FIGURE 70

Charles Scott two-story house, 1889. 207 South Cedar Street. James F. Hutchisson II, architect; G. Overton, builder, $2,800. The house was moved from 103 South Jefferson at the same time that the Scott shotgun (figure 60) was moved, when both buildings were threatened by encroaching commercial expansion. The house is the earliest of the architect's two-story dwellings. It is the only example to have been restored. The small, side balconies are reconstructions based on evidence in the wall of the building and in information from the Sanborn Maps.

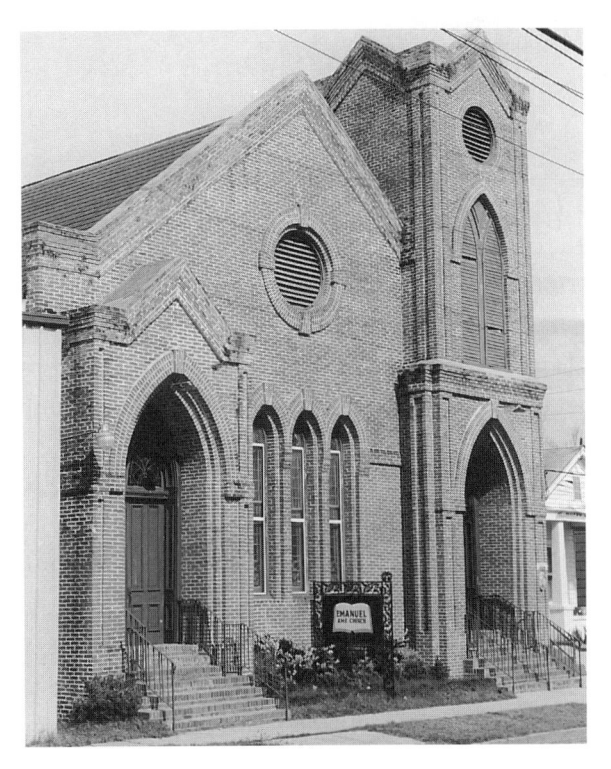

FIGURE 71

St. Emanuel Methodist Episcopal Church, 1890-91. North side of St. Michael Street, east of Washington Street. James Flandin Hutchisson II, architect. Builder not recorded, $10,000. The well-designed Gothic Revival church is crowded in between commercial buildings on a narrow street. The use of brick as both building material and decoration follows in the family tradition as seen in St. Vincent de Paul by James H. Hutchisson (figure 35).

One of the interesting points in the description refers to the chimney construction. It further establishes the skill with which the whole family used the building materials decoratively:

The chimneys, of which there are three, are a special feature of the roof, the design being different from anything heretofore seen here. They are built of rough stone and brick, so arranged that the brick forms panels between the stone, which is built in at the corners, the red of the former contrasts well with the grey of the latter.

The writer of the article describes the interior as well as the exterior. The monumental staircase was formed by a series of broad steps rising to three separate landings. Even the fireplaces attracted his attention. They were designed "in the latest approved pattern, with elaborate hardwood mantels and art tile hearths." That the Boone house was an important structure is also verified by the fact that it had "hot and cold water and gas running throughout the entire building," a luxury only the more expensive homes could afford at that time in history. It is unfortunate that such a house did not survive, for it would have established James Flandin's work on a par with the Victorian homes of Rudolph Benz, as identified by archival photographs.

Three of the churches designed by James Flandin Hutchisson II are extant, though again, the newspapers also give information about his other religious works. He built in both brick and wood, his brick churches averaging in cost from $5,000 to $10,000. The frame churches were more modest, with $5,000 being the top value. He seems to have designed in several styles. In 1890 he did a brick Victorian Gothic Revival Methodist Episcopal Church that once stood on the east side of Warren between Congress and Adams Streets. It had a spire 100 feet high. He erected a frame Baptist Church on the corner of St. Anthony and Warren Streets that had a belfry on the front that rose seventy-five feet.

The St. Emanuel Methodist Episcopal Church on the north side of St. Michael Street, near Washington, has survived. Hutchisson did some work on an older existing church in 1890, and then designed the new facade in 1891 at a total cost of $10,000. This small building's brick patterning of the Gothic lancet arches is unusually fine. It recalls the work of his father, James H. Hutchisson, in his 1874 church of St. Vincent de Paul (figure 35). The plane of the facade (figure 71) is broken on the eastern bay by a projecting, square tower that rises to cut off the right, raking cornice of the gable roof. The tower is divided into two main sections. At the sidewalk level of the tower, a pointed arched doorway forms one entrance into the church (figure 71b). The brick coursing of the doors and windows mark the Hutchisson skill in design. A band of corbelled moldings of white masonry separates the door from the tall, brick-mullioned window in the second level of the tower. An oculus is placed between the tower window and the multimolded angle of the gable over the tower. The raking cornices over both the tower and main building level off in a single corbelled step.

At the western bay of the church is a projecting, one-story porch that contains the large, lancet-shaped second entrance. It is approached by a series of brick steps. Between the porch and the tower, the stepped back facade has three tall lancet windows whose shape and position relate to the openings in the tower and porch and establish a harmony and unity between the three divisions of the facade (figure 71c). The plane of the facade wall continues in unbroken brick coursing up to the peak of the main gable except for a central oculus. The church is not large and rises directly from the sidewalk, crowded in by encroaching commercial developments that mingle with the surviving residences. In spite of this, the church has a dignity and distinctiveness that does credit to the architect who took as much care in designing a church for a small black community as for a wealthy white community.

The only other existing evidence that we have of the religious work of James Flandin is a tower that he added to the 1872 St. Louis Street Baptist Church in 1890. The building is located at 108 North Dearborn on the corner of Dearborn and St. Louis Streets. While the *Mobile Register* for August 31, 1890, gives the information that James Flandin Hutchisson erected the tower for the 1872 St. Louis Baptist Church at a cost of $1,000, it is also known that his youngest brother, Clarence L., worked on the facade of the church in 1908. At this time, it is not possible to separate the work of the two architects.

Of the five members of the Hutchisson family, James Flandin II's professional career in Mobile was the briefest. Yet between 1889-1895, he gave the city a rich heritage through the residences he designed. Now located within the historic districts, his one-story homes are well maintained and much admired. Designing with restraint and selectivity, he created buildings possessing a harmony that blended the past and the future. His buildings helped create Mobile's late nineteenth century street scene. Yet, it would remain for his younger brother to carry on the family tradition in better times.

FIGURES 71B, 71C

In the entrance of St. Emanuel Methodist Episcopal Church, the panels inset in the pilasters, the corbelled areas, and the crown-like keystone of the architrave create subtle decorative effects. The triple-row of voussoirs and strongly accented keystone in the central bay windows are essential to the understated decorative design. The deep arch repeats the shadowed, cut-glass window above the door.

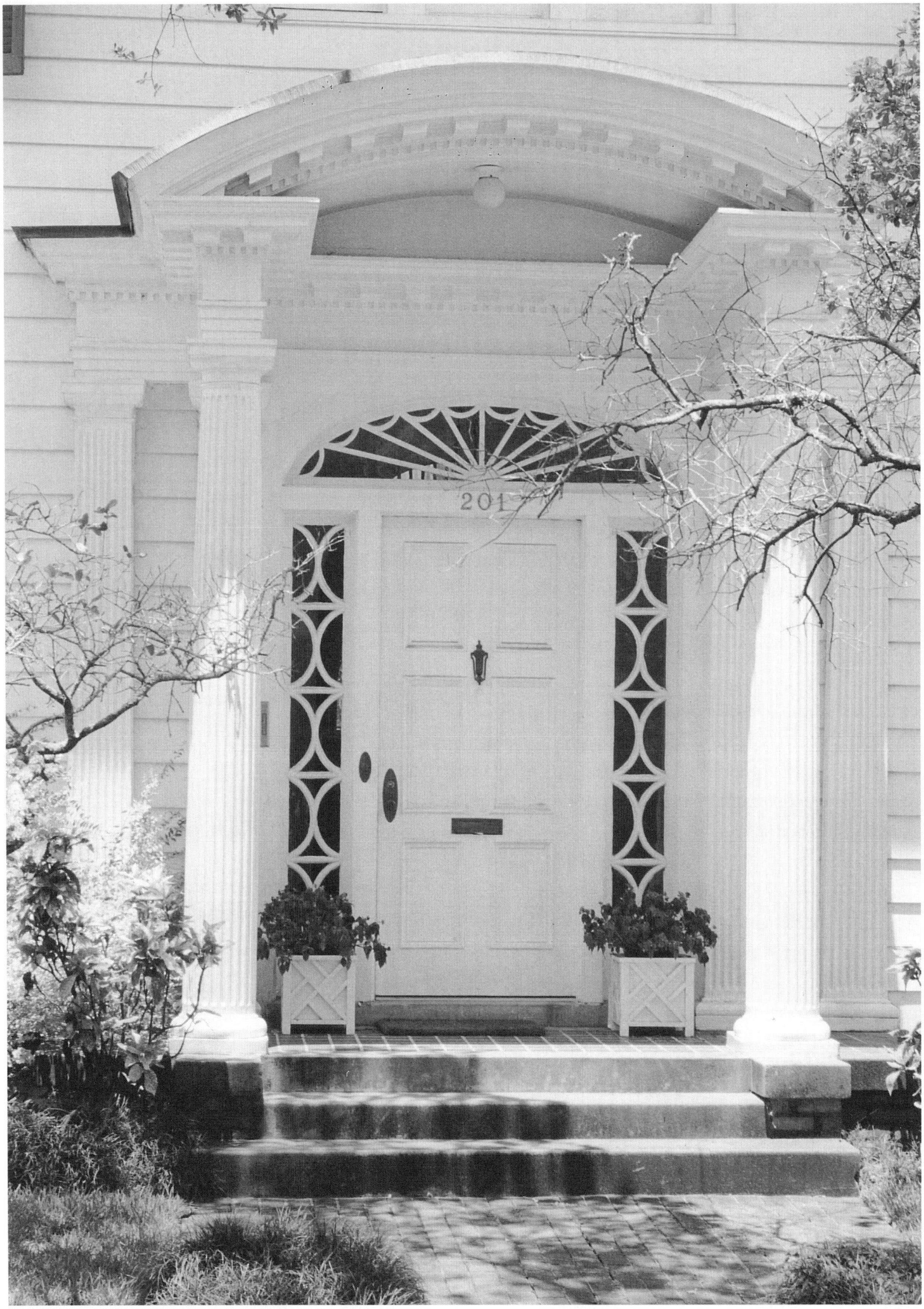
201

Chapter 5

Clarence Lindon Hutchisson, Sr.

(1872-1953)

THE twentieth-century Mobile in which Clarence L. Hutchisson, Sr., lived was a very different city from that in which his grandfather and older brother had worked during the nineteenth century. The first dozen years of the twentieth century were a turning point in Mobile's fortunes. There was not a sudden economic growth but a slow and steady progress that made possible an active architectural program. The increase in commerce and the development of industry required new construction. Old stores were either replaced by modern types or were greatly renovated in the prevailing fashion. Thus the street scenes lost their previous regional characteristics. Large plate glass showcase windows extended along the sidewalks instead of the old windowed doors with their shutters. In spite of the short-lived 1908 trade depression, Mobile was in better financial condition than it had been since before the Civil War. This economic improvement is reflected in the extension of the city limits (figure 72) to include new suburban developments. Newspapers reported the finances spent on building programs.[1]

From 1900 to 1910, the *Mobile Register* contained city and county reports of building permits and their costs. In 1901, the paper stated that half a million dollars had been spent on new construction that included the building of hospitals, schools, municipal buildings and houses. The amount was broken down into two categories: the city expenditure of $500,000 as well as private investment in Spring Hill and Dauphin Way of $100,000. In 1905, the *Mobile Register* listed the increase in the city's building permits covering the years from 1895 to 1905.

    1890-91 — 176 permits
    1895-96 — 278
    1900-01 — 201
    1902-03 — 250
    1903-04 — 418
    1904-05 — 520

With the total evaluation for 1904-1905 being $1,094,538.

Since many buildings were erected without permits, the above figures re-

PLATE V (opposite)
Detail of the entrance to the Maumanee House, 1922, 201 Levert Street, Ashland Place. C. L. Hutchisson, architect. The adaptation of the classically derived porch detailing is typical of the stylistic taste of the early twentieth-century decades.

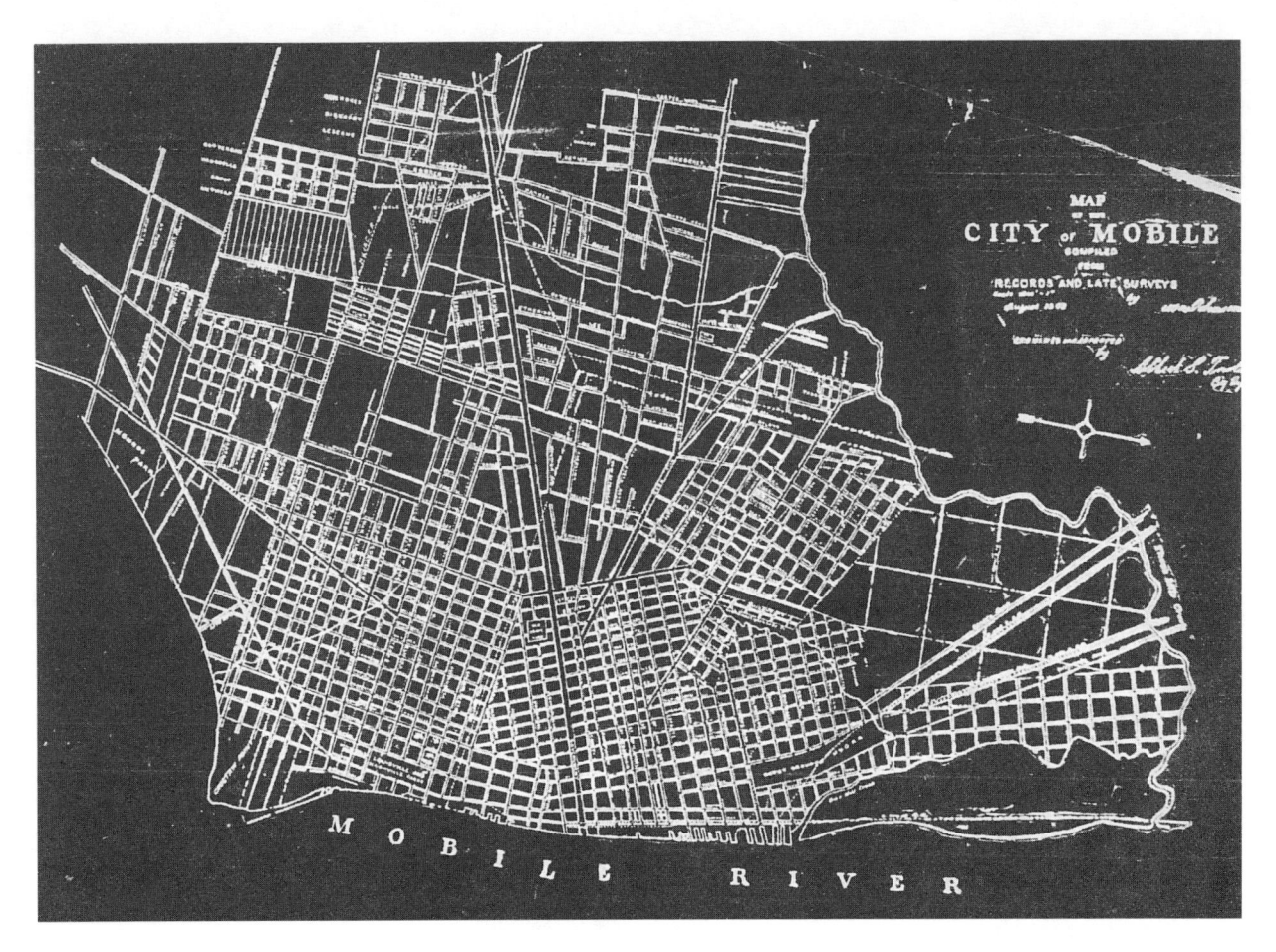

FIGURE 72

The William Johnson Map of Mobile, 1905, printed in the *Mobile Register*, 1905, September 1, section 2, pg. 1. The map delineates the city boundaries at the time C. L. Hutchisson, Sr., was establishing his career in Mobile.

flect only a portion of the activity. The 1905 report went on to say that "a large number of houses for the working classes were built averaging in cost from $2000 to $5000."[2]

In the trade journal for 1907, two million dollars was reported for building programs. Heading the article was a statement "This is the greatest building year in Mobile History."[3] The expenditure listed in 1908 was divided up into categories: brick buildings and wood frame. New brick construction involved $260,000 with repairs to brick buildings amounting to $23,866. New wood frame buildings totalled $385,320 with repairs amounting to an additional $36,912. In addition, the county spent $150,000.[4] The entire value for the year was over $900,000.

In 1910, the journal reported $500,000 spent for public improvements as well as for the growing suburbs. To quote the heading of the article, "The City Beautiful in Recent Suburbs, Houses are Built for Comfort in Semi-Tropical Climate are Artistic Reproductions of Mission and Colonial Architecture with Bungalow Types Popular for Cottages."[5] The large, turreted Victorian homes were replaced by classically inspired mansions with columns rising the full height of the porticoes. Less pretentious homes had one-story porches. The cottage was replaced by the bungalow and the half-cottage of the lower working classes was replaced by the shotgun.

To satisfy the need for new housing, real estate investors and land developers began to open up the western suburbs. Until 1906 the land that comprised the old McDonald Place was still a large farm. It covered the area south of Government Street and west of Catherine. The property was bought by the Lowenstein Investors, who platted the land, laid out streets, paved the sidewalks and constructed entrance gates to the complex. It was named Flo-Claire after the wives of the investing brothers.[6] The Flo-Claire area and the blocks to the north of Government Street along Hunter Avenue and Houston Street were where housing developed the most rapidly. C. L. Hutchisson, Sr., designed many homes in these suburbs, varying from a small bungalow in Flo-Claire to an impressive mansion in Ashland Place.

Not only white residents sought new housing. With segregation resulting from Reconstruction, blacks were largely settled in the Orange Grove area. During the early years of the twentieth century, this suburb was enlarged with new streets opened up east and west of Ann Street and north and south of Davis Avenue (See figure 72). Here newly built single and double shotguns lined the new streets and on earlier streets they infilled between older cottages. Some of the new construction was the result of investors who built for rental income, others were individually constructed by home owners (figure 73).[7] It was the latter group that often had some decorative architectural feature such as porch brackets and better trim. While the homes were largely built by local carpenters, some of the public buildings were designed by architects. C. L. Hutchisson, Sr., was responsible for two of the churches in the area.

A major architectural change that occurred in Mobile with the advent of the twentieth century was the great increase in the number of architects. With the economic improvement and the growth in commerce, the city attracted more than a dozen nonresident architects as well as supporting a half dozen local ones. During the first fifteen years of the century there were more out-of-city architects designing special buildings than in any other time in Mobile's history. Among these were:

- Stone Brothers (Samuel and Guy) of New Orleans, who designed about a dozen buildings including the 1902 Hammel's Department Store that formerly stood on Royal Street; the Masonic Temple of 1901, still standing at 8 St. Joseph Street; the Bienville Brewery, now destroyed; the 1904

FIGURE 73
Advertisement by the Mobile Improvement and Building Company, printed in the *Mobile Register*, 1905, July 16, pg. 16. A typical, company-constructed house of the early twentieth century. The square form of the house with one-story porch extending the full width of the facade was popular throughout the nation.

Leinkauf Bank; the 1903 Lowenstein Bank; and the 1906 Lyric Theater, all three destroyed. Besides public buildings they also designed several large homes along Government Street.
- Andry and Bendernagle of New Orleans were responsible for the City Bank and Trust Building, now destroyed.
- Andrew Downey (b.1873) of New Orleans and William Denham of Mobile designed the 1909 St. Joseph's Chapel at Spring Hill College, and the Izard home at 977 Government Street.
- Frank Andrews (1867-1948) of New York and Cincinnati was the architect for the 1906 Battle House that is now threatened with demolition due to deterioration and vacancy.
- Reuben Harrison Hunt (1862-1937) from Chattanooga designed the 1906 Government Street Baptist Church for which C. L. Hutchisson, Sr., designed the Annex.
- Frank Lockwood (1865-1936) and Walter Seymour of Montgomery were responsible for the 1903 Burgett Memorial Building of the Government Street Presbyterian Church, which was enlarged and renovated in 1917 by C. L. Hutchisson, Sr.
- Philip Thorton Marye (1865-1936) from Atlanta designed the elaborate Spanish Revival GM&O Railroad Station in 1909. It stands at the corner of Beauregard and Royal Streets but is no longer used as a station.
- George Pearson (1849-1920) of Raleigh, N. C., designed the 1900 Fidelia Club that formerly stood on the southeast corner of Government and Conception Streets.
- G. L. Norrman from Atlanta designed the Bienville Hotel in 1900, now destroyed.
- James Knox Taylor from Washington, D. C., designed the 1916 United States Post Office, now destroyed.
- R. M. Mulligan (origin unknown) did the plans for the Providence Infirmary, now destroyed.
- B. B. Smith (1869-1930) from New York and Montgomery added an annex to Barton Academy that still stands at the rear of the 1836 building.

While many buildings were constructed by local builders, there was also an active practice carried on by local architects. Of these, the following were leaders:

- Watkins and Hutchisson, 1903-1905, joined in 1906 by the engineer Joseph Garvin. With Watkins' death in 1907, there followed several different Hutchisson firms. Hutchisson and Chester, 1910-1912. Hutchisson and William Denham, 1912-1916. (For a complete list of firms see Appendix 13).

- Benz and Sons, after the death of Rudolph Benz in 1906, his practice was carried on by his sons.
- George B. Rogers, moved to Mobile about 1902. His name first appeared in the *Mobile Register* for a building in 1903.
- William Haddon, a former partner of James Flandin Hutchisson II, continued to work in Mobile during the early twentieth century.
- McCreary and Slater designed many homes in the Monterey-Reed area. McCreary designed the First Christian Church.
- George D. Hulburt and Co. was responsible for the first design of the Knights of Columbus building, a project that was never built. His design was replaced by one in 1909 by Hutchisson and Garvin.
- P. C. Scheible was responsible for several residential buildings.

Of the group listed above, the firms of Hutchisson and of Rogers were the most active, designing buildings in all categories — religious, civic, commercial and residential. Their commissions were for specific clients not for investors, so each building was individually designed with its own architectural characteristics. C. L. Hutchisson, Sr., was responsible for the greatest number of residences. Of the 233 homes that are known to be Hutchisson's design, 90 are still standing. Within the historic districts, 37 are in Old Dauphin Way, 9 are in Leinkauf, 17 are in Ashland Place, 7 are in the Oakleigh Garden District, 3 are in Church Street East and 17 are not in any district. These homes have survived in good condition and are still in demand, demonstrating their design popularity and their good condition.

In addition to the above residences, Mr. Hutchisson and/or his firm were responsible for 127 commercial buildings that included banks, stores, warehouses, and recreational buildings, as well as a railroad station. Of these only 18 still stand. Of the 16 civic buildings only one is extant. The 1904 Pythian Castle, the 1908 Knights of Columbus Building, the 1910 Mobile Infirmary, the 1915 County Poor House, and the 1921 Tuberculosis Sanitarium have all been destroyed.

In all, he designed nine churches or memorials. In addition to these, he was responsible for seven church improvements and four auxiliary buildings attached to existing structures. He added the Bestor Building to the rear of the First Baptist Church, and the addition to and complete renovation of the Government Street Presbyterian Annex. His schools were also an important contribution to the city and county. Seventeen have been identified, of which nine still stand. In addition to the large and important contracts that came from his firm, his records list some 126 remodelings and renovations of older buildings, and even 29 miscellaneous structures of mundane character, such as chicken houses, residential garages, river camps, and voting booths.

It would seem that this enormous amount of work would have been enough to keep any architect working at fever pitch, but Hutchisson's clientele extended to areas outside of Mobile. He designed 71 buildings in 29 different Alabama cities, 21 buildings in 13 different locations in Mississippi and three as far away as Wisconsin, South Carolina and Panama.[8] Adding the 95 out-of-city buildings to the 568 within Mobile, Mr. Hutchisson's contribution to the art of building makes a grand total of 663.

With 132 known standing Mobile buildings and other important structures now destroyed, it becomes necessary to select only those examples that characterize his work. There was, however, no gradual evolution in the work of Clarence L. Hutchisson, Sr. Even his earliest examples show the skill of a mature architect.

To better present his work, his professional life will be divided up logically into those periods when he had partners and those when he worked alone. By doing this, the designs that came from him or his firm can be better related to contemporary architects and to the local and national trends of the times.

Early Life

Clarence Lindon Hutchisson, Sr., the youngest son of James Henry and Matilda Steele Hutchisson, was born November 4, 1872, in Saint Elmo, on the outskirts of Mobile. Following in the footsteps of his father and older brother, he showed a gift for architecture at an early age. His father recorded in his diary, January 4, 1886, when Clarence was only fourteen years old, that the boy had been paid for making drawings for the contractor W. O. Pond. Pond had constructed many of James Henry Hutchisson's designs, and was well acquainted with the family. The preparation of plans for a contractor implies that the boy was already capable of making working drawings when he was still quite young. After his father's death in 1887 and into the early years of the 1890s, Clarence continued to work in the office under his older brother James Flandin II. His name was included along with that of his brother on several contracts, such as the rectory of the Trinity Episcopal Church standing on Joachim Street.

During the last five years of the century, Mobile's economy could not provide the capital for an active building program, so Clarence left the office of his brother to seek further education elsewhere. By 1897-98, he was working in the firm of McAdoo and Worley in San Antonio, Texas. This experience away from his father's "atelier" enriched his knowledge with differing ways of designing. Two of the known houses by McAdoo and Worley furnished some ideas that later appeared in his own work. Unlike the Italianate and Gothic Revival of his father and the Victorian and Queen Anne of his brother, in San Antonio he came in contact with the Spanish mission influence. He brought this influence back to Alabama as early as 1908 and it is seen in his design for the Masonic Lodge in Brewton, Alabama. This building appeared long before that style became popular in the 1920s.

His Neoclassical movement into the twentieth century may have been in-

FIGURE 74

George Hall, 1902. Mississippi State University campus. P. J. Krouse, architect, with Hutchisson as consulting architect. The earliest-known surviving example of a building with which C. L. Hutchisson is associated.

spired by the two-story porch McAdoo designed for the Alex Joske home, still standing on King William Street in the San Antonio Historic District. The Baroque scrolls that form the crown of the dormer windows of that house certainly impressed him, for he later used the same device. The 1890 Adams house in San Antonio, also by McAdoo and Worely, had a one-story porch that extended over only a part of the front elevation, an architectural component that was successfully applied in the 1904 design for the St. John Episcopal Rectory (figure 76), by Watkins and Hutchisson.

When the Spanish-American War broke out in 1898, Hutchisson joined a Texas Regiment. When mustered out of the Army, he spent another year in Texas. He then moved to New Orleans to work in the office of Favrot and Livauctais. This experience further moved him away from his nineteenth-century training.[9]

Late in 1901 he was offered a partnership with P. J. Krouse, a successful architect in Meridian, Mississippi. In April of 1901, Hutchisson married Henriette Elkin Homer and in 1902 his son, Clarence L., Jr., was born in Meridian. While his partnership with Krouse was a bare two-years duration, it seems to have been a very cordial one. The two architects kept in touch after Hutchisson returned to Mobile. As late as 1915, Hutchisson was the consulting architect with Mr. Krouse on the Meridian City Hall (See figure 115). Not long after Hutchisson joined the Krouse firm, they designed George Hall, 1902, now on the campus of Mississippi State University[10] (figure 74).

George Hall is unusual in the way the end gables are twinned on either side of the truncated hip that forms the main roof of the central block. Round, simplified Tuscan columns support the roof of the three-bay porch of which the central bay projects. The only elements in the design that suggest a later influence on Krouse's young partner Hutchisson is in the repetition of shapes in the different elements of the elevation. Examples can be noted in the triangle of the vent on the main roof that is repeated in the shape of the end gables. This same device can be seen in the rectangle formed by the three central windows of the second story that seems to reflect the rectangle formed by the projecting bay of the porch. Both porch and upper central windows are accented by a similar, strongly emphasized, horizontal cornice. Most of the work of Krouse drew inspiration from Neoclassical developments, which can be traced through the later work of Hutchisson. While Hutchisson was influenced by his experiences in San Antonio, New Orleans and Meridian, he incorporated these influences in his own individual way.

It was also during this time that the working files of Hutchisson contain a reference to designing some buildings for the Industrial College of Mississippi, a complex that later became the Mississippi University for Women. None of the buildings now standing on that campus have been associated with the name of Hutchisson.[11]

The year 1903 brought Clarence L. Hutchisson and his family back to Mobile where he spent the rest of his life. In the family archives is a photograph of the young Hutchisson that must have been taken about this time (figure 75).

FIGURE 75
Portrait of C. L. Hutchisson, Sr., as a young man at the start of his architectural career.

Watkins and Hutchisson 1903-1906

About the time that James Flandin Hutchisson II was getting established in Chicago, George Watkins invited C. L. Hutchisson to return to Mobile as his partner. Watkins, a New York-trained architect, had been working in Mobile for some twenty-five years. Most of his designs were either in the Renaissance or Classical Revival styles, but he also brought to Mobile some new concepts, especially in the design of commercial buildings.[12] Not much information has survived of the buildings done by the new partners until 1904. There is a reference to a house being built on Springhill Avenue near Gilbert Street,[13] but there are no surviving photographs of it.

Another early work, a post office, by the Watkins and Hutchisson firm was for a Mennonite community at Yellow Pine, Alabama. Yellow Pine has now been combined with Fruitdale. Mennonites came to the area to farm. All, including men, women and children, worked by hand to clear the land. They established homes, a bank, a school (known as an academy), and a church. How many of these buildings Watkins and Hutchisson designed is not known since neither the community nor the buildings remain, and it is not possible to establish what existed. According to local residents of Fruitdale, there is an old building thought to be the academy, but no research has been done on the structure.[14]

FIGURE 76
St. John's Episcopal Church Rectory, 1904. Formerly at 205 South Dearborn Street. From the *Mobile Register*, 1904, September 1, section 2, pg. 6. The rectory was one of the first homes designed by Watkins and Hutchisson after the latter returned to Mobile to live.

In the *Mobile Register* for 1904 is a small photograph of a rectory the firm designed for St. John's Episcopal Church.[15] The house once stood at 205 South Dearborn, next to the 1853 Gothic Revival Church designed by David Cumming, Jr. According to church records the first rectory was a small board and batten cottage. The 1904 design of Watkins and Hutchisson shows the change in styles as the twentieth century turned to elements of the Classical and Colonial Revival styles and away from the late-nineteenth-century Queen Anne. Even though the newspaper photograph is poorly preserved (figure 76), the twin columns with their simple classical capitals can be seen. The balustraded-deck of the three-bay porch is the major element in the decoration as opposed to the highly decorative brackets and spindled friezes of the 1890s. The one surviving element from the past is the three-sided, two-story bay at the north end of the facade.

The popular move away from the Victorian can be seen in other examples of the same year. One example by the Stone Brothers of New Orleans makes an interesting comparison with the Watkins and Hutchisson design. The New Orleans firm planned the Norborne Clarke home that once stood on Government Street (figure 77). The Stone Brothers' house has a more complex massing with the bays projecting at both ends of the facade. At the second story, the middle window recalls a Renaissance influence in its semicircular head. Both houses, the rectory and

FIGURE 77
The Narborne Clarke Home, 1905. Formerly at 251 Government Street. The Stone Brothers, New Orleans, architects. While containing the same components as a company-built house (figure 73), the architect-designed home incorporated more individualistic and complex detailing. The building makes an interesting comparison with the St. John's Episcopal Rectory (figure 76).

FIGURE 78

The Henry Hall House, 1905. Formerly at 972 Government Street. The Stone Brothers, New Orleans, architects. The Henry Hall house illustrates how historically derived details, such as the Ionic columns and upper Palladian window, were used by architects to enrich the basic early twentieth-century house.

(FACING PAGE PHOTOS)

FIGURE 79 (top left)

Leinkauf School, 1904-05, 1907-08, 1912. 1451 Church Street. Leinkauf School occupies the southwest corner of Church and Stocking streets. The building faces on Church and extends most of the block along Stocking Street. In 1904-05 a one-story school was designed by Watkins and Hutchisson.

FIGURE 79B (top right)

Three years later Hutchisson and Garvin inserted a second story, resulting in the building illustrated. The cost was $10,444.

FIGURE 79C (center)

In 1912 Hutchisson and Chester were retained to add a two-story annex to the south side of the building. During the course of the century, other additions were made until it now includes a large auditorium-gym at the south end of the complex.

FIGURE 79D (bottom)

Angle view of the east facade of the Leinkauf School as it stood in 1992.

the Clarke home, have a balustraded, one-story porch, a feature that will become increasingly popular throughout the first quarter of the new century.

The design of the Watkins and Hutchisson firm is more tightly integrated in its various components than the Clarke home. The major elements of the Stone Brothers' design, the porch, the two end bays and the central upper window are less related and create a slightly fragmented design. A simpler house by the Stone Brothers built for Henry Hall (figure 78) also illustrates the classical tradition in the porch columns with a Palladian-inspired, central, second-story window. The Pythian Castle of 1904 is another well-known building with which the names of Watkins and Hutchisson were associated. Although described in the *Mobile Register* there was no accompanying photograph. The building appears to have been a major renovation of an older structure.[16]

The most interesting commission of the firm was for a 1904 public school of which the first story still survives. Leinkauf is the oldest extant Mobile school that still serves the purpose for which it was built. Fortunately, the successive enlargements of the school have been documented by existing photographs (figures 79,b,c,d). The first stage was a one-story, brick building designed by George Watkins and C. L. Hutchisson, Sr., soon after their partnership had been established (figure 79).[17] While the details are not very clear, it shows the massing and the general design that formed the basis for all the additions. The single story was raised on a high basement that allowed for indoor recreation in inclement weather. The main rectangular form was penetrated by cross-axes terminating in slightly projecting pavilions that formed the central bays of each of the four elevations. Above each pavilion was a gable roof that intersected the main truncated hip roof. The deck formed by this cutoff of the hip served as the base for a lantern. It is the pyramidal roof of this lantern and the flag pole that seem to unify the complex lines of the gables and hip.

Some of the architectural details have roots in the Italian and French Romanesque, including the stepped molding along the raking cornice of the gable and the corbel tables that connect the heavy hood molds over the windows. These moldings and the shaped bricks that formed the corbels of the hood molds illustrate the design possibilities of brick that were evident in the work of James H. Hutchisson (figure 33).

A clearer picture of the details can be seen in a photograph taken after the second story had been added in 1907-08 (figure 79b). The architects Hutchisson and Garvin maintained the same general design in the second story as had been in the first. From the two photographs, it looks as if the roof had simply been raised and a second story slipped under it. The new wall area on the sides and rear elevations did not present a design problem (figure 79d). It was a different matter with the entrance bay of the facade pavilion. The original tall semicircular entry was retained. In the new space above it, the architects chose the motif of the quarter sections of a circle that were in the gable above and combined them into a semicircular window. Above this, on either side, an oval-shaped panel was placed. The panels were related by an inverted V and by their frames, which were incorporated in the corbel table that extended across the pavilion. Whether the architects intended it or not is unknown, but the final design seems to have a morphological effect of big eyes watching you. The second story was built at the cost of $10,444.

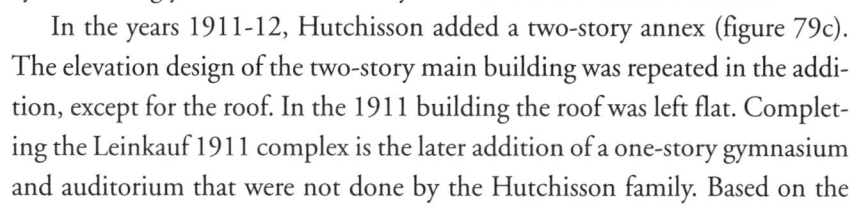

In the years 1911-12, Hutchisson added a two-story annex (figure 79c). The elevation design of the two-story main building was repeated in the addition, except for the roof. In the 1911 building the roof was left flat. Completing the Leinkauf 1911 complex is the later addition of a one-story gymnasium and auditorium that were not done by the Hutchisson family. Based on the

FIGURE 80

The Cawthon Hotel, 1905-06, formerly on the southwest corner of Conception and St. Francis Streets, Mobile. Watkins, Hutchisson and Garvin, architects. Jett Brothers, contractors, $265,000. Some of the most impressive of the early twentieth-century commercial buildings were designed by Watkins and Hutchisson. The architects' employment of new concepts in construction and form, with detailing that harmonized with the historic Mobile styles, can be seen in the elevation of the hotel.

fact that the original design of the first story was continued in the later renovations, Watkins had much to do with establishing the style selected. It is also interesting to note the number of books on school design that Mr. Hutchisson had added to his library. Three of them were *School Architecture, A General Treatise for the Use of Architects and Others*, by Edmund March Wheelright, Boston, Rogers and Manson, 1901; *Modern American School Buildings*, by Warren Richard Briggs, FAIA, New York, John Wiley Pub. Co., 1902; and *A Handy Manual for Architects and School Authorities*, by George Bruce, Milwaukee, John Service Company, 1903.

The building was virtually destroyed by fire in April 1993. Only the damaged exterior walls remained and those are the basis for a rebuilding campaign that duplicated the exterior appearance of the school.

Watkins, Hutchisson and Garvin, 1906-1907

One of the first commissions undertaken by the new firm, after the addition of Garvin, was the Cawthon Hotel of 1906. While it had been commissioned in 1905, the first records of drawings were in 1906 with the construction continuing in 1907 (figure 80,b,c,d,e).[18] The hotel once stood on the southwest corner of St. Francis and Conception Streets, opposite Bienville Square. It was constructed by the Jett Brothers at a cost of $265,000, not counting the furnishings and the $40,000 top floor that was added almost immediately to meet the needs of the hotel. The skeletal framing was a new concept in hotels in Mobile. For many years the building was one of the finest hotels in the entire South, taking its place along with the 1906-1908 Battle House designed by Frank M. Andrews of New York and Cincinnati (figure 81). While the Battle House gradually replaced the Cawthon in the society events in Mobile, the Cawthon continued to be highly recommended and a great asset to the city. It is unfortunate that this well-designed early hotel was destroyed for a parking lot.

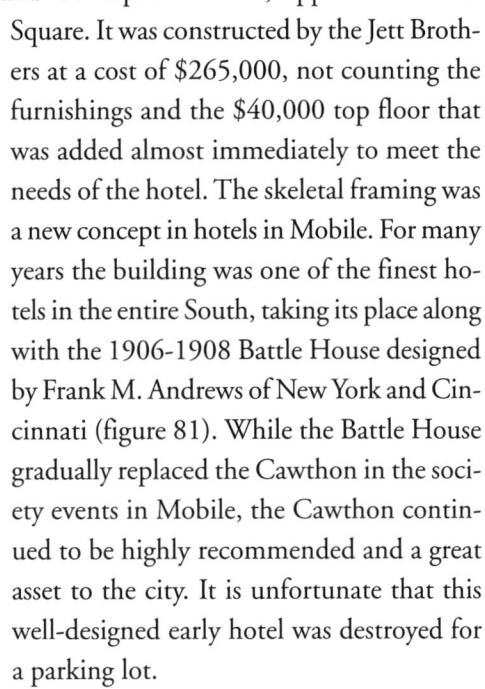

The *Mobile Register* of 1906 had a lengthy description of the Cawthon Hotel, including a reproduction of the architects' rendering of the elevation (figure 80b). The seven-story building was among Mobile's first all-steel frame structures with reinforced concrete floors, and it showed the influence

From Builders to Architects: The Hobart–Hutchisson Six

FIGURE 80B

Architects' drawing of the Cawthon Hotel. The details of the elevation are clearly indicated in the drawing. The surface treatment of the ground level and of the sixth story is similar, relating them to each other. The bay windows unite the five stories containing the hotel rooms. The top story was added after the hotel had been finished. Drawing is from the *Mobile Register*, 1907, August 31, section 2, pg. 2.

of the Chicago Commercial style that developed at the turn of the century. Once again Hutchisson's library demonstrates his continuing self-education. The books include: *Architecture and Engineering with Special Reference to High Rise Building Construction, Including Many Examples of Chicago Office Buildings,* by Joseph Kendall Freitage, New York, John Wiley Pub. Co., 1895; *The Planning and Construction of High Office Buildings*, by William Birkman, New York, John Wiley Pub. Co., 1894; and *Skeletal Structure in Buildings*, by William Birkman, New York, John Wiley Pub. Co., 1904. In addition to other books on steel construction, there were seven on reinforced concrete. His collection was put to use in the planning for the Cawthon Hotel. But unlike the Battle House (figure 81), which had no stylistic ties with Mobile's past, Hutchisson combined twentieth-century concepts with some decorative features that tied into Mobile's history.

The Cawthon was a monumental block with its elevation divided into three zones. The ground level for the public rooms had a relationship in which the first story is oriented to the street, while the upper stories with the private rooms were differentiated from the first floor by a change in the surfacing and in the fenestration. The added seventh story and the projecting cornice formed a third zone in the elevation. The prototype for this configuration can be seen in buildings such as Louis Sullivan's 1890-91 Wainwright Building in St. Louis and the 1899, 1903-04 Carson, Pirie, Scott Department store in Chicago. But while the Cawthon reflects this new concept of relationships, the Mobile building still has reminders of the previous century in the decorative detailing (figure 80b,c).

The first floor of the Cawthon was covered by granite blocks set in strongly marked horizontal courses. The window lintels were formed by flat arches of

FIGURE 80C

Architects' drawing of the entrance of the Cawthon Hotel. The multiple-molded pilasters, the panelled abacus block, the art glass set in designs in the cast iron architrave, and the elaborate balustrade are evidence of the complex decorations designed by the architects.

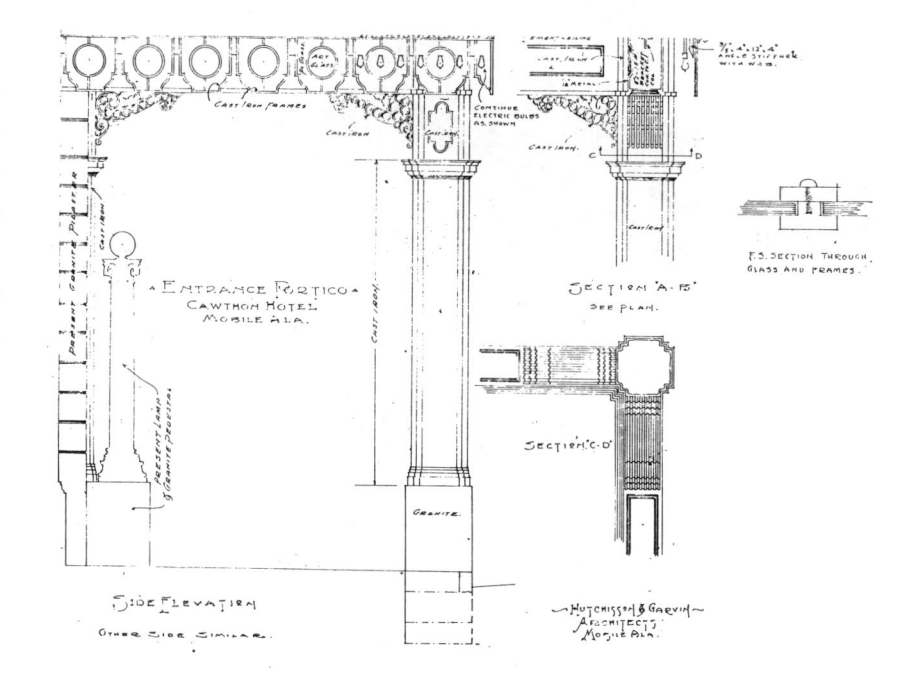

which the voussoirs were lengthened, the central ones rising to the height of the band marking the level of the second story. In contrast to the first story, the upper five levels were surfaced with grey brick. The window lintels were also flat arches, with the end voussoirs and central key stones enlarged, elements that harmonize with the nineteenth-century buildings near by. Two vertical rows of bay windows rose from the level of the second story, further differentiating the upper rooms from the ground story. A white molding delineated the level of the sixth story, echoing the horizontal lines of the first story and making a visual transition to the projecting cornice above. Thus the different elements of the elevation were both differentiated and related.

The main entrance was on the Conception Street side (figure 80c). The

FIGURE 80D

Architects' drawing of a detail of the wall screen around the hotel reception window. The wall screen, where the registrar's window was located, was made of oak supported on a brass railing and surfaced with carved oak panels, above which was a frieze of art glass centered by a clock set under a semicircular frame.

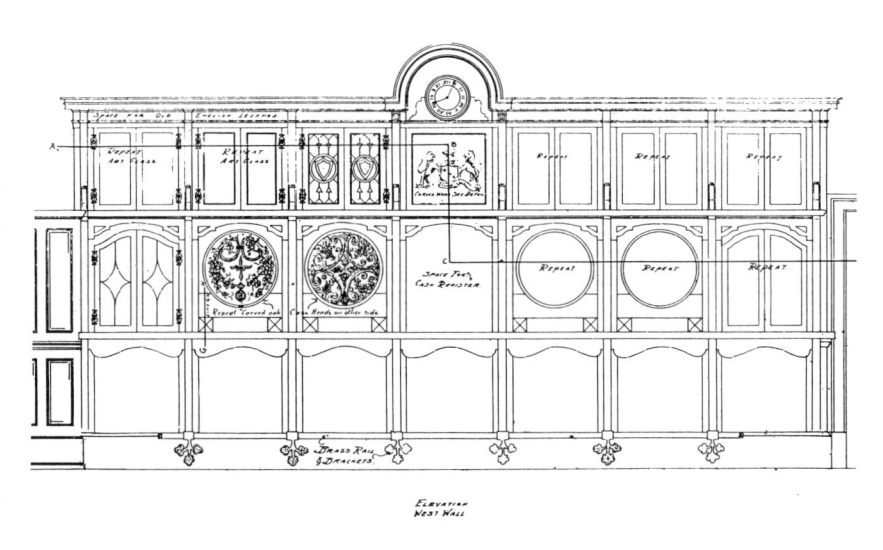

116

From Builders to Architects: The Hobart–Hutchisson Six

FIGURE 80E

The Vineyard Cafe. The Cawthon had a variety of eating accommodations from informal grilles, a tap room and a bar to a formal dining room with a musicians gallery.

doorway was framed by granite piers supporting a cast iron architrave that contained cut glass set in varying geometric designs. Above this a cast iron balustrade extended between short panelled corner piers. This same type of cast iron, art glass decoration was continued in the foyer where it formed a wall screen around the cashier's window (figure 80d). This foyer screen was further embellished by a brass railing at floor level and crowned by scenes of old English legends. On the first floor were various other rooms such as the barber shop, an English grille, a bar, a billiard room, and a fine restaurant. The lobby walls were painted with scenes of New Mexico, by F. Norton, an artist from Boston (figure 80e). A musicians' gallery provided space for live performances before the days of radio and piped-in music. Marble covered the floors of the hall, lobby, and other public rooms. The ladies' entrance was on the St. Francis Street side. Here, parlors and rest rooms provided for their comfort and convenience.

FIGURE 81

The Battle House, 1906-08. 26 North Royal Street. Frank M. Andrews, New York, architect; General Supply and Construction Company, contractor. In a comparison with the Battle House design, the Cawthon has components that relate the building to Mobile's historic past, while the Battle House reflects the national trends of the time.

An interesting comment on the times are the noted points of the article that we now take for granted. The newspaper reporter from the *Mobile Register* 1906 remarked on the facts that all the windows were screened, the heating and ventilation were carefully considered, and that an elevator was "precisely in the right place."

During his lifetime, Hutchisson alone or with his firm carried out several renovations and later additions to existing hotels, including the Battle House (figure 81). The last one with which he worked was the mid-

ELIZABETH BARRETT GOULD

117

FIGURE 82

The First National Bank, 1906, 68 St. Francis Street, Mobile. Watkins, Hutchisson and Garvin, architects; Interstate Construction Company of Mobile, contractors. The white brick and glazed terra cotta moldings of this late Renaissance-inspired bank still dominates the street in spite of the new high-rise hotel and parking garage that towers over it toward the south. The building with historic architectural elements fulfilled the bankers' intent to have a structure that expressed the "solidity and firm foundation of the business within."

FIGURE 82B

Drawing of the 1875 building occupied by the First National Bank, destroyed in 1906 to make way for the Watkins, Hutchisson and Garvin building. The Marion Acker drawing was taken from the First National Bank Publication: *Highlights of One Hundred Years of Mobile History*, page 25.

nineteenth-century building that comprised the La Clede. The two C. L. Hutchissons, father and son in partnership, were commissioned to extend the hotel with three additional bays to the west of the existing facade. The work was so skillfully done that it took considerable research to discover the year of the addition was 1940.

In the same years that Watkins, Hutchisson, and Garvin finished the Cawthon Hotel, they designed the third home for the First National Bank. It still stands at 68 St. Francis Street (figure 82). Now serving the Bank of Mobile, it has been restored following the original plans as drawn by the architects. An older 1865 building that had originally occupied the site was demolished because it no longer met the needs of the twentieth-century expanding bank business (figure 82b). The new building would be fire and burglar proof. The directors rejected the new bank styles that were then going up, and instead, wanted a "distinctive structure, one that would strike the observer as the home of a bank and indicating its solidity, the firm foundation of the business within."[19] To the minds of the conservative First National Bank directors, the two banks that had just been constructed in the city, the Leinkauf Bank of 1903, designed by Stone Brothers of New Orleans and the 1904 Bank and Trust, designed by Andry and Benderbagle also of New Orleans with George Rogers associated in Mobile, were too modern and unrelated to acceptable historic styles. The six-story Bank and Trust with its narrow, tall proportions, its complete break between the first story and the offices above, and the pilasters that rose to the cornice, separating the three bays was too revolutionary to suggest stability. The Stone Brothers' Leinkauf Bank was a less radical change. Its three-story rectangular form was more in keeping with the usual Mobile skyline but the rest of the design was definitely twentieth century with its flat pilasters separating the three bays. Even though they were given pseudo-Ionic capitals, the buildings were still too modern. In the minds of the trustees of the First National these two (both destroyed) looked more like stores than banks. So Watkins, Hutchisson and Garvin designed what the bank trustees wanted, a building that was based on a recognized classical inheritance with architectural elements that had survived throughout the ages. The architects began the plans to satisfy this request in 1905, and the building was completed in August 1906.

The two-story building is fifty feet wide and more than seventy feet deep, with a wing extending from the northeast corner (figure 82). The facade of the bank reflects the influence of the late Italian Renaissance, in which a gabled, vertical rectangle with classic detailing was superimposed on a horizontal rectangle that extended on either side. The central section that projects slightly from the rectangle behind it is framed on either side by a full-height Ionic column, the shafts of both are surfaced with white-glazed terra cotta. Rising to the outside of each column is a white-glazed brick pilaster. On either side of the central section, both the column and the pilaster share the same granite base. Originally the granite was continued across the bay between the columns. During some subsequent occupancy, the granite dado was removed to make way for a large double door. The columns and pilasters rise to the classic entablature, the frieze of which is inscribed with the name of the bank. The gable that covers this portion of the facade has widely projecting cornices accented by heavy, blocky modillions. The horizontal cornice of the gable continues in a step-back across the side bays linking the two rectangles together. All the decorative details were formed of terra cotta, including the

FIGURE 82c

Detail of the doorway to the First National Bank building by Watkins, Hutchisson and Garvin. The door framing is elaborated by scrolled brackets supporting the short returns of the horizontal cornice and the broken pediments. Above the door frame is a panel embellished with a graceful swag.

wreath encircling the pediment oculus, the capitals, and the swags above the doors. A plate glass window, eight by twelve feet, now occupies the central bay of the first story. Above it three windows are located at the second story.

The bank was entered by a door located in each of the side bays (figure 82c). The broken pediments above these doors, with their cartouches and swags, give a decidedly Baroque feel to the facade. The interior was as luxuriant as the exterior suggested. The floor was laid in a mosaic tile; the wainscoting, seven feet high, was of English veined marble with a base molding of green marble. Above the wainscoting, the walls were covered with green burlap stencilled with gold designs. The counters were of marble, and the cages were protected by bronze grills. Mahogany desks were provided for the comfort of the patrons who wished to carry on written business. The director's room behind the main section had an interesting hand-painted ceiling done by a Mr. Folley, an artist from St. Louis.

The second story consisted of a vestibule that had the same decorative features as that on the first story. Fifteen offices were arranged on either side of a central hall, with a cross-hall at each end. The rear wing was equipped for the use of the employees and contained lounges, rest rooms, dressing rooms, a lunching area, and lockers.

Hutchisson's churches fared little better than his commercial buildings. As the population of Mobile moved west, so did the churches, leaving behind buildings that no longer could serve their members. In Hutchisson's list of churches there are six complete structures, four annexes, seven major renovations and alterations, and three memorials. Some of the churches have been described in the newspapers of their time, including the Black Mission Church of 1908 that seated 500 people. It was a frame construction, with four doors leading into the vestibule. The auditorium rose to a height of twenty-six feet with windows filled with art glass.[20] In 1909 the Lily Baptist Church on Kennedy near Basil was constructed. This building was of brick and stone and constructed at a cost of $13,000.[21]

A photograph has survived of the 1906 Sha'arai Shomayim Temple that once stood on the southeast corner of Government and Warren Streets (figure 83).

The temple was designed by Watkins, Hutchisson, and Garvin and served the Jewish community until 1956. The building was beautifully con-

FIGURE 83

The Sha'arai Shomayim Temple, 1906. Formerly on the south east corner of Government and Warren Streets in Mobile. Watkins, Hutchisson and Garvin, architects; Nicol and Legee, builders. The temple was destroyed soon after it was sold in 1952. The brick walls rose above the high foundation of stone. All window hood-moldings, cornices, tower balustrades and trim were of terra cotta. The low domes over the towers were of lead and the roof of slate. Centered in the apex of the front gable was a panel with tablets inscribed in Hebrew.

FIGURE 83B

The architect's drawings of the front (north) facade of the Sha'arai Shomayim Temple, facing Government Street. In the drawing, the low domes over the square corner towers and the detailing are more clearly defined than in the photograph. The pilasters beneath the multiple-molded terra-cotta arches are linear patterns inspired by the deeply splayed openings of twelfth-century Romanesque buildings.

structed of Indiana limestone, Georgia granite, and light-colored pressed brick. At the time of its dedication in 1907, the *Mobile Register* contained a photograph with a brief description.[22] In style, the temple reflected the sixth century of Asia Minor and the twelfth-century Romanesque of France. From the east came the shadowed, recessed entrance between heavy, square corner towers such as in the Louzeh in Syria, the sixth century Basilica of Der Turmanin, also in Syria, and the Bin-dir-Killisse in Anatolia (figure 83b). From twelfth-century France came the deeply splayed and multiple-ordered windows that had been flattened to linear patterns in the temple. The medieval colonnettes standing beneath their respective orders in the temple were reduced to applied, thin, slightly rounded strips and, on the west end, to pilasters (figure 83c).

Three large doors led into the building vestibule. The axis of the auditorium ran parallel to the street so that it faced east and west. It was a large room, sixty by eighty feet with a ceiling fifty feet high. In addition there was a balcony in the auditorium that seated 300 people. The rostrum that was located at the eastern end of the sanctuary was wainscoted with white marble as was the location of the ark. The curving steps leading up to the sacred end were also of marble.

In the east tower was space for a study that opened on to a corridor behind the auditorium. A row of classrooms was in this area. In the western tower the space was divided between the north entrance to the

FIGURE 83C

The Warren Street side elevation of Sha'arai Shomayim Temple. The three divisions of the west side elevation are composed of the tower on the left, the sanctuary in the center and the education building on the right. The small, multi-arched window in the gable of the education building repeats the pattern of the tower window.

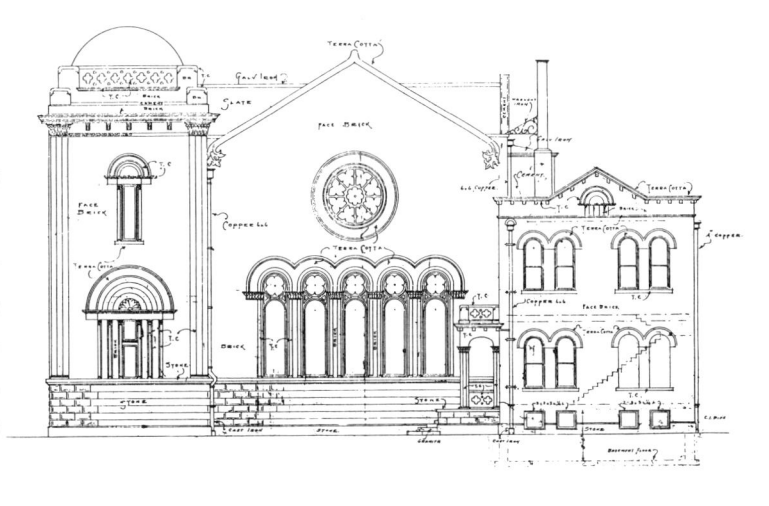

ELIZABETH BARRETT GOULD

gallery and a "retiring" room, so labelled on the plans. These arrangements were repeated in the southern corner of the building beyond the central foyer. Unfortunately, some mildew smeared the plans making them difficult to reproduce clearly on a small scale.

The Sha'aria Shomayim was the last large commission carried out before the death of George Watkins. His firm was carried on by Hutchisson and Garvin. It is not known how many residences the firm of Watkins, Hutchisson and Garvin designed. A few references to them are recorded in the newspapers. One such was on Springhill, near Gilbert Street.[23] Fortunately another one designed while Watkins was alive still stands, but as it was not constructed until after his death, it is usually attributed to Hutchisson and Garvin. It is the impressive home designed for William and Agnes Lott, located on the corner of Church and Rapier Streets where it has excellent exposure on all sides. The large lot on which it is now located was once part of the old Rapier Tract in the Oakleigh Garden Historic District. With the Lott house the account of the life of Clarence L. Hutchisson moves into his next partnership with Garvin.

Hutchisson and Garvin, 1907-1910

The Lott house was reported in the *Mobile Register* of 1906.[24] It is a large wood frame home of two stories with a full width front portico whose square columns with Ionic capitals rise the full height of the facade (figure 84). A two-story porch on the south contains the secondary entrance that is approached from a curving driveway leading off of Church Street. Another two-story porch is located on the north side, off of the rear bays. Behind the house stands the original carriage house, though it has been modified as a studio.

FIGURE 84

The Lott House, 1907. 160 Rapier Street, Mobile. Hutchisson and Garvin, architects. One of the earliest of the classically inspired porticoes built in Mobile during the first decade of the twentieth century. The four, square columns have capitals derived from the Ionic order. Behind them the gracefully curved balcony relieves the severity of the vertical and horizontal lines of the facade.

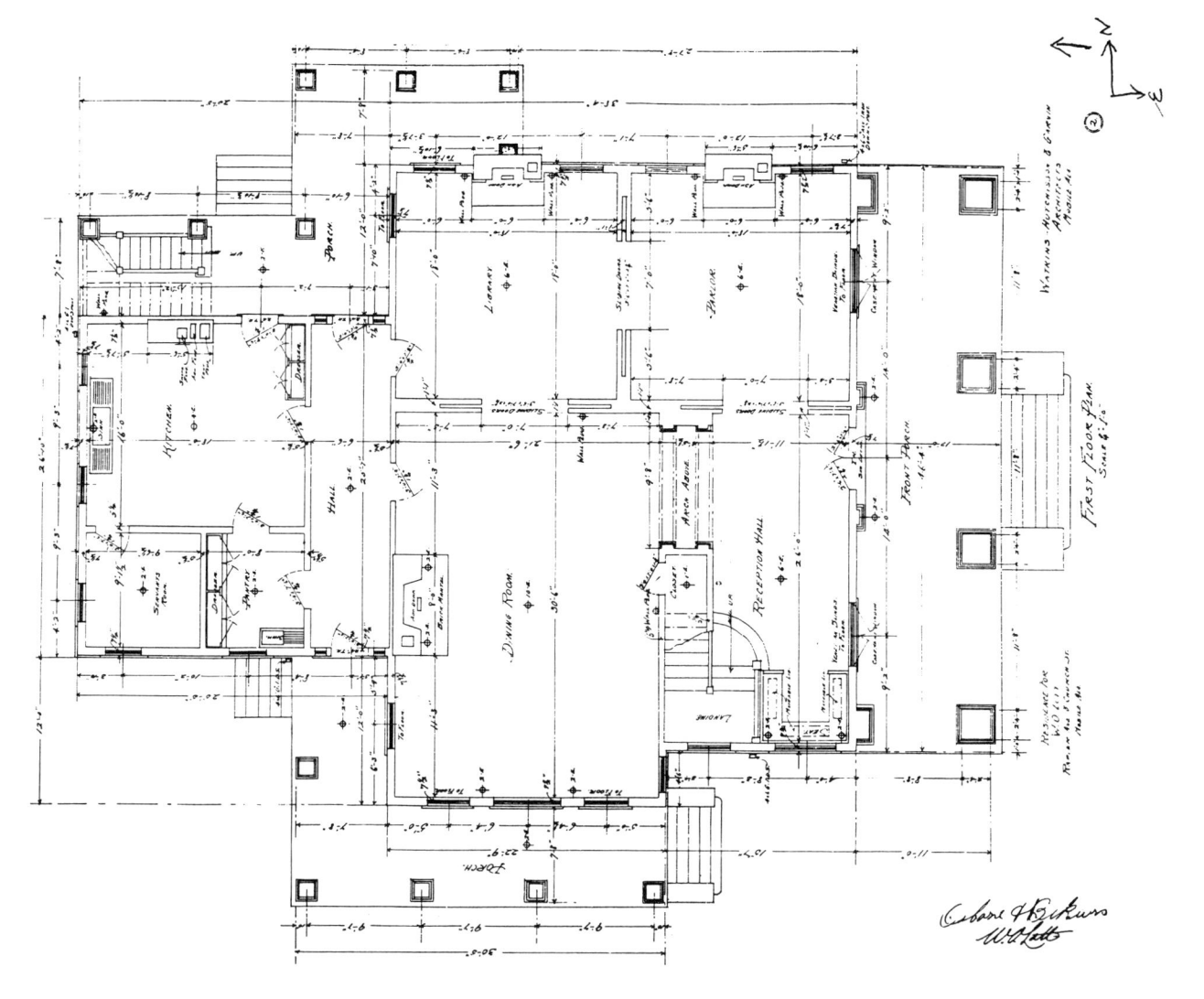

The design of the Lott home reflects the classical revivals that had become popular in Mobile during the first decade of the twentieth century. While the massing and detailing are derived from these historic sources, the architect's skillful interpretation and individuality is evident in how the Greek Ionic capitals are adapted to the square columns, the overhanging cornice using shaped rafters instead of modillions, and the variation on the Palladian theme in the central dormer window. The large scroll brackets that visually support the balcony are from the Greek Revival, but unexpectedly Hutchisson has given the balcony a gentle, undulating curve that adds grace to an otherwise strictly vertical and horizontal movement (figure 84d).

In plan, (figure 84b) the main block of the house has four rooms. There is no hallway and the entrance opens directly into the reception room, twenty-six feet long by eleven feet, one-and-a-half inches wide. Along the south wall is a seating nook that fills the space up to the edge of the two-run stairway that is approached by two curving steps. At the landing is a stained glass window that casts prismatic color patterns into the room. The window is visible in the left side of figure 84. At the rear of the room on the right is an ornamental

FIGURE 84B

Plan of the Lott House as drawn by the architects. Unlike most of the formal porticoed homes of the 1910 decade, the Lott house has no central hall that divided the rooms equally on either side. Instead rooms are arranged by size and position that best serve their purpose.

ELIZABETH BARRETT GOULD 123

FIGURE 84C

Architect's drawing of the front elevation facing Rapier Street. The slate-covered roofs with their iron ridge caps are not visible from ground level but are clearly defined in the drawing. There are no modillions beneath the overhanging cornice but the extended rafters have shaped ends

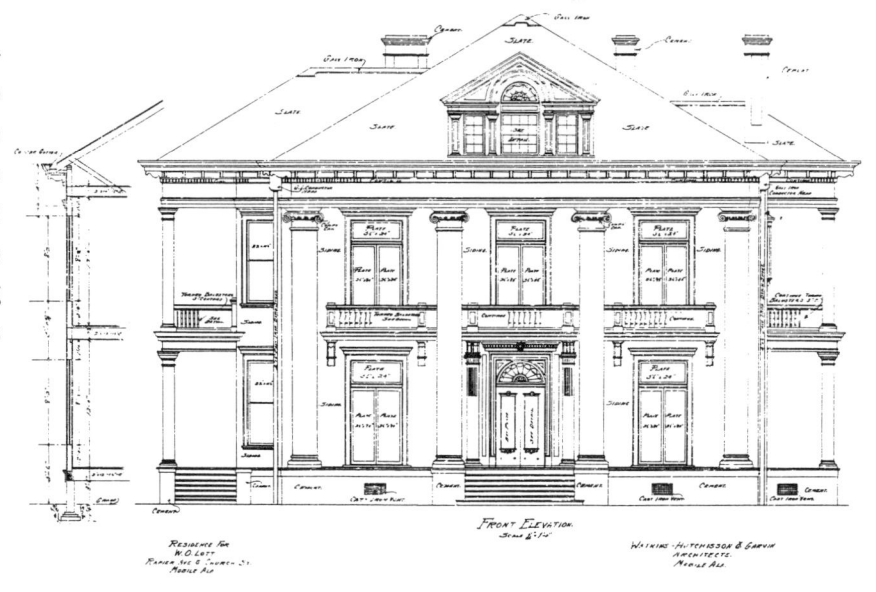

FIGURE 84D

The curved balcony of the Lott House is supported on brackets. Details are difficult to see in the building because of the deep shadows cast by the portico.

archway that leads into the dining room, the largest room on the first floor, being thirty feet, six inches by twenty-one feet, six inches. The room is dominated by a large fireplace on the rear wall with a brick mantel that rises to the ceiling. Hutchisson made use of the brick mantels in several of his houses, each differing in the patterning of the brick coursing.

To the north (right) of the reception room is the parlor, eighteen-feet square. It connects to the library by sliding doors. Both rooms have a fireplace. Sliding doors also connect the library with the dining room. When all the doors are open, a fine flow of space exists through the four rooms.

In the central, rear square wing is a cross-hallway that extends to the porches on either side of the house. Behind this are the service rooms, kitchen, pantry, and the servant's room. The servants' stairway to the upper floor is located outside the walls of the wing, under the roof of the extended north porch.

The second-story bedrooms follow the same partition plan as the rooms downstairs, plus spaces for bathrooms and closets. Some minor changes have been made over the years to accommodate for modern plumbing and heating, but basically the plan remains as originally designed.

During World War II when the population of Mobile "burst its seams" by war workers flooding into the port city, every available space was adapted for minimal living conditions. The Lott house, having fallen into the hands of subsequent owners, was divided into small apartments by inserting partitions and lowering the ceilings. After the war the house continued as low-income housing. It was in deteriorating condition when bought by Mr. and Mrs. Mark Tapia. The new owners tore out all the temporary partitions and false ceilings. The Tapias restored the house to its original condition, according to the architect's plans. The only major change they made was turning the old extant carriage house into a studio.

The elevation drawing (figure 84c) clearly shows the symmetry of the three-bay facade with the elaborate entrance and single dormer accenting the central axis. The side porches, though at unequal distance from the front, do not appreciably detract from the formal balance. The two-story high portico is supported by tall, square columns that seem to give strength to the massiveness of the design, and repeat and harmonize with the rectangular shape of the elevation. The second-story balcony, that extends between the end pilasters, is partially hidden by the columns and the shadows cast by the overhanging roof. Unlike the Greek Revival balconies with their squared lines, the Lott house balcony, as noted before, forms an undulating curve that gives an unexpected grace to the otherwise strictly horizontal and vertical lines (figure 84d). Beautifully shaped scroll brackets beneath the balcony are placed to form an accent on either side of the full height first floor windows. Heavy plate glass fills the windows and the transoms.

The roof, which is not visible from the ground level, is clearly identified in the drawing. The large, central dormer is more successful in the drawing than in the actual construction, since it is set too far back to see the relationship of dormer to roof when viewed from the ground. The three-part dormer window with its curve over the central opening suggests a Palladian influence. The overhanging roof has a row of small dentils running beneath the scroll-shaped rafters, which, except for their close positioning, suggest modillions.

Framing the entrance (figure 84e) are fluted pilasters with Ionic capitals connected by a heavy lintel. In the center is a cartouche design that seems to pull the various parts together, unifying the separate components of the doorway. A semicircular transom filled with art glass completes the entry.

The 1907 home of Judge M. Wilson that stands at 106 South Georgia

FIGURE 84E
The entrance of the Lott House. The details of the door framing are derived from the classical vocabulary: fluted pilasters; scroll brackets; dentil course; and the semicircular transom.

FIGURE 85

Judge J. M. Wilson House, 1907. 106 South Georgia Avenue, Mobile. Photograph also shown in *The Mobile Register*, 1907, September 2, section 4, pg. 5. The architect is unknown, but the design suggests either Hutchisson or someone influenced by him. The portico covers only three bays of the elevation but the curved balcony, the shaped rafter ends and the Palladian division of the gable vent repeat the patterns of the Lott House.

Avenue makes an interesting comparison with the Lott house (figure 85). A photograph of the home appeared in the *Mobile Register* of 1907 along with the William Gordon home that was attributed to Hutchisson and Garvin.[25] However, unlike the Lott house, no mention was made of the architect of Judge Wilson's house, nor has it been possible, as yet, to identify the designer. The outward curve of the central bay of the balcony, the small dentil molding with the scroll-shaped rafters under the overhanging eaves, and the simplified Palladian division of the vent in the porch gable are details found in both homes. The transom is oval — more in the Federal style than in the Georgian-derived, semicircular transom of the Lott house.

The most obvious difference is in the massing. The Wilson home is more contained with the portico covering only the central bays of the elevation instead of extending the whole width of the house. From the ground level, the porch roof is well integrated with the main truncated hip. The circular, Ionic columns with their traditional bases are less a variant on the classical prototype. The result is a greater sense of enclosure in the Wilson house than in the Lott portico.

But the similarities certainly suggest that the Wilson home was a Hutchisson and Garvin design. If it was not, then it was designed by someone adopting some of the firm's devices. This would have been easy to do since the Wilson home was constructed some time later than the Lott home.

During the time of the Hutchisson and Garvin partnership, they built a few other fine homes along Government Street and in the western suburbs. In style their buildings covered the full range of the national as well as the local

FIGURE 86
The George Poetz House, 1907, 100 South Ann Street. Hutchisson and Garvin, architects. The *Mobile Register* of September 1, 1908, mentioned the completed building as a "large, ten room house, semi-colonial in style, with galleries." The tall, square columns are panelled, casting a thin shadow line that breaks the squareness of the shafts. The three homes, the 1906 Lott House, the 1907 Wilson House and the 1908 Poetz House, illustrate the variety achieved by the use of elements derived from the same classical source.

trends, from the classical influence with the Poetz house (figure 86) to the eclectic Tudor Revival with the Dickens house (now destroyed). It was also during the 1907-08 years that the firm received commissions for buildings in parts of Alabama, Mississippi, and Panama (a girl's school).

Locally, 1907 was a very busy year for the firm with the rapidly developing suburban areas opening up. About as fast as the lots were platted, they were sold and houses begun. Two of these by Hutchisson and Garvin have been selected to represent the type popular in the Old Dauphin Way Historic District and also along Michigan Avenue. They are the George Poetz home at 100 South Ann Street (figure 86), and the I. M. Metzger house at 107 Michigan Avenue (figure 87). Built the same year, they illustrate the variations in style, from the continuation of traditional classical influence of the previous century to a typical early twentieth-century residence.

The George Poetz house is a simplified version of the Judge Wilson home. The two-story portico has square-panelled columns with simple capitals and bases of square blocks. A small, straight balcony extends between the columns, and the balusters are a square section. There are no decorative moldings, dentils or shaped rafters beneath the overhanging eaves. A simple, three-part square vent is located in the gable end of the porch. Even without embellishment, the pleasing design makes an impressive house on its corner lot. In the newspaper of 1908, it states that it was a ten-room home "semi-colonial in style, with galleries."[26]

In contrast, the I. M. Metzger home on Michigan Avenue (figure 87) is early twentieth century with its porch reduced to a single bay entry.[27] Twin

FIGURE 87

The Metzger House, 1907, 157 Michigan Avenue, Mobile. Hutchisson and Garvin, architects. The Metzger Home design is a later development of the square house with a one-story porch that was first noted in the St. John's Episcopal Rectory (figure 76). The design has become symmetrical with the centered porch balanced on either side by the windows. The rafter-supported roof has a wider overhang. The porch and door show such details as more slender balusters than would have been found in earlier examples. The geometrical designs of the mullions and window tracery are breaks from the classical prototype.

pairs of fluted, Ionic columns support the balustraded deck of the one-story porch. The balusters are more slender than in the classical older types. The low-hipped, overhanging roof with its plain exposed rafters foreshadows the American Foursquare of the next decade.[28] The low, wide, horizontal lines of the dormer repeat the lines of the main roof to which it is attached at the ridge. The double-hung windows of the second story are typical of the twentieth century. Each first-story window with its single large glass pane is surmounted by a smaller one that is an integral part of the opening, not separated as a transom would have been. Most of the details of the porch are classical in origin but the interweaving triangles of the tracery in the window above seem unrelated to the rest of the elevation.

The home that Hutchisson and Garvin designed for William Gordon once stood on Michigan Avenue (figure 88). It more closely anticipated the American Foursquare with its full width one-story porch supported by triple columns at the outer corners.[29] In 1908, Hutchisson began a thirty-year span of building activity in Ashland Place. During this time, he designed seventeen houses, of which thirteen are still standing. The three houses that were planned by Hutchisson and Garvin were the S. P. Marsh home at 151 Levert Street, the James Coleman residence at 155 Levert Street, and the Lott House at 204 Lanier. Designed in 1908, the Coleman House (figure 89) was the firm's first residence here. Though the columns of the porches are derived from the Greek Ionic order, Hutchisson broke with the strict classical symmetry of the facade by moving the porch off center. The informality of the design is largely achieved by the change from a formal portico to an intimately conceived front porch. The design of the Coleman house is typical of the growing popularity throughout the United States of a large, comfortable home that could easily be enlarged by rear or side wings as an increase in the family required.

At first glance, the porch of the Coleman house appears as a wrap-around, but in reality the front porch is only two bays wide, with an independent porch on the north elevation that joins the house at the northeast corner. There is another two-bay porch on the south elevation. The columns of all the porches are of the Ionic order.[30] There is a low, wood frame balustrade that extends across the two bays of the front porch at the second story. Twin-capped piers that divide the railing into two parts are placed directly above the twin columns making a subtle relationship between the two levels. The slightly off-centered entrance has a one-leaf door with a three-part leaded glass transom above it and sidelights with a single panel of glass matching the leading of the transom.

Just as the various elements of the facade are asymmetrical, so too are the windows. At the second story, the window of the first bay is double hung, with small lights of nine panes over one, a change from the six-over-six of the previous century. Below, the window is a large single pane with a transom leaded like that of the door. In addition to the spacious rooms of the main block, the house plan includes an additional wing at the rear. The casement windows of this wing suggest that it was a later addition.

In contrast to the Coleman House, the S. P. Marsh home (figure 90) is

FIGURE 88
The William Gordon House, 1907. Formerly on Michigan Avenue. The surviving evidence of the Gordon home is a photograph published in the *Mobile Register*. It is evidence of the popularity of the square, two-story house with a one-story porch during the first decade of the century.

FIGURE 89
The James Coleman House, 1908, 155 Levert, Ashland Place, Mobile. The Coleman House is the earliest of the thirteen standing homes designed by Hutchisson. The off-center porch is typical of the more informal treatment of the Neoclassical styles of the early twentieth century. Two-story houses with their one-story porches line Levert Street. They all derive from the same basic form but differ in details so there is a pleasing variety within conformity.

FIGURE 90

The Sam P. Marsh House, 1909. 151 Levert Street, Ashland Place, Mobile. Hutchisson and Garvin, architects. The Marsh House, standing south of the Coleman House, illustrates how the architect altered his designs while still using the same basic components.

FIGURE 91

The Walsh House, 1909-1910. Formerly in Ashland Place, Mobile, now destroyed. Hutchisson and Garvin, architects. The first floor plan shows the typical, informal arrangement of the rooms in Neoclassical homes which were designed without a large central hall. The parlor and reception hall are connected by wide sliding doors that, when opened, created a space the full width of the house. A more private living room is entered from an outside stairway as well as from the interior rooms, a great advantage for family members who can enter without disturbing any social functions in the formal reception hall or parlor.

more formal.[31] Its central block is unbroken by any bays on the front as was the case in the Coleman dwelling. In the Marsh house, the regularity and the placement of the windows add to the effect of the uncluttered outlines of the block. The one-story porch wraps around the front and the south side of the house in a unifying line that repeats the horizontal emphasis of the roofs and windows. The slightly projecting porch entrance bay creates enough of an accent to give the design vitality that might have been monotonous without it.

A set of drawings by Hutchisson and Garvin for the R. Walsh house survived, though the house no longer stands in Ashland Place. The plan (figure 91) is a good example of the changes made in room arrangements from those of the previous century. No longer is there a wide hall, opening on both front and rear porches and dividing the rooms equally with two on one side and two on the other. Only in those homes built in some Colonial Revival style, such as the example of the Rapier-Boone home (figure 103c) was this older plan continued. Instead, the plans of the early decades of the new century were more informal with no

FIGURE 92

The Winslow Partridge alterations and construction, 1909, 1119 Dauphin Street, Mobile. In 1889, Rudolph Benz designed a home for Daniel Partridge. In 1909, a descendent, Winslow Partridge, retained Hutchisson to enlarge the house by adding rooms to form a new front area and new facade in the Neoclassical tradition. The result is an unusual use of a second-story addition to the central bays of the wraparound porch. Without this second story, the long line of the porch would have been monotonous.

through hallway but only a small entrance foyer. Rooms were arranged for convenience of use as in the Walsh House. This plan more easily suited the life styles of the new century.

As a result of this plan, there was a difference in the ratio of wall surface to openings. The Gulf Coast cottage and the Greek Revival buildings had more open space than wall surface. The large number of slide-by windows, interior as well as exterior transomed doorways and open-ended hallways made the difference. When the national trends arrived at the Gulf Coast, this ratio was reversed resulting in a more enclosed dwelling creating the need for air conditioning. Even with the presence of porches, the old vernacular developments of the openness of the Gulf Coast were gone.

All three Hutchisson and Garvin houses symbolize the social and economic status of Ashland Place. While there are smaller houses in the area, such as the Otts house designed by Hutchisson, all are sited on large lots, and shaded by magnificent old oak trees that the developers had the vision to preserve. All are equally distant from the sidewalk, creating a street view of green lawns softened by the shadows of oak trees. The compatibility of the house designs, most being derived from the classical vocabulary, establishes a residential ambience of peace, harmony and comfort.

During the course of Hutchisson's life, he carried out several extensive renovations of older buildings. Three of these are included in this survey under various partnerships. The first was the Winslow Partridge home on Dauphin Street (figure 92). Originally it had been an 1889 Victorian home by Rudolph Benz.[32] It had been built for Daniel Partridge whose descendent, Winslow Partridge, commissioned Hutchisson to enlarge the house in a style commensurate with the 1909 date. To carry out the commission the house was enlarged by adding rooms to the front and designing a one-story porch that wrapped around the front and west side elevations. Accenting the horizontal lines of the porch was a balustraded deck, broken by a slightly projecting three-bay section of the porch that had been raised to the second story. Columns of the Doric order supported the roof of the first story of the porch and the Ionic order was used in the second story section. There is no exterior sign of the original Victorian building.

The same year that Hutchisson and Garvin were beginning work in Ashland Place, they designed a building for a Masonic Lodge in Brewton, Alabama (figure 93). It is impossible to even imagine what the original building looked like when seeing it as it now stands at 220 Belleview Avenue. The building was

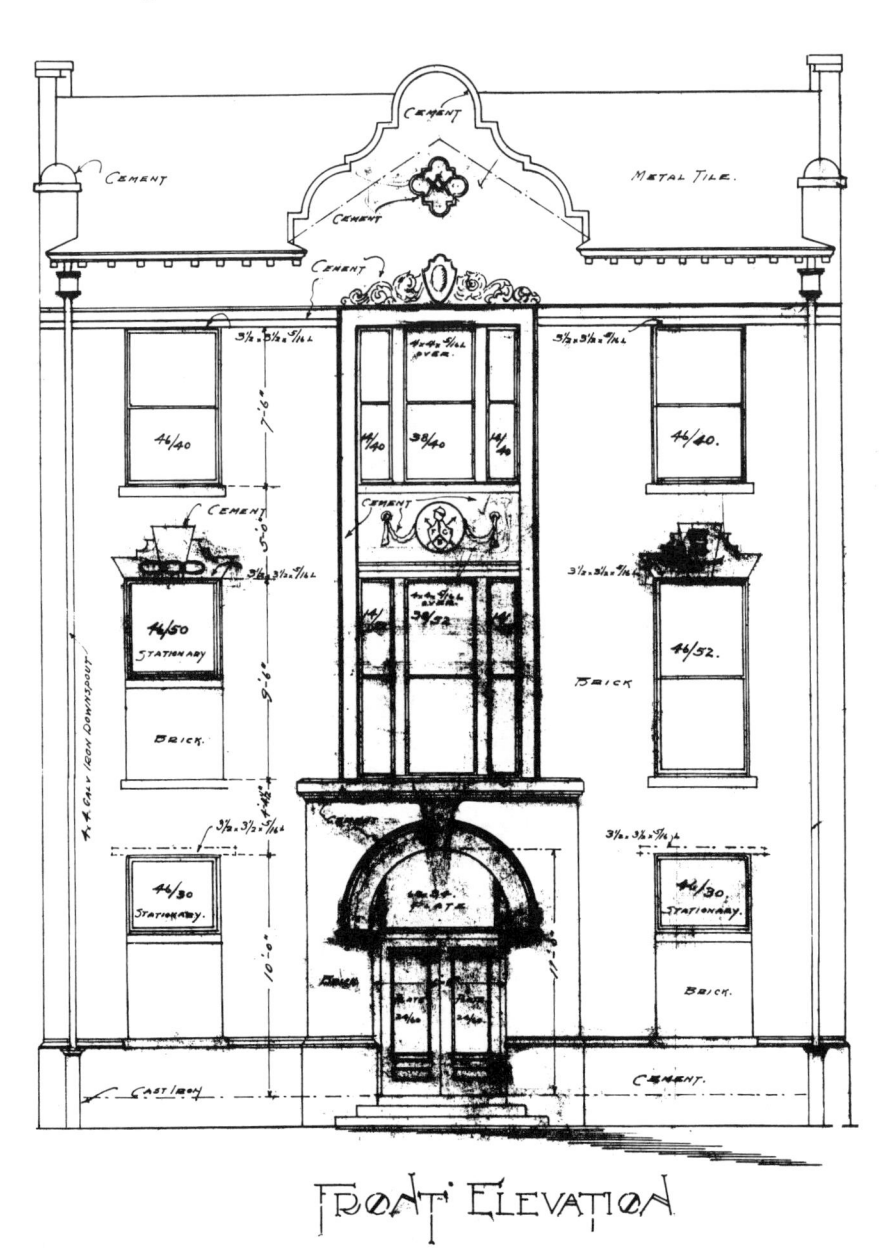

FIGURE 93
Architects' drawing of the front elevation of the Masonic Lodge, 1908, 220 Belleview Avenue, Brewton, Alabama. Hutchisson and Garvin, architects. The three-story Masonic Lodge at Brewton was an unusual combination of brick and cement. The walls were of brick. The hood mold over the two-leaf door, the stepped-lintels over the side windows, the cartouche above the third-story central window, and the parapet were all of the Mission style that did not reach the height of its popularity until the 1920s.

From Builders to Architects: The Hobart–Hutchisson Six

recently "renovated" by covering it with metal sheathing. Only the insignia of the Lodge indicates its purpose (figure 93b).

In the plan, the doors opened up into an entrance hall, at both ends of which the stairways led to upper levels (figure 93c). Check rooms were located at either end, under the landing of the stairways. Beyond the entrance hall, the space was divided into two rooms, a reception room on the left and a library on the right. These were connected by sliding doors. Each room also had a fireplace. Lavoratories and cloak rooms were located between the two rooms and the banquet hall. Occupying the full width of the building (32 by 37 feet), the banquet hall had four square concrete piers to support the floor of the second story, as seen in the drawing. Completing the plan at the rear were three rooms, a kitchen, pantry and store room.

The eighteen-inch-thick concrete walls were covered on the exterior by stucco. This is one of the earliest buildings in which Hutchisson used concrete as the building material instead of his traditional brick or wood frame. However the half-dozen books on concrete construction that he had added to his library attests to his growing interest in the material.

In elevation, the facade design incorporates a Spanish Mission influence, a style that did not fully develop in Mobile until the early 1920s. Though a Spanish-style home was built in 1909 in Monterey Place by McCreary and Slater, Hutchisson's inspiration must have come from his few years of internship with McAdoo in San Antonio. He used a more developed form of the style in his Masonic Home in Montgomery, Alabama, in 1911. Above the central bay of the three-bay facade, the parapet is embellished with a Spanish-Baroque, double-curve crown. Further emphasis to this bay is given by the wide two-leaf door with a transom above framed by a heavy, concrete, semicircular arch. The central window of the second and third stories are united by a common frame, but separated by a panel with the insignia of the order. The enlarged, stepped-architraves of the second-story side windows balance this emphasis on the central bay. The decorated second-story side windows may have been a symbolic gesture since this level housed the secret ceremonial

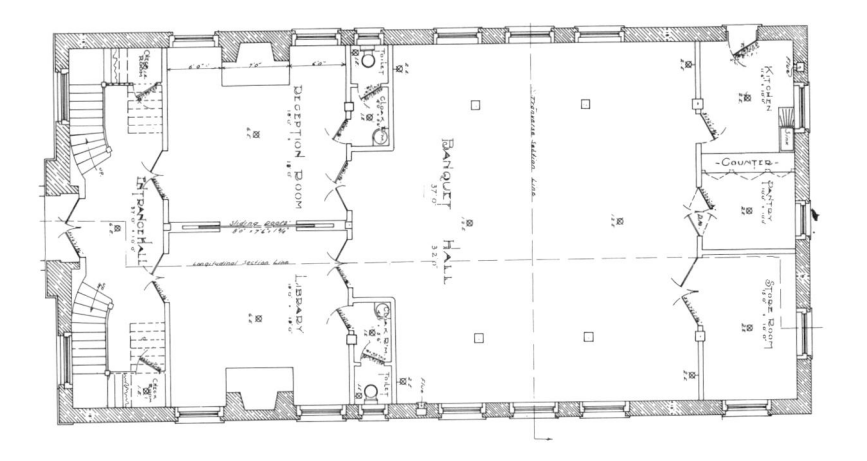

FIGURE 93B

A 1991 photograph of the Brewton Masonic Lodge, now encased in a sheathing of metal siding. The building has been "preserved" at a cost of completely destroying all its historically architectural importance.

FIGURE 93C

The architects' plan for the first floor of the Brewton Masonic Lodge. The interior space was divided. An entrance hall contained two stairways. The hall doors opened directly into the reception hall on the left and a library on the right. Beyond these was the large banquet hall, occupying the full width of the building. Kitchen and service rooms were located at the rear. The Lodge's private and ceremonial rooms were on the second and third stories.

FIGURE 94

The Knights of Columbus Building, 1908. Formerly on St. Joseph Street, between St. Michael and St. Louis Streets, Mobile. Hutchisson and Garvin, architects. The three-story building has nineteenth-century Italianate details such as the dentil molding and corner brackets beneath the cornice. It also has twentieth-century elements in the distinction made between the street-level wall surfacing and that of the two stories above.

rooms of the Lodge. The use of metal sheathing to cover this building was no doubt an economic move, but it destroyed the record of an early twentieth-century Alabama building.

In 1907 Hutchisson and Garvin were given an unusual commission (figure 94). In 1906 The Knights of Columbus had employed George D. Hulbert and Company to design a new building for their organization.[33] Their design was published in the *Mobile Register* of September 1, 1906, Section 3, page 6 and also published in the "Society Journal" (figure 94b). It was an elaborate design and makes an interesting comparison with the 1901 Masonic Lodge by the Stone Brothers of New Orleans, a building that still stands on St. Joseph Street opposite Bienville Square (figure 95). While the Stone Brothers retained some nineteenth-century decorative details, their building was definitely early twentieth century. The steel framing and division of the facade into two main sections are all early 1900s. So, too, is the upper three stories, united by the extension of the pilasters rising unbroken to the overhanging cornice. The general effect was of a flat elevation with windows only shallowly set in the wall.

Hulbert, while retaining the general division of the stories, created elaborate revivalist details that resulted in a nineteenth-century aesthetic. Why this plan was not carried out has yet to be explained. Perhaps the expense made it prohibitive. In 1907, the Knights of Columbus asked Hutchisson to take over the project. Judging from the resulting design (figure 94c), it would appear that the society asked the Hutchisson firm to keep the general division of the parts but to simplify the whole idea.[34] The result is the building as it was constructed in 1908 (figure 94). Now destroyed, it once stood on St. Joseph Street between St. Michael and St. Louis Streets.

The division of the facade into the street level and unified upper stories of the Hulbert drawing was retained, but all the heavy decorative detailing and the massive balcony were greatly reduced and simplified. There were no applied pilasters to mark the bays but a simple small oculus was placed between the bays at the upper level of the tall windows whose frames continued unbroken through the two upper stories. Some traditional Mobile characteristics were continued: the slightly overhanging cornice with its dentil molding and brackets and the parapet that rose to the height of the firewalls. The upper two levels were skillfully united by the three-part windows. Though the framing was continuous, the window levels were separated by a narrow panel on which the insignia of the order was located. While the Hutchisson design does not have the dynamic movements of the Stone Brothers Masonic Lodge, it did suc-

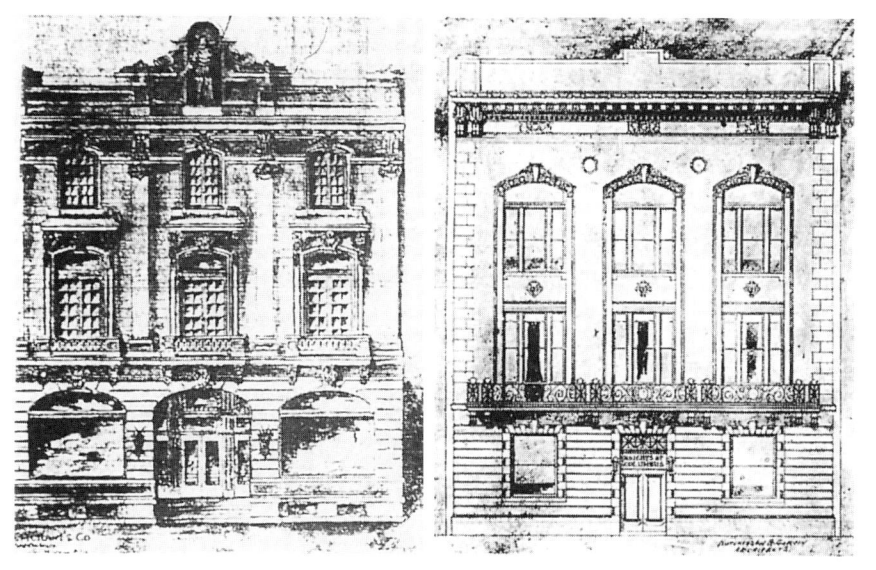

FIGURES 94B, C

The Knights of Columbus Building, left, as first designed by George D. Hulburt in 1906 (the *Mobile Register*, 1906, September 2, section 3, pg. 6). The elaborately detailed elevation, while originally approved, was never constructed. Right, the building as simplified in 1907 by Hutchisson and Garvin (the *Mobile Register*, 1907, September 2, section 4, page 8). The architects were asked to retain the basic divisions of the Hulburt design but to simplify it. The modified building by Hutchisson and Garvin was constructed in 1908.

ceed as a definitive, early twentieth-century building.

The plan of the first story consisted of an eight-foot-wide hall that extended for ninety feet from the vestibule to the back of the building. On either side were offices occupied by physicians. The description of the upper two stories can best be given by a quote from the *Mobile Register*, September 1, 1908, Section 3, page 4:

> The second floor is occupied by the club rooms of the council. Here are found large, airy and well lighted receptions rooms, billiard room with four tables, reading rooms, coat room, baths hot and cold, needle and shower, steward's department, and in fact everything necessary for an up-to-date club. —— On the third floor is the council chamber, a large and beautiful hall measuring 40 x 70 feet in the clear. In addition there are large ante rooms, toilets and other apartments tending to promote the social features of the order.
>
> The electric fixtures are unique and handsome, especially in the council chamber where fifty lights encircle an ornamental dome in which there is placed a large ventilator. There are also wall brackets in the hall to make interiors brilliant and on the lower floors there are numerous chandeliers and brackets illuminating the various rooms. The building taken as a whole is one of the most complete structures of its kind in the South and is the first hall constructed by the Knights of Columbus in the Southern states.

The contractors for the construction of the Knights of Columbus building were S. E. Dupree and Company.

In 1908 Hutchisson and Garvin were asked to design a small bank in Artesia, Mississippi. The bank still stands but has been so altered that a photo-

FIGURE 95

The Masonic Temple, 1901-1902, 8 St. Joseph Street, Mobile. The Stone Brothers of New Orleans, architects. In contrast to the Hulburt-Hutchisson design for the Masonic Lodge building (figure 94), the Stone Brothers building was closer to the national trends, though the architects still retained some revivalist details.

graph would no longer illustrate the Hutchisson design. The exterior has been "modernized" by metal-framing the doors and windows. The original space above the street level has been divided into two sections, the lower by a flat canopy above which is a band of ceramic tiles supported by iron posts. The wall surface above the tiles was plain stucco. Nothing original remains on the exterior except, possibly, the three, short, Doric-derived pilasters that separated the bays. The original interior has been altered by the addition of drop ceilings. By climbing a stairway the original ceiling with its decorative moldings can still be seen. It is the hope of the bank personnel that someday they can restore the building to its original design.

The last major building designed by the firm of Hutchisson and Garvin was the 1910 Mobile Infirmary.[35] The building, now destroyed, once stood on the north side of Springhill Avenue, just east of Ann Street in an area known as Skinner Place. The idea for the Mobile Infirmary was inaugurated in a meeting held in January 1896, initiated by the writer Augusta Evans Wilson. The meeting resulted in the formation of the Mobile Infirmary Association that was legally incorporated in April of the following year. The association's purpose was to obtain the land and sponsor the building's construction. The building was to contain paying and charity facilities and a training school for nurses. The first charity ward had beds for four patients that were donated by Augusta Evans Wilson in memory of her husband, L. M. Wilson.

By 1908 the association acquired land and was in position to proceed with plans for the actual building. Of the several architects who submitted plans, those of Hutchisson and Garvin were selected. Nothing is known of the other plans submitted. Interestingly, Hutchisson seems to have enlarged his library at this time with several books on hospital design including, *The Organization, Construction and Management of Hospitals* by Albert J. Storm, architect, published by the Cleveland Press, 1909.

The building, unusual for its time, was begun in late 1909 or early 1910. It was designed in three separate units, instead of the formerly popular single block buildings (figure 96). The central section was three stories high and the side units were only two stories. These side units were not centered on the

FIGURE 96
The Mobile Infirmary, 1909-10, formerly on the north side of Springhill Avenue, four east of Ann Street, Mobile. Hutchisson and Garvin, architects. The Infirmary was unusual for its time in plan and in consideration paid to the comfort of the patients. Adequate ventilation, some hours of sunshine and convenient plumbing facilities were available for every room. Charity patients were provided for and, in addition, the stated purpose of the Infirmary was to devote all income above the necessary expenses to the increase in charity work.

same main axis as the central one but diverged from it at about a forty-five degree angle, forming arms reaching out to partially embrace the space between. There was an additional building at the rear for the nurses. The architects called their design the "Pavilion Plan."

The photograph taken shortly before the building was replaced by a new infirmary does not show the original roof line. The original roof is illustrated in the architect's drawing of the building that appeared in the *Mobile Register* of 1910 (figure 96b). The original hip roof of the central unit was heightened by two small central dormers and a low square belvedere at the crown. The later change in the roof line further altered the curved end parapets that originally rose above the ends of the two-story wing porches. The original balcony at the third story of the central section also was removed by the time of the photograph. The surviving photograph has thus preserved the basic forms of the infirmary but eliminated the decorative refinements that were important in bringing the three units into close unity.

The buildings were constructed of light-colored pressed brick, with stone trim and a red tile roof. The main floor of the central section contained the offices, reception rooms, and quarters for the resident physician. A stairway and elevator led up to the upper floors. The third floor contained two operating rooms, the x-ray room, and the laboratories.

The side buildings contained wards and private rooms for the patients. Both stories of these wings contained four wards, thirty-two private rooms and a sun parlor at the end of each floor. Most of the private rooms had baths. The four charity wards each had four beds, two of the wards being free and two of the wards with a charge of one dollar per day. The income from all paying patients was used to help cover the hospital expenses. As quoted in the news release of 1910, "The purpose of the institution being first, last and all the time charity." Many of the furnishings of the rooms as well as that of the operating rooms were donated as memorials. The basement contained the kitchen, dining areas, storage rooms and an emergency room near the ambulance entrance.

The architect planned every room to receive some sunshine and every space to have adequate ventilation. The whole complex, including the cost of the site was completed for $80,000 with G. A. Chablin as contractor. It was during the construction of the infirmary that Joseph Garvin left the firm and was replaced by Alan Chester.

FIGURE 96B
The drawing of the Mobile Infirmary from the *Mobile Register*, 1910, September 1, section 7, page 9. Here reproduced from the publication by the First National Bank, *Highlights of One Hundred Years of Mobile History*, page 73. Marion Acker, illustrator. In the drawing, the original roof lines are shown. They were an important unifying element of the design. The small balcony below the central, third-floor window was essential in the relationship of the porch to the roof above. The destruction of these components completely altered the unity of the original design.

FIGURE 97

The Vincent-Walsh House, 1828, 1912, 1927-28. Hutchisson and Chester, architects. In 1912 Hutchisson was retained by J. T. McNamara to make extensive alterations in the 1827 home of Benjamin Vincent. The drawings of his work have been preserved and show the original plan and the changes that he carried out. Even with the changes made, the house retains the basic elements of the early-nineteenth-century Gulf Coast plantation home in which a wood-frame story was raised above a high, brick foundation.

FIGURE 97B

The architects' drawing of the ground level plan of the Vincent-Walsh house as altered in 1912. The original 1827 walls of the house are in light lines. The new enclosure of the rear gallery is indicated by the dark lines.

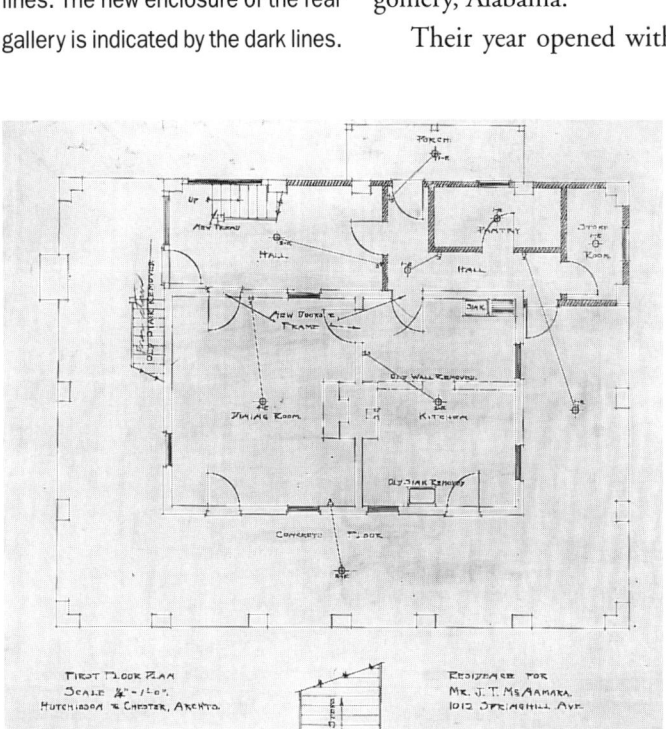

Hutchisson and Chester 1910-1912

In 1910 the firm of Hutchisson and Chester began a two-year partnership. Records indicate that for a short time both Alan Chester and W. L. Denham were in the firm for part of 1911 and early 1912. In 1910 Hutchisson and Chester designed the Hamilton house, now destroyed, in Ashland Place. The busiest year of their partnership was 1911 when they did several large homes, an extensive renovation, and the planning for the Masonic Home at Montgomery, Alabama.

Their year opened with the plans for the alteration of the old Vincent country house of 1828.[36] Originally the house was a raised cottage of three rooms surrounded by galleries. Hutchisson received the commission from J. T. McNamara to almost double its size (figure 97). The plans for this alteration have survived and show the changes made. The plan of the ground level clearly indicated the difference between the original walls and the alterations (figure 97b). The light lines traced the original walls, the dark lines were those of Hutchisson and Chester. With the changes, the lower level was divided in half, the western part served as a dining room and the eastern half turned into a kitchen. One of the original adzed beams can still be seen in the ceiling of the western room. The once open space under the rear gallery was enclosed to form a hall with a stairway to the upper level. To the east of this hall were a pantry and a storage room. The architects removed the 1828 stairway on the northwest corner that once led from the space below the gallery to the floor above. In its place they cut a door into the new hallway, with a stairway on the inside. To complete the plan, the architects added a porch to the rear of the newly infilled portion of the space beneath the rear gallery. The old galleries on both the east and west sides and on the front were left open. An impressive high stairway was built at the center front elevation giving access to the open gallery above (figure 97c).

More extensive were the alterations of the second story (figure 97d). The second-story gallery was enclosed on three sides, at the back, west and east. Only the south part of the gallery on the front was left open. These enclosed spaces were turned into bedrooms with the central rear bay as a hall with the ascending stairs and a bathroom. The original two rooms were adapted as a parlor on the west and the master bedroom on the east. A beautiful, wooden mantelpiece was designed for the parlor fireplace and another, slightly less elaborate one, was made for the master bedroom.

The house remained this way until 1927 when a later firm, Hutchisson, Holmes and Hutchisson, did further alterations for the owner, Alabama Walsh. During her ownership the first floor dining room was changed into a living room. The side galleries of the first story were further enclosed, making a kitchen off the exterior dining area that had formerly been a large kitchen. The front exterior stairway was removed and a new entrance formed on the west side by the driveway. An additional stairway to the second story was cut from the space of the gallery's first level to the floor of its second story. This is the way the house now stands (figure 97). The shape of the old kickoff, broken roof line and the open front galleries recall the original 1828 building, but time and the need for space and modern conveniences have altered the home to make a livable modern dwelling.

Of all the other homes designed by Hutchisson and Chester, the Arnold house on Government Street exemplifies the national and local trends of 1911 (figure 98). The home is a simple, rectangular central block. With the overhanging roof having exposed rafters, the building's height is two stories. A one-story porch extends across the front elevation. Triple, half-length Doric columns stand on brick plinths, dividing the porch into three bays. For the

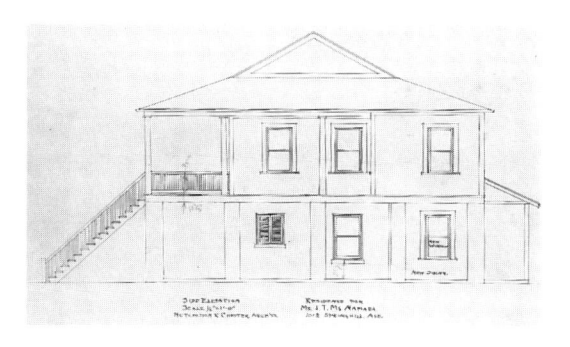

FIGURE 97C

Drawing of the east side elevation showing the 1912 construction of the front stairway leading up to the family living quarters on the second level.

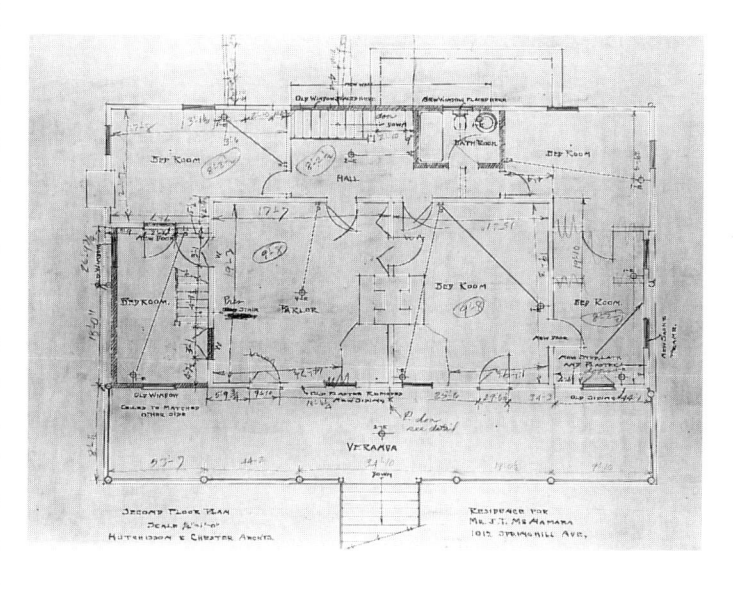

FIGURE 97D

Drawing of the second-floor plan for changes made in 1912 by the firm of Hutchisson and Chester. In the final enlargement, all the galleries at both levels except on the facade were enclosed. The front stairway was later removed and a stair to the second level constructed to open on the deck of the second-story gallery. This is visible in the 1991 photograph (figure 97).

FIGURE 98

The Arnold House, 1911, 1651 Government Street, Mobile. Hutchisson and Chester, architects. By 1911 the architects and builders had evolved a satisfactory way to incorporate classical detailing in the porch and house designs. In the early examples of the century, these historic details seemed awkward and applied, and not an integral part of the design (figure 77).

most part, the design has few local or vernacular characteristics that might distinguish it from another home in the eastern part of the United States. The large transoms over the first-story French doors and the main entrance could be considered southern. Unlike the eighteenth- and nineteenth-century Mobile homes, before the Victorian period, these early twentieth-century homes were more enclosed with less provision for cross-ventilation. Earlier homes were built to catch every breeze in the semitropical climate.

The major commission that came to the Hutchisson and Chester firm was the Masonic Home in Montgomery, Alabama. In 1911 the Masons acquired 276 acres on Vaughn Road for the purpose of establishing a home for their members.[37] As can be seen in the architect's drawing of the plan (figure 99), the complex consisted of three main buildings. The central building was three stories plus a basement and measured 92 feet wide by 36 feet, 4 3/4 inches deep. Attached at the rear was a two-story wing, 48 feet, 9 1/2 inches wide by 88 feet, 9 3/4 inches deep. In front was a one-story veranda, 50 feet, 4 3/4 inches long and 11 feet deep.

One hundred feet to either side of this main building were two-story residential buildings, each being 125 feet long by 32 feet, 9 3/4 inches wide. The residential buildings contained rooms of several different sizes. The rooms were arranged on either side of a long, centrally located corridor. The main entrance was on the side porch that opened up into a cross foyer containing the stairway to the upper level. There were additional porches at either end of the two buildings.

The main building contained the public rooms for the residents. To the

FIGURE 99

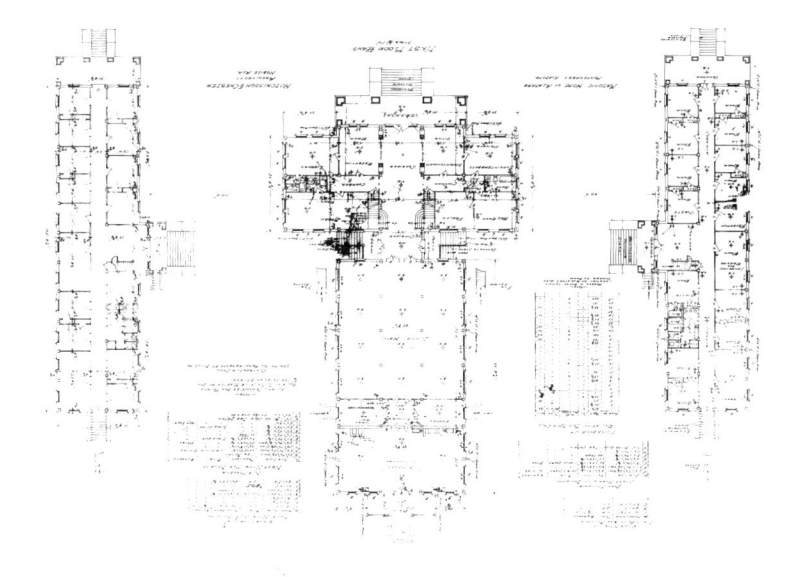

The plan of the Masonic Home, 1911, Montgomery, Alabama. Formerly on Vaughn Road. Hutchisson and Chester, architects. The Masonic Home complex consisted of three buildings. The large three-story central building contained the administrative quarters, reception room, library and common dining hall. Other lodge facilities were on the upper stories. To each side of the central building was a long two-story structure containing the private living quarters of the residents.

right of the central corridor were a reception room, library, toilet, and large rear room. To the left of the corridor were private quarters for the superintendent and his office. Curving stairways leading to the upper stories were located on either side of the rear wall, by the entrance to the dining room that was contained in the rear wing. Beyond the dining room were the kitchen and service rooms.

The walls of the building were made of tile, stuccoed on the exterior and plastered on the interior. Reinforced concrete slabs formed all the floors of the main rooms and were also covered with tile. By 1911 Hutchisson had added to his library more books on concrete construction and was increasingly more involved in using the material in his building.[38] The front elevation of the main building (figure 99b) is a combination of a traditional three-story structure with nontraditional decorative features. The central bays form a pavilion that projected slightly from the plane of the main wall. The long three-bay, one-story porch had square, stuccoed, hollow tile piers. The capitals were pierced by flat brackets that rose through the architrave to the multiple moldings that formed the cornice below the deck. The deck was surrounded by a low balustrade whose solid surface was pierced by a series of quatrefoil cutouts. The same balustrade design was used around the balcony beneath the twinned windows of the third story.

It was at the roof level that the most complex of the decorative features were concentrated. Running parallel with the main tiled roof was a lower secondary roof over the pavilion. A large rectangular panel projected in front of the pavilion roof cutting through the side slopes. The panel was framed by rectangular capped piers and

FIGURE 99B

The architects' drawing of the front elevation of the main building of the Montgomery Masonic Home. The rectangular shaped three-story building was centered by a projecting pavilion. This was crowned by an elaborately detailed parapet in the Spanish Mission style. A solid balustrade, with a pierced design, extended the length of the three-bay, second-story porch. A balcony with the same balustrade design was located below the central third-story window. All surfaces and details were of stucco.

FIGURE 99C
The architects' drawing of the front elevation of the dormitory wings. These wings faced the central building. Their design was a simplified version of the facade of the main building.

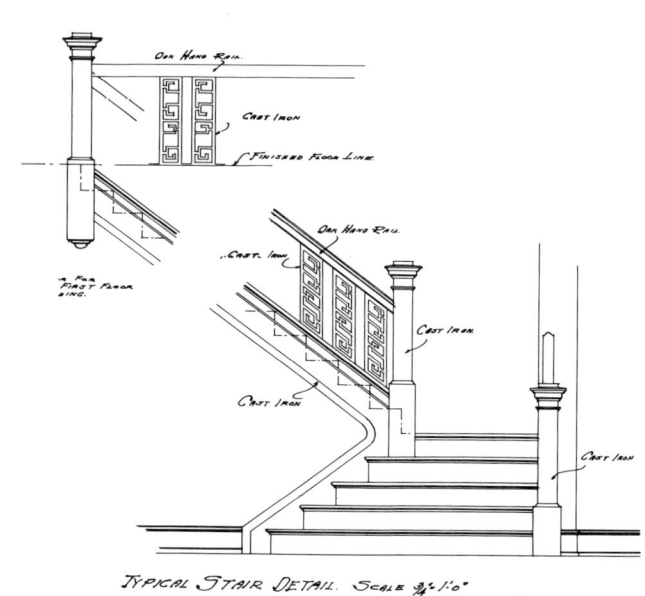

FIGURE 99D
One of the many drawings of the interior details. The stairway was made of cast iron with oak handrails. The panelled balusters were cast in a vertical fret design.

crowned by a double-curved, Mission-style crest. From this panel projected a narrow, tiled, shed roof that was supported by two Tuscan-Doric type columns. The effect was that of a small temple entrance. To add to the complexity of the roof line, small pagoda-like shapes extended above the outer edges of the pavilion roof. The Spanish Mission style elements were similar to those in his Brewton Masonic Lodge (figure 93). Unfortunately, no photograph yet has been found to better display how these diverse decorative elements might have looked in the actual building.

The facades of the residential buildings were much simpler in design, with the main parapets centered by the double-curved Mission designs. The porches formed decks with the same type of balustrade as those on the main building (figure 99c).

All the details were carefully drawn in the complete set of plans made for the building: each bracket was delineated, each molding was detailed, etc. An illustration of the staircase was selected from all the details (figure 99d). The newel posts formed vertical panels filled with an ascending series of Greek fret designs. The handrails were of polished oak making an interesting contrast with the iron in texture and color.

In 1912, Alan Chester left the firm and he was replaced by W. L. Denham who remained with Hutchisson for four years, the longest period of time for any of the young, aspiring architects to train with him.

Hutchisson and Denham 1912-1917

The partnership of Hutchisson and Denham was a most successful one. The firm attended to the architectural needs of a population growing rapidly due to the influx of World War I workers in the ship building industry and the port activities. The architects were involved with designing religious, commercial, civic, recreational and residential buildings.[39] (See Appendix 14)

Churches and a chapter house in Mobile and in other parts of the state came to their drawing boards. In 1913 St. John's Episcopal Church engaged the firm to design their new chapter house, to be located east of their 1858 Gothic Revival Church. In 1904 Watkins and Hutchisson had designed the

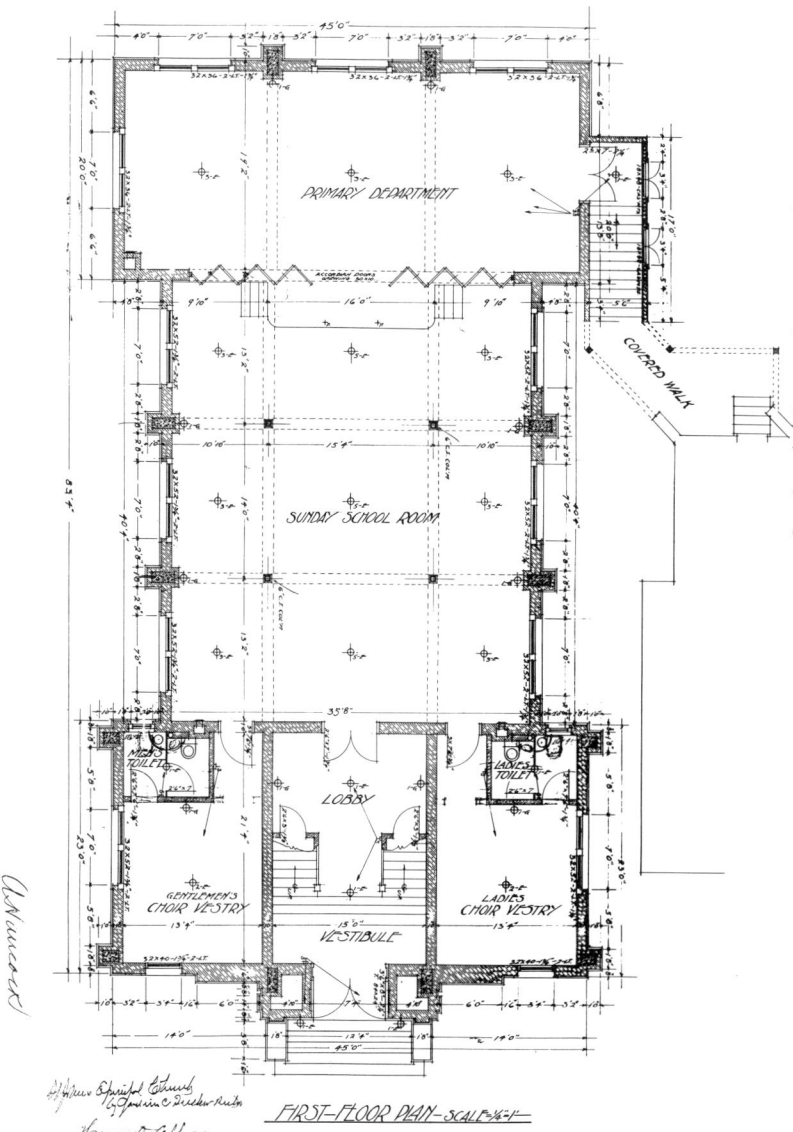

FIGURE 100

Plan of St. John's Episcopal Parish House, 1913. Formerly at 605 Monroe. Hutchisson and Denham, architects. The I-shaped plan is divided into three sections, each serving a particular function. The first section contained the lobby, the staircase and the two choir rooms. The large open middle section had provisions for classrooms formed by sliding curtains. At the rear was the primary department.

Church's Rectory (figure 76), which was located just south of the church on Dearborn Street. In 1913, at 605 Monroe, a lot east of the church, the new chapter house was built. The Sanborn Fire Insurance Map of 1957 shows it still at that location, but it was destroyed sometime after that. Though the building is now gone and no photographs have been found, the drawings have survived and are dated July 13, 1913. They illustrate Hutchisson's continued interest in decorative details based on the Spanish Mission style, as noted in his Masonic Lodge of 1908 (figure 93) and Masonic Home of 1911 (figure 99).

The plan of the chapter house (figure 100) depicts an "I" shaped building whose overall dimensions were 45 feet wide by 83 feet, 4 inches long. The front and rear sections projected on either side of the central section that was 35 feet, 8 inches wide. The main entrance opened up into a lobby that contained the stairway. On the left was the gentlemen's choir vestry, with lavatory,

FIGURE 100B

Detail of the stairway of the St. John's Episcopal Parish House. The stairway balustrade is composed of a continuing series of balusters forming a Latin cross, united above by a handrail and below by the stair treads.

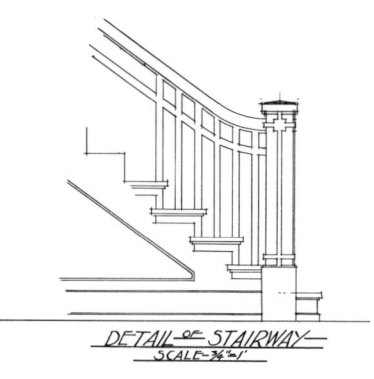

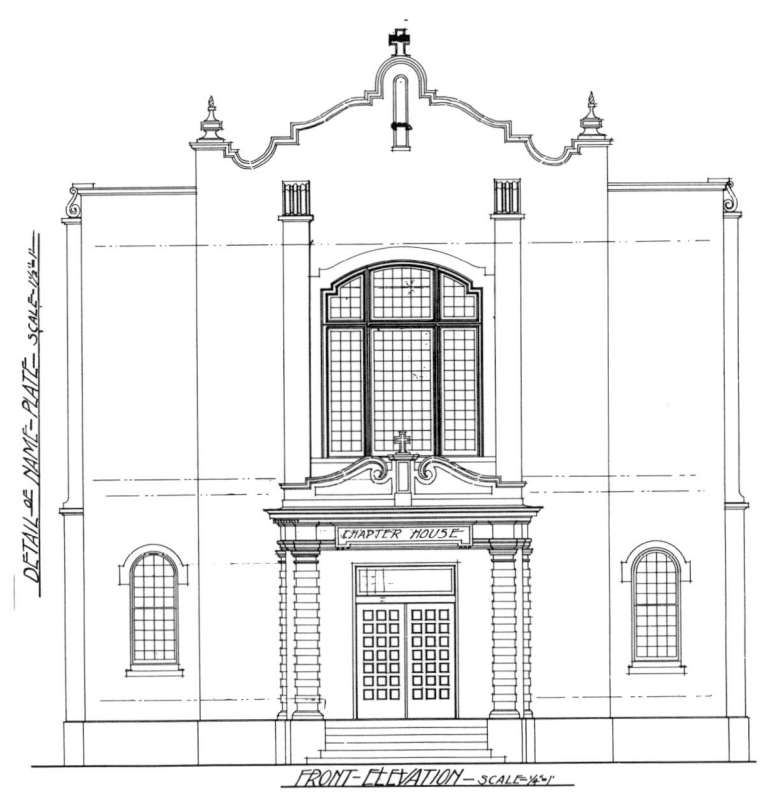

FIGURE 100C

The front elevation of the St. John's Episcopal Parish House. The Spanish Mission style influenced Hutchisson's designs from 1908 to the mid-1920s. In his public buildings, he concentrated the elements of the style in a central pavilion. Every line and shape are essential to the design and could not be eliminated without a loss to the overall composition.

and on the right was a similar room arrangement for the ladies' choir vestry.

The central division of the building was planned as a large Sunday school room. The four square piers supporting the ceiling were equipped with hardware for curtains that could separate the space into nine small rooms for individual classes.[40] The rear section was devoted to the primary department with the same provisions for curtaining off private classrooms. Leading out of the back was a door to the cloister of the church. Figure 100b is a drawing of the detail of the stairway off the lobby. The architect subtly used the Latin Cross as a basis for the design of the balusters and applied it to the newel post.

The central bay of the three-bay facade projected from the plane of the main wall and contained Spanish decorative detailing (figure 100c). The entry was framed by banded applied columns with stylized Doric capitals and a strongly marked fillet at the neck. Similar pilasters were engaged on the side walls of the entry. Above the porch a broken, double-scrolled pediment was centered by a cross standing on a rectangular pedestal.

On either side of the entrance, round-headed windows were covered with moldings. The large three-part, multiple light window at the second level was framed by pilasters whose capitals were formed by vertical channels that resembled the three-part division of a Doric triglyph. The parapet over the central bay was crowned by a double-curved, stepped design and centered by a cross. At each side of the parapet rose a small flamelike figure mounted on an urn. The side elevations of the building were divided into bays by applied shallow buttresses; at the top of each a scrolled bracket made the transition to the eaves.

The Baptist church standing in Bay Minette, Alabama, is very different. The building, no longer used as a church, is located on D'Olive Street on the City Hall Square (figure 101). It is built of red brick with white trim. The plain gable end of the porch is supported by two Doric columns forming the

FIGURE 101
Baptist Church, now used for non-religious purposes, 1914. Bay Minette, Alabama. Located on d'Olive Street opposite the City Hall Square. Hutchisson and Denham, architects. For the Baptist Church, Hutchisson returned to the Greek temple for inspiration. He created a distyle-in-antis portico. The extended side walls of the portico have partial columns closely tied in to the wall surface. The horizontal cornice of the pediment extends so that it forms a shallow roof over the steps.

three bays and an additional Doric column engaged at either end of the porch's projecting side walls. The horizontal cornice of the pediment projects out into a shallow roof over the steps. Though the church is no longer used for religious purposes and has passed through several hands since it was sold, it is still well preserved and is an excellent example of a classically designed building.

Three years after completing the chapter house for St. John's, the firm of Hutchisson and Denham was asked to design the Robinson Memorial Chapter House for Trinity Episcopal Church, at the time, located on St. Anthony Street. The little building was given in memory of Edward Walter Robinson and still stands at 257 State Street (figure 102). For some time the building was unoccupied, suffering some vandalism and a small fire in the rear. It was rescued and restored by the firm of Knodel and Thomas to serve as their archi-

FIGURE 102
The Robinson Memorial Parish House of the Trinity Episcopal Church, 1916, 257 State Street. Hutchisson and Denham, architects. When the Trinity Episcopal Church was moved out to Dauphin Street by C. L. Hutchisson, Jr., (see Chapter 6) the little Parish House experienced a series of mishaps, from vandalism to fire. The architectural firm of Knodel and Thomas restored the exterior. The original interior space was preserved by using one-half height walls to form the individual offices, thus leaving the upper half of the interior unaltered. The building is one of the two best Spanish Baroque designs found in Mobile.

FIGURE 102B

The rear of the former Trinity Episcopal Robinson Memorial Chapter House. A fire destroyed most of the last bay of the building; it was not rebuilt. When restoring the building, the architects sealed off the remaining bays and constructed the framing and truss of the bays that had been destroyed, paying tribute to what had been, and furnishing an interesting trellis over the rear of the property.

tectural office. The original plans, beautifully preserved and mounted, hang in their small reception room. Instead of rebuilding the rear bay that had suffered fire damage, the architects constructed the framing and trussing and left them exposed, finishing a wall between them and the interior (figure 102b). The interior ceiling and beams were left exposed, and half walls erected to cordon off space for the offices.

The little building was constructed of stucco over hollow tile (figure 102c), one story in height and consisting of an open space for the Sunday school with committee rooms partitioned off on either side. At the far end of the building was a stage with a kitchen to the left and a vestry room and lavatory on the right. A rear door led to the cloister that separated the chapter house from the church.

The three-bay facade, facing north, shows the influence of the Spanish Mission style in the porch details and the gracefully curved parapet (figure 102d). The twin fluted columns of the porch have an interesting fillet encircling them about one third of the way up the shaft. It is an important and subtle detail that keeps the columns from appearing too tall in relation to the rest of the building. Half-columns of the same order are attached to the side walls of the porch, and pilasters decorate the corner at the front wall. The entablature over the columns steps back over the entry. The parapet above the porch is framed on either side by short piers supporting two finials. The crown of the parapet rises in a series of "S" curves to meet at a cross on top. The roof is concealed by another curved parapet that extends the width of the facade. A Baroque influence is evident in the framing of the windows with their curved lintels and double-curved aprons. While the building is small, it is so skillfully designed that it takes on a monumental character (figures 102d).

The demands for housing kept builders as well as architects busy. The

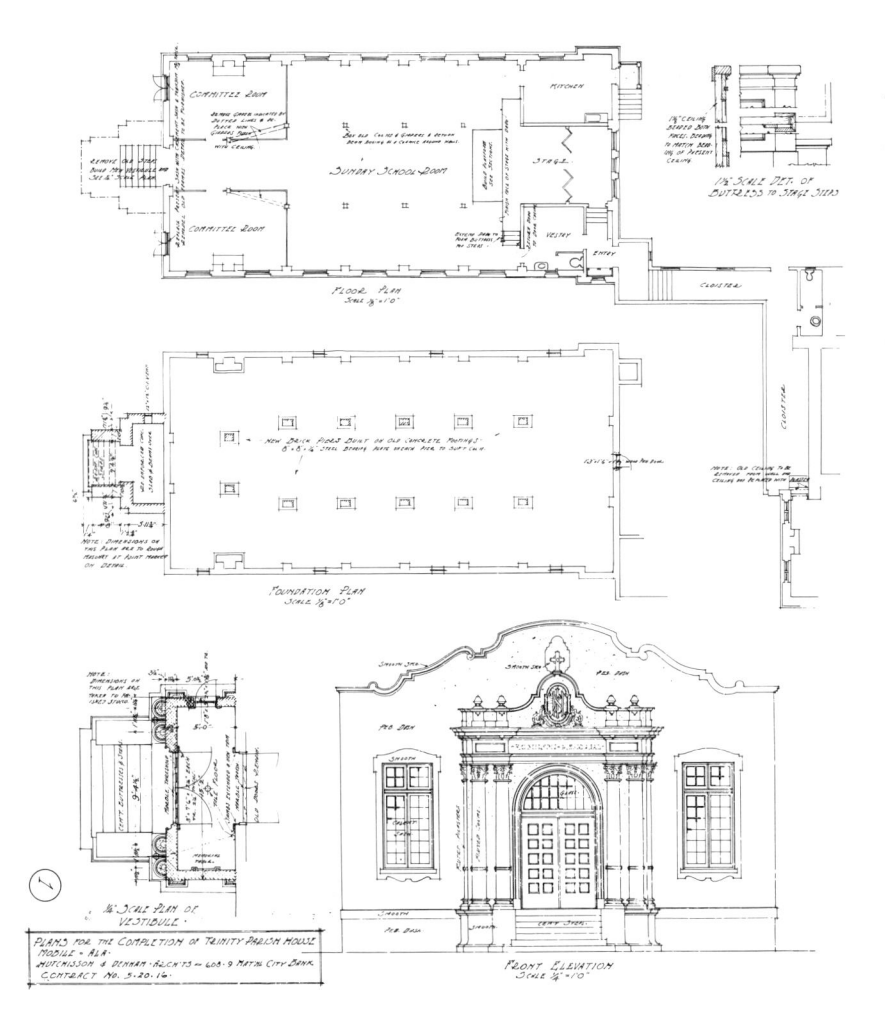

FIGURE 102C

The architects' drawings of the foundation and floor plan of the Robinson Memorial Parish House showing the division of the space into the committee rooms, a Sunday school room and a stage. A vestry and kitchen were located in the rear bay.

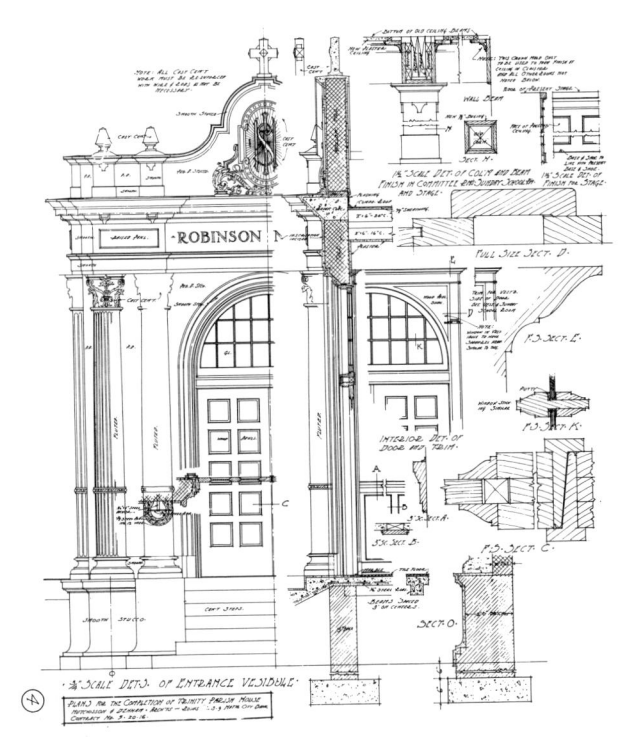

FIGURE 102D

The architect's drawing of the details of the front elevation for the Robinson Memorial Chapter House. The drawing includes details of the construction and the fully developed design. The Spanish Mission style and the exterior stucco were revivalist, but the construction was twentieth century with a reinforced concrete floor, hollow tile walls, and cast cement decoration in the pavement.

FIGURE 103

The photograph of the original Rapier cottage. Built in 1878 and enlarged in 1885. The cottage was transformed into an imposing mansion that stands at 1207 Government Street, Mobile.

homes designed by Hutchisson and Denham can be roughly categorized into three types: large, wood frame homes continuing the Neoclassical traditions; bungalows and other small one-story homes; and some masonry structures of which several were of stone, a rare building material for Mobile. Of the examples chosen to illustrate these three types, all except one home on Government Street are still standing and in good condition. Of the first group, the firm's earliest Neoclassical commission was for an extensive remodelling and altering of an old one-and-a-half-story Victorian cottage that once stood at what is now 1207 Government Street.

An old cottage built by the Goldthwaite family was burned and rebuilt as a one-and-a-half-story cottage by the same family. In 1885 the property was purchased by John Rapier, who added a wing on the east side. An old, faded photograph of the Rapier cottage still is in existence in that family. It shows the cottage to be of Victorian style, but whether these details were the result of the Goldthwaite or Rapier renovation is not known (figure 103). In 1912 Hutchisson was retained to turn the cottage into a two-story Classical Revival house for Thomas Boone (figure 103b). There is nothing left of the old cottage that can be seen except some foundations and the 1885 side wing. The firm of Hutchisson and Denham created an impressive, large, two-story house raised on a series of shallow terraces and located toward the middle of the lot.

FIGURE 103B

The Rapier-Boone House, 1912, 1207 Government Street. Hutchisson and Denham, architects. In 1912, Thomas Boone asked Hutchisson to transform the 1878, 1885 Victorian Rapier cottage into a two-story Greek Revival home. As can be seen in figure 103, only the east side wing of the cottage was retained and this was redesigned to harmonize with the impressive portico of the main house.

In plan (figure 103c) it is typical of its style, with a large central hall and double rooms on either side. The drawing of the plan shows the parlor and the living room on the left (east side) and the library and dining room on the west. A bedroom was located in the one-story wing on the east and a pantry and kitchen in the one-story wing to the rear. The room arrangement for the second story followed the same general division with two bedrooms joined by a common bathroom on either side of the central hall. A small sewing room was formed at the front end of the hall overlooking the balcony.

The full-height portico is supported by four Ionic columns with well-designed bases and with decorative detailing at the capitals between the volutes. At the central window of the second story, a wood balcony is supported by scrolled brackets. Just below the cornice of the hip roof, a molding of small brackets and dentils surrounds the house. The main central entrance draws on the Federal style, with an oval transom covering both the door and the sidelights. The transom and sidelights are filled with leaded glass. The original side wing of the Rapier era was retained and given Greek Revival detailing by two Doric columns.

The drawing of the front elevation (figure 103d) clarifies the design better than the photograph in which the dark shadows of the deep portico hide the details. While the inspiration for the design was derived from Greek Revival, Hutchisson took liberties with the style, creating a twentieth-century version. The popular return to the architecture of the pre-Civil War plantation homes came at a time when Mobilians were feeling a strong nostalgia for past glories and seeking some kind of historic security as they faced the changes of the next century. Between about 1908 and 1916 most of the Victorian homes along Government Street were destroyed and homes of Greek Revival inspiration replaced them.

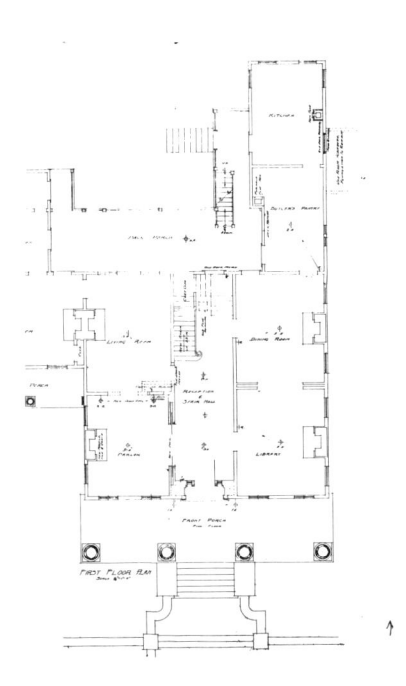

FIGURE 103C

The plan of the first floor of the Rapier-Boone House. The plan is typical of the Colonial Revival and Neoclassical Mobile homes in which symmetry was achieved by a central hall, with equal rooms on either side.

FIGURE 103D

The architects' drawing of the front elevation of the Rapier-Boone House. From about 1910 to 1915, there were several large mansions built on Government Street. In style they were a nostalgic recalling of the old plantation homes of the pre-Civil War days.

FIGURE 104

The Burke House, 1912. 1835 Dauphin Street. Hutchisson and Denham, architects. The architects successfully combined elements of several historic styles to make a harmonious design that could only have been built in the early twentieth century. The original open porch on the west has been enclosed with windows, detracting from the architects' design.

FIGURE 105

The Ernest Ladd House, 1913. Formerly on Government Street, three west of Monterey, Mobile. Hutchisson and Denham, architects. Drawing of the front elevation. Before World War I, classic detailing dominated in many of Hutchisson's designs for large homes. In the Ladd House the architect created a good twentieth-century elevation while still employing the classic device of the superimposed orders of the porch columns, Doric below, Ionic above.

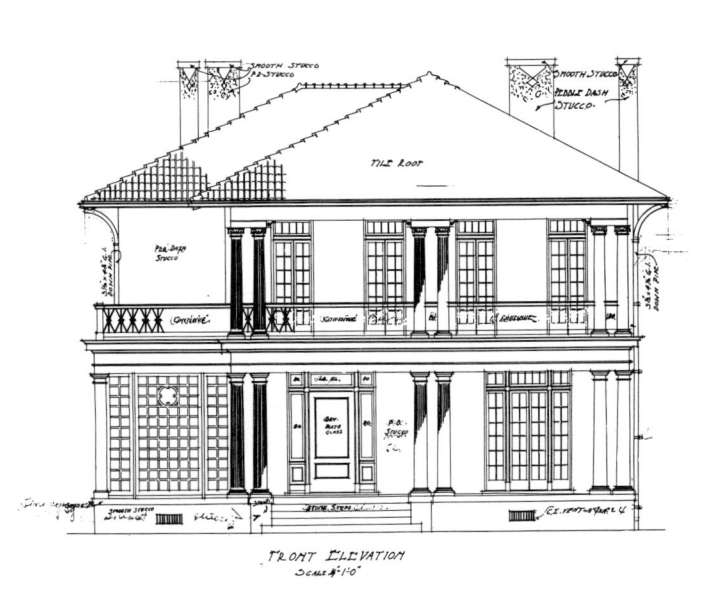

Another example is the 1912 Burke home standing at 1835 Dauphin Street. Hutchisson moved farther away from the original models (figure 104). The wood frame house is made even larger by the addition of a two-story bay on the east, a two-story bay on the west and a two-story wing on the rear. Little has been altered in the original design over the past years except for enclosing the west porch with glass. The effect of a home planned for gracious living was enhanced by the use of a soft, moss green color tile roof. When the house no longer served as a home, it was occupied by the Mobile Garden Club who maintained it in excellent condition. After the garden club moved the house was vacant for a time and recently suffered a serious fire in the upstairs. Fortunately the building was saved, although the tile roof was replaced with a modern one.

In 1913 Hutchisson designed a home for Ernest Ladd that was a definite break with the past in method of construction and in general style (figure 105). Unfortunately this house that once stood on Government Street is now gone, but the drawings have survived. Built in the Flo-Claire subdivision it was one of several homes that Hutchisson planned for different members of the Ladd Family. The design of the Ernest Ladd home was definitely of the twentieth century, though the historic two-story porch was retained. Transoms and classically derived columns also survived. But these details were not handled in traditional ways, nor would they have been so used in Mobile before the second decade of the twentieth century.

The walls were constructed of hollow tile with their holes infilled by iron bolts set in concrete that could have withstood any hurricane. The founda-

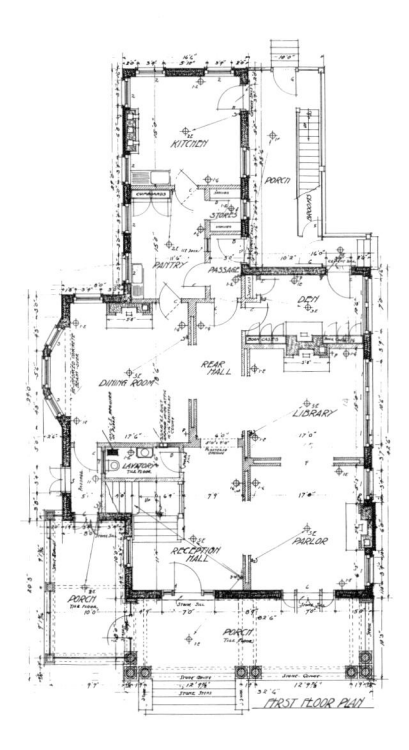

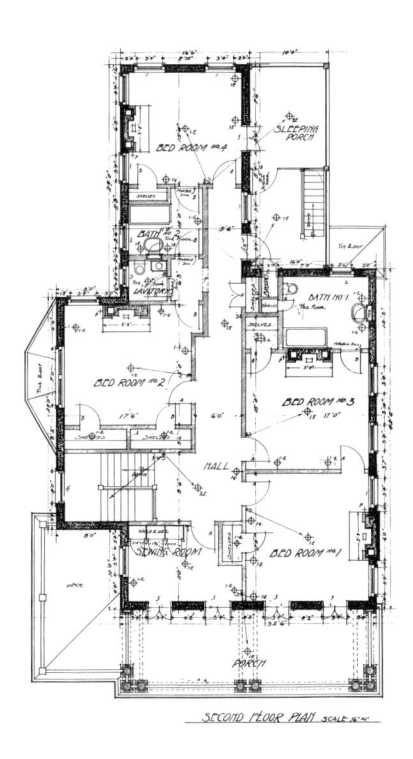

FIGURE 105B

Plan of the first floor of the Ladd House. Unlike the plans for the formal, porticoed homes, the Ladd House plan was asymmetrical with an unusual private and public entrance to the dining room. Guests could enter the dining room by way of a glassed in porch and short corridor, or if more informal, could enter through a doorway off an interior hallway.

FIGURE 105C

Second-floor plan of the Ladd House. Opening onto the second-story porch was a sewing room on the left and a bedroom on the right. Two large bedrooms with baths occupied the main section of the house. An additional bedroom and sleeping porch were in the rear wing. In the semitropical south, the screened sleeping porch was a popular feature before the days of air conditioning.

tion was of reinforced concrete with a brick footing below tile walls. A moisture barrier between the footings and the wall was inserted. This is the first time that this has been noted in the drawing, a valuable addition to an area where tropical rains often soak the earth. Reinforced concrete beams were used to span some of the wider, open spaces as in the bay of the dining room and across the expanse of the porch. The exterior of the walls was covered with a pebble dash stucco except around the windows where the stucco was left smooth. Interior walls and ceilings were plastered and floors were of wood. Exterior steps were formed of twelve-foot blocks of stone set in concrete, and stone was used for doors sills and porch coping. Built to withstand any natural catastrophe, it could only have been destroyed by men.

The main block of the house measured about thirty-two feet, six inches by forty-two feet, six inches with a rear wing projecting another twenty-nine feet. The long two-story porch was divided into two bays by Ionic columns on the second floor and Doric columns on the first, with three grouped at each end of the porch and two in the center. The capitals were of composition and ordered from the Seifert Company.[41] Steps led up to the left bay of the porch deck. The porch gable was covered with Spanish Mission-type tiling as was the main truncated hip roof.

A secondary porch, ten by twenty feet and five inches, was located on the front, east side with an entrance from the front porch and another on to a deck from the second story. The first story of the side porch was enclosed with glass and formed a corridor along the east wall and led directly to the dining room (figure 105b). The tiled roof of the truncated main hip extended out over the upper deck of the side porch. Details of the porch can be more clearly seen in figure 105d.

The plan of the first and second stories were similar in room arrangement (figures 105b,c). The hall of the first story was divided into a wider front section, narrowing to the rear. It was seven feet, nine inches wide in front and six feet in the rear. On the left, between the reception room and the corridor leading to the dining room were the stairway and the lavatory. The dining room was enlarged by a three-sided bay on the east. All rooms had fireplaces. In addition, there was a hot air system with a floor and ceiling register shown in the drawing of the lavatory, each ten by sixteen inches, as indicated in the plans. Heat ducts were set into the walls.

On the right of the central hall were the parlor, the library and the den. The rear wing, twenty-nine feet long by twenty-six feet wide housed the kitchen, pantry and storage rooms. A two-story porch was located on the right (west) side of the rear wing to which two separate sets of stairs gave access to the yard with a third stairway to the sleeping porch above the wing.

At the second level were four large bedrooms (figure 105c) each with a clothes closet. A walk-in closet was included in the master bedroom, a decidedly modern idea. One of the bathrooms was divided into two sections, one for the lavatory and one for bathing. The front (north) end of the upstairs hall was partitioned off for the sewing room. All the front rooms, both upstairs and downstairs, opened on to the front porch. By today's standards, this eighty-year-old house was well adapted for modern living. That it was demolished, leaving an empty lot, is unexplainable. It may have resembled Dr. Rutherford's home in Oakleigh Garden District, a house that was modeled after the Ladd dwelling.

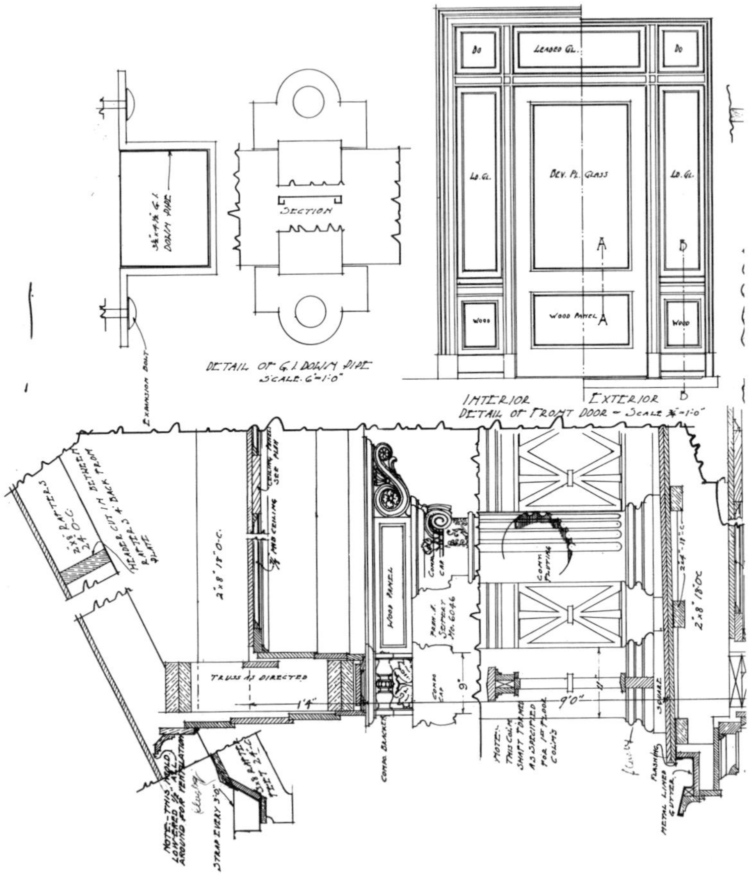

For those who did not want a large home, Hutchisson designed a variety of one-, and one-and-a-half-story houses that can be seen in various suburbs, especially Ashland Place and Flo-Claire. As early as 1909, he planned a bungalow for Henry Hamilton that once stood on the west side of Levert.[42] Nothing is known about the house that was destroyed

FIGURE 105D

Architects' drawing of the Ladd House porch details showing the designs of the brackets, columns, capitals and balustrade.

around 1940. It was an early date for a bungalow in Mobile, where this type did not reach its greatest development until the 1920s.

The bungalow was the ideal twentieth-century substitute for the nineteenth-century Gulf Coast cottage. As with the cottage, this easily constructed house could be built by a carpenter or designed with elegance and refinements by an architect. The simple bungalow could be built with mass-produced, precut materials, stock window and door parts and other easily assembled components. A real estate investor built block long rows of bungalows intended for either sale or rent (figure 106). But for those who could afford it, architects designed bungalows with refined, specially ordered moldings, hand cut, decorative, wood detailing inspired by the California architects, Greene and Greene.

The bungalow type began in California about 1905 and rapidly spread across the United States. Workbooks and pattern books proliferated, providing plans and elevation drawings. Such a publication was the *Craftsman* that was available from 1906-1916. In 1907 compiled examples were published in *Bungalows, Camps and Mountain Homes, 80 Designs by American Architects*.[43]

It is not hard to distinguish between a "jerry" built bungalow and one designed by an architect, even if the latter did not approach the complexity of a Greene and Greene design. Compare the examples in figures 106, 107, 108 and 109, the last three being the work of C. L. Hutchisson. His concern for pleasing proportions, relationship of the different elements, and care in the detailing required careful workmanship.

There are certain characteristics that are present in all bungalows, regardless of who built them. All have a simple, central square or rectangular block with one-bay porch that has a distinct type of pier at each end to support the roof. These wood piers are short and stocky, standing on a plinth or pedestal that rises a little higher than the solid balustrade that is left open only at the entrance steps. The piers are usually square and tapered. They may be made of a single large column or of smaller shafts grouped to form a square pattern (figures 106,107,108). The solid balustrade encloses the porch on both sides and on the front, opens up only at the stairway to provide privacy from the street traffic, and also allows space for a neighborly chat across to the next bungalow.[44]

The position and the size of the porch requires a different handling of the roof. The most typical bungalow porch extends only over half of the front elevation. Its overhanging gable roof, similar in pitch to that of the main gable, has one slope following the rake of the main roof and the other cutting down at a line parallel with the opposite roof rake (figures 106,109). All the roofs are fairly low-pitched with a wide overhang, having brackets at the apex and at one or more positions under the raking cornices. A less common type of porch

FIGURE 106

A typical Mobile bungalow, 60 Demouy, Mobile. Architect or builder unknown. The bungalow gradually replaced the Gulf Coast cottage as the preferred home of the working middle class. Typical of the style is the one-story elevation, a one bay porch supported by short, tapered, square piers standing on plinths, and a solid balustrade. One slope of the porch roof could be contiguous with the slope of the main gable or the main roof could extend out over the porch.

FIGURE 107

Sam Pounsey Bungalow, 1921. 213 Lanier Street, Ashland Place, Mobile. C. L. Hutchisson, architect. While many bungalows were constructed "en masse" for speculative purposes, those designed by architects had subtle refinements and excellent craftsmanship derived from the influence of the Craftsman Movement. Such details can be noted in the long brackets connecting the entablature blocks above the clustered piers making a subtle transition from vertical to horizontal.

extends the full width of the front elevation, in which case the roof is either a continuation of the front facing main gable or follows its contours closely (figure 107).

Hutchisson designed both types of bungalows and several are still standing in various parts of the city. One of his earliest was built by Hutchisson and Denham, but the greatest number were designed between 1919 and 1924 when Hutchisson was working alone. The early example (figure 108) was built in 1914 for G. Russell Hollinger at 60 Fearnway. The house is located on a rise of ground that once formed the banks of a bayou and now overlooks a drive that follows the contours of the old waterway. The house does not have all the characteristics of a true bungalow as that form developed some half a dozen years later. The porch is typical, but the main part of the house with its roof running parallel with the axis of the building could well have started out as a cottage. One of the variations that can be seen in all of Hutchisson's bungalows is the difference in the piers. In the Hollinger house he grouped three shafts in an L-shaped pattern, connecting them near the top with a wood crossbar. The short piers are raised on plinths that continued the height of the side enclosing the solid balustrade. In front where the balustrade meets the steps, the height of the enclosure is lowered and drops down in the side cheeks that frame the steps. Subtle details, like the corner brackets that visually connect the piers with the entablature of the porch, make a nice transition from the vertical to the horizontal. Brackets

FIGURE 108

The G. Russell Hollinger Bungalow, 1914. 60 Fearnway, Mobile. Hutchisson and Denham, architects. One of the earliest examples of the use of the bungalow-type porch. Here, it is attached to a rectangular building that more closely reflects a cottage tradition.

154   *From Builders to Architects: The Hobart–Hutchisson Six*

FIGURE 109

The Bodden Bungalow, 1919. 308 West Street, Mobile. C. L. Hutchisson, Sr., architect. In and around the Flo-Claire subdivision, houses were constructed on fairly small lots and located close to the sidewalks. To avoid the crowding of the usual bungalow front entry, Hutchisson moved the steps off to one side, thus allowing a continuous balustrade across the porch and providing greater privacy from the street.

beneath the extended roof are terminated in a star-shaped cap. The wood filled, gable end projects slightly, supported by smaller brackets that echo those of the roof. In the center of the triangle are framed, four, small casement windows set in a panel that, in turn, projects beyond the gable and is further supported by twinned brackets. This attention to detail is what gives added charm to a well-designed bungalow.

More typical of the style is the 1919 Bodden bungalow standing at 308 West Street in Flo-Claire (figure 109). Again, Hutchisson used the clustered pier but has also infilled the space above the crossbar with a pattern that repeats the shape of the window lights in the two gables. The architect chose to continue the solid balustrade across the front of the porch with the entrance steps rising from the side. In this way he secured greater privacy from the sidewalk and traffic of the street. Even the line of the single wood strip that connects the porch entablature with the rake of the porch roof is important in establishing a relationship between the piers and the slanting lines of the roof rake.

The last example, figure 107, was a bungalow built for Sam Pouncey and stands in Ashland Place at 213 Lanier. It was built in 1921, and is an excellent example of the wider porch type. Distinguishing the Pouncey home from the mass-produced bungalows are small details of moldings and refined craftsmanship, such as the way the transition is made from the vertical line of the piers to the horizontal of the porch opening. Instead of a single, wide beam spanning the distance, there is an additional narrow molding, making an abrupt angle with the piers, that resolves into a bracket, which increases to form the entablature extending over the capitals of the front two piers. This kind of attention to detail adds interest to the simple bungalow form.

The three-bay division of the facade is repeated in the three-part design of the large attic vent, which projects from the pediment and is supported by four small brackets. With the limited attic space caused by the low slope of the roof, adequate ventilation was achieved by the enlargement of the vents, a necessity in the hot climate. One of the unifying elements in the overall design is the use of the same siding to infill the pediment around the vents and to surface the balustrade, the walls, and the south rear wing.

In plan, the main, central entrance leads directly into the living-room. No space was wasted with a hallway in these small homes. The door is covered by a narrow five-light transom; the framing is plain except for a slight pedimentation of the lintel. On either side of the door, three narrow casement windows are framed with the pedimented lintel that matches the door.

All of the bungalows were planned so that there was no wasted space. Rooms were arranged so that one could pass from room to room without any outside passageway. They were compact, easy to maintain, and required no servants to assist in the maintenance.

The year 1915 seems to have been a turning point in the work of the Hutchisson and Denham partnership. While they were building their bungalows, they were also moving into a concentration on masonry construction either for small buildings as the 1916 Robinson Memorial (figure 102) or for large, fashionable homes. The change in material may have been caused by the World War I ship construction companies' orders for Liberty Ships. If the demand for ship construction used the best lumber available, wood would not have been readily accessible for private homes. Whatever the cause, the firms masonry structures of 1915-16 brought about a completely new style of design.

An example of the change can be seen in the homes of the Creagh sisters (1915) and Elmer Maddox (1916) (figures 110, 111). The strong horizontal lines and deeply shadowed porches emphatically suggest the gravitational weight of the material used. The wide overhang of the heavy tile roofs seem to tie the building securely to the ground. The accent on the horizontal reflects a derivation from the Prairie style. The difference between the wood frame and the

FIGURE 110

The Creagh House, 1915. 1202 Government Street, Mobile. Hutchisson and Denham, architects. The heaviness of the stucco over thick masonry walls is expressed in the design of the building. In sharp contrast to the light verticality of the Burke House (figure 104), the Creagh House has deep shadows created by the overhanging roof and the horizontal belt coursing that give a sense of weight.

FIGURE 110B

Architects' drawing of the front elevation of the Creagh House. The unusual brackets on the capitals and the triglyph motif above the columns and piers are more noticeable in the drawing. Multiple-moldings form the cornice of the roof deck. The relationship of the triple roofs can be appreciated only in the drawings since it is not visible from the ground.

156 *From Builders to Architects: The Hobart–Hutchisson Six*

FIGURE 110C

Detail of the porch and balustrade of the Creagh House. Much of the effectiveness of the design is a result of the contrast in textures of the smooth wood against rough stucco. The short, squat, vase-shaped wood balusters add to the feeling of heaviness noted in the whole elevation.

FIGURE 110D

Close up photograph of the porch of the Creagh House. The design is a study of contrasts, light against shadow, smooth against rough, circles against straight lines.

masonry construction can be seen in sharp contrast between the Burke home (figure 104) and the Creagh sisters home (figure 110). The latter is located at 1202 Government Street opposite a Neoclassical house also designed by Hutchisson. It was finished in 1915 during the partnership of Hutchisson and Denham. Where the Burke house has a light, spatial quality, with its open porches and pastel colored paint, the Creagh house is dark and deeply shadowed, walls of pebbly stucco and dark green trim add to the somberness. The home of the Creagh sisters is located far back on its lot with plantings along either side of the approaching sidewalk. The building is almost a cube in mass, with a wide, deeply set front porch and a correspondingly wide rear wing. The level between the first and second story is marked by a concrete belt course with a narrower one above it running along under the second story windows (figures 110, 110b).

The two-story porch covers the central three bays of the house. The first-story deck extends out to the sides to form a terrace. Between the heavy masonry corner piers that support the porch roof are two short Tuscan columns that stand on square pedestals, forming the short piers that divide the balustrade (figure 110c). Inset in the face of the piers is a panel surfaced with the heavy pebble stucco of the walls. The resulting contrast in texture among the panels, and the smooth wood frame railing, and the squat, vase-shaped balusters provides much of the decorative effect of the elevation. An unusual feature in the design can be seen in the very narrow architrave formed by a series of linear divisions. In front of the capitals of each of the Tuscan-derived columns is a small T-shaped block, forming a transition between the vertical column and the horizontal architrave. The wider frieze above the architrave has stylized triglyphs above each end pier. These details are difficult to see because of the shadows cast by the projection of the deck of the porch's second story. As though to emphasize the weight of this masonry-stuccoed home, the upper balusters are heavy cast iron in an open rectangular panel supported by iron bars. The widely overhanging, red-tiled hip roof of the porch and of the main house seem to bare down, anchoring the home to the ground.

Figure 110d more clearly shows the contrast in the texture between the stucco and the wooden elements used in the design. This use of building materials for decorative effect is a characteristic of the family's work noted before in the brick construction of James H. Hutchisson as well as James Flandin II.

The Creagh sisters home is one of five historic houses that stand side by side on the north side of Government Street. Together they form a sequence of stylistic changes from the late nineteenth-century Victorian to the developments of the second decade of the twentieth. Note the contrast between the simplicity of a Neoclassical doorway and the complexity of the entrance to the Creagh home as shown in the Hutchisson drawing (figure 110e). Such details can be appreciated by an on site examination at the house but are lost in a photograph.

The drawing of the Creagh home plan is somewhat blurred by age and mold (figure 110f) but is still clear enough to recognize the room arrange-

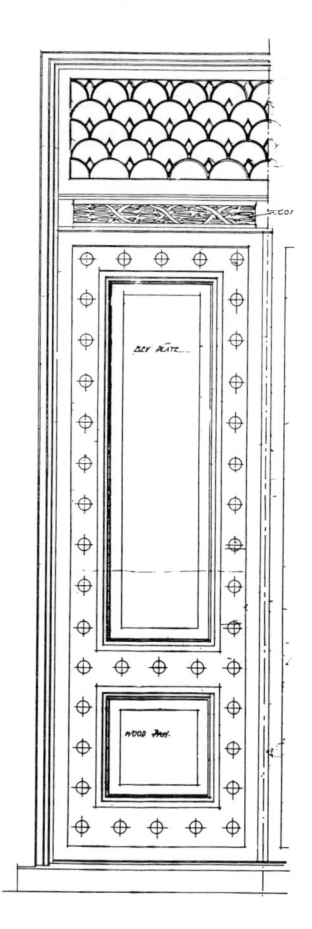

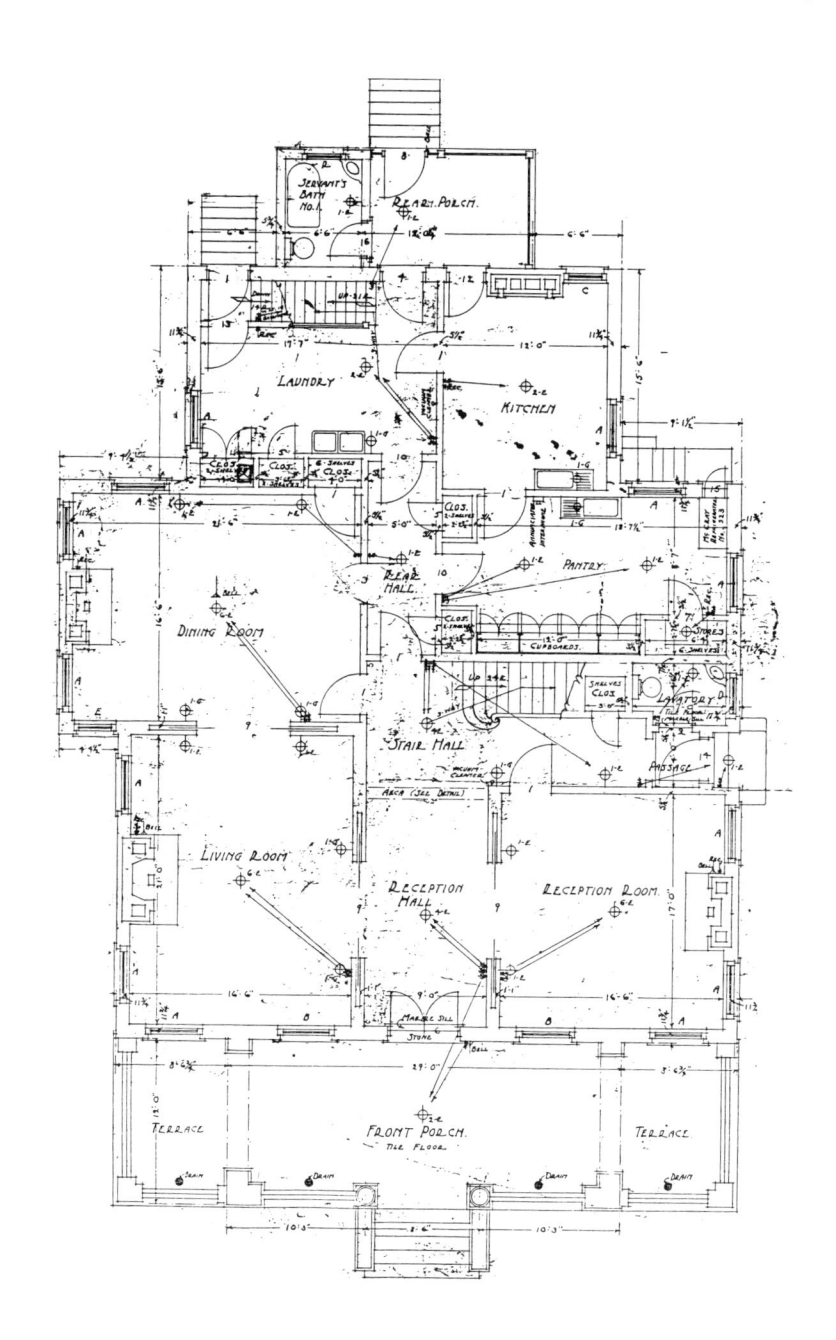

FIGURE 110E

Drawing of one front-door panel. The bevelled plate glass and the wood panel below are framed by a series of small circles cut with cross-axes. They recall the use of rosettes in the Greek Revival. The transom is filled with art glass in a fish scale pattern.

FIGURE 110F

First-floor plan of the Creagh House. A central hall is divided into three parts. The front reception hall is connected to the central stair hall by an archway. The rear hall opens onto the dining room on one side and a large pantry on the other, then continues back through the wing. Large fireplaces are located against the outer walls of the reception room, the living room and the dining room.

From Builders to Architects: The Hobart–Hutchisson Six

ments. From the twelve-foot-wide porch with its side terraces, the entrance opens into a reception hall. On the right is the reception room, seventeen by sixteen feet and six inches. On the left is the larger living room, sixteen feet and six inches by twenty-one feet, both rooms entered from the hall through wide, sliding doors. To the back of the reception hall is an archway that opens into a cross-hall containing the monumental stairway. In the space beneath the stairway, there is enclosed a lavatory and clothes closet, and beyond the stairs is the pantry. At the rear of the living room is the dining room, twenty-one feet, six inches by sixteen feet, six inches, with sliding doors leading to it from the living room. From this room a door opens on a rear hallway. A rear wing, twenty-nine feet, seven inches by fifteen feet, six inches, contains the kitchen, laundry and servants' lavatory, and the rear porch completes the plan.

Much less elaborate is the Elmer Maddox home built of cut stone with main walls rusticated and the trim dressed. The house stands at 816 South Broad (figure 111). Stone houses are rare in Mobile; the material must be brought in from other areas of the country. Most stone was reserved for details on brick buildings, such as lintels and sills of windows and doors, and for coping on fire walls. The Maddox house is made of large blocks of rusticated stone and combined in a design that reflects the heaviness of the material used. The pronounced horizontal line of the stone coursing, the wide belt course that marks the level of the second story, the small belt course that

FIGURE 111

The Elmer Maddox Stone House, 1916. 816 Broad Street, Mobile. Hutchisson and Denham, architects. Mobile is a city of wood and brick houses. Stone of building quality had to be imported and was used sparingly for trim, window sills and lintels. Not more than a half-dozen stone houses were ever constructed, and of the three still standing, Hutchisson built two.

ELIZABETH BARRETT GOULD

connects the windows of the second story and the wide overhang of the low-pitched roof, all contribute to the sense of massiveness and weight. A very shallow dormer extends across the central section of the roof, barely visible above the eaves when seen at ground level. The slight projection of the central bay of the house is repeated in the one-story porch that extends nearly the full width of the facade. The rusticated piers that support the porch rise up through a balustrade that surrounds the deck at the second story. Even this balustrade is designed to reflect the heaviness of the stone. The balusters connecting the extended piers are cut to frame square openings. The one release from this massiveness and rectangularity is the presence of a round, stone Tuscan column standing on either side of the central opening to the porch. Marble steps lead up to the porch entrance bay; the marble forms a textural contrast with the walls.

Maddox was the owner of a marble and stone company, so he could furnish the material for his home. The building has been vacant for some years, but it is so solidly built that there is little vandalism to the main structure. It stands on a large corner lot with two rusticated stone piers marking the rear line of the property.

Public buildings as well as private residences claimed the attention of the Hutchisson and Denham firm, but, unfortunately, only a few have survived. Among those now gone were two designed for the Gulf Coast Fair that opened from October 30, 1914 to November 5, 1916.[45]

The Fine Arts Building (figure 112) incorporates characteristics of the Italian Renaissance phase of the classical revivals that spread across the United States

FIGURE 112

The Fine Arts Building constructed for the Gulf Coast Fair, 1915. None of the fair buildings have survived. Hutchisson and Denham, architects. For his Fine Arts Building, Hutchisson used the architecture of fifteenth-century Italy as his inspiration.

FIGURE 113

A general view of the County Poor Farm complex taken from the *Mobile Register,* August 20, 1978. All buildings are destroyed. In 1915 Hutchisson designed the keeper's lodge, the hospital and a dormitory. Hutchisson and Garvin, architects.

following the 1893 Chicago World's Fair. The style continued into the first years of the twentieth century. The central section of the Fine Arts Building is fronted by a semicircular arcade that recalls the fifteenth-century Florentine Hospital of the Innocents by Brunelleschi. From the front elevation, the end pavilions resemble corner towers. This tower effect is enhanced by the upper level open deck that is balustraded and shaded by a widely overhanging low-hipped roof. From the corners of the tower-like bays and along the roof edge of the main section stretch a row of flag poles. Characteristic of the style was the contrast in size of the tall windows on the first story with smaller ones on the second. The large end window was elaborated with a decorative surround.

Hutchisson kept in close touch with these national trends as noted in the architectural magazines and books in his library. He undoubtedly was familiar with the influence of the Chicago World's Fair buildings. In addition to the Fine Arts Building, Mr. Hutchisson designed the Merchants and the Auto Display Buildings for the Mobile Fair.

Another example of a civic structure was the Poor House and Farm designed in 1915, but now destroyed. Located on Stanton Road, it covered considerable ground with a variety of buildings (figure 113).[46] Whether the Hutchisson firm planned the whole complex is not known and all that remains is a photograph of a portion of it reproduced in the *Mobile Register* in 1978. Based on the information in the Hutchisson files and the memory of C. L. Hutchisson's son, the firm was responsible for the keeper's lodging, a dormitory, a hospital and the entrance gates.

Fortunately, some of the schools of this period have survived, such as the Tanner Williams School of 1915 in Mobile County (figure 114). It makes an interesting contrast with the 1904 Leinkauf School (figure 79b). During the expansion of the suburbs, new school districts were laid out with ample lot sizes. This is reflected in the architectural change from a multiple story, tightly contained building of the inner city to a more open, one-story structure composed of a main section and several wings (figure 114). The plan provided for more window space and hence better lighting. It made quieter passage of in-

FIGURE 114

Tanner Williams School, 1915, Mobile County. Hutchisson and Denham, architects. One of the many county schools designed by C. L. Hutchisson, Sr. In contrast with the self-contained, multi-story, blocky structure of a limited city site, Tanner Williams illustrates the trend toward the single story, elongated plan with wings centered by the administration offices.

coming and outgoing pupils possible. Most importantly, it created a quicker exit in case of fire. Aesthetically, the open plan seemed to express the gradual relaxation from earlier schools' austerity.

The Tanner Williams School was an early example of the change, and while it was designed on the one-story idea, there were details that reflected the Italianate Revival trends. These details include the bracketed gable end over the entrance, the semicircular recessed entrance with its strongly accented keystone, corner blocks forming a white contrast to the color of the bricks, and a fan light over the door (figure 114b). Characteristic of the Hutchisson tradition is the use of white details contrasting with the darker brick and the varying ways bricks were laid.

His use of variegated, colored brick enlivens an otherwise plain wall surface. To add interest to the central entrance bays, small, square, white masonry blocks are set at the midpoint and at the upper corners of the window framing. This accent is repeated at the ends of the main axes of the central oculus window (figure 114b). Except for the change in the window types, the building stands much as it did when originally designed.

The most interesting project during this time was one in which Hutchisson

FIGURE 114B

The central section of the Tanner Williams School. The contrasting color and texture between the bricks and the masonry insets at windows, impost blocks, and oculus liven the otherwise strictly functional design.

From Builders to Architects: The Hobart–Hutchisson Six

FIGURE 115

The Meridian City Hall, 1914-15. Meridian, Mississippi. Designed by P. J. Krouse, architect. C. L. Hutchisson, Sr., consulting architect. The Meridian City Hall is an impressive Neoclassical building occupying a full block. Above a high podium, Ionic columns divide the windowed bays. The entablature extending over the recessed entry is supported by two full-height Ionic columns. Above the wide cornice, a solid balustrade has panels with geometrical designs in low relief. The major change in the exterior of the building has been the installation of modern windows replacing the originals.

was a consulting architect for the Meridian City Hall in Meridian, Mississippi, designed by P. J. Krouse (figure 115). The architect was the same Krouse with whom Hutchisson, at the start of his career, had been a partner in 1902. Information on the part Hutchisson played in the city hall construction is based on information contained in the minutes of the Meridian City Council, researched by Fonda K. Rush, the historic preservation consultant for the city of Meridian.[47] In addition C. L. Hutchisson, Jr., has a vivid memory of the plans being studied in his father's office, and of the many visits his father made to Meridian. But neither of these sources gives any information as to whether Mr. Hutchisson had anything to do with the Krouse original design. He was responsible for some changes made on the interior and on the wall construction. His contribution is further noted on the bronze plaque on the interior wall at the head of the entrance stairway. On this, his name is embossed as consulting architect.

From the council minutes, it is known that there were three architects vying for the commission. On March 18, 1914, R. H. Hunt and C. L. Hutchisson appeared before the city council and presented their claims for the position of architects on the new city hall. On March 19, 1914, P. J. Krouse appeared before the council and presented his claims, and "on April 15, the Council selected P. J. Krouse as architect but in June the Council decided that the law required them to have a consulting architect to consult the Council and architect Krouse in the preparations of the plans for the new city hall." Just when Hutchisson was appointed is in question. It was August before Krouse

FIGURE 115B

The architect's drawing of the rear elevation of the Meridian City Hall. The original window configuration can be seen here.

presented his specifications and September before the bid of the contractors, Hancock and McArthur, was accepted. The last payment to Hutchisson for services rendered was on October 6, 1914. Since the building was not finished until the next year, it can be assumed that Hutchisson was not involved in the actual construction of the building, but was working with Krouse during the planning stages.

Meridian had two other city halls prior to the 1914 construction, an early one in 1860, followed by one built in 1885 and designed by Gustav Togerson, a native of Sweden who had been working in Mississippi since 1880 as a carpenter and architect. The general style of the 1914 building followed the national trends of combining Italian Renaissance tradition with some influence of early Beaux Art. The recessed, entry porch has fluted Ionic columns rising through the height of the two stories. The bays of all the elevations are articulated by applied Ionic columns. The dentilled cornice projects beyond the surface of the wall but not far enough to require brackets in the true Italianate manner. The solid parapet has an interesting series of panels in which are embossed geometric patterns of lines following the axes and diagonals of the square. As can be seen from the drawing of the rear elevation (figure 115b), the division of the bays by applied classical columns is continued. The major change in the building is the replacement of the original double hung windows by large panes of multiple lights. Undoubtedly, this was helpful in furnishing more interior light, but it also altered the original rhythm of the fenestration.

C. L. Hutchisson, Sr., 1917-1927

The years following the Hutchisson and Denham partnership were the most productive of Hutchisson's career, reaching a high point in 1921. It was a time when all categories of buildings were in demand, especially residences, from Mobile's first apartment houses to single-family dwellings, both large and small. Mobile industries found it necessary to construct company housing for their employees of which Mr. Hutchisson planned two buildings. Churches were expanding with annexes and educational buildings to meet the needs of growing congregations. Adding to new commercial interests, the automobile industry played an important part by requiring various types of buildings, sales and display buildings and gas and service stations. Of the eleven motor display buildings planned by Hutchisson, four still stand, though altered for other uses.

The Dodge and Graham Brothers building is a large, deteriorated one-story building at 400 St. Louis Street. The structure is brick, with brick pilasters framing the large display windows. Still visible are the initials, DB and GB, forming an octagonal cartouche above the entry. Another building was done in 1937 for a Mrs. Festorazzi at 500 St. Louis Street. It was designed by Hutchisson and Hutchisson during the last years in which Hutchisson, Sr., was active. The building still has the Art Deco style parapet on the main south-facing elevation and stepped parapets at the ends, but the general effect of the design has been altered by filling in the large showcase windows with bricks.

Least altered of the four is the building located at 200 Government at the corner of Government and Conception streets. Originally it was built for a Mrs. Kirkbride and occupied by the Gale Motor Company, which handled the Maxwell automobile agency. It is now known as the Herndon Building. There is nothing spectacular about the building, but it is a good commercial structure with understated aesthetic elements in the brick wall of the four-story building (figure 116). The first story has large, plate glass, display windows. Above this, the three stories have identical wide windows, set in panels slightly recessed from the plane of the wall. The white cement of the sills makes a strong accent with the color of the bricks, as does the concrete molding separating the windows from the parapet above. Between the stories, the wall surface is given interest by a slightly recessed panel in which

FIGURE 116

The old Kirkbride Garage, now known as the Herndon Building, 1921, northwest corner of Government and Conception streets, Mobile. C. L. Hutchisson, Sr., architect. The Kirkbride Garage was one of eleven that the architect designed. With the growing popularity of the automobile, the dealerships were prospering. The buildings were all large, of brick construction, with display windows along the sidewalks.

ELIZABETH BARRETT GOULD

FIGURE 117

The architect's drawing of the AT&N Railroad Station, 1921, York, Alabama. C. L. Hutchisson, Sr., architect. During the hey-day of the railroads, small stations dotted the countryside. Few have survived. The York AT&N was an example of the typical southern station with racially divided waiting rooms and ticket windows.

two, small, diamond-shaped blocks are located toward the edges of the panels. The severely angular building is softened by the gentle curve of the parapet, the surface of which has a series of five panels per bay. Though the building was designed for a utilitarian purpose, the architect did incorporate some unobtrusive decorative effects. The building has been restored for offices.

In the year 1921, Hutchisson was also active in other parts of the state. In York, Alabama, he designed three buildings, a bank, a Baptist church and the Alabama Tennessee and Northern (AT&N) Railroad Station.[48] The station is gone now and the AT&N Line, first bought by the Frisco Line, is now owned by the Burlington Northern System. Though destroyed, the station plans have survived. Some information was given for this publication by Jud Arrington, a former train dispatcher for the original line. The building was small as were many of the local stations of that day (figure 117).

In plan, the first story (figure 117b) was divided into three main parts. The first section had two waiting rooms, one marked for whites, the other for "colored," a comment on the social customs of the 1920s. In the center was a large ticket office connected with the waiting rooms by windows for separate races. Beyond the ticket office was the baggage room, the large door of which can be seen in the front elevation (figure 117). The plan of the second story was divided into various offices, including one for the train dispatcher. In addition there were lavatories and file storerooms.

York was a railroad town. The York Coleman Cultural Center is organizing a history of its railroads to be housed in an old caboose. Since so many of the small stations that once dotted the country are now gone, it is important to preserve as much of this history as possible. Later in his career, Hutchisson

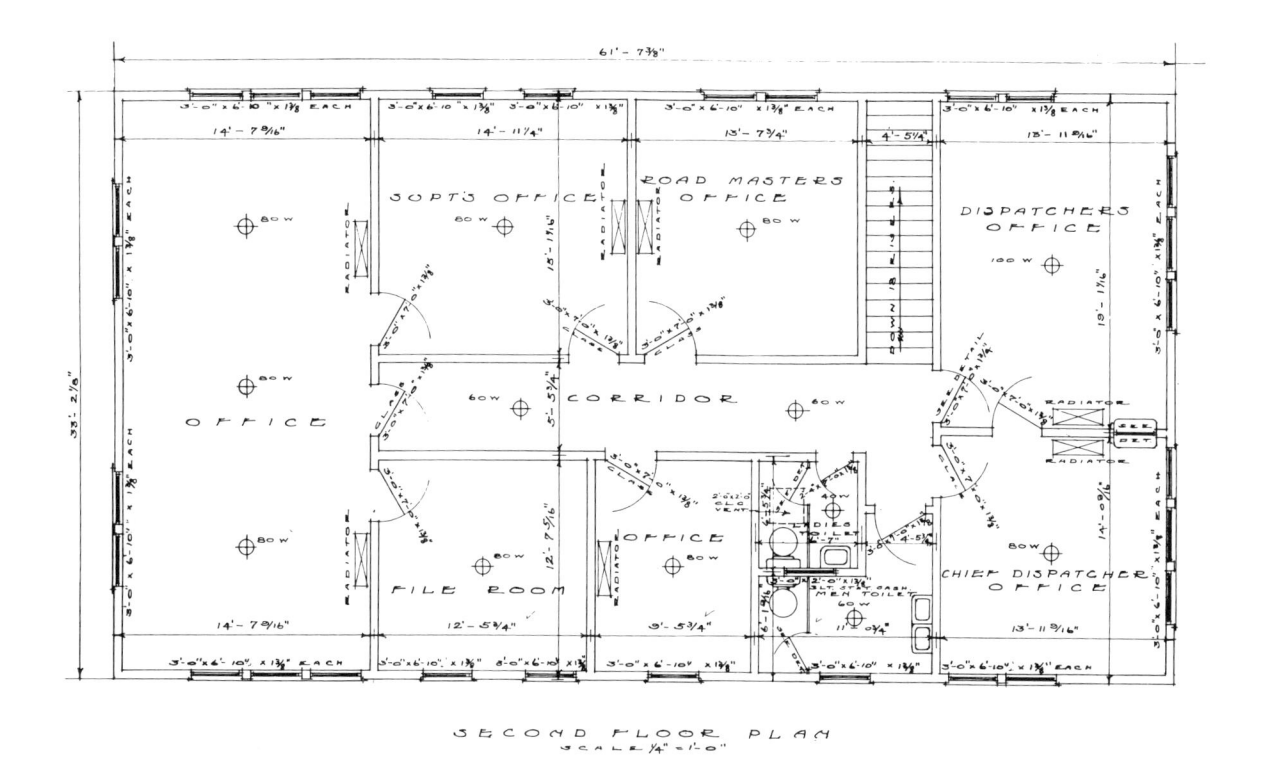

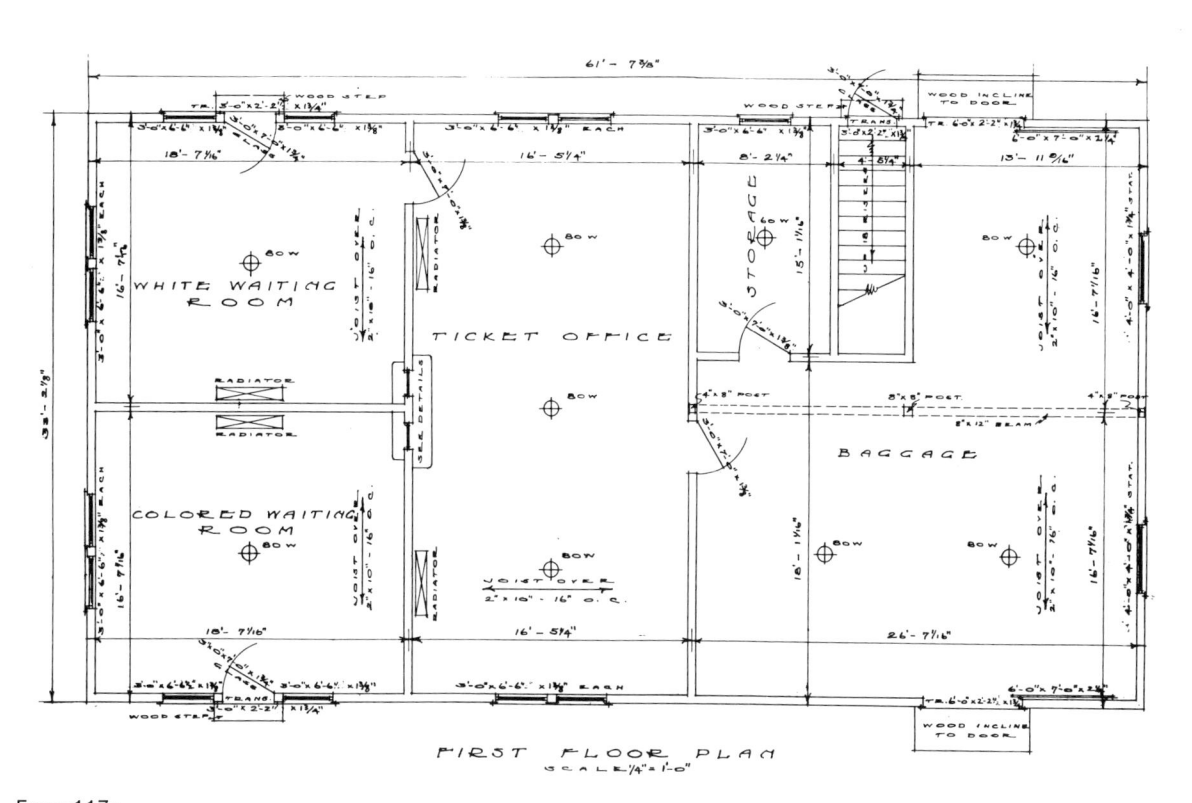

FIGURE 117B

Plan of the first and second stories of the York AT&N Railroad Station. The first floor contained the waiting rooms, ticket offices and baggage areas. Offices and storage rooms were arranged along a central corridor on the second floor.

ELIZABETH BARRETT GOULD

FIGURE 118

The St. Charles Apartments, 1921, 963 Government Street, Mobile. C. L. Hutchisson, Sr., architect. The only surviving apartment complex of the four that were designed by Hutchisson, Sr. Mobilians preferred individual housing whether a mansion or a shotgun. Apartment dwelling did not grow in demand until after World War II. The St. Charles apartment is still in great demand, being located just west of Broad, a street that divides the commercial from the residential areas of Government Street.

designed other stations, including the 1927 AT&N Freight Depot in Mobile.

To do justice to the many homes Hutchisson designed between 1917 and 1927 would take a volume in itself. To illustrate his contribution, a few representative examples from each of his residential categories have been selected.

Until the last quarter of the twentieth century, Mobile was not a city of apartment dwellers. The population preferred private homes, even if they were only small shotguns standing in a row like those on Caroline Street in Old Dauphin Way, or in the Davis Avenue community. Of the few multiple units that were built before midcentury, Hutchisson was responsible for four: The Sherman Plaza; the Spotswood Apartments; the Weinecker Apartments; and the St. Charles. Only the last still stands.

The St. Charles is located at 963 Government Street (figure 118). In the September 1, 1921, *Mobile Register* is a reference to the apartment building being under construction. It is a six-story, red brick complex that occupies all of its corner except for a narrow green strip on the two street sides. The first story is visually related to the public way and separated from the apartment levels above by a heavy, white concrete belt course that surrounds the build-

168

From Builders to Architects: The Hobart–Hutchisson Six

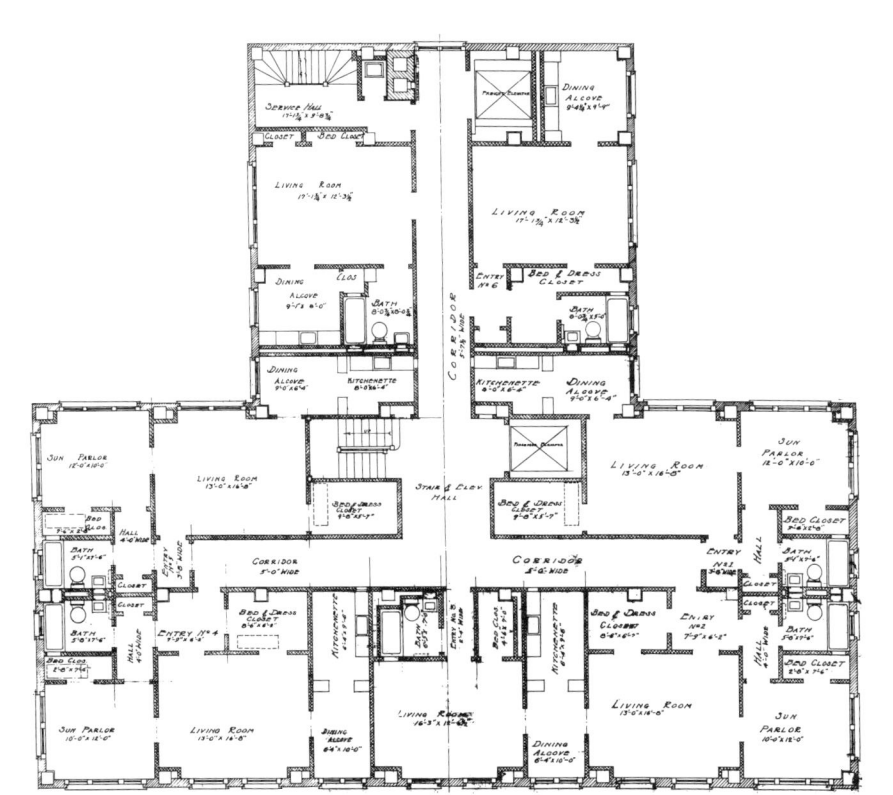

FIGURE 118B

The architect's plan for the apartments in the St. Charles. Each floor had a similar plan that consisted of five apartments in the main building and two in a rear wing.

ing. Above this strongly accented horizontal line is a smaller string course that runs under the windows of the second story. These two courses are important elements in the design. The larger belt differentiates between the public and private areas, and the smaller one makes a subtle transition to the second story, thus reuniting the two levels. As noted before, this division of elevation recalls the early commercial buildings of the Chicago School, in which the first story is related to the street but is differentiated from the upper stories that are given anonymity by rows of similar windows. In the prototype, the building was then crowned by some form of strong cornice or roof treatment. Hutchisson caps his building with a string course that runs below and above the windows of the sixth story, and by the bracketed, overhanging cornice and parapet.

The single entry from Government Street has a wide two-leaf door with a bevelled glass pane and a single-light transom above. The concrete door framing is sufficiently strong to maintain its importance in the overall design. It is formed of two, square pilasters on either side of the door that support a classic entablature with a parapet above. The position of the parapet is such that it ties in with the line of the heavy belt course.

The windows of the apartment levels are arranged in groups of triples, doubles, and singles, instead of rows of similar openings. At the central bay, which projects slightly, are two single windows placed side by side. The plan of the apartments follow the same scheme on the different floors (figure 118b). The individual apartments are located along a central corridor with a cross-

FIGURE 119

H. F. Warren House, 1919, 155 Levert, Mobile. Between the years 1919 and 1923, C. L. Hutchisson, Sr., was in great demand by new residents in Ashland Place. The Warren home is an example of his designs in which he did not include a porch, but instead employed a simple, one-bay stoop that harmonized with his use of the gambrel roof.

corridor leading back to the rear wing. All the rooms are a comfortable size, a thirteen-by-sixteen-foot living room with an attached bed-closet, dining alcove, kitchenette and corner sun room. There is adequate clothes storage. An elevator and a stairway give access to all levels.

Single-family dwellings were of two types, two or more stories and small one-story dwellings. They included a variety of styles all reflecting the national trends of the times: Neoclassic, Italian Renaissance, Spanish Mission, Craftsman and the American Foursquare, the latter influenced by the Prairie Movement of the Chicago School.

From 1919 to the mid-1920s, Hutchisson was busy in Ashland Place, building large and small homes. One of his 1919 homes is the two-story house for H. F. Warren, which still stands at 155 Levert (figure 119). The basic rectangle of this two-story home is covered by a gambrel roof; the side slopes of which extend down to the level of the first story of the house. From the front slope of the gambrel roof, a wide dormer of three bays projects above the first story. The slope of the dormer roof forms a wide overhang, shading the east-facing windows from the heat of the summer sun. Instead of a porch, there is a one-bay stoop over which a small gable forms a protection from the weather. Instead of the traditional pediment, a graceful curve replaces the usual horizontal cornice. Adjoining this stoop gable on either side is a narrow shed roof that extends across the house above the first-story windows and wraps around the

170   *From Builders to Architects: The Hobart–Hutchisson Six*

side elevations. If it were not for this wrap-around shed roof that seems visually to bind them together, the unconventional combination of the gambrel and gable roofs could be a fracturing element in the unity of the design.

The R. A. Christian house (figure 120) at 1605 Government Street is completely different in terms of aesthetic effect from the Maddox house (figure 111), although both are of similar materials. The Maddox home is built of rough-cut stone set in regular horizontal coursing. The 1921 Christian home is made of natural field stone, set in random patterns with no porch to break the beauty of the stone wall. The differing tints of the grey-and-earth colored stone, some showing natural veining, provide the decorative element of the design. Where the Maddox House declares the pull of gravity, the Christian house settles peacefully in a well-planted yard shaded by an enormous oak. Mr. Christian, who owned a hardware business, imported the field stone from South Carolina.

A curving, randomly placed, stone sidewalk leads up to the slightly recessed entrance (figure 120b). The door framing is formed by alternate lengths of cut, cast stone that merge into a corbelled arch capped by a horizontal slab

FIGURE 120
The R. A. Christian Stone House, 1921, 1605 Government Street, Mobile. C. L. Hutchisson, Sr., architect. Polished, riverbed field stone was imported from South Carolina by Mr. Christian for his home. In designing the stone walls in random coursing, Hutchisson kept away from any decorative elements that would distract from the natural veining of the stones.

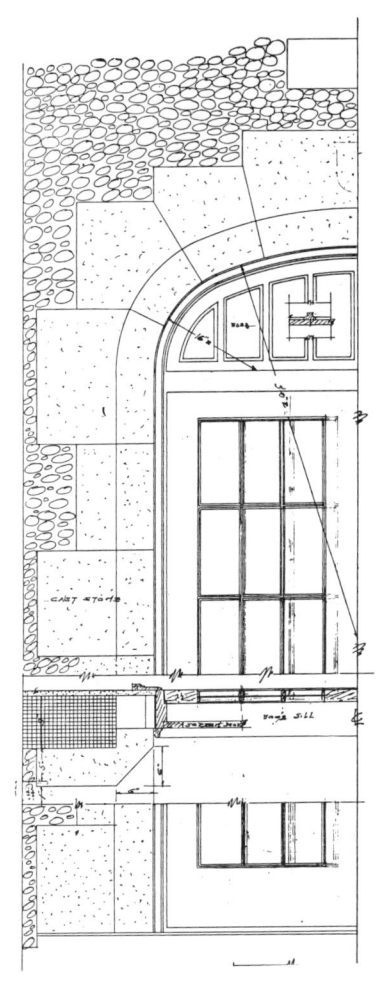

FIGURE 120B (ABOVE RIGHT)
Detail of the entrance to the Christian House. The slightly recessed entry has a cast stone frame that is proportioned to maintain its importance within the expanse of the stone wall.

FIGURE 120C (ABOVE)
Architect's drawing of the front door of the Christian House.

(figure 120c). The wide, two-leaf door is covered by a transom. The house has been recently restored, following the original plans that had been preserved in the Hutchisson family archives.

Many of the houses that Hutchisson designed between the First World War and the Great Depression are still standing. Along West and McDonald Streets in the Flo-Claire subdivision, he built several varieties of the bungalow, as well as two-story homes on Hunter Avenue, Demouy Street, South Ann, Michigan Avenue and Broad Street. The Christie House at 4 Demouy is a 1921 example of the American Foursquare (figure 121). The blocky massing with the widely overhanging eaves, the full width, single-story front porch, the low central dormer and the exposed rafters under the overhang roof are characteristic of the style. Hutchisson put his own stamp on the design in the unusual treatment of the piers at the outer corners of the porch (figure 121b). The upper half of the heavy, square corner piers has a decorative panel of which the center is a lozenge with a cross-shaped drop below, and a shaft connector to the abacus block above. In contrast with the large piers, two circular columns support the center of the three-bay porch. The first-story casement windows and their transoms repeat the lines of the French doors that lead onto the porch.

FIGURE 121

The Christie House, 1921, 4 Demouy Street, Mobile. C. L. Hutchisson, Sr., architect. The blocky American Foursquare house with its overhanging roof and wide front porch was popular during the years before and after World War I. It could easily be enlarged as needed by the addition of wings both to the sides and to the rear. Detailing could be as simple or elaborate as the purse allowed. While these homes were designed by architects, most were constructed by building companies and investors.

FIGURE 121B

Detail of the corner pier of the Christie House. Hutchisson varied the designs of his piers so no two houses were the same. Here the pier is elaborated by geometric panels that occupy the upper half of each face.

In the January 1982 issue of *The Old House Journal*, page 7, there is a summary of the American Foursquare and its derivation. In the article is the statement that the type is "simple, honest, substantial, practical and economical." It lent itself to a variety of treatments. It could be given details adopted from any of the historic styles at the discretion of the owner or it could be left plain. As was the case with the bungalows, the house could be constructed by local contractors or designed by architects. The type became very popular and can be found in all parts of the country. As was stated in *The Old House Journal*, it was the most house for the least money. Adopting elements of the horizontal emphasis found in the Prairie School, it was not out of place in any street scene of the 1920s.

FIGURE 122

The J. A. McGowin House, 1923, 1957 Government Street, Mobile. C. L. Hutchisson, architect. As the commercial interests of the city expanded to the west, they overtook the residential areas. Homes, in turn, moved out farther and farther into the Spring Hill area. Left behind were houses that were either demolished or adapted for some commercial use. One of the few large homes that remains is the McGowin residence, standing now quite isolated on a large lot in the busy Loop area.

FIGURE 122B

Porch detail of the McGowin House. Though Hutchisson designed in all the national trends of his day, those derived from the classical tradition were the most popular with Mobilians. Here twin columns support a pediment with short returns of the horizontal cornice.

Some of the large homes designed by Hutchisson in the early 1920s seem to be an attempt to combine the sheltering overhanging roof of the Foursquare with the proportion of the more traditional Neoclassical home. Such a residence is that built for J. A. McGowin in 1921 (figure 122). It still stands in the middle of a crowded commercial development. The large two-story rectangular block of the house is covered by a widely overhanging roof, whose low-pitch seems to bear down on the house rather than protect it. But the tripled casement windows with their transoms and the one-bay entry porch are a successful early twentieth-century adaptation of the older tradition. In the detail of the entry (figure 122b), the fine moldings of the gable's raking cornice, the short returns of the horizontal cornice and the oval fanlight should be noted.

Not all of the homes of the period followed in the tradition of the bungalow, American Foursquare, or Neoclassic. There were some of unusual design and construction. One of these is a large log home, built in 1919 on the west side of Dog River, near where it empties into Mobile Bay (figure 123). Ferdinand S. Frederick, who owned a dry cleaning business, bought some eleven acres of pine covered river-front property and employed Hutchisson to design his log house. In doing so, the architect drew on the old French-galleried cottage style, creating a one-and-a-half-story dwelling with galleries on three sides. It is constructed of yellow pine logs, with double saddle-notched ends and caulking between the logs (figure 123b). In plan, it has a central hall with two bedrooms on the first floor, one of which has been adapted as a den. In the upper half-story there are three bedrooms. A kitchen is attached as a rear wing.

A fire in the kitchen destroyed most of the original rear wing, but the

FIGURE 123

The Frederick-Bender Log House, 1919-1920, 3619 Riviere du Chien, Mobile County. C. L. Hutchisson, architect. As the century developed, the rivers and water ways attracted the city dwellers for summer retreats. Many became year-round residences as did the log home of the Bender family. The long, one-and-a-half-story house with its galleries is located on the west bank of Dog River, facing out to overlook the water. Behind it, a large grove of trees isolates it from the road. Adding to the rustic effect of the log house are the gallery posts made of cedar, some of which still retain their bark.

FIGURE 123B

Photograph of the north side elevation of the Bender Log Cabin. The double saddle notching of the logs can be seen at the corner of the house.

present owners, Dr. and Mrs. T. I. Bender, were able to restore it based on the original plans. The long, gable roof covers the main building and swings out over the front, east-facing porch. Exposed beams with diagonal bracing support the porch roof. Seven cedar posts divide the porch into six bays. The posts were left in their natural shapes without cleaning off the stubs of branches and some even have retained bits of the original bark, showing one of the ways in which the Hutchisson family of architects incorporated the aesthetic qualities of their building materials. The portion of the gallery that wraps around to the south side has been screened and winterized. It is the only noticeable alteration to the original design of the cabin.

Opening on the front porch from the inner rooms are three pairs of French doors. Above each pair is a five-light transom. In addition to the double sash windows on both the north and south elevations, there is a low, two-section dormer across the central axis of the roof. These allowed the house to take advantage of the cooling breezes off the water.

The home of Dr. J. U. Reaves at 1862 Government Street (figure 124) was another unusual building, but it was destroyed in 1985 to make way for a Burger King Restaurant. During the early 1920s, the Spanish Revival reached its greatest popularity in Mobile as well as throughout the state. The Reaves home, built in 1923, reflects this influence, though not in the usual manner. Its location was on a narrowing stretch of the block close to the point where two converging streets meet. The result of this site was a building roughly on a Greek Cross plan, with the south wing incorporating the main entrance on Government Street and a secondary entrance at the north side on Airport Bou-

FIGURE 124

Dr. J. U. Reaves Home, 1924, formerly at 1862 Government Street, Mobile. Destroyed in 1985 to make way for a Burger King. The Reeves home was a good example of the Spanish Revival style that was popular in Mobile in the early 1920s. It is one of the fine Hutchisson homes that fell victim to commercial encroachment.

FIGURE 124B

A photograph of the Reaves Home taken when the building was occupied by the Casbah Restaurant. Stuccoed walls, grilled balcony, and Spanish tiling all reflect the origin of the style.

levard. The west wing was longer than the one on the east, producing an uneven massing. Instead of having the main entrance on the southern facade, it was located at the angle where the front and west wings met (figure 124b).

The two-story walls were stuccoed up to the peak of the gable of the red-tiled roof. Rafters of the gables were exposed but shaped. Quoining accented the corners of all the wings. The small entry at the angle of the wings was covered by an awning. The pediment of the door frame is Baroque in style with embellishments including scrolls and garlands. At the second-story level, above the entry, the window has a pediment supported on scrolled brackets. A simpler stoop forms the rear entry with an awning over the deck. On the south face of the west wing is a cast iron balcony with a French door leading to it from the large inner gallery room (figure 124).

Over the years, as the Loop area became more and more commercial, houses were either torn down or adapted for commercial uses. The Reaves home contained several fine restaurants in succession, the best known being the Casbah. The irregularity of the different room levels of the interior made an ideal arrangement for private parties and intimate dining, though it must have been difficult to do the serving. After the last restaurant folded, the building was vacant for a time. When the request came from a fast-food company to demolish the home, efforts were made to persuade the company to adapt the building, but it was no use and the Reaves House was destroyed. It its place stands a nondescript, characterless building. It is interesting to note that the draftsman for the Reaves home was the son of C. L. Hutchisson, C. L. Hutchisson, Jr.

FIGURE 125

Architect's drawing of the R. R. Long House, 1921, Atmore, Alabama. The Long home is a good example of a 1921 design in which no revivalist details remain.

FIGURE 125B

Architect's plan of the second story of the Long House. The plan reflects the informal living patterns of the 1920 decade with bedrooms clustered around a small cross hallway. Bathrooms and clothes closets are conveniently arranged, and a large sleeping porch is provided for hot summer nights.

One of Hutchisson's two-story homes that was built outside the Mobile area was constructed for R. R. Long in Atmore, Alabama (figure 125). More informal than the 1913 Ladd House (figure 105), the 1921 home no longer had the classically derived detailing such as columns, but it resembled the Mobile house in general massing and in the horizontal emphasis of the elevations. The double hung windows with their nine-over-one panes of glass belong to the 1920s rather than the 1910s. Though a transom and side lights around the door were retained, their arrangement would not have been found in the earlier period. Unbroken by the vertical lines of the columns, the horizontal emphasis is augmented by the spreading roof of the low dormer, the strongly accented horizontal cornice, the lines of the fenestration with the string course extending beneath the windows, and the porch roof deck. The thin posts supporting the porch roof are hardly noticeable. The only break from this horizontal emphasis is the railing of the deck in which the crow's foot pattern changes line directions. Though the house could not be classified with the Prairie style, nevertheless it is influenced by it.

In a comparison of the second-story plans of the 1913 Ladd house (figure 105c) and the 1921 Long house (figure 125b), the change from the more formal to the more infor-

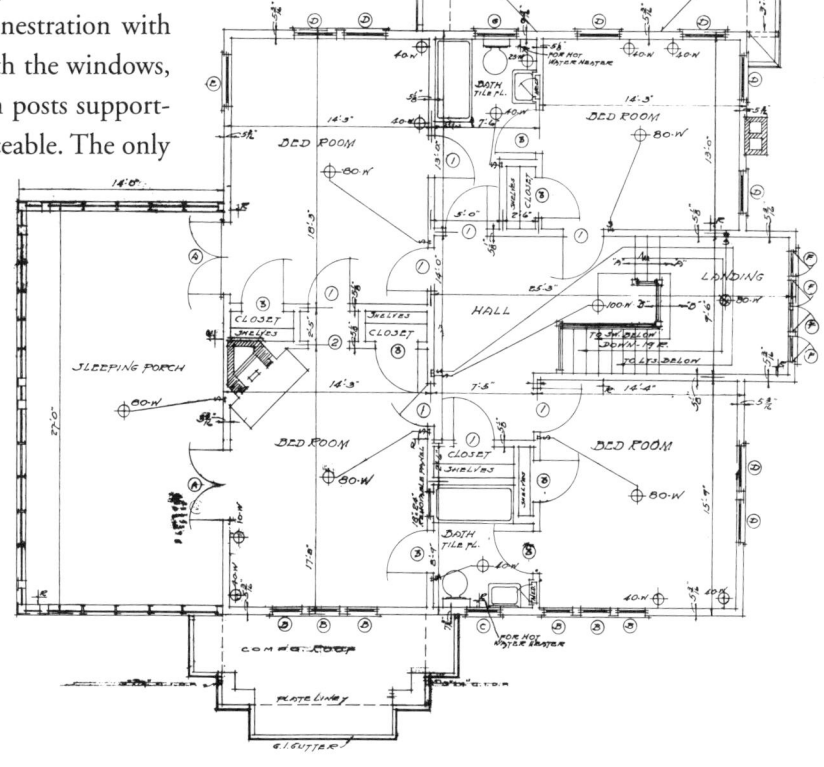

ELIZABETH BARRETT GOULD   177

FIGURE 126

The J. L. Gardiner House, 1921. 200 Lanier Street, Ashland Place, Mobile. During the 1920s, Hutchisson designed several one-story homes for residents in Ashland Place. Some are constructed of wood framing as is the Gardiner home. Others had walls of tile with exterior stucco.

FIGURE 126B

Entrance to the Gardiner House. In order to adopt a classically derived entry to the low elevation, the architect used an archway to make the transition between the twin columns and the broken pediment above.

mal room arrangement is obvious. Instead of the long, central hall of the former, the latter has only a small, I-shaped cross-hall with the rooms grouped around it rather than beside it. Also note in the Long plan, there was no longer a fireplace in every room. Only one fireplace existed, and it was in the master bedroom, tucked away in a cozy corner. It looks as if it were for relaxation rather than for heat.

For those who wanted smaller homes, Hutchisson designed a number of one-story houses, some traditional wood framing with classical porch entries and others with hollow tile construction and stuccoed walls. Several of the traditional wood homes are still standing in Ashland Place.

The general form of these one-story dwellings consisted of a rectangular building with an overhanging roof. A one-bay entrance usually projected from one of the front-end bays. Additional space was gained either by side wings or a front bay (figure 126). The Gardiner house at 200 Lanier is an example.

The Gardiner house plan was unusual in that the owner requested that her kitchen be at the front where she could see what was happening on the street. This posed a problem for the architect, since in those days before modern refrigerators, ice was delivered through a service door directly into an icebox in the kitchen. By harmonizing an ice door with the rest of the side elevation, Hutchisson reconciled the owner's request with the rest of the design.

The Gardiner entry porch with its pair of twin fluted Tuscan columns that supported the entry roof also presented a problem. For the porch gable

FIGURE 127

Sal Rosen House, 1921. 1656 Dauphin Street, Mobile. C. L. Hutchisson, Sr., architect. Unlike the Ashland Place lots, the city lots are narrow and deep. The Rosen House with its narrow front elevation is well adapted to this site limitation.

to reach the height necessary to intersect the main roof, it would have required very tall supports that would have been out of proportion with the general design. To resolve this, the architect chose to use twin columns of pleasing size and to insert a large block above them to fill in the gap (figure 126b). Then, instead of a horizontal line across the opening connecting the two ends of the gable, he swung an arch which added a feeling of lightness. This semicircle is repeated in the transom over the doorway and relates the porch more effectively to the wall of the house.

His hollow tile construction houses can be represented by the 1921 Sol Rosen home at 1656 Dauphin Street. In style it is derived from the bungalow rather than any classical tradition (figures 127,b). The triple overhanging gables with their shaped brackets derive from the bungalow, but while a bungalow has a main porch, the Rosen house has a projection that forms a thirty-four-foot-long front wing containing the living room, den, entry hall and a long side porch. A one-story porch occupies the east front bay of the house with its roof line complementing that on the front of the living room. Thus, instead of the usual two gable roof lines, the Rosen house has three, each one smaller than the one above but repeating the same contours. All the roofs, including a shed over the front living room windows, are tiled.

FIGURE 127B

Architect's drawing of the front elevation of the Rosen House. The porch, front living room and main section of the house are covered with separate gables forming a typical bungalow relationship.

The main section of the house contains the dining room, kitchen, the three bedrooms, two baths and a rear porch. The home is eighty-six feet and three

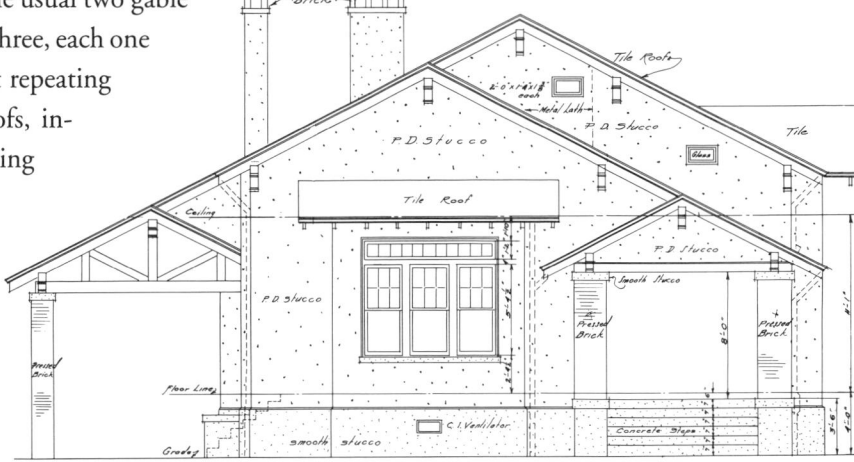

ELIZABETH BARRETT GOULD

inches long, thus creating a house well adapted to a narrow, deep city lot.

The wall construction drawing (figure 127d) clearly indicates the methods of construction used. Bolting the tiles together at the corners are iron bars set in concrete. Three-quarter-inch rods are set in the rest of the wall tiles. Eight-by-eight-by-twelve-inch tiles form the lintels, all stuccoed on the exterior. The drawing of the fireplace (figure 127e) illustrates how Hutchisson used the coursing of the bricks to create the decorative effects. Contrasting with this type of private, commissioned residence, Hutchisson was employed to design housing projects for two different companies.

During the years of the First World War, there was a critical shortage of housing, as Mobile became a center for ship building. The Mobile Ship Building Company was formed in 1918 and purchased most of the lots in three blocks comprising the area between Monterey and Hannon Streets and along Laurel. Here they erected small, simple homes for their employees. In 1919, Sayner and Allen contractors asked for building permits for twenty houses designed by C. L. Hutchisson, Sr. He submitted five different plans, with four homes built from each of the five plans. They were all similar in design but differed in size and price (figure 128):

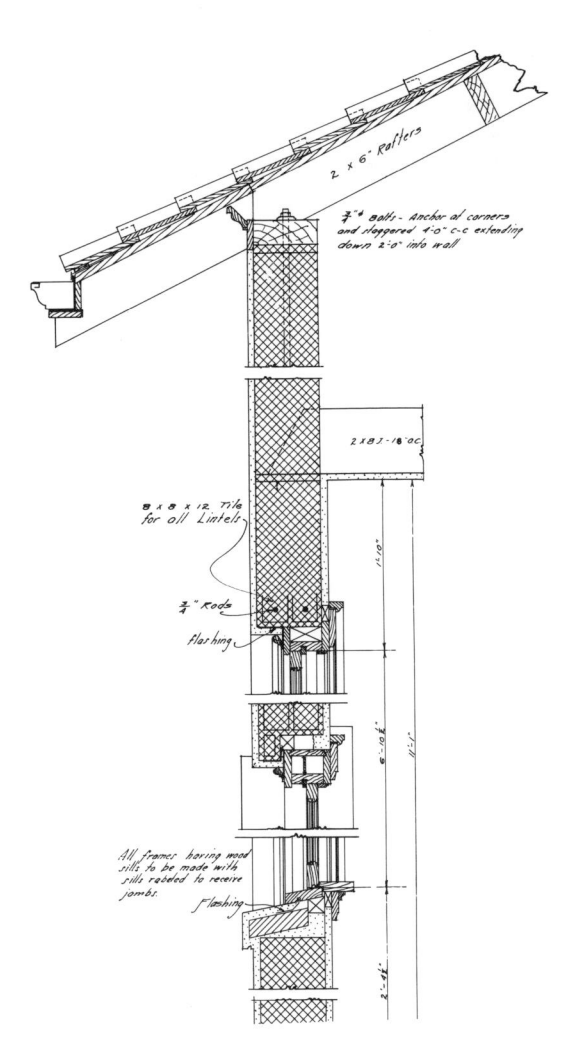

FIGURE 127C

Architect's drawing of the hollow tile wall construction of the Rosen House. Three-fourths-inch iron bolts anchor the tile to the wood roof framing. Three-fourths-inch rods cemented in the holes of the tile form a secure structure. Walls built like this survived Camille and Fredrick hurricanes as well as several less severe storms.

FIGURE 127D

Architect's drawing of the fireplace in the living room in the Rosen House. Bricks laid in different coursing constitute both the structure and decoration of the fireplace.

From Builders to Architects: The Hobart–Hutchisson Six

25' x 32'; $2,000 each
25' x 36'; $2,250
28' x 45' 4"; $2,400
24' 10 7/8" x 57' 1 3/8"; $2,750
33' 2 1/3" x 40' 7"; $2,750.

The five types were intermingled so that there was some variety within the street scene. The twenty houses still stand along Laurel, Houston, Monterey, and Hannon Streets, though some have been altered by aluminum siding, modern roofing, and porch screening. The one selected here to illustrate the group (figure 128) is located at 100 South Monterey Street. Like the others, it is one-story in height, with a full-width front porch that is covered by the extension of the main gable. All originally had wood shingles and wood siding. Rafters are exposed, and the gable is bracketed. The square corner piers that support the porch roof are of an unusual design and distinctive to the company housing. The detail

FIGURE 128
Workman's cottage, Mobile Ship Building Company housing, 1919, 100 South Monterey. C. L. Hutchisson, Sr., architect; Sayner and Allen, contractors. With Mobile booming during World War I, the shortage of housing became acute. Two city blocks still contain twenty houses designed by Hutchisson for company employees. Based on five different plans, they differed in price and size, though they can be recognized by their porches and piers. In this example, the porch has been screened.

FIGURE 128B
The company houses can be recognized by the design of the porch piers. The square supports for the extended roof are infilled with wall siding. At the upper coursing, a bracket projects from the outer face and two, wooden, circular panels decorate the square capital block.

FIGURE 129

Workman's shotgun house, built for the employees of the Gulf Coast Produce Exchange, 1918, Johnson and Airport Roads, Mobile County. The complex planned by C. L. Hutchisson, Sr., included the manager's home and housing for the laborers in this early agricultural experiment. Only two of the small houses still exist and while they are of no architectural merit, they represent an early extensive attempt in Mobile County to carry out company housing in an agricultural setting.

FIGURE 130

The McGowin Memorial Mausoleum, 1921, Magnolia Cemetery, Mobile. C. L. Hutchisson, Sr., architect. The McGowin Memorial is a beautifully designed mausoleum. The refinement of its proportions and detailing are a tribute to the skill of the architect. The repose and dignity sometimes found in large memorials is here encapsulated in the small, personal, family mausoleum.

in figure 128b gives an idea of the pattern. Over the years some of these piers have been replaced by simple square posts.

A second commercial company for which Hutchisson designed homes was the Gulf Coast Produce Exchange, founded in 1918 and controlling some thousand acres of land west of the extension of Airport Boulevard. It was a horticultural venture to grow fruits, especially satsumas. The large home for the manager designed by Hutchisson has been destroyed by fire, and only two of the little workmen's cottages have survived on Johnson Road (figure 129). Architecturally, they are of little significance, being shotguns of one-story, with a gable roof and simple entry. They are significant because they represent one of the few attempts at agricultural company housing in Mobile. Most of the workmen's homes were built by real estate investors for rental income, though some were privately owned. The Gulf Coast Produce Company had barely gotten started with their satsuma trees just beginning to mature, when an unusual early freeze hit the Gulf Coast and destroyed the orchards putting the company out of business by 1920.

Last of the pure Hutchisson buildings to be presented in the 1917-1927 period is the McGowin Family Mausoleum, located in the southwest corner of Magnolia Cemetery (figure 130). Designed in 1921, it is individually listed on the National Register, as are many of Hutchisson's buildings. The square structure is located on a stone terrace. The mausoleum's walls are of grey, cut, granite blocks. The base of the mausoleum walls flare slightly above the foundation. The top member of the foundation is molded like the base of a column. The entrance is a double-leaf, heavy door inset with grilles that cover a glass door (figure 130b), so when the outer grilled doors are opened, one can see through the central aisle to a stained-glass window on the eastern wall (figure 130c). The front grille is matched by one over the back window. In the architrave above the entrance is carved the name, McGowin. Above the rear window is a monogram, a letter "M," on either side of which is carved a form that looks like an inverted torch.

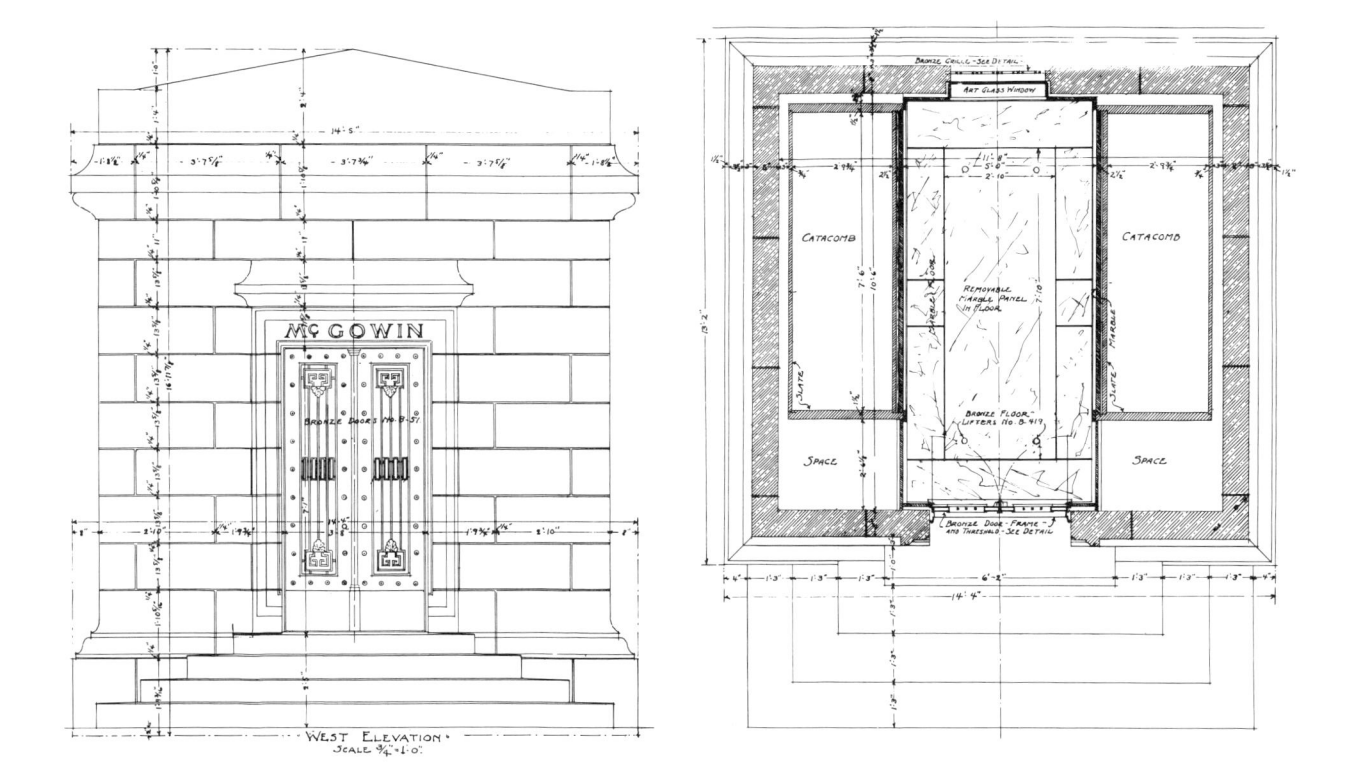

In plan (figure 130c), the little building is roughly a square, thirteen feet, two inches by fourteen feet, four inches. Behind the bronze doors the space opens up into an aisle, the floor of which is paved with removable marble slabs supported on bronze lifters. Behind the two-and-a-half-inch-thick marble walls of the aisles, catacombs are lined with three-fourths-inch slate. The morning sun, shining through the rear stained-glass window casts a glow of color on the interior. The grace and refinement of this memorial is a tribute to both the McGowin family and to the architect who created it, becoming a memorial for both. One of the last buildings Hutchisson had a part in before the Great Depression struck was with a team of architects designing the dormitory for Spring Hill College.

The group, all from Mobile, consisted of Hutchisson, Hutchisson, March, Downey and Roberts. Three generations of Hutchissons worked for the college during their respective lifetimes, beginning with James H. (Chapter Three).

FIGURE 130B

Architect's drawing of the McGowin Mausoleum. Blocks of grey granite form the walls of the mausoleum. A bronze door with a grille covering plate glass forms the entrance. On the rear wall, a bronze grille covers a rear window filled with art glass that casts prismatic colors into the interior.

FIGURE 130C

Architect's plan for the mausoleum. The interior of the central aisle is lined with marble. Removable marble floor slabs are lifted by a bronze mechanism. The catacombs are lined with lead.

FIGURE 131

Mobile Hall Men's Dormitory, Spring Hill College, 1927, Old Shell Road, Mobile. Hutchisson, Hutchisson, March, Downey and Roberts, architects. The long men's dormitory was designed to harmonize with older existing campus buildings. The use of the projecting central and end pavilions repeats the elevation of the Administration Building of 1869 designed by James Freret of New Orleans. Photograph of the south and east end elevation.

FIGURE 131B

The main entrance on the north side of Mobile Hall. Above the entry porch with its simple Tuscan columns and entablature is an elaborate scroll window frame with a broken pediment above.

In designing Mobile Hall, the architects succeeded in combining a well-planned dormitory that was still stylistically compatible with the nineteenth-century buildings nearby (figure 131).

In mass, it is a large, three-story, rectangular-shaped building raised on a high basement. It follows the format of the college's French-inspired administration building in having three projecting pavilions, each with corners accented by quoining. The main hip roof is intersected by a large gable covering a central entry pavilion that has doors on both the north and south elevations. There are also entries at the east and west ends of the building. The main doorway is located on the north in the central pavilion. It is elaborated by classical detailing (figure 131b). Two, large, unfluted, Tuscan-Doric columns with matching wall pilasters frame the entrance. Scrolled brackets support the broken pediment of the second-story windows. The whole framing is crowned by a decorative ornament on a pedestal.

The southern entrance is similar to that on the north, but without the columns. The doors at the east and west end are double leaf, with a semicircular transom framed by an arched molding with a scrolled keystone. One of the unusual elements in the design is the fenestration. Large twin windows with six-over-six lights are interspersed with small twins with four-over-four lights, forming an ABA ABA ABA rhythm over the facades of the north and south elevation.

Hutchisson, Holmes and Hutchisson 1927-1932

It was during the early, lean years of the depression that Nicholas Holmes, Sr. and C. L. Hutchisson, Jr., joined the firm. One of the first buildings planned by the new firm was the Methodist Church at Atmore, Alabama. It was also the last large public building by the firm until 1938 (figure 132). The drawings for the church are dated June 15, 1927. The understated style can be traced back to the Spanish Mission influence noted in such earlier work as the Robinson Memorial Chapter House (figure 102), but in the 1927 church the earlier Baroque detailing is omitted. The brick wall surface is left plain. The semicircular-headed dows and doors, the stepped and double-curved parapets on all four elevations and the tiled roof all incorporate the Mission characteristics. Only the white trim of the openings give contrast with the wall surface. Even the transoms are infilled with brick laid in a vertical, zig-zag pattern. The building is fifty-two feet wide by eighty-six feet, eight inches long, not counting the balustraded deck that extends across the front and around the first bay on the right side (figures 132b,c).

The wall construction shows the developments of the post-World War I years (figure 132d). Between the concrete foundation and the one-and-a-half-foot-thick brick walls is inserted a "damp course." The support for the basement and the auditorium slab floors was formed by steel trusses bedded in the brick walls. To quote from the drawing concerning the slab construction "Vertical and horizontal rods shall be wired together at every intersection. Rods shall be blocked out from forms and wired to hold in position shown during pouring of concrete." (figure 132d) The interior of the brick walls is covered

FIGURE 132

The Methodist Church, Atmore, Alabama, 1927. Hutchisson, Holmes and Hutchisson, architects. One of the last public buildings designed by the firm before the Great Depression made any such structure impossible. The design is a simplified version of the Spanish Mission style.

FIGURE 132B

Architect's drawing of the front elevation of the Methodist Church in Atmore. The stone coping of the porch balustrade and the double-curved parapet form a contrast of color and texture with the brick walls. Semicircular transoms over metal doors are filled with bricks set in a herringbone pattern.

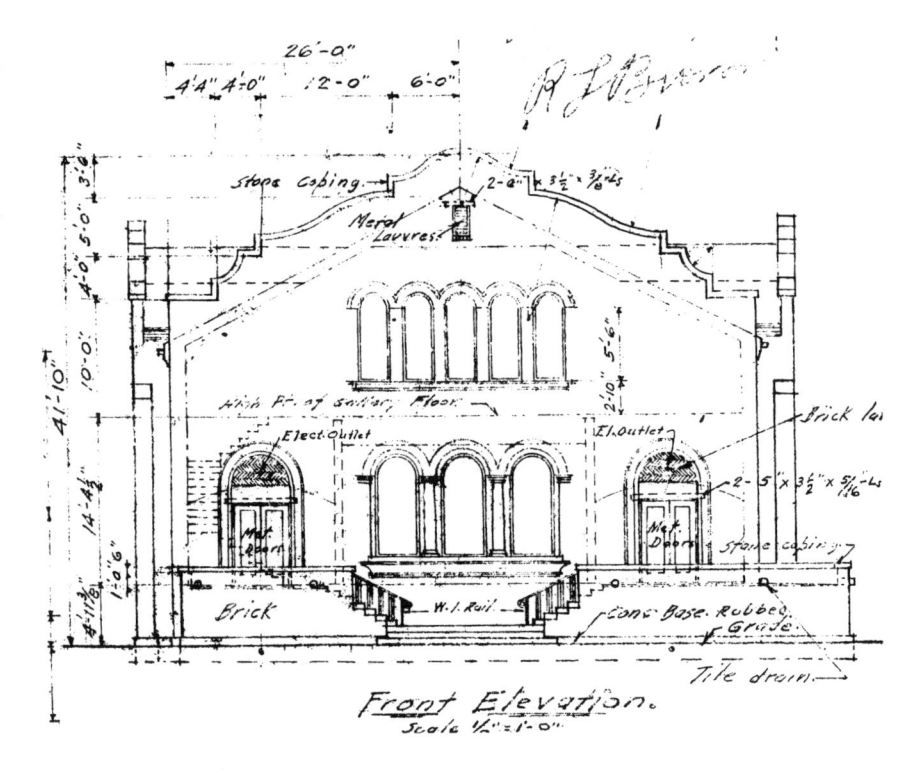

FIGURE 132C

Side elevation of the Methodist Church, Atmore, Alabama. The Spanish revival design is repeated in the parapets above the transept and the sanctuary end. The porch balustrade wraps around the first bay of the side elevation providing for a secondary entrance. All the semicircular-headed windows have brick sills.

with celotex. The doors and window frames were of steel. All these building materials, except the bricks, were products of the postwar era.

The building was entered through any one of the two front doors or the right side bay. In plan the church was the usual Latin division of the entry, foyer, nave and a cross transept toward the sanctuary end. On either side of the central foyer were smaller square rooms, the one on the left having a stairway to the basement. The auditorium was the full width of the building, without side aisles. To provide for better visibility, the floor of the auditorium was sloping, 5/8 of an inch for every 2 feet and 2 3/4 inches until about 10 feet from the sanctuary where it leveled off. The sanctuary end was shallow and of unusual shape with sloping sides sealed off at the back wall. To either side of the sanctuary were small vestry rooms with a double lavatory behind the sanctuary. Over the years, the church has done modifications, but the exterior is much as it was originally designed, as can be seen by comparing the photograph of 1992 with the original drawings.

In any depression, the building industry is one of the first to suffer. In the years of the

186   *From Builders to Architects: The Hobart–Hutchisson Six*

Great Depression from 1929 through the 1930s, only a few homes and the most essential of repair work were undertaken. The commercial world tried to weather the depression with what it had. Suburban development halted as residential building declined. Two programs were sponsored by the government that, to a degree, helped the situation. One was the Historic American Building Survey (HABS) that was initiated in 1933 by the joint efforts of the American Institute of Architects (AIA), the Park Service, and the Library of Congress. In 1934-35 this was funded by the Work Projects Administration (WPA). To stimulate the construction of low-cost housing, a second act, the Federal Housing Authority (FHA), was passed. But, at best, there was little work for builders and even less for architects. Yet somehow the firm Hutchisson, Holmes and Hutchisson survived through 1932. It is a tribute to the firm's adaptability in using the materials available that kept them going. In 1932 Nicholas Holmes left the firm and the Hutchissons, father and son, continued separately, rather than as a listed firm. Nicholas Holmes became involved with FHA and C. L. Hutchisson, Sr., went into partial retirement.

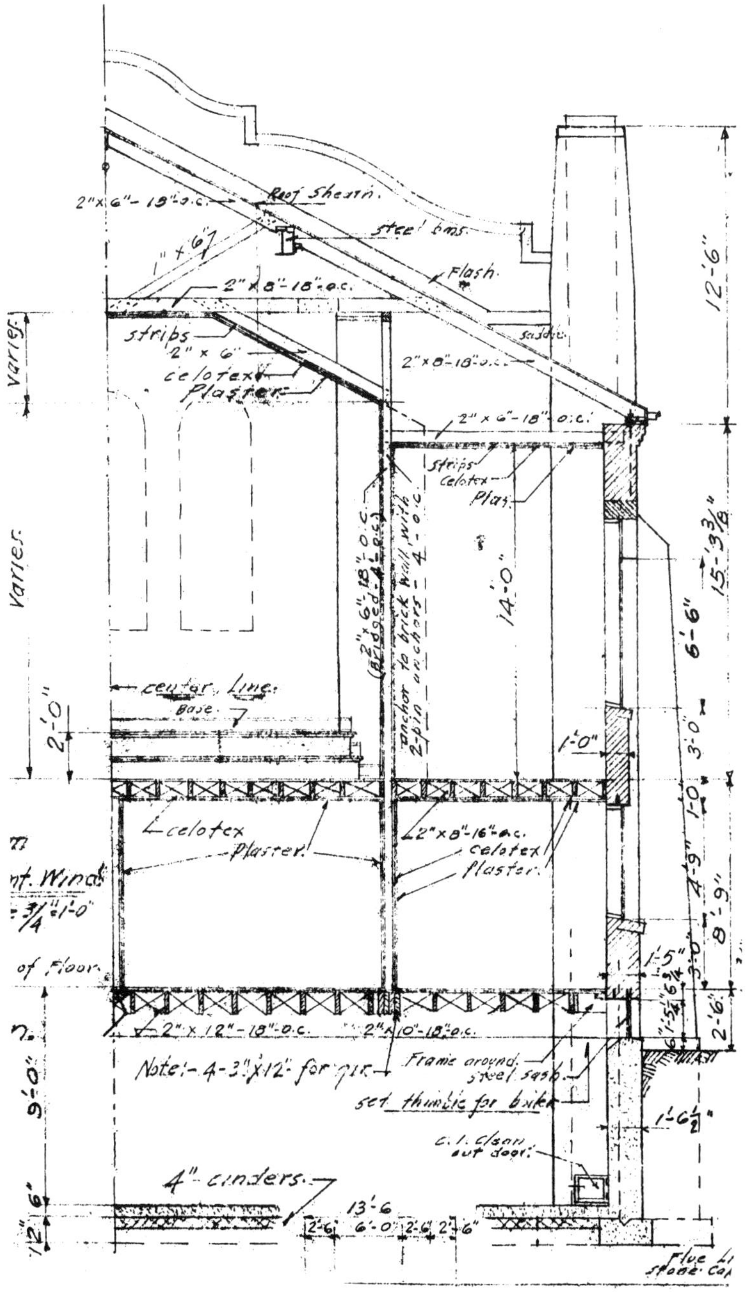

Of the homes by the firm of Hutchisson, Holmes and Hutchisson, seven are within historic districts, well preserved and still occupied.[49] Three of these illustrate the range of their work.

In the Country Club section of Spring Hill is the 1928 Charles Meredith house. It is situated on a wide lot, located back on its site and approached by a concrete drive and parking area that is surrounded by grassy plots and low shrubbery that complement the long, low line of the house (figure 133). The stained shingled walls of the house are low, sheltered by a steeply pitched gable roof that covers the front section containing the living room. The entrance to the house is located in a projecting left side wing. The gable of the wing intersects that over the living room. A high roof line that covers the rear wing is

FIGURE 132D

Architect's drawing of the wall construction, Methodist Church, Atmore, Alabama. The construction is a combination of traditional brick walls and modern steel supports.

visible in the photograph beyond the two front gables. The rear wing contains the kitchen, an inset side porch, three bedrooms and two baths (figure 133b). At the time, these dimensions could have been accommodated only in the Spring Hill or Ashland Place suburbs. The use of shingles as a wall covering was the most frequently used material throughout the depression years.

Somewhat smaller than the Meredith home of 1928 is a one-and-a-half-story stuccoed house built for B. C. Anderson at 252 West Street in the Leinkauf Historic District (figure 134). The two, front-facing gables, one over the entry and the other over the left side bedroom, follow the bungalow relationship with one slope for the two contiguous gables (figure 134b). They intersect the steep slope of a high, truncated hip forming an unusual roof configuration (figure 134c). The high, truncated roof allows for the use of part of the attic for a bedroom, bath, servant's room and storage area.

The front door is formed of vertical boards set flush with the wall of the house, and approached by a series of brick steps. A small window of leaded

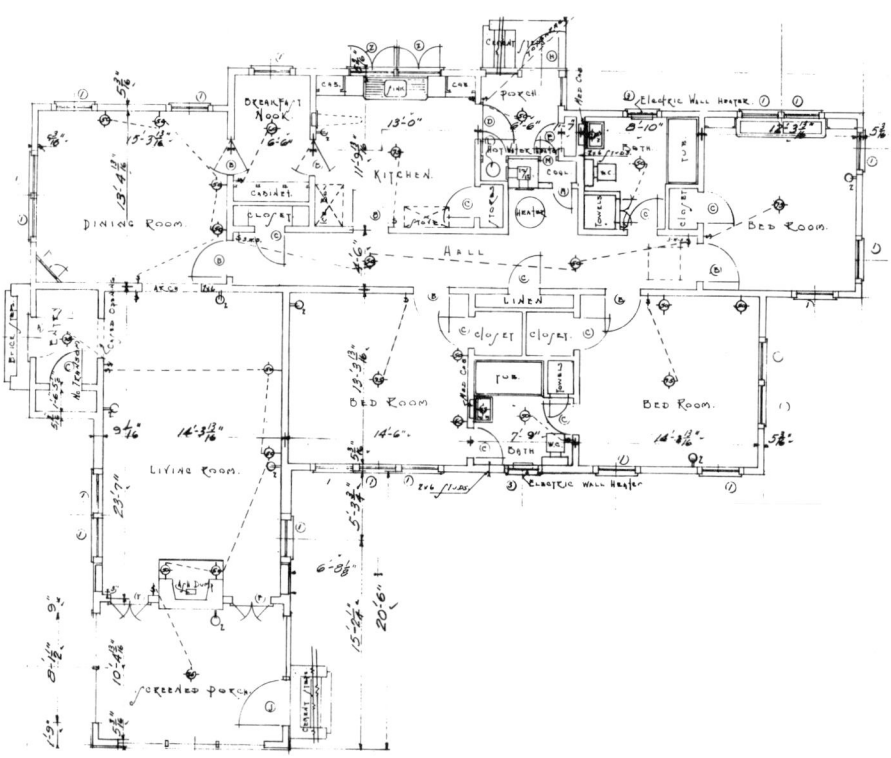

FIGURE 133

The Charles Meredith House, 1928, 15 Wildwood Drive, Mobile. Hutchisson, Holmes and Hutchisson, architects. One of the largest of the homes built before the 1930s Depression years. Shingles played an important role in wall cladding during this time. Although wood shingles were used in this home, manufactured shingles such as asbestos frequently were employed. The home is located near the country club in the expanding southern area of Spring Hill.

FIGURE 133B

Architect's plan of the Meredith House. The long L-shaped plan with the slightly projecting left entrance is well adapted to its large lot. To the left of the entry is the dining room with the living room occupying the rest of the front elevation. Bedrooms, kitchen and utility rooms are located in the rear. A porte-cochère on the right has replaced the closed garage popular earlier in the century.

From Builders to Architects: The Hobart–Hutchisson Six

glass is just large enough to give a view of who might be standing outside. The windows of the house are steel casement types with brick sills. Only one of the gables has a decorative treatment at the upper angle.

The plan of the house is compact in room arrangement. The living room opens from the right of the entry. The living room has two adzed beams extending across the ceiling. At the far end a large fireplace fills most of the wall, with doors on either side leading out to the porch. From the living room, an archway on the left opens onto a dining room with a kitchen beyond. The left front bedroom with its bath is entered from a narrow passageway off the living room. Space for the heating equipment is located between the front and rear bedrooms. Off the rear bedroom is a sleeping porch. There is no wasted space in this house.

FIGURE 134

The B. C. Anderson House, 1930, 252 West Street. Hutchisson, Holmes and Hutchisson, architects. The Anderson home was constructed of hollow tile and surfaced with stucco, a commonly employed practice when good, heavy wood framing and siding were scarce. In this house, manufactured steel-framed casement windows were used, another development that became popular after World War I. Awnings, placed over the east-facing door and window, alter the original design.

FIGURE 134B

Architect's drawing of the front elevation of the Anderson House. With the 1930 and 1931 Depression years, houses were built smaller. The high-truncated roof and side dormers provided for additional bedroom space above the first floor.

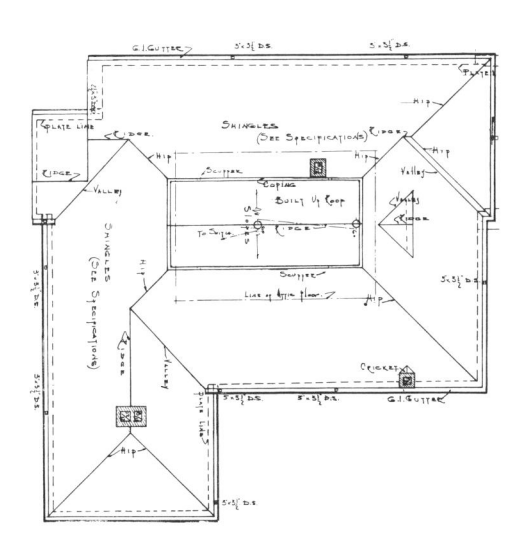

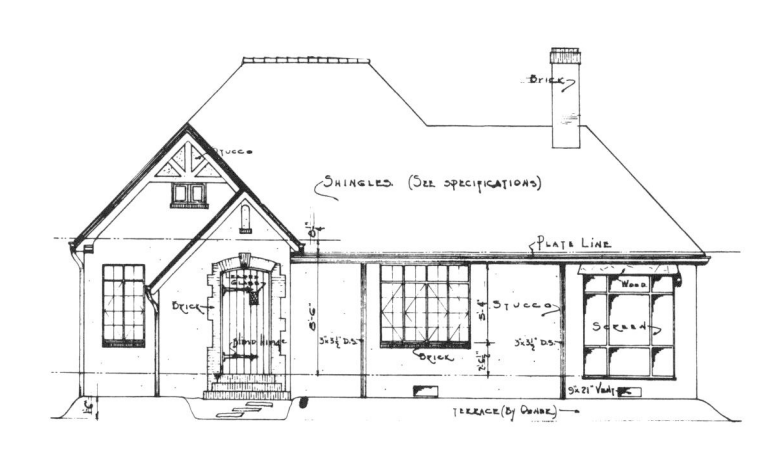

FIGURE 134C

Architect's drawing of the roof of the Anderson House showing the complex relationship of the different roof levels. The high-central, truncated hip roof has a scupper hole cut in the coping to allow for adequate drainage from the deck.

ELIZABETH BARRETT GOULD

FIGURE 135

The Steele Partridge House, 1931, 306 McDonald Avenue, Mobile. Hutchisson, Holmes and Hutchisson, architects. The compact L-shaped house of Steele Partridge is typical of the homes built during the lean years of the Depression, when no materials were wasted on non-essential spaces like halls and porches. Yet within the limits of the plan, the architects achieved a pleasing and comfortable design.

The last house selected from this period is the smallest of the three and is typical of the less expensive homes of the depression years. The Steele Partridge home was built in 1931 and is located at 306 McDonald Street, in Flo-Claire, now in the Leinkauf Historic District (figure 135).

It is a one-story shingled building, with a right front projecting bay forming something of an "L" plan. The three-bay porch forms an arcade over the main section of the house. Gable roofs cover both parts, the one over the right bay being at right angles to the main axis of the house. This "L" plan seems to have dominated most of the buildings of the period. The plan is simple and has reduced all unnecessary space, such as hallways or entrance foyers, though it could easily be enlarged by another forward wing on the opposite side. Being a Hutchisson building, however, it had its elements of individuality. The chimney on the north elevation has double stacks rising from a common base. The square stacks are set on the diagonal to the wall, making a diamond pattern. The gable end over the right wing has a flared barge board that rests on corbels. All the materials in the Partridge house are typical of those made available following World War I. Good lumber for siding of the prewar type was hard to find and shingles became the most common form of wall covering.

With the depression discouraging any building of note, the firm of Hutchisson, Holmes and Hutchisson was dissolved. Except for the FHA houses, the years from 1932 to 1938 had little to offer an architect, but by 1938 there were signs of improvement.

It was in 1938 that the Alabama State Docks commissioned C. L. Hutchisson, Sr., C. L. Hutchisson, Jr., Nicholas Holmes, Sr., and William March to design their new office building (figure 136). The building still stands in the center of a complex of railroads, truck lines, and dock facilities. The two-story, rectangular-shaped building of fourteen bays has had an addition on the north that carries out the same elevation design as that of the original building. The concrete walls are stuccoed, with the bays framed by pilasters that rise the full height of the facade. The interior of the walls were lined with cork insulation to help keep the interior cool. A concrete canopy covers the main entrance, on the west side. Twin scrolled brackets of metal support it at the wall. In the frieze above the entrance, the name, The Alabama State Docks Administration Building, is carved in Art Deco lettering, and the emblem of the state docks is centered in the parapet. There are secondary entrances on both the north and south ends of the building, each with a cantilevered canopy. The heavy plate glass door in a steel frame is a replacement. The building was well thought out and efficient. It planned for the future and today still serves its original purpose.

The State Docks Office Building was the last major commission in which C. L. Hutchisson, Sr. participated. He retired from active practice but remained a member of the Mobile Housing Board throughout World War II and several more years after that. It seems fitting to close the record of his long career with his delightful Chinese Gas Station of 1926. It was during his active years that the automobile changed the American way of life, creating ever more distant suburbs as well as transforming the commercial world. In the earliest years of the architect's life, carriage houses were still in demand. Eventually, private garages and many small contracts followed where he either had to renovate the carriage houses or build new structures. He introduced the

FIGURE 136
State Docks Administration Building, 1938, State Docks Complex, Mobile. Hutchisson, Holmes, Hutchisson and March, architects. Located on the west side of the Alabama River, just at the entrance to the bay, the State Docks buildings stand on ground reclaimed from early marshy land. Without any protective trees to shade from the hot summer sun, the architects lined the interior walls with cork insulation. Now with air conditioning and additional bays added to the north, the building still serves its original purpose.

FIGURE 137

The Chinese Gas Station, circa 1926, formerly on the north side of Government Street, in the 650 block. Hutchisson, Holmes and Hutchisson, architects. All of the many gas stations designed by Hutchisson or his firm had some distinctive style. Some were given classical detailing, others less reflective of any particular period. One of the most fanciful was the Chinese Gas Station, destroyed only a few years ago to make way for the increasing demand for parking, ironically being demolished by the needs of the machine that it was originally constructed to fuel.

porte-cochere that became more popular than the closed garage in the South.

Among the new demands brought about by the advent of the automobile was the need for gas stations. Of the ten designed by Mr. Hutchisson all are gone. The only one for which drawings have survived is the charming Chinese Gas Station that once stood on the corner of Government and Dearborn Streets (figure 137,b). How boring are the repetitive duplications of modern gas stations that now dot the corners of so many of our streets. None of Mr. Hutchisson's gas stations were in the same design. Unlike some of the anthropomorphic and imaginative style stations that can be found in California, all his designs came from the pages of architectural history. Surviving evidence indicates the charm of his stations and renders their loss all the more regrettable.

Versed in the nineteenth-century building techniques, Hutchisson had to learn by his own efforts the changes taking place in other parts of the country. He kept in touch with the prevailing trends in styles and adapted them to his clients needs and wishes. He was not a style originator but his designs always were harmoniously planned with individual elements in each building. No shoddy workmanship ever got by his eagle eye and he was known to have a substandard piece of work done over at the builder's expense. The end of his life coincided with the end of the depression and the coming of World War II. With the growth of architectural schools and the spreading influence of the International style promulgated by Walter Gropius at Harvard, the time of the builder-architect was drawing to a close. It is doubtful that even if he had lived to move with the times, he would have accepted the new developments in his world. The deep conservatism of the old South clung, and still clings, to its traditional roots. For every 100 homes designed in some historic style, there may be one built of concrete, steel and glass. So the whimsical and fanciful Chinese Gas Station with its Imperial Spanish tile roof, its upward tilted cornices and its pagoda-like spire is a gracious close to a long and successful career. It is both ironic and a comment on our times that the building was destroyed to make way for a parking lot.

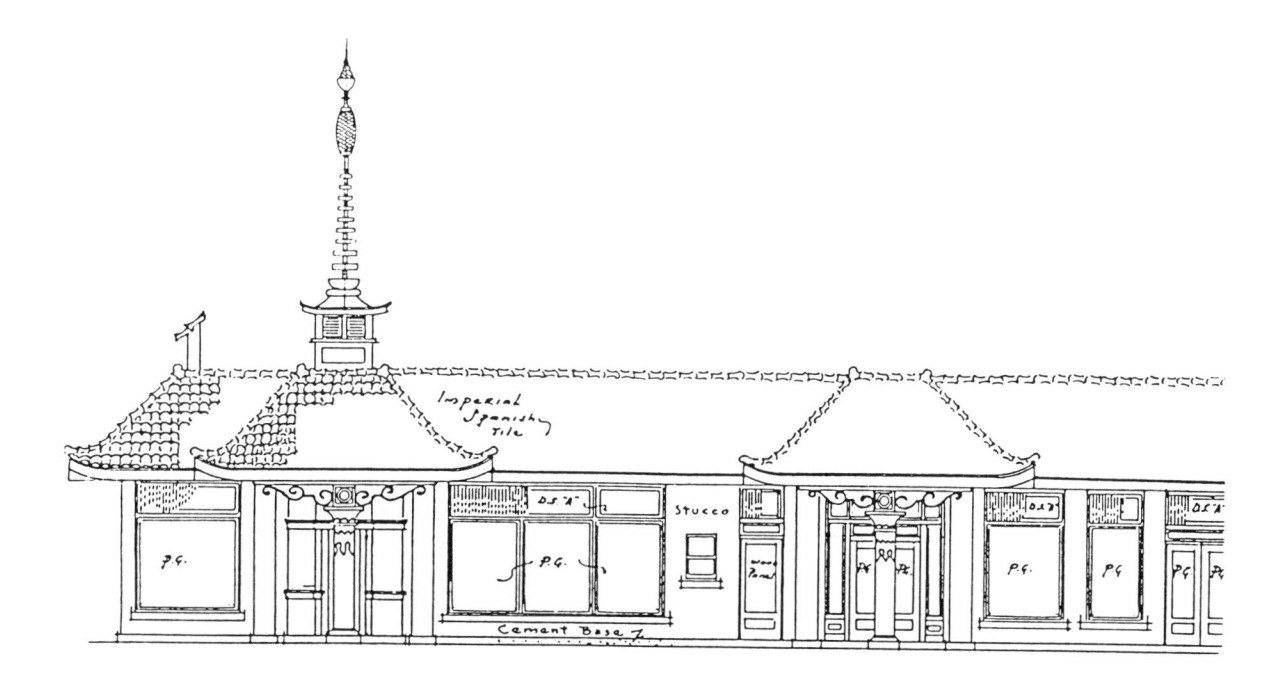

FIGURE 137B

Architect's drawing of the Chinese Gas Station. It was the coming of the automobile age that contributed to the expansion of the suburbs in which Hutchisson designed so many of his fine homes. It seems fitting to close the drawings, illustrations and photographs of his career with this drawing of his delightful Chinese Gas Station.

PLATE VI

The Quinlivan House, circa 1940. 1908 Hunter Avenue. FHA house. Clarence L. Hutchisson, Jr., architect. One of the finest of the FHA houses designed by the architect.

Chapter 6

Clarence L. Hutchisson, Jr.

(1902-1993)

CLARENCE L. Hutchisson, Jr., was the last member of the long family line of builder-architects who first began their work in Mobile in 1797. He was born in Meridian, Mississippi, during the time that his father was in partnership with P. J. Krouse. Only a year old, he came to Mobile when his father joined the firm of George Watkins. Introduced to construction at an early age — at six years old — he began accompanying his father on inspection trips to numerous building sites. Besides both consciously and unconsciously absorbing a craftsman's knowledge, he also showed an early interest in anything mechanical. After a traditional education in Mobile's private schools, he began a two-track training as an architect in his father's office and as an engineer. For many of the buildings mentioned in Chapter Five, C. L. Hutchisson, Jr., was the draftsman. In addition, to further his childhood fascination with machines and anything mechanical, he began to study mechanical engineering and at the same time served a four-year machine apprenticeship.

To further his engineering training, young Hutchisson went to Chicago to study heating and ventilation problems. He also attended the University of Alabama from which he received a certificate of graduation from a special program in Aerial Bombardment Protection. As a result of this engineering training, he developed several structural devices for which he received three United States patents and one Canadian.

The work of C. L. Hutchisson, Jr., can be divided into three main periods. The first period covered the years from 1932 to World War II. The second period extended through the war years, from 1941 to 1945 when he was the chief architect for the Mobile unit of the United States Army Corps of Engineers. The last period covered the postwar years to the time of his retirement in 1967-68.

During the Depression and pre-World War II years, two tracks of architectural development took place within the United States. One of these was an isolated movement in the northeast and in Chicago that introduced the nation to modern architecture. In the northeast, Walter Gropius came to America

FIGURE 138

The Muscatt House, 1936, 1825 Old Shell Road, C. L. Hutchisson, Jr., architect. One of the sixty-five FHA homes designed by C. L. Hutchisson, Jr., during the 1930s. The two-story home has a one-bay extension on the east side that has been altered by being enclosed. Other changes from the original design are the new aluminum siding and the installation of cast iron supports for the porch, replacing the original square columns that matched the existing wall pilasters.

from the Bauhaus, to become chairman of the Harvard Architecture School. In 1937 he introduced the concepts that functionalism should be a determinant factor in architectural design. About the same time, Mies van der Rohe came from the same German school and chaired the Architecture School at the Illinois Institute of Technology in Chicago. van der Rohe built his famous Crown Hall in 1939. With him, there was a renewal in skyscraper developments using all steel and glass construction.

While these embryonic movements were forming in the early 1930s, the rest of the country was bogged down in the post-Depression years. Employment remained at an all-time low with architects and engineers joining the ranks of the unemployed. Building had come to a halt and was rescued, as in other areas of the economy, by the United States government. With all the training that C. L. Hutchisson, Jr., had in engineering, one might expect that he would have pursued this profession. However, in postwar Mobile, there was little opportunity to continue this line of work. There was, however, a need for new low-cost housing and a demand for renovation and restoration of older buildings, both residential and commercial. Some of C. L. Hutchisson, Sr.'s structures were restored by C. L. Hutchisson, Jr., who had his father's plans and drawings preserved in the family archives. He returned to his early education in his father's firm and concentrated in the field of architecture during the first and third periods of his professional life.

During the years of his independent practice, Hutchisson was responsible for thirty-six houses of which twenty still stand, not including the sixty-five FHA houses he built; forty commercial buildings of which nine are extant; and seven civic buildings of which three still are standing. Outside of Mobile and the county, thirteen other structures have been documented, some in Alabama, Florida, and Mississippi.[1]

The New Deal, under President Roosevelt, passed many legislative acts to improve the economy of the country. Among these was the Federal Housing Authority that guaranteed loans for low-cost house construction. At this time, C. L. Hutchisson, Jr., was beginning to carry out commissions of his own. He found it a challenge to see how well he could design a building within the government guidelines. Proof of his success can be seen in the large number of his FHA homes that have survived and are prized by their owners, who have kept them in excellent condition. Few have had any changes made from the original construction. There is no duplication in their designs. They vary from small, one-story wood frame bungalows to two-and-a-half-story brick houses. Some have porches, as in figure 138. Others have only a series of steps or a stoop in front of the entrance (figure 139). For some, he invented special architectural features that were patented (now expired), such as the "expansion strip," which he used along the edges of plastered walls where cracking is most like to occur. He first used this device in the Perkinson house at 1610 Lamar Street near the Flo-Claire subdivision. Unless deliberately destroyed by the hand of man or by hurricane, the Hutchisson houses survived both the wear and tear of time and the changing styles.

As might be expected, most of the FHA houses were modestly small, and

FIGURE 139

The Booksch House, 1938. 1922 Hunter Avenue C. L. Hutchisson, Jr., architect. This one-and-a-half-story home stands on a terraced lawn. The steps of the simple stoop entry lead to a door that is framed by pilasters and a pediment whose short returns form the capitals of the pilasters.

FIGURE 140

The Phillips House, 1936. 2056 Dauphin Street. C. L. Hutchisson, Jr., architect. The first of the FHA houses built in Mobile is a modified bungalow-type. Unlike the usual, tapered-wood porch piers of the typical bungalow, the architect designed corner brick piers formed of four shafts joined at the top and bottom by a block of bricks.

FIGURE 141

E. P. Martin House, 1938, 128 South Street. C. L. Hutchisson, Jr., architect. The home is known as the Martin House, since Martin bought the property soon after it was constructed in 1938. It is a two-story, brick veneer building. The first floor windows have an interesting suggestion of the old style with panels that look like jib doors but in reality are casements. The windows of the second story are unusual as they break through the line of the eaves with the crowning molding gently curved like an eyebrow.

designed in one or more of the traditional styles and types, such as bungalows, cottages, American Foursquare and simple Colonial Revival. Some were perfectly plain or had details around the doors that derived from Neoclassical prototypes. This continuing interest in classical detailing was especially true in the deep South, where tradition has always been a dominant characteristic.

The first of C. L. Hutchisson's, Jr., FHA houses was the Phillips bungalow, constructed in 1936. It was also the first FHA home built in Mobile. Located at 2056 Dauphin Street, it is one of the smallest structures and the only one of the group that no longer serves its original purpose. It has been adapted as a chiropractor's office, with the steps divided by an iron railing to assist patients in their ascent (figure 140). The small building is a modified bungalow of simple design, with the gable roof extended over the wide, one-bay porch. Unusual for this type of house are the square, brick, corner piers that support the porch roof. The heaviness of their mass is relieved by the hollow center, which opens up in long, semicircular-headed channels on each of the four faces. The result suggests a group of four slender shafts that rest on a common base and are headed by a common block serving as a uniting capital. Another feature is the brick coursing in the porch balustrade, where a single coursing of bricks, laid as headers set on the vertical, forms a cap for the balustrade.

Two other FHA single-family homes and one apartment have been selected to represent the sixty-five FHA houses he designed. Both houses were constructed in 1938 and are located on South Street. The residence at 128 South Street (figure 141) is a square, two-story house of brick veneer painted white. The house stands on a corner lot that provides ample space for the two two-story rear wings that are connected by an enclosed one-story porch with a balustraded deck. The recessed front entrance on South Street is framed by louvered shutters and is approached by a few low steps. The windows of the first story of the facade are casements over molded panels that suggest jib doors. The windows of the second story are unusual. They project up through the cornice of the roof, suggesting dormers. Their hood moldings that rise above the eaves look like eyebrows. A brick belt course marks the level between the two stories. The name of the original owner has not been found, but the house was bought by E. P. Martin in 1940, just two years after the residence had been completed. The Martin family still owns the property and have kept it in excellent condition.

The Wheeler House is the second 1938 FHA home selected, as it represents the smaller wood frame types. It is located at 188 South Street (figure 142). It is one-and-a-half stories, with a one-story wing extension. The house is raised from sidewalk level by terraces on concrete retaining walls. A porch is located in the southeast bays of the building. Instead of columns, the porch bays are formed by arches resting on brick piers. Somewhat altering the original intent of the architect, these bays have now been infilled with casement windows. The semicircular-headed door was made of vertical boarding with a small window filled with diamond-shaped lights.

FIGURE 142

The Wheeler House, 1938, 188 South Street. C. L. Hutchisson, Jr., architect. The Wheeler House is a good example of the smaller FHA homes. It fits snugly on its small-terraced site. The narrow-arcaded terrace at the south end replaces a porch. One of the characteristics that gives individuality to the architect's FHA homes is the variety of porches and entries that he employed.

FIGURE 143

An apartment house, 1936, 188 South Carlen Street. C. L. Hutchisson, Jr., architect. The coarsely textured brick apartment building is the only FHA. multiple-housing example by C. L. Hutchisson, Jr., that still stands. A two-story central rear wing and the main front section form a T-plan. The simplicity of the facade is given interest by the decorative treatment of the entrance framing.

FIGURE 144

The S. H. Goldman House, 1938, 111 Beverly Court. C. L. Hutchisson, Sr., and C. L. Hutchisson, Jr., architects. This was the last home in which C. L. Hutchisson, Sr., participated in the design.

The FHA apartment building was constructed in 1936. The two-and-a-half-story brick structure stands on a corner lot at 188 South Carlen Street (figure 143). The central bay of the facade projects, forming a pavilion that contains the entrance at the first story and a twin double hung window at the second. This pavilion, with its shadows, gives interest to an otherwise plain design that is symmetrically balanced by an equal number of windows on either side of the entrance pavilion. It is covered by a gable that intersects the main gable at right angles. The small dormers rest low on the roof. As a whole, the design is quite simple, but some details add much to the general effect. The corners of the projecting central bay are quoined. Considerable attention was paid to the main entrance. The single-leaf door has a five-light transom. A double row of six glass panes forms twelve side lights on either side of the door. Above each pair, two glassed openings continue the line of the main transom. The whole doorway is crowned by a projecting architrave that is accented by dentils. Fluted pilasters form the side framing. The short returns of the horizontal cornice in the front bay gable are supported on multiple moldings.[2]

By 1937 some homes were constructed without the aid of the FHA. Among these, C. L. Hutchisson, Jr., designed the 1938 brick home of S. H. Goldman at 111 Beverly Court. It was the last home in which C. L. Hutchisson, Sr., had input (figure 144). The two-story home has the complex brick coursing that characterized several of the buildings by the younger Hutchisson. The roof sections differentiate the various parts of the house as

FIGURE 144B
Detail of doorway of the Goldman House at 111 Beverly Court. The complexity of the brick coursing is evident in the colors and sizes of the bricks in each of the changing contours of the recessed entrance.

was seen in the Meredith House (figure 133) and the Anderson House (figure 134) designed during the Hutchisson, Holmes and Hutchisson years. The asymmetrical plan of the Goldman house is composed of four different sections: the main section under the hip roof; the right cross-wing under a gable roof; the entry with gable; and the extended sun porch on the left covered by a shed-like extension of the main hip. Above this porch is a large dormer whose roof intersects the main hip and shed. The bricks used for the veneered wall are in varied colors and the coursing of the bricks around the entry is given decorative treatment by the way the bricks are laid (figure 144b). The voussoirs of the semicircular entry are accented by elongated bricks that resemble a sunburst pattern. From the entry opening, the wall curves back to a semidome above the doorway. Here the bricks are laid in an unusual way, the arches diminishing in size until they form a blind oculus.

Even more complex brick coursing can be seen in the W. D. Evans home of 1937, at 112 Lanier, Ashland Place. It is a two-and-a-half-story, red brick

ELIZABETH BARRETT GOULD

FIGURE 145

W. D. Evans House, 1937, 112 Lanier, Ashland Place. C. L. Hutchisson, Jr., architect. The brick patterning of the large Evans home is complex, with the variations in the coursing and color forming linear designs on the surface. This two dimensionality of line is balanced by the broken massing of the form and the variations in the roof.

building with wood trim painted a dark brown (figure 145). The facade faces west and is roughly divided into two parts. The northwestern portion is a wide projecting bay that covers almost half of the front elevation. Here, triple double-hung windows are set into a wall in which the horizontal mortar joints of the brick are white and the vertical joints of the brick are colored, resulting in a strong horizontal emphasis. The right, southwest half of the facade contains a small projecting entry that is tucked in the angle between the bay and the recessed right half (figure 145b). The single-leaf door is surrounded by a frame of which the brick heading forms a segmental curve. This brick arch springs from white masonry impost blocks. The keystone is also white, and both imposts and keystone make a sharp accent against the red of the brick. A vertical panel of bricks above the entry gable has two diamond-shaped blocks that repeat the white contrasts. Gables cover the projecting bay, entry, main roof, and the dormers that are located in the roof of the southwestern half of the facade. The barge boards of the dormer gables form a wide ogee arch.

The brick patterning is the most complex of any in the city (figure 145c).

In the bay gable, panels of bricks are set in different patterns. The window sills and lintels are all formed by bricks laid in the vertical as headers and stretchers, respectively. A unifying element in the complexity of the brick coursing is that, except for the window sills, the bricks are laid flat to the plane of the wall

FIGURE 145B
Detail of the entrance. No decorative detailing has been added to the wall surfaces or window. Aesthetic qualities are determined by the coursing and patterning of the bricks and the few structural elements of contrasting color.

FIGURE 145C

Detail of the wing facade of the Evans House showing the complex brick patterning in the gable end.

FIGURE 145D

Chimney detail of the south elevation of the W. D. Evans House. Bricks are laid in horizontal, vertical and diagonal patterns in the wall and double stacks of the chimney. Note the inset brick panel in the chimney base in which the bricks form a chevron pattern.

From Builders to Architects: The Hobart–Hutchisson Six

with no projecting moldings, and the design becomes a two-dimensional pattern of thin lines formed by the mortar joints. The brick coursing in the chimney side of the Evans house is especially notable (figure 145d).

About this same time, C. L. Hutchisson was designing the Neal home in Brewton, Alabama. Though employing varied colored bricks, it has much simpler detailing (figure 146). The brick coursing is done by contrasting the color of the bricks in a Flemish bond pattern in which headers and stretchers alternate in shape and color.[3]

Two of the last prewar buildings commissioned with which Mr. Hutchisson, Jr., had a part were projects under a HUD grant. The Orange Grove community was planned for black residents and was located on the north side of town. On the south side in the Woodlawn subdivision was a housing project for whites. The architects involved were Cooper Van Antwerp, Harry Inge Johnstone, C. L. Hutchisson, Jr., and William March.

The Orange Grove Complex covers the blocks between Bloodgood, Morgan, Jackson, and North Conception Streets, with Joachim Street dividing the area into two parts. The general layout consists of groups of six one-story and seven two-story brick tenements, with open spaces left at strategic locations (figure 147). The buildings are arranged in rows. Each row faces out on a street which provides for off-street parking by extending a shallow curved drive into the narrow front yard of each structure. The backyards are separated by a concrete, public walkway that terminates at each end in one of the open communal areas (figure 147b). The brick buildings are all on concrete slabs and with uniform fenestration. The simplicity of the elevations is relieved by the

FIGURE 146

The Neal House, 500 Douglas Avenue, Brewton, Alabama. C. L. Hutchisson, Jr., architect. A brick home in Brewton in which the two different colored bricks are laid so that the stretchers in a dark color alternate with the headers of a lighter color to form the pattern of the Flemish Bonding.

FIGURE 147

The Orange Grove Housing Complex, 1940. Two blocks bounded by Bloodgood, Morgan, Jackson and South Conception Streets. Johnstone, Hutchisson, Jr., March and Van Antwerp, architects. Designed for the Mobile Housing Board under a grant from the United States Housing Authority, the complex contains both one- and two-story brick buildings with open community areas between the block divisions. Photograph of a street view of one of the sections.

FIGURE 147B

View down the central walkway dividing the properties at the rear.

vertical coursing of the bricks in the rain table and in the molding beneath the eaves. The Orange Grove Complex is constructed for low-income housing for the black community. A similar complex was designed for whites in the Oakdale area, about halfway between the inner city and Brookley Field, a neighborhood now largely integrated.

The Second World War, 1941-1945

During the years that C. L. Hutchisson, Jr., was in the Mobile Unit of the United States Corps of Engineers, Mobile was undergoing an upheaval that permanently changed the city. As a port location, it became a major ship building and aviation center. Alabama Dry Docks, with a government contract for 19,000 ships, and the Gulf Coast Ship Building Company in Chickasaw, where destroyers were constructed, were two of the large ship building companies.

An aviation center was constructed during 1941 at Brookley Field. Here the Army Air Force opened an air service depot and a modification plant. Large bombers from the Asian theater of war were brought to Mobile for repair. To service this center, 17,000 civilians were employed in addition to Air Force personnel.

By 1943 the Alabama Dry Docks was employing 30,000 workers and the Gulf Coast Ship Building Company had 11,600. By the end of 1944, the population of Mobile had been swollen by migrant war workers to 102,000 people.[4] Even before the influx, Mobile was hardly able to service the city with adequate public facilities. In the *Gulf Coast Historical Review*, Mary Martha Thomas wrote that by 1944 the population of Mobile increased by 75 percent.[5]

The housing shortage became critical, and though the government erected sixteen housing units to provide for 11,000 dwellings, it fell short of the growing population needs. Tent cities grew. Shacks were thrown together and people were asked to make every spare room in their homes available. It was at this time that the Lott house (figure 84) was subdivided. During the war years, C. L. Hutchisson, Sr., no longer active in his profession, served as an advisor and as a member of the Mobile Housing Board. C. L. Hutchisson, Jr., was fully employed in the Corps of Engineers and did not carry on a private practice.

From this period, only one building by C. L. Hutchisson, Jr., survives in Mobile — the hangar at Bates Field, now occupied by Aero-One. Before the war, he was commissioned by the City of Mobile to design a hangar at the new Bates Field, now the Municipal Airport. Before the building was completed, the project was stopped, and, with the advent of war, he enlarged his original design for the Corps of Engineers. This hangar still stands at the east end of Bates Field (figure 148). The hangar is constructed of concrete, with an overhanging, shallowly arched roof that was formed of asphalt felt covering corru-

FIGURE 148

The Old Army Corps of Engineers Hangar, 1941-42, east end of the Municipal Airport, Bates Field, now occupied by Aero-One. Originally planned as a hangar for the City of Mobile by C. L. Hutchisson, Jr., it was redesigned and enlarged during World War II when Hutchisson was in charge of the architectural department of the Mobile Division of the United States Army Corps of Engineers.

FIGURE 148B

Interior view of the hangar trussing that supports the arched roof.

gated metal and was manufactured by the H. H. Robertson Metal Roofing Company. The edge of the roof has an outward swing that recalls the roof of the Chinese Gas Station that was designed by Hutchisson, Holmes and Hutchisson in 1938 (figure 137). The building originally had a row of offices along the inside of both the north and south walls. Only those on the north wall are still intact. In 1982 an administration building by a different architect was semi-attached on the south side by Aero-One, a company with a crew of mechanics to service private planes housed in the hangar. Aero-One also runs a training program for private pilots.

The hangar remains in excellent condition and serves as a good example of an early aviation structure. The exterior of the north and south walls is divided into six bays by applied buttresses. The large, six-part sliding doors enclose the building at the east and west ends. At the four corners of the building are bays with recesses into which the doors can be slid when opening the hangar. In the interior, six great trusses support the vaulted roof (figure 148b). High in the walls, clerestory windows admit light into the interior. Later, the inner surface of the vault was covered by boards laid in tongue and groove.

Another building constructed during this period, but not in Mobile, was the Climatic Hangar at Eglin Field, Florida. As an architect for the Corps of Engineers, C. L. Hutchisson, Jr., played an important part in this construction.

Post-World War Years to Retirement in 1967-68

With the close of the war, the inflated number of residents was reduced. By 1946, 55,000 people had left Mobile to return to their original locations. The postwar years left Mobile culturally split between the old residents and the newcomers who remained to make their homes in the city. This was especially true in the middle and upper classes. The old guard wanted to retain much of the former life and the newcomers were intent on developing in other directions. But with all the change that came to the city, the architecture remained essentially conservative.

The influences of Marcel Breuer to the northeast and of Richard Neutra to California did not touch Mobile or the deep South, in general. It was not until 1960 that Paul Rudolph designed the Tuskegee Chapel, breaking with all traditional ecclesiastical norms of the area. In Mobile, even the young architectural graduates of Auburn found it difficult to design in the modern idiom.

It was in this atmosphere that C. L. Hutchisson, Jr., began the last years of his independent career. His first big commission after the war was not a new design but a removal and rebuilding of a historic church, the 1853 Trinity Episcopal Church that had been designed by Willis and Dudley of New York (figure 149). The building originally stood on the northeast corner of Jackson and St. Anthony Streets and was reconstructed at 1900 Dauphin Street during the years 1945-46.[6] The old bricks had to be carefully removed and cleaned before being replaced at the new site. The complex English Gothic Revival detailing of the wood trussing and trim of the nave was marked as to position, tagged with identification labels, and re-established in their original relationship. The delicate cusping of the decorative detailing had to be carefully handled.

The re-erection site provided a good slope, allowing for a basement to be constructed under the rear of the building. C. L. Hutchisson, Jr., with a sensitive appreciation for the original design, insured no disharmony in the addition. The original tower that had been added to the church in 1884 by the New York archi-

FIGURE 149
The re-erected Trinity Episcopal Church, 1945-46, 1900 Dauphin Street. C. L. Hutchisson, Jr., reconstruction architect. The 1853 church was formerly located on the northeast corner of St. Anthony and Jackson Streets. The demolition and reconstruction of the mid-nineteenth century, English-inspired Gothic Revival building was an enormous undertaking. With skill and a sensitive appreciation for the original structure as designed by the New York architects, Willis and Dudley, C. L. Hutchisson, Jr., admirably succeeded in the task.

ELIZABETH BARRETT GOULD

FIGURE 150

Maryvale Public School, 1965, 1901 Maryvale Avenue. Grey and Hutchisson, Jr., architects. A large brick complex with projecting wings is centered by the administration offices. The center bays are approached under a roofed "drop off," a concession to the modern age of the automobile.

tect, Frank Willis, was rebuilt by Hutchisson, but unfortunately the spire was destroyed by Hurricane Frederick in 1979. It was subsequently replaced by one of the new mass-produced steeples of synthetic material.

An extensive alteration that Hutchisson, Jr., carried out was on the Adams Glass building, now destroyed. He removed the top story, gutted the remaining interior and redesigned it to serve new needs. He was the third family member to work on the Southern Express building that had been designed by his grandfather (figure 44). In 1933, he took down the historic old Windsor Hotel, a building of which he had a vivid memory. He used these experiences to study the building methods and the careful craftsmanship of the nineteenth century. This contributed to his success as a restoration architect.

In 1965, the architects Grey and Hutchisson designed the Maryvale School, a large complex at 1901 Maryvale Avenue (figure 150). It illustrates a further development in school planning that was noted in the Tanner Williams School designed by C. L. Hutchisson, Sr. (figure 114). Maryvale is constructed of brick on a concrete slab, one-story in height and with wings projecting both to the sides of the administrative center and to the rear. Provisions are made for parking and a circular drive leads up to a covered "drop off." This entrance has some interesting detailing in an otherwise strictly functional building. The flat-roofed "drop off" is supported by T-shaped concrete piers that have insets of brick paneling harmonizing with the brick coursing of the walls. Special consideration was paid to designing a building that would be as fire-safe as possible, with easy exits in case of need. Since most of the county schools are not air conditioned, adequate ventilation was also an issue. Frequently, construction costs are more than anticipated; however, in the Maryvale School the architects had no cost overrun, but showed a credit balance of $1,500 at the completion of the building.

While Hutchisson was in great demand as a restoration and renovation architect because of his knowledge of historic building methods and his sensitive appreciation of the old styles, he nevertheless was busy designing new homes, especially in the Spring Hill area. For years, Spring Hill had been a summer retreat for Mobilians who escaped the heat of town for the hills of the western suburb. Letters still exist in family collections telling of the treks made to the summer homes — carriages and wagons carrying even dishes and furniture for the season. But as early as 1836, some people built permanent homes in the area, such as the 1836 Beal-Gaillard home and the 1853 Marshall-Hixon home, both still standing.[7]

Over the years, the early five-acre plots of ground first surveyed in 1836 were broken up and rapidly filled with the growing population. By World War II, the area was a thriving community in which there is still an active building program, especially in the western areas.

It was in this section of the city that Hutchisson made his final contribution to Mobile architecture. It is interesting to note that Peter Hobart built close to the waterfront with the 1824-25 county court building, and that successive members of the family were active in each suburb as the city developed to the west, with the last member working in Spring Hill. Beyond Spring Hill is the new area of the city being built up around the University of South Alabama.

The last two buildings selected to show Hutchisson's postwar work are both of brick veneer and in styles typical of Mobile taste. One of the homes is the two-story house of 1947 built for A. P. Ogburn at 28 Hillwood (figure 151). In style, it is a Colonial Revival, standing serene and dignified on its large lot, surrounded by tall pines. Yet, it is typically Hutchisson in the use of colored bricks. The long windows of the first story with six-over-twelve lights contrast with the six-over-six lights of the second story. The door framing with its dentil molding is more clearly defined in the architect's drawing than it is in the photograph (figure 151b). The paneled door with sidelights and transom derive from the nineteenth-century tradition, and the swag in the gable could well have come from some decorative feature of an Adam-designed mantelpiece (figure 151c).

The house has been enlarged since originally designed. Only the central

FIGURE 151

The A. P. Ogburn House, 1947, 28 Hillwood Drive, Spring Hill. C. L. Hutchisson, Jr., architect. In contrast with the complexity of the Evans House, the Ogburn House is the quiet of the classically inspired. The one-bay entry porch with its columns and the dentil coursing along the gable rake are traditional in design.

FIGURE 151B

The architect's drawing of the front elevation of the Ogburn House shows the house as it was originally designed before the addition of the one-story wings.

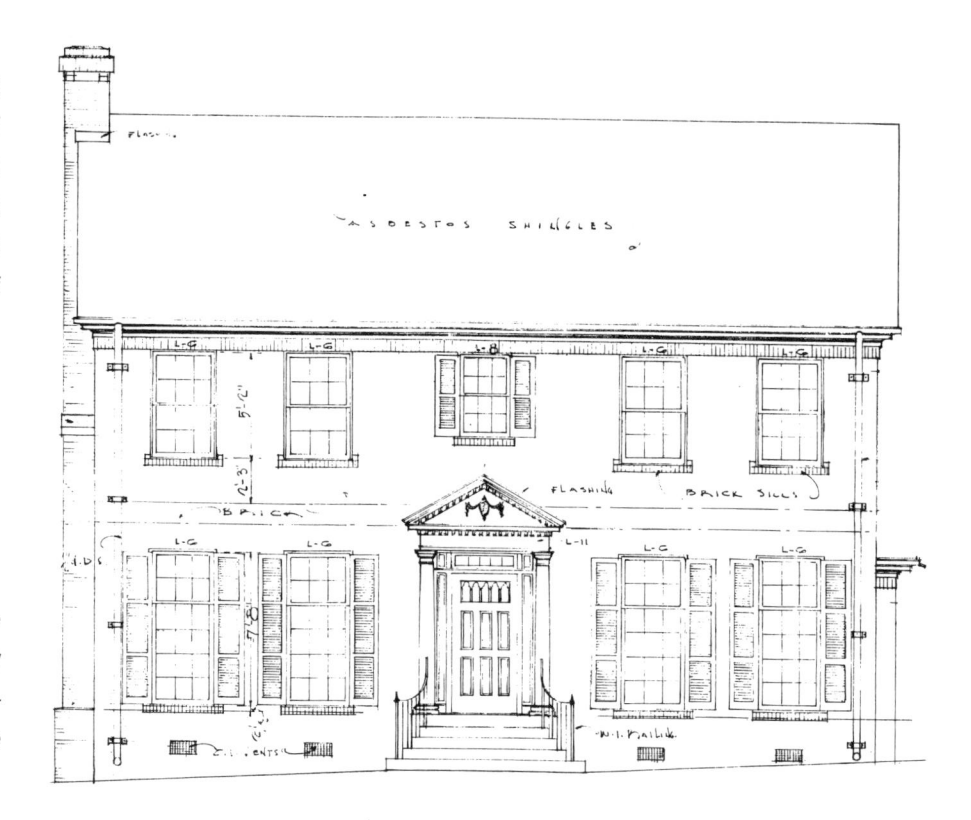

FIGURE 151C

The drawing of the Ogburn House doorway illustrates the refinements designed by the architect.

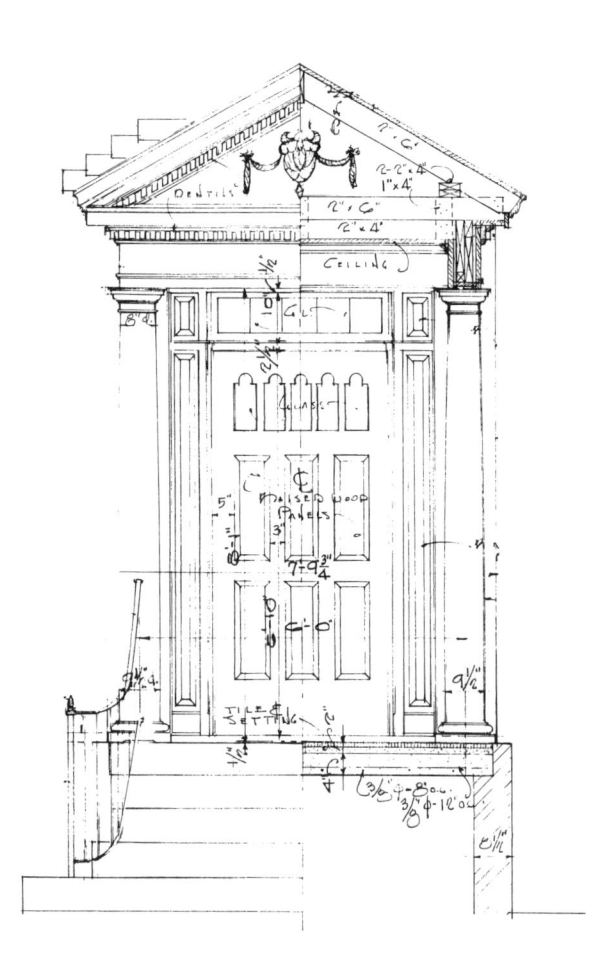

FIGURE 152

Portrait of C. L. Hutchisson, Jr., taken in 1992, the last member of the generations of the Hobart-Hutchisson family of builder-architects who worked in Mobile from 1797 to 1967.

From Builders to Architects: The Hobart–Hutchisson Six

section was shown in the 1947 plan. The first floor consists of a central hall with living room and tile-floored, living-room porch on the left. On the right of the hall is the dining room, a tile-floored breakfast room, kitchen and utility rooms. The two wings, added, one on each side, blend in with the brick work of the original. The large wing on the right has its axis perpendicular to that of the main section and is connected to the older portion by a one-bay passageway. A multiple-paned window fronts this wing and overlooks the wide expanse of lawn in front of the home.

In 1967, C. L. Hutchisson, Jr., (figure 152) designed his last home. It was built for J. D. Quinlivan, for whom both C. L. Hutchisson, Jr., and his father constructed the Crystal Ice Company in Mobile and a branch in Bayou Le Batre. The house is difficult to photograph, since it is on top of several terraces, surrounded by shrubbery, and shaded by large trees (figure 153). The large lot is on the corner of McGregor Street and Springbank Road in Spring Hill. The house is approached by a series of brick steps that cut through the brick-walled terraces, a detail also planned by the architect.

The one-and-a-half-story residence is much larger than it appears from the south-facing facade. The plan extends to the rear, along McGregor Street, with a connector to a large den that runs transversely to the main axis of the building. A bedroom extends to the east behind the den. The rooms are large and the entrance hall is twelve feet wide. Forty pages of drawings for the home are still in the family archive.

The walls are built of subtly variegated brick veneer. Three unfluted Tuscan-Doric columns support each of the outer corners of the porch gable (figure 153b). The columns are matched at the wall by two similar pilasters, with columns standing in front of them. Dentil courses articulate both the raking cornice of the porch and the eaves of the main roof that run parallel to the

FIGURE 153

The J. D. Quinlivan House, 1967, 3908 South Springbank Road, Spring Hill. C. L. Hutchisson, Jr., architect. The last large home designed by C. L. Hutchisson, Jr., was built for the Quinlivan family, for whom he and his father had done other structures. It is a handsome, brick residence built on a high-terraced lot and shaded by large trees and plantings. The plan forms an "L" with a long rear extension in which the den runs at right angles to the main axis of the house.

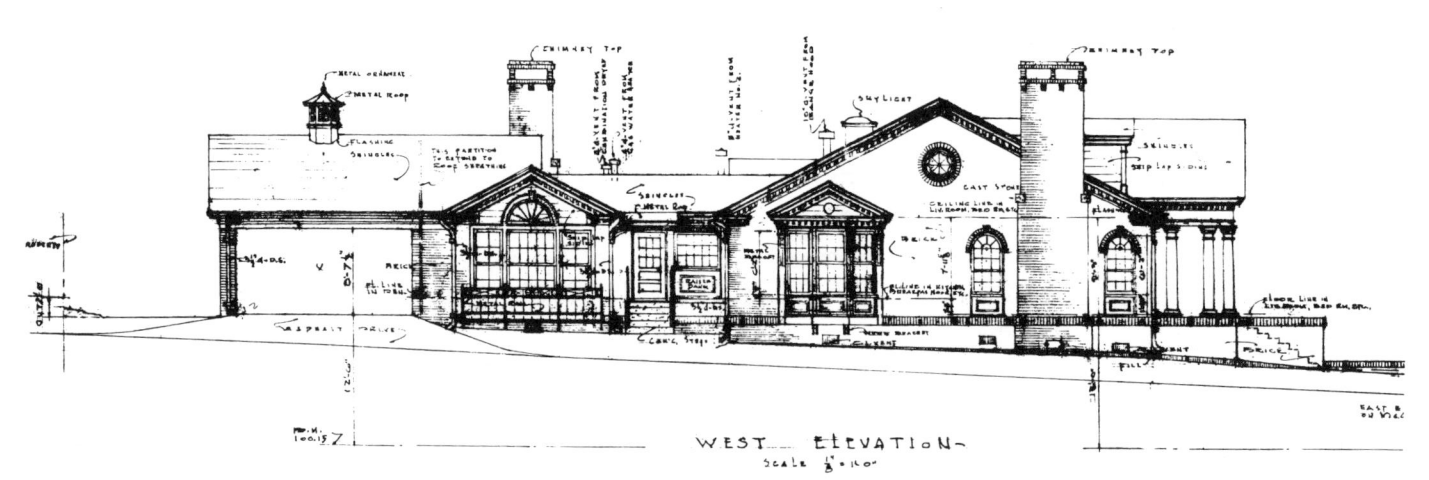

FIGURE 153B

Architect's drawings of the front (south) and the side elevations of the J. D. Quinlivan House. The upper drawing shows the front porch with living room windows on the left and the bedroom windows on the right. The lower drawing shows the west side elevation with the living room, the bay window of the dining room, a side entry and the Palladian window of the breakfast room off the kitchen. A later den replaced the porte-cohere shown in the drawing.

street. The double-leaf front door has glass lights in the upper half, with molded blind panels below. A wide, oval transom extends over both doors and side lights, a design derived from the Federal style. An oculus is centered in the pediment of the porch gable, as is the case with all the gable ends (figure 153c). The dormer windows are semicircular-headed, and framed on either side by unfluted Tuscan pilasters. The main windows of the house are also semicircular-headed with the central keystone in white marble contrasting with the brick voussoirs (figure 153d). This treatment is elaborated in the Palladian window on the west elevation (figure 153e).

The house measures 180 feet front by 92 feet deep. In plan, the central hall is divided, half is eight feet wide but opens up to a cross-hall and then continues in a large rear hallway sixteen feet wide. The rear wall of this section has a large, bowed-window that overlooks a courtyard with a barbecue facility. To the left of the front hall is the living room with a fireplace and a fine mantelpiece. To the right extends the bedroom wing that is entered by a cross-hallway that extends the full width of the house. Behind the living room and

FIGURE 153C

The bay window of the dining room of the Quinlivan House. Details of the porch are adapted to the bay window design.

FIGURE 153D

The Palladian window of the breakfast room in the Quinlivan House with lower panels hidden by shrubbery.

cross-hall is the dining room with the three-sided window shown in figure 153c. The details of this triple-sided window repeat the design of the entablature of the front porch. Next, on the west is the kitchen with unusually well-designed accommodations for storage and cabinets. The left section of the kitchen has a breakfast nook on the outer wall of which is the Palladian window seen in figure 153d. A large room with a fireplace has been added to the west, opening onto the courtyard.

In the last house designed by a Hutchisson, only the finest of available materials were used. This solidly constructed brick home, adapted to the needs of the client and the site, brings to a close the Hutchisson tradition of good design and excellent craftsmanship. It is a fitting tribute to the history of one family of builder-architects who influenced a city from 1797 to 1967. C.L. Hutchisson, Jr., retired a

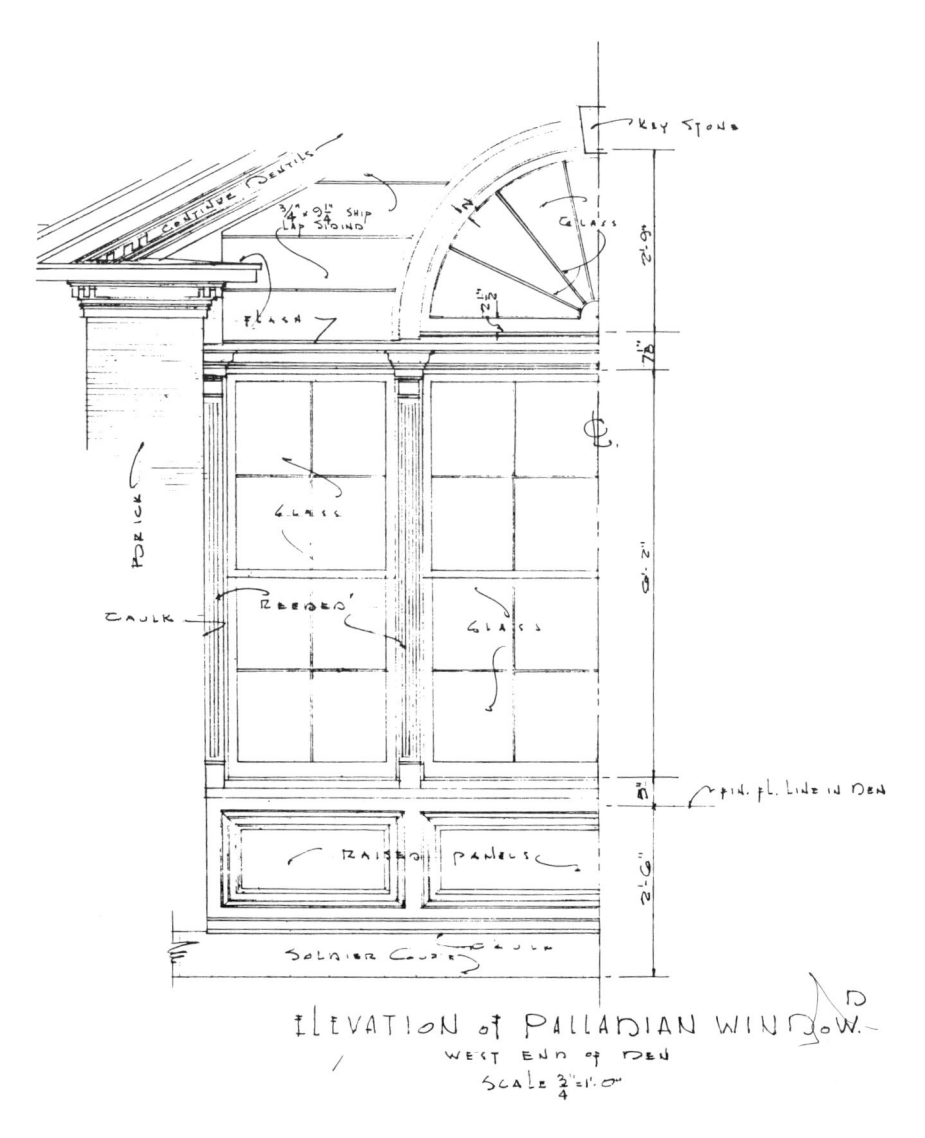

FIGURE 153E
Architect's drawing of the Palladian window details.

few years after the construction of the Quinlivan home. He died December 18, 1993.

Each member of the family lived through a crucial age in the history of the United States that affected their lives and their work. C. L. Hutchisson, Jr.'s., great, great, great grandfather came to Mobile in the age of the sailing vessel and stage coach, bringing to a primitive fort town its first classically inspired courthouse. His great, great, grandfather contributed his skill to building the early steam-powered river boats and housing for an emerging commercial city. His grandfather made the transition in building styles from the pre-Civil War days to the developments of the new South, using the emerging material of iron for both structure and porch details. His great uncle's career saw the coming of steel and the expansion of railroads throughout the United States. His skill is seen in the residential areas of the expanding city. His father's life and work coincided with the automobile age which affected the commercial world and brought about rapid expansion of the suburbs. In both areas his father contributed a lifetime of construction. C. L. Hutchisson, Jr., the last of the line, designed the first city airplane hangar at Bates Field, lived through the lean FHA housing years, and completed his career with the Quinlivan home in Spring Hill. This is a unique record of one family of builder-architects.

APPENDIX

Excerpts and copies of contracts in the Appendixes follow the format of the originals. Since there were no rules for punctuation or for the use of capital letters in the contracts, both were used at the discretion of the individual scribes. In copying the contracts, these idiosyncrasies have been incorporated. Also the double "s" was often signified by the "F" sign.

EBG

Appendix 1

Historical records from the American State Papers 1789-1838, Public Lands, Vol. III, pp. 12-13, place Peter House Hobart in Mobile in 1797. [See line 29 in the illustration below.]

Appendix 2

Contract, Frame Store, constructed on a lot 36'x120', located on the sw corner of Dauphin and Royal. The lot was not owned but rented for $125.00 per year in a ten-year lease.
Misc. Bk. A/13-14, March 18, 1817
James Innerarity, owner; Th. Kellogg of the Mississippi Territory, Builder.

— will complete on the above premises one good framed building of the dimensions of twenty two feet in width on the front on Royal by 45 feet in depth, bounded easterly by — brick foundation of at least five layers and two bricks thick: that it shall be two stories in height besides the garrett and that the lower and second stories may each be at least eleven feet high, that the whole building shall be throughly framed and well braced, that the Sills, Sleepers, Joists, Posts, Braces, Rafters shall be of fully sufficient strength and as stout dimensions as are usual in buildings of this size, and that all the material used shall be of the best quality and the lumber free of sap or defects, that the Building will be covered with shingle Roof, the shingles to be of Juniper or Cypress of Eighteen Inches long by four to six Inches broad, shaved at both ends and perfectly tight, that the wall of the lower story shall be filled in with brick or moss and clay mortar between the posts and shall be ceiled inside with plank & that the whole building shall be weatherboarded with half inch quartered [?] board neatly painted with at least two coats of paint, and completed and finished in a workmanlike manner — and that said Theron Kellogg — shall have the building fully completed by eighteen months from and after the date here of the aforesaid business shall be fully completed.

[To clarify the reading of the first contract, commas have been placed in the original "run-on" sentences. Courtesy of the UAP.]

Appendix 3

Misc. Bk. B, pp. 42 ff Contract for the County Courthouse

August 30, 1825

Commissioners of the County of Mobile by William Hale, Benjamin Smoot and Isaac Johnson of the first part and Peter H. Hobart and Lewis Judson of the County of Mobile, parties of the second part.:

that the parties of the second part for and in consideration of the covenants herein after mentioned to be done and performed on the part of the parties of the first part do covenant and agree to and with the said parties of the first part that the said Peter H. Hobart shall on or before the first day of September in the year of our Lord, one thousand eight hundred and twenty six, at his own proper coste and charges, erect, build, complete and finish a Courthouse for the County of Mobile according to the specifications written to wit:

The size of the building to be seventy five feet long by fifty feet broad. The foundations to be three inch plank laid transversely. Whole height of the walls to be thirty four feet. The stories to be divided in the following manner to wit Basement story to be five feet high to the top of the first floor and the walls to be three bricks thick. First story to be twelve feet in the clear and the walls thereof to be two and one half bricks thick, the Second story to be fifteen feet in the clear and the walls thereof to be three Bricks thick, the Gable ends to be one and a half bricks thick and raised to a pitch proportionate to the building and the roof to be covered with the best Welch Slate. The partition walls, say two walls across the whole length of the building to be one and a half bricks thick in the basement Story and two walls across the building of the first story of the same thickness as the walls across the basement story. The building to have two fireplaces, the one in the Orphan's Courtroom and one in the principal room in the second Story. The building is to have one room in the center thereof of forty two feet and five rooms on the sides that is to say three rooms on one side and two rooms on the other with doors leading from each room to the centre room, One leading from the Sheriff's Office to the room in the rear of it. Three doors in front of the building say one large door leading to the center room with side and fan lights, eliptic heads, one to each end room with square heads and Transom lights, The second story to be divided into four rooms, one of which to be fifty eight feet to be used as the principal Court Room, the others to be of equal size and taken off the west end of the building with doors leading from each to the principal room, one larger door in the center of the front leading from the Court Room to the piazza. The whole number of windows to be twenty eight double hinged sash of twenty four lights each, of twelve inches by fifteen with marble heads and sills. The floors to be of one and a fourth inch plank tongued and groved. The base and trimming of the doors and windows to be done in a neat style corresponding to the style of the rest of the building. All the doors to be pannelled, also the window shutters of the windows of the lower story to be pannelled. A platform in the rear of the large lower room and stairs to run each way from it to the second story. The timbers employed in the floors and roof to be substantial and of good heart pine. Four turned posts in the large room below for the support of the second floor. Two story piazza projecting pediment from the roof in front of the building of twenty feet long and to extend eight feet from the front with steps and railing leading up each side of it to the large door in the center. A neat fence to extend from the foot of the railing to the end of the building. The Columns for the support of the piazza to be of brick and plaistered with Roman cement and to extend to the roof. The whole of said building to be plaistered with three coats inside.

———

Peter Hobart shall at his own proper costs and charges provide the material——and shall complete in the same workmanship manner

———

in consideration of the sum of $13,000

$5000.00 to be paid on the first day of January next

$5000.00 to be paid on the first day of January, 1827

$3000.00 to be paid on the first day of January, 1828

———

the basement to be finished on or before the first day of January next.

Appendix 4

Building Contracts for James F. Hutchisson (1838-1852)

Misc. Book	Date	Owner	Building
C/52-53	Jan. 17, 1838	Aaron Livingston	Cabin on the steamer, *Tallapoosa*; $1,200.00
C/86-87	April 6, 1838	Oliver Pittfield	Frame House, 1 story; Conception Street south of Canal; with specs.; $650
C/159/160	Aug. 24, 1838	James Sills	Frame House, 1 story; Bayou Street between Government and Dauphin; $675
C/160-162	Aug. 24, 1838	George Patterson	Frame House, 1 story; Bayou Street between Government and Dauphin; $725
C/162-163	Aug. 5, 1838	Barth Skates	Frame House, 1 story; Bayou Street between Government and Dauphin; $675
C/184-185	Oct. 3, 1838	C. S. Hale	Frame House, 1 story; St. Francis Street across from the Church; Plan and specs; $1,300
C/311-313	June 7, 1839	Edward O'Connor	Frame House with outbuildings; Dauphin Rd., west of City Limits; specs; $3,350
D/85-86	July 19, 1840	M. Eslava and A. Dumée	Warehouse, brick, 2 story; specs; Block of Water, Commerce, Monroe & Eslava; $16,250
D/152-153	Feb. 20, 1841	John Marshall	Store/Dwelling, 2 story; Jackson Street; $3,350
D/153-154	Feb. 22, 1841	James Burns	Store/Dwelling, 2 story, with cellar and passageway between double complex; specs; $5,000
D/173-174	Mar. 3, 1841	A. Dumée	Double store and dwelling with passageway; w.s. Water St. between Monroe and Eslava; specs
D/344-345	July 6, 1842	A. C. Wilson	Cabin on steamship; specs; $1,842
E/388-389	July 24, 1849	Charles Cullum	2 story brick addition, Mansion House, Conti St.
E/453-0455	May 1850	Second Contract	specs; $7,000
E/474	May 29, 1850	Jobu Carter	2 frame, 1 story with kitchen; Franklin St. between Government & Church; $1,600
F/11	Oct. 2, 1852	J. Bloodgood	3, 2-story kitchens 15x30 ft.; Orange Grove area
F/41	Dec. 30, 1852	Mathew Anderson	Brick house; NW cor. Church & Lawrence; $1,500

Appendix 5

Contract, cottage, one story frame
Misc.Bk. C/86-87; April 6, 1838
J. F. Hutchisson, architect-builder for Oliver Pittfield
On Conception Street, south of Canal.
Excerpts from contract:

— of the following size and description 24 ft front and rear and 20 ft deep with a gallery of six feet in depth in front of the building to be one Storie high, said Story to be nine feet in the clear, said house to have one front room with front door and transom sash over it leading to gallery, one door leading to front bedroom and one door leading to rear of house in dining room without transom sash overhead. These three Doors are to be panneled doors, to have one window of 10 by 14 glass 12 lights, Chimney piece, washboards.— The front bedroom to have two windows of the same size as front Room with a batten door leading to hall way or Dining Room, to have windows and doors Cased throughout, — There will be a small room partition off on the opposite side of the rear bedroom for Pantrie or Clossett as the said Pittfield may designate, the lower floor laid thruout with good inch and a quarter floor plank Tongued and groved and the upper floor laid of ruff inch boards as far as is necessary under the rafters, to be weatherboarded on one side and each way on the Rear as far as the steps with ruff weatherboarding not plained, the opposite being the south side to have the weatherboarding plained. Corresponding with the front which is to be plained, also the gallery overhead will be Ceiled with half inch weatherboarding, Plained Tongued and Groved. The front of gallery to have a wooden Cornice. The gallery supported by five turned Collums, Rail and Bannisters, to have front and rear steps leading to yard —

[The contract stated that the builder was to furnish all the materials including hardware but that the owner, Mr. Pittfield would have the piers erected in the foundation and be responsible for the chimneys. $650.00]

Appendix 6

Contract Misc. Bk. C pp. 184-185, plan drawn on p. 183; October 3, 1838. James F. Hutchisson, for C. S. Hale.

The cottage was located on St. Francis Street. Excerpt:

— 36 feet front and 28 feet deep with a Gallery 7 feet in depth on the front of the building furnished with 6 ten inch pillars a bannister & railing and a suitable flight of Steps to ascend said Gallery. Said house to be erected on 22 brick pins 3 1/2 ft high and to have one double chimney with two fire places below, for two front rooms and two in the Garret, Said house is to be one Story high 11 feet clear in the rooms - having two front doors suitably panneled & finished, also two windows in front and three on each end Containing twelve panes of glafs 10x16 - also two Garret windows Containing the Same number of panes 6x10. Two rooms on the base of the building, one in front sixteen feet square, the other in rear twelve by thirteen feet and to be finished in good Style - the rooms having a fire place is to be furnished with a chimney piece, Two panneled doors on one side and one in rear Connecting with the back Room, Wash boards painted & plastered with two Coats, the other room to be finished in a Similar Manner with the exception of a fire place, having only the aforesaid door for communication and an outer door leading to the back of the building. There is also to be another back door from the unfinished part of the house, In other respects the whole of the western part of the building is to be finished to wit Shingles, weatherboards and properly painted and the outer doors are to be finished with transom lights the remainder unfinished.

The whole materials for the above building are to be furnished by said Hutchisson and to be such as are of good quality and suitable for the purpose for which they are appropriated Said Hutchisson also further agrees to complete said building agreeable to the above description in or before the seventh day of November next under a forfeiture at the rate of two hundred dollars per month according to the time the work delayed.

[There followed the business agreement in which Mr. Hale promised to pay Hutchisson $1300 in installments: $700 on laying the frame, $500 on the first of December, $500 on the first of April in the year 1839.]

A portion of the contract between Hutchisson and C. S. Hale, showing their signatures and seals.

Appendix 7

Contract Misc. Bk. D, pp. 173-174. Contract for a store-residence with kitchen dependencies. Miguel D. Eslava and A. S. Dumée, owners, and James F. Hutchisson, builder. March 3, 1841, located on the west side of Water Street between Monroe and Eslava Streets.

Specifications for a building to be erected on the west side of Water Street between Eslava and Monroe Streets. Sizes. The main building to be of brick covered with Slate, to be fifty two feet in front and fifty feet deepth in the clear, to be divided into two stores and a corridor, the corridor to be nine feet, the first story to be (13) thirteen feet between the floor and ceiling, second Story divided into two tenements, the south side divided into 4 rooms and one corridor, the north side into 3 rooms and one corridor and twelve feet between the main building and the kitchens to be covered the same size as the kitchens and the stairs which lead to the second floor to be in said space, the kitchens to be two, divided by the continuation of the wall which divides the two stores of the main building. The kitchens to be two stories high each (28) twenty eight feet by (12) twelve feet divided into two rooms below and two rooms upstairs. The first story to be eleven feet high between floor and joists. The second story to be 10 feet between floor and ceiling walls. Walls. All walls to be 1 1/2 bricks thick except the walls forming the second story of the kitchens and the gable ends of the main building above the second story which may be one brick thick, the south dividing wall to extend (36) thirty six feet further west than the main building wall and be eight feet high. All the bricks used in this building to be good hard Mobile bricks, the mortar to be made with gritty sand and good lime in the porportion of one Bbl to each thousand bricks used, the front piers and walls to be made with good smooth Mobile bricks and white mortar, Straight joints, the foundations to begin two feet below the floor and to be footed four courss on & two thicknesses of boat plank. Floors. The floors to be on a level with the warehouse opposite, laid on good hard brick well laid in sand and double floor, first to be 1 1/4 inch thick rough and top planks to be 7 + 1 1/4 inches plained and jointed, the first floor of the kitchens to be paved with good hard bricks and laid so as to stand without plank floor on the top, the second floor of the main building to be 7 + 1 1/4 inch planks, plained, tongued and grooved. Joints. to be 2 1/2 + 10 inches 16 inches apart from center to center, rimmers to be double joists, the floor of the second story of Kitchens to 7 + 10 inch plained, tongued and grooved, joists to be 2 1/2 + 8 inches 16 inch apart from center to center and extending out to form a gallery in front 4 feet wide which is to be floored with seven inch stuff plained and jointed and faced in front with railing and banisters, all stuff used for floor and joists to be good stuff mainly clear of sap and knots and that for gallery to be clear stuff. Openings. The front doors of stores to be six in number, three to each store, to be 5 + 10 double sash 2 1/2 inches thick with portable shutters, the front door of corridor to be double door, imitating the front door (the outside) on stores, the back doors of stores, one to each to be a sash door, with portable shutters also one window back of each store 12 + 16 glass 15 lights with shutters, all the windows of the second story, nine in all, to be 12 + 16 glass 15 light, there will be two doors with transoms at rear of second story for entrance from the landing of stairs, there will be six panel doors in south side 3 feet four inches by eight but with transoms and five doors same size with same transom for the north side, the window frames are to be made with hanging Styles, so that blinds may be adapted hereafter, without extra work, there will be four doors to coll kitchen of 3 feet 6 inches by 7 feet high to be batten doors and four windows in all to each to be 8 +10 glass 12 lights. Chimneys. There will be six fire places in the main building, two of which will be below, the four upstairs to have good mantles in imitation of marble, mantles to be painted black and four in the kitchens, two large ones below and two smaller above. Stairs. The stairs to lead to second story of the main building to be in the space of eight feet between the kitchens and the main building, to have risers, hand rails and bannisters, the stairs for the kitchens to be without risers but with hand rails and rails in lieu of banisters. Finish. The Caps of the first story to be 7 inches beveled, door and window casings to be plain, Caps of second story to be 7 inches with 3/4 beed and all the casings to have 1/2 inch beed, the partitions to be studded 3 + 4 inches plastered. Roof. The roofs to be slate, main building 13 feet pitch with one scuttle for each tenement, the eaves to extend 3 to 4 inches out of the front and rear, to have tin sizeable gutters and leaders, the roof of the kitchens and space between the building to have 7 feet pitch and extend over the gallery and leders, all the gutters to be held with good strong hooks and secured to the hooks by wire. Plastering. The whole of building to have two coats of plastering, white finish inside except the kitchens which will be whitewashed below with one coat of plastering whitewashed to the ceiling and one coat of plastering to walls and ceiling smooth and whitewashed to the second story. The ceiling of gallery of kitchens to be plastered too coat works. Painting. All the front doors to be painted two coats grained imitating sap wood and varnished, all the inside work and outside banisters and window and door frames to be painted two coats of pure white lead, all the outside wood work and gutters and leaders to be painted two coats lead colour, the Caps also to be painted two coats lead colour and mantle to be black N. B. The 3rd floor to extend 10 feet in the middle of garret, the well hole to be stopped by a batten trap and the Steps leading to it to be portable; zinc must be used to cover the scuttle and be of one single piece and overlap the frame which will form the scuttle hole to be at least 8 inches above the roof in the upper part and so lined outside that no water can possibly get through the scuttle. the wall which divides the two stores and two kitchens to be all the way 1 1/2 bricks and extend two feet above the roof of the main building and kitchen and to be caped. Fastenings. All the locks for the upper part to be 7 inch locks and each store to have 9 inch lock, the locks to be used to be Carpenter or at least as good in quality, the doors below to be hung with Clark's patent 6 + 6 butt hinges, a three foot monkey bolt to each store opening and two 12 inch bolts also to each store opening, the hinges for the gate or nine foot door to be strongly fitted in the wall when building and the necessary fastenings put to it to hold it closed. W. B. Fire places to have a space of two feet in front paved with good northern brick, the Privy to be made of wood, 8 + 8 divided into two apartments for each tenement with doors to each division neatly finished and painted outside, the pit to be curbed with wood and eight feet deep and two feet each way narrower than the house. the house to be ten feet high with a ventilator in the roof. In presence of A. J. Dumée. Mobile, M. D. Eslava, Jas. F. Hutchisson

This indenture made the 3rd day of March, 1841, between Miguel D. Eslava of the first part and James F. Hutchisson of the second part, both of City and County of Mobile, and State of Alabama. Witnessed that, in consideration of the payment herein after mentioned to be made by the said M. D. Eslava to the said James F. Hutchisson convenent and agrees to build, put up and finish a double house and kitchen on a lot situated on the west side of Water Street between Eslava and Monroe in the City of Mobile and according to the specifications herein annexed, marked and dated the same date as these permits and signed by the parties. to identify them with three permits all the materials to be furnished by James F. Hutchisson and that none but the best material shall be used in the construciton of there in mentioned building, the work to be done faithfully and completed on or before the first day of July next ensuing under a penalty for failure of doing, forfeiting to the profit of said M. D. Eslava the sum of ten dollars a day for each and every day delay in finishing and completing said work on building after the day of July next, and forfeiting, if any, to be retained by M. D. Eslava the sum of ten dollars a day for each and every day of delay in finishing and completing said work on building after the day of July next, and forfeiting, if any, to be retained by M. D. Eslava from and if moneys to be paid by said M. D. Eslava to Jas. F. Hutchisson, and Miguel D. Eslava on his part agrees to pay to the said Jas. F. Hutchisson for the said work well and faithfully done and performed, the sum of six thousand dollars in the manner following: $500 when the walls are about 8 feet high, $500 when the work is about the second floor, a note of A. I. Jude dated the 21st of October, 840, to the order of Bartelly Waring due and payable 10/13 of June, 1841 for $1000, one thousand dollars when the roof is going on, the Balle say four thousand dollars work is completed, in the following manner, to say $432.93 four hundred and thirty two dollars 93/100 in cash ans a note of B. Cutta dated Febuary 10th, 1840 at 18 months, to the order of M. D. Eslava for the sum of $1120, eleven hundred and twenty dollars and a note by William Anderson dated, April 10th, 1840 @ 21 M/date to the order of M. D. Eslava for $2447.07, two thousand four hundred and forty seven and 07/100, in the presence of words that said Jas. F. Hutchisson interlined above the sixth line before sealing.

A. S. Dumée

M. D. Eslava

Jas. F. Hutchisson

Received in Office for Record, March 18th, 1841.

Appendix 8

The list of the standing buildings designed by James H. Hutchisson. The number in parentheses after the name of the building designates the page number from the Diaries of 1885, 1886. The Diaries are located at the University of South Alabama Archives.

1) 1869. The Creole Fire Station Number I, 15-17 North Dearborn Street.
2) 1872-1887. The facade of the Cathedral of the Immaculate Conception, 4 South Claiborne Street.
3) 1872. The Bernstein House, 355 Government Street. Now the City Museum.
4) 1872, 1885. St. Bridget's Church, Whistler, Alabama, 3625 W. Main Street. Spire built 1885 (7).
5) 1874. St. Vincent de Paul, 454 Charleston Street. Renamed the Church of the Prince of Peace.
6) 1883. Hanlon Cottage, 202 South Royal.
7) 1884. The Perryman House, 1000 Dauphin Street.
8) 1884. Dr. Mastin's Office, ne corner Conti and Joachim Streets. Now the building is numbered 9-11.
9) 1884. AME Zion Church, 502 State Street. Only the facade and entry bay belong to the Hutchisson period.
10) 1885. Whiting Ames Cottage (81), 907 Dauphin Street.
11) 1885. Spring Hill College Refectory (89), Spring Hill College. The structure is now the Fine Arts Building.
12) 1885. Anne Williams House (94), 552 Eslava Street.
13) 1885. The South building of the Convent of the Visitation (95 ff). Considerable detail is given in the Diary.
14) 1886. The Turner Building (114). 209 Dauphin Street.
15) 1886. The Dunn Cottage (129), 206 South Royal Street.
16) 1886. Spring Hill College Infirmary (142), east building on the Quadrangle. May be a part of the present Moore Hall.
17) 1887. Junger Building (74, 173), Corner of Government and Jefferson Streets. Hutchisson seems to have built an earlier building for Junger and then either enlarged it or constructed a new one.
18) 1887. Christ Chapter House (128), corner of Conception and Church Streets.

There is a possibility that Mr. James H. Hutchisson has two other buildings still standing. In the 1885 Diary he lists a brick building on the east side of Conception Street, one north of Government Street. This is the location of the rear wing of the Eslava-Zaphiris building that is known to have had the long wing added some time after the original 1850s building. Hutchisson's building was ordered by Mr. Yuille.

In 1887, numbers 174 and 175 of the master list of his works, he records two cottages for a Gonzales located on Canal and Warren, and Canal and Cedar. One of these still stands but it was in deteriorating condition when inspected on the original street survey.

In summary, of the eighteen verified standing buildings: four are cottages; two are houses; eight are religious structures; four are miscellaneous.

ELIZABETH BARRETT GOULD

Appendix 9

Obituary notice of James H. Hutchisson, August 26, 1887.

DEATH OF CAPTAIN JAMES H. HUTCHISSON

Captain James H. Hutchisson died yesterday afternoon at 6 o'clock, after a lingering illness.

He was the son of the late James F. Hutchisson, who was a prominent builder in his day, and who was at one time sheriff of this county. The subject of this sketch served an apprenticeship under his father, and became expert in the trade of a house builder. He was born in New York at [sic] 1830, but came here with his father at the age of twelve years. He was active in his trade until the war broke out, and at once he enlisted in Battery B, Alabama State Artillery, and served with gallantry at Shiloh. Later he was transferred to Mobile and promoted to a lieutenancy, and later to a captaincy, and to the command of Battery McIntosh. He served also in command of the outer works for the defence of the city.

After the war he resumed his work as a builder, but in 1866 abandoned the trade and devoted himself exclusively to the profession of architect, in which he achieved an immediate success, and for twenty years designed many of the most prominent buildings in Mobile and vicinity. Among these are St. Vincent's Church, the later additions to Spring Hill College, to the Convent of the Visitation, etc. He was an excellent designer, and his work was always satisfactory.

The deceased was a prominent fireman. He signed as member of Fire Company No. 3 on the 8th of February, 1853, and was afterwards foreman of that company. In 1855 he was elected second assistant chief under A. M. Quigley. In 1856 he was chosen first assistant under J. F. Jewett, and in 1857 was elected chief. Under him was D. Gerow, first assistant, and Chris Smith, second assistant. Capt. Hutchisson was one of the original organizers of Fire Company No. 9 on the 2nd of April, 1866.

His wife was Miss M. M. Steele, of this city, and she, with two daughters and four sons, survives to mourn the loss of a kind husband and good father.

Captain Hutchisson was a man among men, of excellent traits of character, generous, brave and courteous. He was a tireless worker, and being endowed with an iron constitution he performed prodigies of labor, often sitting up all night to complete some special piece of work. Such practice had, no doubt, much to do with bringing on this last, and almost the only illness of his life. He leaves a host of friends who will long cherish a memory of his warm heart and amiable disposition.

The funeral will take place at the residence of the deceased at half-past four o'clock this afternoon.

Appendix 10

An example of the type of information included in the 1885 Diary of James H. Hutchisson. The original is in the University of South Alabama Archives. A copy is in the Special Collections Division of the Mobile Public Library.

June

1 Made drawings for the mantles at the Convent

3 Received orders for plans for Dick Roper and for Warren Hirsh. Received cash from College, $50.00

4 Worked on plans for Tabor

6 C. Bancroft ordered plans for dwelling

Received cash from Convent for $150.00

8 Completed plans for Tabor

9 Worked on plans for Bancroft

10 Worked on plans for Bancroft

11 Worked on plans for Bancroft and McDonald

Had call from MacMillan [also McMillan] in Stockton for plans for residence [This house is still standing. EBG]

[Hutchisson has several references to travel to towns outside of Mobile to carry on his architectural practice. He records traveling by river steamer, usually taking two days for each way of the journey. With our modern ease of travel, it is easy to forget it was much different in 1885. See notation for June 26. In September he took four days for a trip to Sheffield, Alabama. This house is still standing. EBG]

12 Worked on plans for McDonald

13 Same [EBG]

15 Same [EBG]

16 Cash from McDonald, $25.00

17 Made sketch for Dr. Heustis [He worked on plans for Heustis until July 29, EBG]

18 Began plans for Roper

Worked on plans for MacMillan

19 Worked on plans for MacMillan

20 Gave plans to Bancroft

Received cash from Dr. Michael $30.00 and $50.00 [This was work for Hygeia Hotel, at Citronelle]

Received cash from Goelet, $24.00

22 Worked on plans for Roper

23 Received order for stairs at the Bascomb Race Track

Orders for a church spire from Father O'Reilly

Worked on plans for MacMillan and Roper.

24 Call from Raulston. Wants to discharge Rudolph Benz and wants me to continue with the house. I declined.

26 Made plans to visit residence of Mrs. Jewett, 100 miles up the Tombigbee River. [Subsequent to this note, on July 2nd he left Mobile at 7 in the evening on the steamer, the *May Elizabeth*, arriving the next day at 1:15 p.m. EBG]

27 Worked on plans for Heustis

28 Worked on plans for Heustis

29 Worked on plans for Heustis

Appendix 11

Summary of the work of James H. Hutchisson for the Convent of the Visitation, as taken from his 1885 Diary. The original Diary is at the University of South Alabama Archives.

JANUARY

10 Began plans for church at Convent.

13-31 Worked on plans for the Church at the Convent.

FEBRUARY

2-5 Worked on plans for the Church at the Convent.

6 Had interview with Mr. McKnight about Church plans. [The name of McKnight was faded and may not be correctly deciphered. EBG] Interviewed Bishop Manucy about the interior. Due to submit plans tomorrow.

7 Plans pronounced perfect. Turned them over to Bishop Manucy. [This Church was never constructed. In 1989, the Mother Superior very kindly researched in the Tricennial for 1882 to 1885 and found that the Bishop did not approve of the plans and requested that the money be used in the construction of the building that now forms the south boundary of the cloister. EBG.]

18 Received request for plans for altering a Convent building.

26 Did sketch for Convent building. [The original building was small and Hutchisson enlarged it by adding the two upper stories and the bays on the north end. EBG.]

27 Worked on plans for Convent.

28 Worked on plans for Convent.

MARCH

3 Worked on plans for Convent building.

5 Submitted some plans for Convent building.

16-26 Continued working on plans for Convent.

27 Received cash from Convent for $100.00.

31 Gave estimate of cost for building to Convent.

APRIL

2 Began to take off roof of old building. Made plans for the framing of the Convent building.

3-10 Worked on plans for Convent.

13 Gave drawings of Convent framing.

20 Gave contract for Convent to Heuston.

MAY

12 Commenced putting in joists for second floor.

13 Continued work on second floor framing.

13-25 Construction work continued.

25 Worked on stairs for the Convent.

JUNE

1 Made drawings for the mantels of the Convent.

3 Made drawings for the moldings of the Convent.

3-10 Worked on drawings for the Convent.

13 Worked on drawings for the cornices of the Convent.

29 Hired four white carpenters for the Convent.

AUGUST

5 Made drawings for the bookcases at the Convent.

14 Received $100 from the Convent.

OCTOBER

13 Finished plans for balustrade.

30 Made drawings for the doors. [Last decipherable entry. He also continued with the construction of the clock cupola and the gazebo that stands on the south lawn. EBG]

Appendix 12

List of extant buildings for James Flandin Hutchisson II

One story cottages:
1. M. C. Rooney House, 1888; 908 Augusta St. (2 west of Broad). J. F. Griffin & Co., builders, $2,000.
2. Charles Scott Cottage, 1889; 209 South Cedar, moved from 195 South Jefferson Street. G. V. Overton, builder, $800.
3. Kilduff House, 1891; 20 George Street. Sossaman Brothers, builders, $1,800.
4. Peter Brown House, 1891; 51 South Georgia Street. J. Bride, builder, $1,500.
5. M. B. Conelly Cottage, 303 South Dearborn Street. J. Bride, builder, $1,000.
6. Wm. Gordon Cottage-Mobile Mission Office, 1892; 210 State Street. No builder mentioned.
7. J. W. Little House, 1892-93; 1312 Dauphin Street. Sossaman Brothers, builders. $2,200.

Two story houses
8. Charles Scott House, 1889; 207 South Cedar moved from 103 Jefferson Street. G. V. Overton, builder, $2,800.
9. M. V. Smith House, 1889; 550 St. Michael Street. C. E. Chamblin, builder, $3,800.
10. Trinity Episcopal Church Parish House (Bartolli House), 1893; designed with brother Clarence L. Hutchisson, 263 North Joachim. H. C. Fonde, builder, $2,250.
11. B. R. Tunstill House, 1894; 1202 Dauphin Street, in partnership with Hammond. G. Chambers, builder, $2,000.
12. Farley-McAleer House, one-and-a-half story for Farley, 1894. Second story added in 1908. 115 South Dearborn Street. 1894 portion built by Thomas Savell, $2,800.
13. The Petronovich House, 1894, with Hammond. Listed as on the north side of Church, two west of Lawrence, 504 Church. Greenwood, builder, $2,500. There is a question about this house, for the MHDC dated it 1901.

Churches
14. St. Emanuel Methodist Episcopal Church, 1890-1891; North side St. Michael Street, 2 east of Washington [listed as Wilkinson in the *Mobile Daily Register*]. Builder not given, $10,000.
15. Cathedral of the Immaculate Conception, 1888-1895. Finished the facade; stone steps and stuccoing, 1890, $6,000. Stone by McDonald Company; stuccoing by Pat Houston.
    Towers of the Cathedral, 1895; no builder mentioned, $12,800.
16. St. Louis Street Baptist Church Tower, 1890; 114 South Dearborn. Church, 1865; tower, 1890; facade renovated 1906. Tower, $1,000. No builder mentioned.
17. St. Bridget's Church spire, 1885, Whistler, Alabama.

Appendix 13

List of the partnerships of C. L. Hutchisson, Sr. From 1903 C. L. Hutchisson was in residence in Mobile, Alabama.

1901-1903	C. L. Hutchisson and P. J. Krouse, Meridian, Mississippi
1903-1906	George Watkins and C. L. Hutchisson, Mobile, Alabama
1906-1907	George Watkins, C. L. Hutchisson, and Joseph A. Garvin
1907-1910	C. L. Hutchisson and Joseph Garvin
1910-1912	C. L. Hutchisson and Alan Chester
1912-1917	C. L. Hutchisson and W. L. Denham
1918-1927	C. L. Hutchisson worked alone
1927-1932	C. L. Hutchisson, Nicholas Holmes, Sr., and C. L. Hutchisson, Jr.
1928	The firm was joined by William March in a limited association for designing the Alabama State Docks Administration Building
1933-c1940	C. L. Hutchisson and C. L. Hutchisson, Jr.; after 1940, C. L. Hutchisson, semi-retired, occasionally working with his son who began his independent practice after four years as chief architect in the U.S. Army Corps of Engineers during World War II.

Appendix 14

From the *Mobile Register*, September 1, 1910, section 5, p. 8.

Appendix 15

From the *Mobile Register*, September 1, 1912.

C. L. Hutchisson — W. L. Denham

Hutchisson & Denham

Architects

Rooms 1 and 2 Peoples Bank Building

MOBILE, ALABAMA

Architects for the Following Buildings

Jewish Temple
Cawthon Hotel
C. J. Gayfer & Co.
Mobile Infirmary
First National Bank
Pythian Castle Hall
F. M. Ladd, Residence
Central Trust Company
J. T. Burke, Residence
L. H. Metzger, Residence
Masonic Home of Alabama
Knights of Columbus Home
Mobile Gas Company (Machinery Building)

Notes to the Text

Chapter 1 Notes

1. American State Papers, 5:713 (May 24, 1796), records the commissioning of the Ellicott and Freeman boundary line to run at the 31st degree latitude.

2. Pensacola Restoration and Preservation Commission, *Historical Architecture of Pensacola*. Earle M. Newton, editor. (Pensacola, 1969) p. 1.

3. Elizabeth B. Gould, *From Fort to Port, an Architectural History of Mobile Alabama, 1711 to 1918* (Tuscaloosa: University of Alabama Press, 1988) pp. 21-25.

4. Peter J. Hamilton, *Colonial Mobile*, (3rd ed. 1879; reprint, Mobile: First National Bank, 1952), p. 322.

5. Ibid., pp. 331, 353.

6. Ibid., p. 362.

7. The deed to this property is still in the family archives. The site was visited by the author with C. L. Hutchisson, Jr., and Judy Leventhal during the initial street survey in 1987.

8. ASP, III, 12/22/1815 to 5/26/1824. pp. 12, 13. Properties obtained by Peter Hobart are listed in the years 1797 and 1798. One was for lands previously owned by Gabriel Tixerrant, dated April 11, 1797. The other was for a house and lot from Thomas Powell, 1798. Hobart also took out land on Bayou Sara and Dickens Pasture, the deed for which is in the family archives. The July 26, 1828, death notice of Peter Hobart in the Mobile Commercial Register states that he arrived in Mobile in 1804. This is incorrect as shown by the land purchases recorded in the ASP.

9. Hamilton, *Colonial Mobile*, p. 352 and genealogical records in the Hutchisson archives.

10. Gould, *From Fort to Port*, p. 22.

11. Ibid., p. 9. The letter from Josiah Blakely was quoted on p. 23 and taken from Misc. Bk. B, p. 467. See Gould note p. 272, n. 47.

12. Hamilton, *Colonial Mobile*, p. 349.

13. Gould, *From Fort to Port*, For a history of the development of the Creole cottage see pp. 9-13.

14. Ibid. p. 28. The contract for the building can be found in Misc. Bk. A, pp. 13-14.

15. Pensacola Commission, *Historical Architecture of Pensacola*. The drawing for the elevation of the Lavalle house is on p. 12. The house is not the Widow Toulette's Cottage as previously thought.

16. For a history of the development of the Alabama log cabins and their types see Robert Gamble, *The Alabama Catalog: the Historic American Building Survey*. (Tuscaloosa: University of Alabama Press, 1987) pp. 24-29. The log cabin was introduced into the Colonies by Swedish settlers in Delaware.

17. Ibid., pp. 271-272.

18. Hamilton, *Colonial Mobile,* p. 360.

19. The series of historical events were compiled from the following publications: *Encyclopedia of World History*, William Langer, compiler and editor (Boston: Houghton and Mifflin Co., 1940. 5th ed. 1972), pp. 642, 643, 646-47, 649, 810-11; *Pictorial Atlas of United States History*, Hildreth Kagan, editor in charge (New York: The American Heritage Publishing Co. 1966), pp. 23-24, 26, 53, 62-63, 120-24, 138-39, 199, 202, 205, 210-11, 214, 218, 245, 264, 271, 285, 287, 290, 335, 339, 351; Melton McLauren and Michael Thomason, *Mobile, The Life and Times of a Great Southern City* (Woodland Hills, Calif.: Windsor Books, 1981), pp. 24-34; Hamilton, *Colonial Mobile*, pp. 354, 383, 397, 401-402, 410, 426, 435-37.

20. Judge Harry Toulmin, *Digest of the Laws of Alabama*, compiled by John G. Aiken. (Cahawba, Alabama: Ginn and Co., 1873) pp. 781, 784. Also see Gould *From Fort to Port*, p. 273, n. 2.

21. Hamilton, *Colonial Mobile*, pp. 439-448.

22. Gould, *From Fort to Port*, The development of architecture during the Territorial Years see pp. 26-30, 273-274, nn. 1-12.

23. *The Territorial Papers*, Vol. XVIII; *Alabama Territory* 1817-1819.

24. Ibid., Jan. 20, 1817. Also Gould, *From Fort to Port*, pp. 30, 274, n. 17.

25. Police records of the Night Patrol, 1822. Mobile City Archives 33-3-2-1. (L-2).

26. Gould, *From Fort to Port*, for the architectural development of early statehood, pp. 30-56.

27. Census for Mobile in the *Mobile Commercial Register*, Feb. 7, 1822, pp. 3-5.

28. Gould, *From Fort to Port*, p. 275-276, n. 41 for the attribution of the Theatre to Isaiah Rogers. Also Talbot Hamlin, *Greek Revival Architecture of America* (New York: Dover Publication Inc., 1944), p. 111.

29. Contract for the Mobile County Courthouse, in Misc. Bk. B, pp. 42-44.

30. Gould, *From Fort to Port*, the drawing for the city market, p. 43. The drawing for the brick store, p. 35.

31. William H. Pierson, Jr. *American Buildings and Their Ar-*

chitects: The Colonial and Neoclassical Styles (Garden City, New York: Doubleday and Co., 1970) pp. 243-47.

[32.] Gamble, *The Alabama Catalog*, pp. 46, 52, 330-331, 351.

[33.] Gould, *From Fort to Port*, for a History of the Mobile County Courthouses see Appendix 3.

Chapter 2 Notes

[1.] Mary Wallace Crocker, *Historic Architecture of Mississippi*, (Jackson: University Press of Mississippi, 1973, 5th reprint 1988), Introduction, p. xi.

[2.] Elizabeth Gould, *From Fort to Port, an Architectural History of Mobile, Alabama, 1711 to 1918*, (Tuscaloosa: University of Alabama Press, 1988), p. 38.

[3.] Ibid., p. 28.

[4.] Peter J. Hamilton, *Colonial Mobile*, (3rd ed. 1897; reprint, Mobile: First National Bank, 1952), pp. 472, 473.

[5.] Melton McLaurin and Michael Thomason, *Mobile: The Life and Times of a Great Southern City*, (Woodland Hills, Calif.: Windsor Books, 1981), p. 42.

[6.] The census was given in the City Directories for 1839 and 1855.

[7.] McLaurin and Thomason, *Mobile*, p. 44.

[8.] Gould, *From Fort to Port*, p. 69, figure 45a. There is still disagreement as to the architect of Christ Episcopal Church. Tradition credits C. Butt as the architect but the church minutes state that the building was designed by Frederick Bunnell.

[9.] Gould, *From Fort to Port*, pp. 156-160.

[10.] Marriage records for Hutchisson's two marriages were given in the *Deep South Genealogical Society Journal*, "Marriage Records," Vol. II, pp. 293, 296. There were three major outbreaks of yellow fever in Mobile during the nineteenth century. They occurred from 1821 to 1822, 1837 to 1843, 1853 to 1856. During the last two epidemics, whole sections of the population were decimated. Those that had the money fled to summer homes in Spring Hill where the disease did not strike. The middle and lower classes that had to remain in the city died by the hundreds. Hutchisson's first Mobile wife died in the summer of 1837, presumably of the fever. The Health Department of the City merely recorded her death, not the cause. At the time it was impossible to keep up with all the usual notations on various documents due to the large number of deaths.

[11.] In the City Archives is an 1837 bill for taxes due by Mr. James Flandin Hutchisson for $24 on real property and Poll Tax of $4 with no tax on personal property. This establishes that he was already living in Mobile by 1836.

[12.] City Archives, Box 18003, Env. 1, Folder 141. The permission for the reconstruction of Hutchisson's carpenter shop was in Box 18002, Env. 7, Fol. 373.

[13.] Receipt is in the City Archives, Box 18003, Env. 3, Fol 383.

[14.] Mobile Probate Court Records, Misc. Bk. C, pp. 52-53.

[15.] Ibid., Misc. Bk. D, pp. 344, 345.

[16.] For an explanation of the development of the Creole and Gulf Coast cottages see Gould, *From Fort to Port*, pp. 81-89.

[17.] Misc. Bk. C, April 6, 1838, pp. 86, 87. Contract between Oliver Pittfield and J. F. Hutchisson, with specs. $650.

[18.] Misc. Bk. C, October 3, 1838, pp. 184, 185. Contract between C. S. Hales and J. F. Hutchisson with specs and plan. $1,300.

[19.] Misc. Bk. A, May 23, 1825, p. 230. A contract between the Trustees of the Catholic Diocese and the builder George Hilliard for a cottage with a central hall.

[20.] Misc. Bk. C, June 27, 1839, pp. 311, 312, 313. Contract between Edward O'Conner and J.F. Hutchisson, for a large cottage on Dauphin Rd. outside the city limits. $3,350.

[21.] Misc. Bk. D, February 20, 1841, pp. 152, 153. Contract between John Marshall and J. F. Hutchisson for a store/house complex on Jackson Street.

[22.] Misc. Bk. D, February 22, 1841, pp. 153, 154. Contract between the partners James Burns and John Riley and J.F. Hutchisson for a large brick building containing four stores and an upstairs residence with a central passageway between the stores.

Misc. Bk. D, March 3, 1841, pp. 173, 174, 175. Specifications and a contract between Messieurs M. Eslava and A. Dumee and J.F. Hutchisson for a store and house complex consisting of two stores with a corridor between and residences above, a double kitchen and a privy. Payment was for $6,000.

[23.] Misc. Bk. D, pp. 85, 86. Contract between M. Eslava and A. Dumée and J. F. Hutchisson for a warehouse occupying the block between Water, Commerce, Eslava and Monroe Streets. Two-story brick. $16,250.

[24.] Gould, *From Fort to Port*, pp. 110, 111.

[25.] Misc. Bk. E, July 24, 1849, pp. 388, 389, 453, 454. Contract between Charles Cullum of the Mansion House and J. F. Hutchisson for an enlargement of the Mansion House.

[26.] The silver pitcher is in the possession of William Hutchisson of Albany, Ga., the grandson of James Flandin Hutchisson II and great-great-grandson of James Flandin Hutchisson I.

27. Misc. Bk. F, Oct. 2, 1852, p. 11. Contract between J. Bloodgood and J. F. Hutchisson, for three two-story kitchen houses in the Orange Grove area. Each building 15 by 30 feet. $1,800.

28. Anderson and J. F. Hutchisson for a brick house on the northwest corner of Church and Lawrence Street. $1,500.

Chapter 3 Notes

1. Russell E. Belous, "The Diary of Ann Quigley," from *Gulf Coast Historical Review*, Spring 1989, Vol. 4, No. 1, pp. 97-98.

2. Gould, *From Fort to Port*, see Chapter 5 for the architecture of the years from 1850 to 1860, pp. 128-163.

3. Daniel Blueston, *Winterthur Portfolio*, Vol. 25, no. 213, 1990, for a discussion on the architect of the United States Custom House, pp. 141-144.

4. The lists of the architects and master builders were compiled from the City Directories for the decade and from the building contracts.

5. Building documentation has been compiled from the contracts found in the Miscellaneous Books at the Mobile County Probate Court, architectural records found in the contemporary newspapers, the Hutchisson family archives, and records in the archives of the Catholic Diocese and Parishes. For a complete list of the work of James H. Hutchisson contact the author.

6. Turpin Bannister, *The Architects at Mid Century, Evolution and Achievement*, (Vol. 1, New York: Reinhold Publishing Co.), pp. 94-101 and charts #56 and #58. Chart #56, for 1930, shows that 4,622 architectural students were enrolled in academic courses in the United States, of which only 67 were in Alabama. Chart #58, for 1930, states that only 507 architectural degrees were granted in the United States, of which only ten were in Alabama.

7. The list of books that are in the Hutchisson library was taken from a master list compiled by Clarence L. Hutchisson, Jr. Some of these books have recently been sold locally and a few have been sold to architectural firms in New York.

8. Belous, *The Diary of Ann Quigley*, pp. 91, 94.

9. The military records for James H. Hutchisson are from the official records of the *Confederate Military History*, Vol. 7, edited by General Clement A. Evans, *United States War Documents*. The records were collected by Mr. Burney Crooks of Pensacola, Fla., who also obtained Hutchisson's portrait and other memorabilia. The quotation describing Hutchisson in action was from the *Mobile Advertiser and Patriot*, March 18, 1862. Other descriptions of the battle can be found in the same source for April 11 and 18.

10. Belous, *Diary of Anne Quigley*, p. 93.

11. McLaurin and Thomason, *Mobile*, p. 69. Other information of the postwar era was compiled from Dan H. Doyle, Chapel Hill, University of North Carolina Press; Articles from *Gulf Coast Historical Review*, Vol. 2, No. 1, 1986, Stephanie Hardin, "The Climate of Fear, Violence, Intimidation and Media Manipulation in Reconstruction Mobile," pp. 39-53; Ibid.: Vol. 4, No. 2, 1989. Frank I. Owsley, Jr., "Incidents on the Blockade of Mobile," pp. 38-49; Ibid.: Vol. 5, No. 2, 1990. Harriet E. Amos, "From Old to New South Trade in Mobile. 1850-1900," pp. 114-127; Ibid.: Vol. 7, No. 1, 1991. Joseph E. Brent, "No Compromise. The End of Presidential Reconstruction in Mobile, Alabama," p. 19 ff.

12. From the *Mobile Register and Advertiser*, May 10, 1866, p. 3.

13. A party wall was one that connected two buildings, serving as a dividing wall between them. When the wall was extended above the roof, it was called a fire wall and kept flames from crossing over from one unit to the next.

14. The membership of the Creole Fire Company, founded in 1819, was quite cosmopolitan in nature, being made up of whites and those of mixed blood that were descended from the original colonial French families. They were bilingual, speaking both English and a dialect of French. During succeeding years, nine other companies were formed. They bought their own equipment, maintained their own stations and had considerable rivalry as to which company could get to a fire first. The City Fire Department, organized in 1888, absorbed the Creole Fire Department but the rest of the companies were disbanded. The Creole Fire Station continued to serve the community until 1960, when it was abolished. See *Souvenir History of the Mobile Fire and Police Departments 1819-1902*. Reported by Thomas F. Price, chief of the fire department and C.W. Soost, chief of police (Mobile: Commercial Printing Co., April 1902). Also, the *Azalea City News*, "Parade of the Creole Fire Station," July 30, 1981. The reporter was Frank Daugherty.

15. Misc. Bk. H, June 23, 1869, p. 67, Mobile Sugar Refining Co.
    Ibid., Aug. 11, 1869, p. 85, Mobile Fertilizer Manufacturing Co.

16. Ibid., July 22, 1871, pp. 329-330, The Phoenix Foundry.
    Ibid., January 1, 1872, pp. 365-366, Mobile Wooden Ware Co.

17. In 1872-78 James H. Hutchisson served on the Manufac-

turing Committee of the Mobile Board of Trade. Recorded in the *Deep South Genealogical Society Journal*, Vol. XVII, p. 87.

[18] Don H. Doyle, *New Men, New Cities, New South*, (Chapel Hill: University of North Carolina Press, 1990), pp. 78, 79.

[19] For the general development of the architecture of the 1870s, see Gould, *From Fort to Port*, Chapter 7, pp. 183-193.

[20] The contract signed between Claude Beroujon and the Catholic Diocese Building Committee can be found in the Misc. Bk. D, pp. 636-637, dated August 7, 1843.

[21] *MCR*, September 1, 1895, gives the date of the finishing of the towers and the cost at $12,000.

[22] *MCR*, August 31, 1890, gives the date of the finishing of the Cathedral and the paying of Pat Houston for the stucco work and the McDonald, March and Co. for the stone.

[23] Gamble, *The Alabama Catalog*, pp. 114-116, for reference to the Wetumpka, First Presbyterian Church, see p. 227, for the Orion Church see p. 337.

Crocker, *Historic Architecture of Mississippi*, pp.112, 115.

[24] *The Catholic Week*, "Parish Histories: Vincent de Paul," November 23, 1979, p. 25.

[25] Contract for the construction of the Bernstein House by Charles Fricke upon the designs of James H. Hutchisson, January 16, 1872. The original contract is in the possession of a descendent of the Bernstein family. A copy is in the files of the Mobile Historic Development Commission.

[26] The deeds for the property are to Ruth S. Bush, Deed Book 76, p. 186 and from Bush to Frank Roche, Deed Book 125, p. 522.

[27] Copies of the Sanborn maps are in the archives of the City of Mobile. They are for the years 1885, 1891, 1915. Bernstein House Block 370, p. 47 of 1915.

[28] For a complete list of all J. H. Hutchisson buildings, both standing and destroyed, contact the author.

[29] *Mobile Daily Register*, August 28, 1877, p. 3.

[30] Doyle, *New Men, New Cities, New South*, p. 114.

[31] For more on Victorian architecture in Mobile, see Gould, *From Fort to Port*, pp. 195-225.

[32] Gould, *From Fort to Port*, for the Benz County Courthouse, p. 197 and figure 173; for two of his houses, figures 207, 208; pp. 222, 223.

[33] The Forcheimer Building, *The Mobile Daily Register*, Sept. 1, 1886, p. 3.

[34] *Mobile Daily Register*, September 1, 1885, p. 5. Quotes the "north side of Theatre, between Royal and St. Emanuel Streets, two-story carriage factory, G. Lauber, owner, Pond builder, James H. Hutchisson, architect, $1300.00."

[35] The drawing of the Lauber House and entrance to the carriage factory is from *Where Time Bears Witness to Sound Building*, (Mobile: First National Bank, 1935). No pagination.

[36] For information on the Aldrich house that burned, see the City Planning Commission of Mobile Publication, *Nineteenth Century Mobile Architecture, an Inventory of Existing Buildings*, 1974, p. 52, figure 110.

[37] Crocker, *Historic Architecture of Mississippi*, Rosalie, p. 24.

[38] Gamble, *Alabama Catalog*, Kenan House, pp. 60, 223-224.

[39] Ibid., the Kitchen-McMillan House, p. 195. A very deteriorated set of plans was found in the house and was largely illegible except for the name Hutchisson.

[40] The Keyes House. Information on changes to the Keyes House was made available by the present owner, Mr. Bud Harrison, who purchased the home in 1978.

[41] See Gould, *From Fort to Port*, pp. 205, 293, n. 17.

[42] Gamble, *The Alabama Catalog*, the Romanesque influence, pp. 112, 113.

[43] *MCR*, September 1, 1885, p. 5. The south side of Spring Hill Avenue, three and a half miles from the city. The Convent of the Visitation, James H. Hutchisson, architect. P. Houston, builder, $10,000.

Diary of James H. Hutchisson, 1885, January 10, 13, 16.

Ibid., February 6. Records the interview concerning the designing of a chapel. *The Triennial Book*, May 16, 1885 states that it was decided not to build the chapel but to use the money to enlarge the school building. This information was researched in the records of the Convent by Sister Anita, June 28, 1989.

[44] Information on the Academy Building enlargement is contained in J. H. Hutchisson's diary, 1885, beginning with February 18 and continuing throughout the year (see Appendix 11).

[45] *MCR*, September 1, 1885, p. 5. Spring Hill College, two-story brick refectory and one-story brick kitchen, $13,000. James H. Hutchisson, architect. Diary, 1885, April 29, Spring Hill College ordered two-story building, 43 by 113 feet. Reports on progress continued throughout the month. Diary, February 21, 1886. Plans ordered for the Spring Hill Infirmary.

46. Diary, 1886, May 2, orders for plan for Dr. Mastin's office.

   MCR, September 1, 1886. "On the northeast corner of Conti and Joachim Streets Dr. William Mastin is erecting a two-story brick building, the lower floor of which will be used for offices and the upper one as a residence. Cost $6,500. James H. Hutchisson, architect, George Discher, builder."

47. James F. Sulsby, Jr., *Historic Alabama Hotels and Resorts* (Tuscaloosa: University of Alabama Press, 1960) pp. 160-162.

   Diary, 1885, February 13, 14; May 6, 9; June 20.

Chapter 4 Notes

1. McLaurin and Thomason, *Mobile*, p. 79. Harriet Amos, *Gulf Coast Historical Review*, "From Old to New South Trade," Vol. 5, No. 2, Spring 1990, p.120. Don Doyle, *New Men, New Cities, New South*, pp. 133-134.

2. Don Doyle, *New Men*, p. 16. In 1860 Mobile was the fourth largest city in the South. It was smaller than New Orleans (1), Charleston, S.C., (2), and Richmond, Va., (3). By 1880 it was the eighth largest. It was smaller than New Orleans (1), Richmond, Va. (2), Charleston, S.C. (3), Nashville, Tenn. (4), Atlanta (5), Memphis, Tenn. (6) and Savannah, Ga. (7).

3. Amos, *Gulf Coast*, p. 122.

4. McLaurin and Thomason, *Mobile*, pp. 80-81.

5. City Directory, 1890, p. 405.

6. McLaurin and Thomason, *Mobile*, p. 81.

7. Doyle, *New Men*, p. 31.

8. McLaurin and Thomason, *Mobile*, pp. 84-87. Doyle, *New Men*, pp. 247-259.

9. Doyle, *New Men*, pp. 250, 256.

10. Gould, *From Fort to Port*, pp. 202, 211-213. For information on George Watkins.

11. It is known that James Flandin Hutchisson was in Chicago by 1902. He is listed in the City Directory as an architect for the Carnation Milk Co.. The Carnation Milk Co. confirmed this by correspondence, but they could not name the specific buildings he designed since they do not list buildings according to architect. A researcher in the Chicago Public Library has been unable to find any further information about either his life or his work while in Chicago, nor does the AIA have any information.

12. For information on the Victorian buildings such as the recently destroyed German Relief Building and the Pincus Building, see Gould, *From Fort to Port*, pp. 201, figure 17b; 216, figure 196a.

13. The Queen Anne was popularized in England by the architect Richard Norman Shaw and introduced in America about 1874. It became popular along the eastern seaboard, in towns like Cape May, New Jersey. It did not develop in Mobile until the end of the nineteenth century. The only surviving large Queen Anne home in Mobile belongs to the years 1899 and 1901. For the surviving examples, see Gould, *From Fort to Port*, pp. 223, figure 209; 244, figure 230.

14. John Sledge, *Gulf Coast Historical Review*, Fall 1990, Vol. 6, No. 1, "Shoulder to Shoulder," pp. 56-66.

15. The University of South Alabama Archives has some photographs of Victorian buildings now destroyed but not all have been identified.

Chapter 5 Notes

1. The map was prepared by William Johnson for publication in the *Mobile Register* for 1905, September 1, section 2, p. 1. The trade journal was a section of the *Mobile Register* published the first Monday in September or the Monday after Labor Day listing the major constructions with tables or reports of economic progress.

2. The *Mobile Register*, 1905, September 1, section 2, p. 1.

3. Ibid., 1907, September 2, section 4, p. 2.

4. Ibid., 1908, September 1, section 4, p. 1.

5. Ibid., 1910, September 1, section 5, p. 8.

6. Ibid., 1908, September 1, section 8, p. 1.

7. The advertisement was from the *Mobile Register*, 1905, July 16, p. 16.

8. It has not been possible to compile a list of standing buildings that Hutchisson or his firm designed outside of the Mobile area. Most of the churches still exist but only about one half of the residences and commercial buildings remain. A complete list of all buildings is available.

9. The war record of Clarence L. Hutchisson, Sr., was given by his son C. L. Hutchisson, Jr., and confirmed by Mr. Burney Crooks of Pensacola, Fla.

10. The buildings of the Mississippi State University and their architects are included in a publication by Samuel Kaye, AIA, and Dr. Kit Carter, *A Survey of 73 State Owned Landmark Buildings*, 1985.

11. A catalogue of the J. P. Krouse buildings was obtained from the archives of the city of Meridian, Miss., courtesy of Fonda Rush, consultant for the City of Meridian.

12. For examples of the Watkins commercial designs, see Gould, *From Fort to Port, An Architectural History of Mo-*

bile, Alabama, 1711 to 1918, pp. 211, 212.

13. The house was designed by Watkins and Hutchisson. *MR*, 1906, September 1, section 3, p. 1.

14. Information on the Mennonite Community designed by Watkins and Hutchisson was given by the archival records of C. L. Hutchisson. The date has not been established. More information was obtained in correspondence with Carlotta Dunn of Yellow Pine and Fruitdale, Ala., May 21, 1992. Research should be done on this community. A Yellow Pine resident referred to a publication on the Mennonites, *Coming South*, but the person could not furnish the author or publisher.

15. *MR*, 1904, September 1, section 2, p. 6. St. John's rectory with photograph is the only reference found on this building outside of the Sanborn Fire Insurance Maps. For an account of the St. John's Episcopal Church building, see Gould, *From Fort to Port*, pp. 292-4.

16. *MR*, 1905, September 1, section 4, p. 2, "The Pythian Castle." The article refers to it as a major renovation and was so listed in Hutchisson's working files.

17. Ibid., 1904, September 1, section 4, p. 10, contains the story of the first Leinkauf School building with a photograph, designed by Watkins and Hutchisson. In 1908, section 4, p. 1, is the record of the second story added for $10,444.

18. The drawing of the Cawthon Hotel with a lengthy description can be found in the *Mobile Register* issues for 1906, September 1, section 4, p. 1, and in 1907, August 3, section 2, p. 2. The original drawings by the architect are located in the archives of the Historic Mobile Preservation Society, but they are in a deteriorating condition, especially the plan.

19. A photograph of the First National Bank was published in *MR*, 1906, September 1, section 3, p. 9. In the bank's publication *Highlights of 100 Years of Mobile History 1865-1965*, there are drawings of the various buildings occupied by the bank over the years. Unfortunately, the original drawings of the Watkins, Hutchisson and Garvin firm were not made available for this publication.

20. *MR*, 1908, September 1, section 4, p. 1, contains reference to a Black Mission Church on Davis Avenue, and includes a brief description.

21. Ibid., 1909, September 1, section 2, p. 2, lists the Lily Baptist Church on Kennedy Street as costing $15,000. It is built of brick and stone.

22. The Sha'arai Shomayim Temple photograph appeared in *MR*, 1907, September 1, section 5, p. 3. The article contains a brief description.

23. *MR*, 1906, September 1, section 3, p. 1, lists the house at Springhill near Gilbert Street.

24. Ibid., 1906, September 1, section 4, p. 2. A photograph of the Lott house appears in the next year's edition. (September 2, 1907, section 4, p. 5). The plans on linen are well preserved, framed and hung on the walls of the present owner. (Courtesy of Mr. and Mrs. Dent Boykin.)

25. Ibid., 1907, September 2, section 4, p. 5, photograph of the home of Judge J. M. Wilson, but there is no information on the house included.

26. The George Poetz house, 100 South Ann Street was briefly described in *MR*, 1908, September 1, section 4, p. 1.

27. *MR*, 1907, September 2, section 4, p. 5, contains the pictures of the Metzger house and the William Gordon house, both on Michigan Avenue.

28. The term "American Foursquare" was given in *The Old House Journal*, January, 1982, p. 7.

29. *MR*, 1907, September 2, section 4, p. 5, has a photograph of the William Gordon house on Michigan signed by Hutchisson and Garvin.

30. The twin Ionic columns on the front of the porch do not match those on the sides, the latter being smaller could be a later replacement.

31. The Marsh House was listed in Hutchisson's master file (#421), but no address was given. In the *MR*, 1908, September 1, the Marsh House was given as being located in Ashland Place.

32. *MR*, 1889, September 1, section 2, p. 3, and the Sanborn Map of 1904, confirm that the Partridge house was on Dauphin Street and in the newspaper that it was built by Rudolph Benz, costing $4,200. In the *MR*, 1909, section 2, p. 2, is a reference to a remodeling of the house.

33. Ibid., 1906, September 1, section 3, p. 6, has a drawing of the Knights of Columbus Building as drawn by George D. Hulburt and Co..

34. Ibid., 1907, September 2, section 4, p. 8, has a drawing by Hutchisson for the Knights of Columbus Building. *MR*, 1908, September 1, section 3, p. 4, has a photograph of the building as built by Hutchisson and Garvin.

35. Ibid., 1910, September 1, section 7, p. 9, published the architects' drawing of the Mobile Infirmary. For a better copy, the drawing in this publication was taken from *Highlights of 100 Years of Mobile History*, published by the First National Bank of Mobile, p. 73.

36. Information on the original Vincent-Walsh home can be found in Gould, *From Fort to Port*, pp. 50-52.

37. Information for the purchase of the land for the Mont-

gomery Masonic Home was furnished by courtesy of the staff of the Alabama Historical Commission, Montgomery, Alabama.

38. Among the books on concrete construction owned by Hutchisson were: W. B. Henry, *Practical Concrete Work, An Elemental Treatise on Concrete Construction* (Atlanta); *Concrete Age*: (Construction Publishing Co., 1911); Maurice M. Sloan, *The Concrete House and Its Construction* (Philadelphia: The Association of Portland Cement Manufacturers, 1912); Three volumes of George A. Hool and Frank C. Phiessen, *Reinforced Concrete Construction, 1913-1917*; several volumes of works by Albrich and a volume by McKim, Mead and White; a series of copies of *The Architectural Record* and *The Architectural Digest*, as well as publications by the AIA on the subject of concrete construction. For the complete list contact the author.

39. A list of the standing buildings by the firm can be obtained from the author.

40. Some of the books on Sunday School buildings owned by Hutchisson were: Marian Lawerence, *Housing a Sunday School*, (Westminister Press, 1911); P. F. Kidder, architect, *Churches and Chapels* (New York: the William Comstock Co., 1910); Herbert Frances Evans, *The Sunday School Building and Its Equipment* (Chicago: The University of Chicago Press, 1914).

41. On the architect's drawing for the porch details of the Ladd house is the label that the composition capitals of the columns were from Seifert, number 6046.

42. *MR*, 1909, September 1, section 2, p. 2, lists a bungalow for Mrs. Lilian Hamilton. In Hutchisson's files is a record for two dwellings, one house for M. C. Hamilton and another bungalow (File #99 and 225). Other bungalows were being built on Monterey by Downey and Denham.

43. In the Hutchisson library were books on bungalows and the developments in California. For a list contact the author.

44. *Craftsmen Bungalows: 50 homes from The Craftsman*, edited by Gustav Stickley, by the Wm. T. Comstock Press, 1908. Reprinted by Dover Press, 1988, as *Bungalows, Camps and Mountain Homes*.

45. *MR*, 1915, September 1, section 1, p. 14 and in the publication *Gulf Coast Fair* booklet, Mobile, Ala., October 30, 1915 to November 5, 1916.

46. Ibid., 1978, August 20, section 6, is a reproduction of a photograph of the Poor Farm with a short description of it, on file in the MPL(SC).

47. The relationship of Hutchisson and P. J. Krouse in the designing of the Meridian City Hall was furnished by Fonda Rush, consultant for the city of Meridian. Her correspondence of April 16, 1992 included the following information from the City Council Minute Books:

March 18, 1914 — Mr. R. H. Hunt and C. L. Hutchisson, architects, appeared before the City Council and presented their claims for the position of architects on the new city hall;

March 19, 1914 — P. J. Krouse appeared before the Council and presented his claims for the position of architect for the new city hall;

April 15, 1914 — Councilman Owen presented an Ordinance authorizing the Mayor, City Clerk and Treasurer to make and enter into contract with P. J. Krouse for the drawing of plans and specifications for the erection of a new city hall;

April 29, 1914 — voted on contract with P. J. Krouse, all councilmen voted yes;

June 9, 1914 — Mayor John Parker called the attention of the Council and architect Krouse in the preparations of the plans and specifications now being prepared by Mr. Krouse for the new city hall. The Mayor stated that he did not feel competent to pass on the plans and specifications intelligently and that in his opinion, the wise thing for the Council to do was to employ some competent architect who had ample experience in arranging the details of such a building, to guide the Council in their final selection of plans and specifications.

With the above facts in mind, the Mayor made a motion that the Council employ a consulting architect. No action was taken, Councilman Slaughter and Owen asking for more time in which to consider the matter;

August 21, 1914 — Krouse presented specifications which were approved by Council;

September 22, 1914 — The Council awards bids to Hancock and McArthur of Meridian for the construction of city hall. After reviewing bids with architect Krouse and consulting architect C. L. Hutchisson;

October 6, 1914 — C. L. Hutchisson paid $249.00 being balance due for services rendered as consulting architect for a new city hall.

48. Information on the York, Ala., AT&N Railroad Station was furnished by Jud K. Arrington of York, who was the train dispatcher on the railroad. He also furnished information on the bank, designed by Hutchisson, and the Baptist Church, all of which are included in Hutchisson's working files.

49. For a list of standing buildings designed by Hutchisson,

Holmes and Hutchisson contact the author. Of the nine surviving buildings, seven are in Historic Districts: three are in Ashland Place; two are in Old Dauphin Way; and two are in Leinkauf. The others are scattered in different areas of the city.

Chapter 6 Notes

1. For a list of buildings by C. L. Hutchisson, Jr., contact the author.

2. The term "short return" refers to the termination of the midsection of the horizontal cornice that forms the bottom line of the triangle forming the gable end.

3. Flemish bond is a brick coursing in which the stretchers and headers alternate, forming a break in the coursing so that no vertical joints are in a straight line, but alternate. It was popular in the late eighteenth century.

4. Mary Martha Thomas, *Gulf Coast Historical Review*, "The Mobile Home Front During the Second World War," 1986, Vol. 1, No. 2, pp. 55-75.

5. Ibid.

6. For information on the original Trinity Episcopal Church, see Gould, *From Fort to Port*, p. 142, figures 107a-b.

7. Ibid. The Beal-Gaillard House, 1836, pp. 96-98, figures 72a-c. The Marshall-Hixon House, 1853, pp. 150-152, figures 118a-f.

Architectural Terms

A

abacus: The flat block above a classic capital. It varies in detail with the different columnar orders.

acanthus: An ornamental motif derived from the acanthus leaf and used in classic structures, as in the Corinthian capital or in decorative brackets and moldings.

Adamesque: Delicate, refined, decorative, classic detailing in the style of the English eighteenth-century architect Robert Adam.

anthemion: An ornamental design based on the honeysuckle flower and leaf, commonly alternating with a Palmette, common in classical moldings.

arabesque: A decorative molding formed by intertwined vines and scrolls using flora and fauna motifs.

arcade: A series of arches and their supports.

architrave: (a) the lowest of the three divisions of a classic entablature. (b) The framing of an opening.

arris: The edge made by two straight or curved surfaces coming together at an angle, as in a molding, or the raised edge separating the fluting of a Doric column.

B

baluster: The upright member of a balustrade supporting the railing.

balustrade: A railing formed by the balusters, the top hand rail and sometimes a bottom rail.

bargeboard or vergeboard: A facing board, set back and along the edge of a gable of a roof, usually decorative and common in Gothic Revival and Downing cottage styles.

batter: A wall, support or framing that slopes away from the perpendicular.

bay: Divisions of a building marked by structural members—as columns, piers, windows, etc.

bay window: A window that projects from the plane of the wall. If supported on brackets or corbels, and above the ground story, usually called an oriel window.

bead molding: A decorative molding made by a series of half round or half spherical units resembling a string of beads. Common in classic detailing.

belt course or band course: A slightly projecting flat, horizontal band, marking a floor level, or division on the exterior wall of a building.

board and batten: A siding for a structure in which vertical boards are combined with narrower wooden strips covering the vertical joints between the boards.

bonding: The various methods of laying bricks or stones in courses: English bond: alternate courses of headers and stretchers. Flemish bond: alternate headers and stretchers in each course. Common bond: rows of stretches with every sixth course a row of headers.

bracket: A small supporting projection often decorative, used to carry an overhanging weight as a shelf, lintel, cornice, or balcony, etc. *See* console, modillion or corbel.

bull's-eye block: A circular design used to decorate and accent the angles of the horizontal and vertical members of the framing of an opening, such as a door or window.

buttress: A mass of masonry built to give stability to a structure or to counteract the outward thrust of an arch or vault.

C

canopy: A projecting cover or hood over an opening, a niche, altar, or pulpit, etc.

cantilever: A structural member projecting beyond its support.

capital: The top or crowning member of a column, pilaster or pier.

cartouche: an ornamental shield or scroll, usually with an inscription or date.

cast iron: An iron alloy shaped by pouring it when it is in a molten state into a preformed mold.

cavetto cornice: A concave profile forming the cornice of a building—especially characteristic of the Egyptian style.

chamfered: The bevelling off at a 45 degree angle of the sharp edges of two surfaces that meet at an exterior angle, as the edge of a square post or a beam.

clapboarding: A type of wood siding that is thin on one edge and thicker on the other and overlapped horizontally to form a weather proofing—frequently referred to as weather boarding.

coffer: An ornamental, recessed panel in a ceiling or soffit.

colonnade: A row of columns with their connecting arches or entablatures.

column: A vertical supporting member with circular or square section. In classical architecture may be of several different orders or styles. An engaged column is fastened to a wall or flat surface.

composite order: A columnar order of Roman origin combining the Greek Doric and Ionic.

console: A scrolled bracket.

corbel: (a) See bracket. (b) The extension of successive courses of masonry beyond the wall plane.

Corinthian order: A columnar order of Greek origin in which acanthus leaves decorate the bell-shaped capital.

cornice: (a) The horizontal projecting member at the top of a wall or building. (b) The horizontal member of a classic building that crowns the entablature and forms the base of the pediment. (c) A crowning molding of an opening such as a door or window. (d) Raking cornice: the cornice along the slope of a gable or pediment.

crenellation: Battlement in which the parapet has alternate raised panels or merlons and indented areas or embrasures.

Creole cottage: A style of domestic architecture developed in the French colonial period along the lower Mississippi River and the Gulf Coast.

crown molding: The horizontal molding at the top of an interior wall.

cupola: A domed turret rising above a roof or a small domed roof, square or round.

D

deck: (a) An unsheltered floor or porch. (b) A flat roof.

dentil: A molding in a classic entablature formed of small blocks set in a row, like a row of teeth.

distyle-in-antis: A Greek ground plan in which two columns are set between the extensions of the side walls.

Doric: A columnar order of Greek origin in which the column has no base, and the capital is formed by an echinus curve, and the frieze contains metopes and triglyphs.

dormer window: A window placed in a projection from the slope of a roof.

E

eared architrave, shouldered architrave or crossette: The squared, side projection of the upper corners of the architrave of a door or window frame. Found in the Greek key door, locally called an "Egyptian door."

echinus: The curved cushion member of the Doric capital

eclectic architecture: Implies an architecture using varying characteristics from different stylistic sources that are selected because of personal preference.

egg and dart: A Greek molding applied to an ovolo surface in which an egg shape alternates with a dart shape.

elevation: The vertical projection or description of the surface planes of a building.

entablature: In classic architecture the horizontal superstructure immediately above the capitals of the supporting members. Traditionally it is divided into three parts: architrave, frieze, with a taenia molding between in the Doric, and the horizontal cornice.

entasis: The outward or convex curve on the lower profile of a column shaft to counteract the optical illusion of concavity of a straight line profile. Found especially in Greek architecture.

F

facade: Front elevation of a building.

fan light: The semicircular or a semielliptical window above a door common in Georgian and Regency styles.

fascia: (a) A flat horizontal band beneath the eaves covering the ends of the rafters. (b) A horizontal division of the architrave of a classic entablature—using either two or three fasciae found in the Ionic and Corinthian orders.

Federal Style: A style of architecture evolving out of the Georgian during the Post Revolutionary Years popularized by the work of Thomas Jefferson and Henry Latrobe, and incorporating Robert Adam's influence in the delicate decoration of interior detailing.

fenestration: The arrangements of windows in a building.

finials: An ornamental form terminating the top of a spire, pinnacle, gable, etc.

firebreak or fire wall: A low parapet rising above roof level of attached row houses to retard the spread of fire from one roof area to the next.

fish scale pattern or imbricated: Shingles or tiles set in overlapping, curved units, forming a pattern resembling fish scales.

flat arch or straight arch: An arch whose intrados, or inner profile, is a horizontal line; the individual units of the arch may or may not be wedge shaped.

flute, fluting: The shallow, vertical concave grooves on a column, pilaster or other supporting member.

foliated: An ornamental pattern derived from leaves.

fret or Greek Key: A classic decorative band of geometric design made of straight horizontal and vertical lines.

frieze: (a) The horizontal member of a classic entablature between the architrave and horizontal cornice. (b) A decorative band along the upper part of a wall.

G

gable: (a) The triangular upper portion of a wall under the ridge of a pitched roof. (b) A roof formed by two inclined planes meeting at a ridge, forming a triangle.

gallery: A Gulf Coast misuse of the French word galerie, when applied to a porch. (a) galerie: In the French architecture of the lower Mississippi and Gulf Coast area, a term used for the ground level porch either fronting or surrounding a home and roofed by the extrusion of the main gable or lip. *See* veranda. (b) gallery: (1) A long hall, such as an exhibition room; (2) A structure attached to one or more sides of an auditorium or room and projecting over the main floor below.

garconniere or gareonnier: Bachelor apartments.

giant order or colossal order: A column or supporting member that rises through two or more stories to the roof line.

glazed: Used in this book to refer to openings in which glass panes have been installed.

Gothic Revival: The nineteenth-century revival of Gothic decorative motifs and an attempt to recreate the atmosphere of Gothic architecture. In Mobile the form is limited to churches and cottages, popularly called steamboat Gothic, carpenter Gothic or the Downing cottage style.

Greek key door: An opening with eared architrave, frequently with shallow pedimented molding above and with battered jambs.

Greek Revival: The nineteenth-century style of architecture based on classic orders and motifs.

H

hip roof: A roof whose ends are sloped as well as the sides.

headers: The end or short side of a brick

hood mold or dripstone: A projecting molding over the upper portion of an opening. If rectangular in shaped called a label.

I

interstices: A space between certain architectural members, as the triangular area formed by a column, the section of the adjacent arch, and the lintel above. Used here in reference to the location of some cast iron decoration.

Ionic order: The classic columnar order in which volutes are carved on the capital and dentils embellish the cornice.

Italianate: An architectural style of the nineteenth century based on the Italian Renaissance villa.

J

jamb: The vertical side of a door frame, window or other opening.

jerkin head: A roof form in which the ends of the gable are truncated or bevelled off.

jib door: A semiconcealed door, flush with the wall, and paneled so as to appear part of the wall

jig-saw: In Gothic Revival and Victorian architecture, decorative bands and details made possible by the invention of the jig-saw.

K

keystone: The top center wedge-shaped voussoir of an arch.

L

lintel: The horizontal beam over an opening. A beam whose two ends rest upon separate supporting members, in the trabeated system of construction.

loggia: A passageway open on one or more sides, it may be colonnaded.

louvre or louver: A ventilating opening, often with horizontal slats to exclude rain.

lunette: A semicircular window or panel.

M

Mansard roof: A roof that has a double slope, the lower plane being longer and steeper than the upper plane. Developed by the French seventeenth-century architect Francois Mansard.

medallion: A decorative relief carving, usually round or oval. Popular in ceilings above a chandelier.

modillion: (a) A form of bracket or console found under the cornice of a Corinthian or composite order. (b) Commonly used for any bracket beneath an overhanging cornice.

mullion: Vertical member dividing the "lights" of a window.

muntin: Vertical member of a paneled door or screen. Can also be applied to vertical members that separate panes of glass in the window of a door.

O

oriel: A bay window supported on corbels.

P

Palladian window or Venetian window: An enclosed group of three windows, the center one round headed and taller than the two square-headed side windows.

parapet: A low wall, sometimes battlemented, rising vertically above the edge of a roof.

party wall: A wall common to separate buildings that are attached, as in row houses.

pavilion: (a) The projecting subdivision of a large building forming a right angle with the main facade; as a projecting wing. (b) A small unattached building for pleasure or decoration as a garden summer house. (c) A building for temporary use.

pediment: The triangular gable formed by the horizontal and raking cornices. Can be found in classic styles formed by the pitch of the roof or as a decorative device above doors. and windows. It may be closed, or broken if the horizontal cornice is not complete or the raking corners do not meet.

pendant: A carved decorative member hanging from above, commonly from the center of an arch or from the edge of a bracket.

pier: A solid supporting member, usually square in section.

pilaster: A rectangular pier or column, fastened or engaged to a wall and projecting only slightly from it. In classical revival styles can be given attributes of the classic orders.

plinth: (a) The lowest member of the base of a building. (b) The projecting base of a wall.

podium: (a) The platform or continuous base of a building. (b) An elevated station or platform for some specific purpose as for a lecture.

porch: A covered entrace into a building, or a roofed space outside a main wall of a building. If the porch is large and given classic detailing of columns, etc., it is called a portico.

porte-cochere: A porch large enough for a vehicle of transportation as a carriage or a car.

portico: See porch.

prostyle: A Greek building plan with columns across the front. In Greek Revival associated with the columns of the portico.

Q

quoining: The accenting of the external corner angles of a building, especially in masonry by changes in size and textures.

R

rusticated: (a) Masonry in which the surface of individual blocks is roughened, or given an uneven or vermiculated treatment. (b) Masonry cut in massive blocks and set in deep mortar points creating a rich texture to the wall.

S

scored: The mark or indentation on a plastered or stuccoed wall to create the effect of courses of stone. Popular in Greek Revival and Italianate styles.

segmental arch: An arched form in which the profile or intrados is a segment of a semicircle.

sill: (a) The lower horizontal closure of a door or window frame. (b) The heavy foundation timber of a building. It supports the posts and studs of the walls above.

soffit: The undersurface of a projection such as a cornice, or the underside of an arch or lintel.

spandrel: (a) The triangular surface or space between the sides of an arch. *See* interstices (b) A panel between adjacent structural members.

stilt block or dosseret: A high block placed above the abacus, separating the abacus and lintel or spandrel above.

stretcher: The length of a brick

string course: A molding or projecting band running horizontally across a wall.

T

taenia or tenia: The small molding or fillet separating the frieze from the architrave in the Greek Doric order.

trabeated: Construction by the post and lintel principle as contrasted with arcurated.

tracery: The ornamental and functional intertwining and branching mullions of a window, screen or panel decoration.

transom: An opening over a door or window.

turret: A small round or polygonal tower, usually supported on corbels.

Tuscan Order: A simplified Doric developed by the Romans and used in other Italian architecture. It has an astragal molding around the neck and a more shallow echinus curve.

V

verandah: A long porch, sometimes two storied.

vernacular: A native or local style, characteristic of a particular locality.

volute: A spiral scroll motif found in the Ionic capital and in a modified form in the Corinthian and composite. Sometimes it is adapted to consoles and brackets.

voussoir: The wedge-shaped unit of an arch between the springing and the keystone.

W

water table: A projecting course at the base of a wall to throw off water.

weatherboarding: Wedge-shaped boards overlapped horizontally to weatherproof a building with timber-framed walls. The wedge is turned with the thinner edge up so that the thicker bottom part of the board overlaps the upper thinner part of the board below.

wrought iron: Iron that is puddled, rolled and then hammered or forged into the desired shape.

Bibliography and Sources

Selected Books

American Institute of Architects, San Antonio chapter. *San Antonio Architects*. San Antonio: AIA, 1959.

Bannister, Turpin C. *The Architects at Mid Century: Evolution and Achievement*. Vol. 1. Report on the Commission and Regulation of the American Institute of Architects. New York: Reinhold, 1954.

Benjamin, Asher. *American Builder's Companion 1827*. Reprint of 6th edition. New York: Dover, 1969.

Biloxi Historical Survey. *The Buildings of Biloxi: An Architectural Survey*. City of Biloxi: 1976.

Bruhn, Paul A. *A Celebration of Vermont Historic Architecture*. Photographs by Sanders H. Milens. Shelburne, VT: New England Preservation, Inc., 1983.

Burkholder, Mary R., editor. *A History and Guide to the Houses of the King William Area*. San Antonio: The King William Association, 1989.

Condit, Carl W. *American Building Art: The Nineteenth Century*, 5th edition. Chicago: University of Chicago Press, 1975.

Crooker, Mary Wallace. *Historic Architecture of Mississippi*. Jackson: University of Mississippi. 5th edition, 1985.

Doyle, Don H. *New Men, New Cities, New South*. Chapel Hill: University of North Carolina Press, 1990.

First National Bank. *Highlights of 100 years of Mobile History 1865-1965*. Mobile: First National Bank, 1965.

———. *Where Time Bears Witness to Sound Buildings*. Mobile: First National Bank, 1935.

Gamble, Robert. *Alabama Catalog: The Historic American Building Survey*. Tuscaloosa: University of Alabama Press, 1987.

Gould, Elizabeth B. *From Fort to Port, An Architectural History of Mobile, Alabama, 1711-1918*. Tuscaloosa: University of Alabama Press, 1988.

Hamilton, Peter J. *Colonial Mobile*. 3rd edition, 1897. Reprint. Mobile: First National Bank, 1952.

Hamlin, Talbot Faulkner. *Greek Revival Architecture in America*. New York: Dover reprint, 1964.

Higginbotham, P. Jay. *Old Mobile: Fort Louis de la Louisiane, 1702-1711*. Mobile: Museum of the City of Mobile, 1977.

Hitchcock, Henry Russell. *Architecture, Nineteenth and Twentieth Centuries*. Baltimore: Penguin Books, The Pelican

History of Art Series. 3rd Edition, 1968.

Holly, Henry Hudson. *Holly's Country Seats*. New York: Appleton, 1863.

Kagan, Hilda Heum, editor. *Pictorial Atlas of United States History*. New York: American Heritage, 1966.

Kaye, Samuel and Kit Carter. *Survey of 73 State Owned Landmark Buildings*. Jackson, Mississippi, 1985.

Langer, William, editor. *An Encyclopedia of World History*. 5th edition. Boston: Houghton Mifflin, 1972.

Lewis, Arnold and Keith Morgan. *American Victorian Architecture*. New York: Dover, 1975.

Love's Legacy. Marriage Records in French, 1724-1786. Translated and edited by Jacqueline Olivier Vidrine. Lafayette, La.: University of Southwestern Louisiana, Center for Louisiana Studies.

McAlester, Virginia and Lee. *A Field Guide to American Houses*. New York: Alfred A. Knopf, 1984.

McDermott, John, editor. *The French in the Mississippi Valley*. Urbana: University of Illinois Press, 1965.

McLaurin, Melton and Michael Thomason. *Mobile: The Life and Times of a Great Southern City*. Woodland Hills, Calif.: Windsor Books, 1981.

Mills, Lane. *Architecture of the South, Mississippi and Alabama*. Beehive Book Press, New York: Abbeville Press, 1989.

Mobile City Planning Commission. *Nineteenth Century Mobile Architecture, An Inventory of Existing Buildings*. Mobile: City of Mobile, 1974.

Mobile Fire and Police Department Souvenir Report, 1819-1902. Compiled and edited by Thomas F. Price, chief of the fire department and C. W. Soost, chief of police. Mobile, 1902.

Newton, Earl, editor. *Historic Architecture of Pensacola*. Pensacola: Pensacola Historic Restoration and Preservation Commission, 1969.

Peterson, Charles, editor. *Building Early America: Contribution Toward a Great Industry*. Radnor, Pa: Chilton, 1976.

Pierson, William H., Jr. *American Buildings and their Architects*. Vol.1: *The Colonial and Neoclassical Styles*. Garden City, N.Y.: Doubleday, 1970.

Stickley, Gustav, editor. *Bungalows: 50 Homes from the Craftsman*. Comstock Press, 1908. New York, Dover reprint, 1985.

Sulsby, James F., Jr. *Historic Alabama Hotels and Resorts*. Tuscaloosa: University of Alabama Press, 1960.

Toledano, Roulhac, Betsy Swanson and Pat Holdry, editors. *New Orleans Architecture: The American Sector*. Vol. II. Gretna, La.: Pelican Press, 1972.

Toledano, Roulhac, Sally Kitteredge Evanson and Mary Louis Christavich, editors. *New Orleans Architecture: The Creole Faubourge*. Vol. IV. Gretna, La.: Pelican Press, 1974.

Walker, Lester. *American Shelter*. Woodstock, N.Y.: Overlook Press, 1981.

Warner, Lee H. *Building Florida's Historic Capitol*. Tallahassee: Historical Tallahassee Preservation Board, 1977.

Wilson, Eugene N. *A Quick Guide to Rural Houses of America*. Montgomery: Alabama Historical Commission, 1975.

——— *Alabama Folk Houses*. Montgomery: Alabama Historical Commission, 1975.

Wilson, Samuel, Jr. "Colonial Fortifications and Military Architecture in the Mississippi Valley," in *The French in the Mississippi Valley*, edited by J. F. McDermott. Urbana: University of Illinois Press, 1965.

Articles and Pamphlets

Alabama Architect's Newsletter, Vol. 8, no. 2 (March, April, May 1972).

Amos, Harriet E. "From Old to New South Trade in Mobile, 1850-1900." *Gulf Coast Historical Review*, Vol. 5, no. 2 (Spring 1990) pp. 114-128.

Belous, Russell E. "The Diary of Ann Quigley." *Gulf Coast Historical Review*, Vol. 5, no. 2 (Spring 1990) pp. 89-100.

Blueston, Daniel. "The United States Custom House." *Winterthur Portfolio*, Vol. 25, no. 213 (1990).

Brent, Joseph. "No Compromise: The End of Presidential Reconstruction." *Gulf Coast Historical Review*, Vol. 7, no. 1 (Fall 1991) pp. 18-37.

Deep South Genealogical Society Records, Vol. 1-19, references to Hobart and Hutchisson. Index vol. 19.

___ "Marriage Records," Vol. 2.

Fabel, Robin F. "St. Marks, Apalache and the Creeks." *Gulf Coast Historical Review*, Vol. 1, no. 2 (Spring 1986) pp. 4-23.

Guice, John D. "The Cement of the Society Law in the Mississippi Territory." *Gulf Coast Historical Review*, Vol. 1, no. 2 (Spring 1986) pp. 55-76.

Hardin, Stephanie. "Climate of Fear, Violence, Intimidation and Media Manipulation in Reconstruction Mobile." *Gulf Coast Historical Review*, Vol. 2, no. 1 (Fall 1986) pp. 37-53.

"James H. Hutchisson." *Deep South Genealogical Society Journal*, Vol. 17, p. 55.

Jones, Harvey. "The Federal Period in Huntsville, 1805-

1835." *Historic Huntsville Quarterly*, Vol. 7, no. 1 (Fall 1980).

Kniffen, Fred and Henry Glassie. "Building in Wood in the Eastern United States." *Geographical Review*, Vol. 56, no. 4 (1966) pp. 40-66.

Magee, Jacob and Mary. "St. Bridget's Parish, Whistler, Alabama, 1874-1974." Anniversary pamphlet.

Oldenmoppen, Bernadette G. and Genevieve Spafford. "Old St. Mary's Parish." (1967). Pamphlet.

Owsley, Frank I., Jr. "Incidents in the Blockade of Mobile." *Gulf Coast Historical Review*, Vol. 4, no. 2 (Spring 1989) pp. 38-49.

"Parish Histories." *Catholic Week*, Vol. 45, no. 46 (1979) p. 25.

Sledge, John. "Shoulder to Shoulder: Mobile's Shotgun Houses." *Gulf Coast Historical Review*, Vol. 6, no. 1 (Fall 1990) pp. 56-66.

St. Laurent, Addie S. "People Along the Bayou Sara." Undated pamphlet published by the Women's Club of Saraland, Ala.

Thomas, Mary Martha. "The Mobile Home Front During the Second World War." *Gulf Coast Historical Review*, Vol. 1, no. 2 (Spring 1986) pp. 56-75.

United States Papers and Documents

American State Papers: Legislative and Executive (ASP). Vol. 3 (1815-1824), Vol. 5 (1828-1834). Washington, D.C.

"Confederate Military History." *Official Records.* Edited by General Clement H. Evans. Washington, D.C.: United States Department of Military Documents, Vol. 7.

General Catalog of Historic American Building Survey. Washington, D.C.: Department of the Interior, National Park Service, 1972.

Grass Roots of America; A Computerized Index to the American State Papers: Land Grants and Claims (1789-1837) with other Aids to Research (Government document serial set numbers 28-36). Edited by Phillip W. McMullin. Salt Lake City, Utah: Gendex Corp., 1972

Territorial Papers of the United States (USTP). Edited by Clarence E. Carter. Vol. 18. Territory of Alabama, 1817-1819. Washington, D.C., 1952.

Alabama State Documents

Alabama Census. 1820, 1830, 1840.

Digest of the Laws of Alabama. Compiled by Judge Harry Toulmin. Edited by John C. Aiken. Cahawba, Ala.: Ginn and Curtis, 1823.

Living History of Alabama. Official Sesquicentennial Guide, 1963.

Mobile City Records

Burial Records. Vol. 1 (1820-1856), Vol. 2 (1857-1879).

"Burial Records," *Mobile Genealogical Society,* 1963. Mobile Public Library, Special Collections Division.

City Directories. 1839, 1842, 1844, 1845, 1852, 1855, 1869, 1870, 1875, 1876, 1885, 1887, 1888, 1892.

Minutes of the Common Council. Vols. for 1839-40, 1844-50, 1857-61, 1871-9, 1887-9, 1890-1900. City Vault.

Minutes of the Mayor and Board of Alderman. Vols. for 1824-9, 1829-32, 1833-34, 1839-43, 1843-47. City Hall Vault.

Mobile Newspapers

Mobile Gazette and General Advertiser. April 27, 1817; May 11, 1819; September 28, 1820; October 3, 1820.

Mobile Daily Commercial Register and Patriot. 1821-1841.

Mobile Daily Register and Journal. 1841-1849.

Mobile Daily Register. 1850-60.

Mobile Daily Advertiser and Register. 1861-1867.

Mobile Daily Register. 1868 to October 15, 1916.

Mobile Register. 1916-present.

Mobile County Records

Mobile Tax Records. 1829, 1832, 1833.

Will: The Old Will Book. Compiled by Arthur D. Crigler. Reference to Hobart, February 20, 1828, p. 142.

Mobile County Probate Court Records. Receipts for work on the County Courthouse paid to Peter Hobart.

Spanish and French Records. Vol. I: 1715-1812. Translated by Joseph Caro, 1840. Mobile Probate Court.

Mobile County Miscellaneous Books: A: 1821-25, B: 1826-32, C: 1833-40, D: 1841-1845, E: 1846-1852, F: 1852-1858, G: 1858-1866, H: 1867-1873, I & J: 1874-1879. County Probate Court.

Archives

Triennial Book, 1885. Convent of the Visitation.

Hutchisson Family Archives

Letters

Diary of James H. Hutchisson, 1885, 1886.

Family Bible with genealogical records.

Records of works designed by James H. Hutchisson, C. L. Hutchisson, Sr., and C. L. Hutchisson, Jr.

Drawings and ground plans.

Oral information from C. L. Hutchisson, Jr.
Photographs of the family and personal memorabilia.
Newspaper clippings preserved by the family.

Mobile City Archives
Box 18003, Env. 3, Folders 3, 83.

Public Library, Special Collections Division
Files on the Saucier Family.
File on St. Bridget's Church.

Mobile Historic Development Commission
Files on buildings.

Unpublished Material
Lipscomb, Oscar H. "The Administration of Michael Portier, Vicar Apostolic of Alabama and the Floridas, 1825-1829, First Bishop of Mobile, 1829-1859." Ph.D dis. Washington, D.C.: American University, 1965.

Messing, Francis A. "Dominic Manucy, Vicar Apostolic of Brownsville, Texas and Third Bishop of the Diocese of Mobile, Alabama, 1885." Thesis for Masters at New Orleans' Notre Dame University, 1964, Chapter VI-IX.

Sources of Illustrations

Except as noted below, all photographs, drawings, and illustrations are from the research files of the author and/or Hutchisson family archives.

Figure Number
Frontispiece, Plate I: Photograph by Paul R. Thompson.

2. Reprinted by permission from the *Pictorial Atlas of United States History*, by J. J. Thorndike. Copyright 1966 by the American Heritage Publishing Company, pg. 118.

3. Courtesy of the Library of Congress and the University of Alabama Press.

6. Courtesy of the Historic America Building Survey, the Library of Congress.

7. Courtesy of the Library of Congress, HABS.

7b. Courtesy of the Library of Congress, HABS.

8. Reprinted by permission from the *Pictorial Atlas of United States History*, J. J. Thorndike. Copyright 1966 by the American Heritage Publishing Company, pg. 121.

9. Reprinted by permission from the *Pictorial Atlas of United States History*, by J. J. Thorndike. Copyright 1966 by the American Heritage Publishing Company, pg. 149.

10. Reprinted by permission from the *Pictorial Atlas of United States History*, J. J. Thorndike. Copyright 1966 by the American Heritage Publishing Company, pg. 139.

11. Courtesy of the Mobile Public Library, Special Collection Division and the University of Alabama Press.

12. Courtesy of the Library of Congress and the University of Alabama Press.

14. Courtesy of the Library of Congress.

16. Courtesy of the Alabama Department of Archives and History.

Plate II: Courtesy of the Alabama Department of Archives and History.

19. Courtesy of the LC and the UAP.

20. Courtesy of the LC and UAP.

21. Courtesy of the MPL(SC).

25. Courtesy of the University of South Alabama Archives.

26. Courtesy of William Hutchisson, grandson of J.F. Hutchisson II.

26b. Photograph by Devereaux Bemis.

28b, c. Courtesy of the MPL(SC).

29. Courtesy of the owner, Burney Crooks of Pensacola, Florida.
30. Reprinted by permission from the *Pictorial Atlas of United States History*, by J. J. Thorndike. Copyright 1966 by the American Heritage Publishing Company, pg. 211.
31. Reproduced from a photograph published in the *Mobile Press Register*, April 8, 1962. The present location of the sketch book is not known.
32. Reprinted by permission from the *Pictorial Atlas of United States History*, by J. J. Thorndike. Copyright 1966 by the American Heritage Publishing Company, pg. 245.
36. Courtesy of the Library of Congress, HABS photograph.
41. Courtesy of the Library of Congress and the University of Alabama Press.
44. Courtesy of the MPL(SC) from the *Mobile Register*, September 1, 1886.
45. Courtesy of the MPL(SC) and the UAP.
46. Courtesy of the MPL(SC) from the *Mobile Register*, September 1, 1886.
46b. Courtesy of the HMPS Archives.
47. Courtesy of the Mobile Planning Commission and the UAP.
48. Courtesy of the First National Bank of Mobile.
52. Courtesy of the Library of Congress, HABS photograph.
53b. Courtesy of Carl Hixon.
58. Courtesy of the UAP and of the USAA, T.E. Armistead Collection.
72. Courtesy of the MPL(SC).
74. Courtesy of the Historic Preservation Division, Mississippi Department of Archives and History. Photograph by Samuel H. Kaye, AIA.
76, 77, 78. Courtesy of MPL(SC).
79. Photograph from the *Mobile Register*, 1904. Courtesy of the MPL(SC).
79b. Photograph from the Wilson Collection. Courtesy of the Historic Mobile Preservation Society.
79c. Photograph courtesy of the USAA, Erik Overbey Collection and UAP.
80. Courtesy of the Overbey Collection, USAA and the UAP.
80b. Courtesy of the MPL(SC).
80c. Drawings preserved in the archives of the Historic Mobile Preservation Society and reproduced with permission.
80d. Courtesy of the HMPS archives.
80e. Courtesy of the USAA.
81. Courtesy of the Erik Overbey Collection of the USAA and the UAP.
82b. Courtesy of the First National Bank of Mobile, Alabama.
83b. Courtesy of the Dauphin Street Synagogue Archives. Robert Zeitz, archivist.
84b. Courtesy of Mr. and Mrs. Dent Boykin.
89. Photograph by Devereaux Bemis.
94. Courtesy of the USAA.
94c. Courtesy of the MPL(SC).
95. Courtesy of the USAA and the UAP. Photograph by Michael Thomason.
96b. Courtesy of the First National Bank of Mobile.
97b-d. Courtesy of Mrs. Betty Mann Doan and the UAP.
102c, d. Courtesy of Bruce Knodel, AIA.
103. Courtesy of Mrs. Edwin Trigg.
103c, d. Courtesy of Dr. and Mrs. Richard Mazey.
110b, e, f. Courtesy of Colonel and Mrs. Gordon Moulton.
112. Courtesy of the USAA.
113. Courtesy of the MPL(SC).
115b. Courtesy of the Mississippi Department of Archives and History, Division of Community Development.
120c. Courtesy of V. B. and M. H. Blankenship.
124. Photograph by E. B. Gould.
124b. Photograph by E. B. Gould.
127b-d. Courtesy of Mr. and Mrs. Neal Yates.
137. Photograph courtesy of the USAA.
137b. Courtesy of the USAA.

Index

Note: All buildings designed by the Hobart-Hutchisson family are listed alphabetically in the general index, but are listed chronologically under the individual architect's name. Bold face page numbers identify where photographs, illustrations, and plans are found.

A

Acker, Marion, 69
Adams Glass Warehouse, James H. Hutchisson, architect, 68, 210
Alabama Dry Docks, 206-207
Alabama State Docks, 191
Alabama State Docks Administration Building, C. L. Hutchisson, Sr., C. L. Hutchisson, Jr., Nicholas Holmes, Sr., and William March, architects, **191**
Alderson, William S., architect, 40
American Foursquare, 128, 170, 172-174, 198
American Institute of Architects (AIA), 187
Anderson House, Hutchisson, Holmes and Hutchisson, architects, 188-**189**, 201
Anderson, Matthew, 37
Andrews, Frank M., architect, 106, 114
Andrews log cabin, **8**
Andry and Bendernagle, architects, 106, 119
Arch:
    cusped, 94, 209
    jack, 50
    lancet, 100, 101
    relieving, 70
    segmental, 50, 63, 67, 202
Architectural schools, 195-196
Architrave, 91, 117, 141, 157, 183, 200
Arlington Fairgrounds, 68
Arnold House, Hutchisson and Chester, architects, 139-**140**
Arrington, Jud, 166
Art Deco, 165, 191
Ashland Place, 105, 107, 128, 130-132, 138, 152, 155, 170, 178, 188, 201
AT&N Railroad Station (York, Alabama), C. L. Hutchisson, Sr., architect, **166-167**, 168
"Ateliers", 41

B

Balconies, 99, 122-125, 126, 127, 134, 137, 141
    interior, 121
    iron balconies, 176
Baluster, wood:
    flat patterned, 94
    square, 122-125, 127
    turned, 91, 92, 94, 96, 98
Balustraded decks, 97, 111, 117, 128, 132, 161, 185, 199
Bank of Mobile, 16, 51, 118
Banks, 16, 51, 110, 118, 119, 120, 136, 166
Baptist Church (Bay Minette, Alabama), Hutchisson and Denham, architects, 144-**145**
Bargeboard, 94, 190, 202
Barnes, James, 25, 36
Baroque influence, 109, 120, 146, 176, 184
Barton Academy, Gallier and Dakin, architects, 15, 18, 22, 25, 106
Bascomb Race Track, 68
Battle House (1852), Isaiah Rogers, architect, 40, 68
Battle House (1906), Frank M. Andrews, architect, 106, 114-115, 117
Bauhaus, 196
Bay windows. *See* Windows
Bayou Chotage, 13
Bayou Sara, 5
Beal-Gaillard House, 211
Beaux Art, 164
Bender Ship Building Company, 27
Benjamin, Asher, 41, 73
Benz, Rudolph, architect, 20, 51, 61, 65, 70-71, 82, 87-88, 97, 100, 107, 132
Berkmire, William H., 89
Bernstein House, James H. Hutchisson, architect, **58-59**, 83
Beroujon, Claude, architect, 36, 52
Bestor Building, C. L. Hutchisson, Sr., architect, 107

Bienville Hotel, James F. Hutchisson II, engineer, 88, 106
Bienville Water Works, 49
Birkman, William, architect, 15
Black Mission Church, C. L. Hutchisson, Sr., architect, 120
Blakely, Josiah, 6-7
Board of Trade, 51
Bodden Cottage, C. L. Hutchisson, Sr., architect, 155
Booksch House, C. L. Hutchisson, Jr., architect, **197**
Boone, Boykin, house, James F. Hutchisson II, architect, 99
Boone, Thomas, 148
Boundaries. *See* City boundaries
Brackets, 50, 54, 55, 59, 71, 72, 73, 77, 81, 91, 92, 94, 96, 98, 99, 105, 111, 132, 125, 134, 135, 142, 144, 149, 154-155, 162, 164, 169, 176, 181, 184, 191, 200
Bracket style, 94
Breuer, Marcel, 209
Bricks, 23, 35, 49, 62, 77, 83, 113, 162, 165, 198, 201-205
    types and sources
        Mobile, 48, 67
        molded, 50, 198
        pressed, 67, 121, 137
        Zanesville, 67
Bride, James, 95
Briggs, Warren Richard, architect, 114
Brown, John F., 67
Brown House, James F. Hutchisson II, architect, **94-95**, 96
Bruce, George, architect, 114
Bulfinch, Charles, architect, 17
Bulfinch coin, **18**
Bungalow, 104, 105, 152-155, 172, 174, 179, 188, 198
Burgett Memorial Building, Lockwood and Seymour, architects, enlargement and renovation, C. L. Hutchisson, Sr., 106
Burke House, Hutchisson and Denham, architects, **150**, 157
Burlington Northern System, 166
Burns and Riley, store/residence, James Flandin Hutchisson, builder, 32-33
Bush, J. Curtis, 59
Butt, Cary, 25, 36

C

Cartouche, 120, 125, 165
Casbah Restaurant. *See* Reeves House
Cathedral of the Immaculate Conception, Claude Beroujon, architect;

portico, James H. Hutchisson, architect; towers, James F. Hutchisson II, architect, **Frontispiece**, 26, 27, 36, 37, **38**, **52**, 87
Cawthon Hotel, Watkins, Hutchisson and Garvin, architects, 114-115, 118
Census, 15, 24-25, 28, 61, 85, 86, 87, 89, 103-105, 107-108, 209
Center, Henry, 17
Chablin, G. A., 137
Chamberlain, H. B., 16
Chandler Foundation, 59
Chester, Alan, architect, 137-138, 142
Chicago Commercial Style influence, 114-115, 195-196
Chicago School of Architects, 34, 169-170
Chickasaw Indians, 25
Chinese Gas Station, Hutchisson, Holmes and Hutchisson, architects, **192-193**, 208
Choctaw Indians, 4, 12, 13, 25
Christ Episcopal Church, 25
Christian House, C. L. Hutchisson, Sr., architect, **171-172**
Christie House, C. L. Hutchisson, Sr., architect, 172-**173**
Church of St. Bridget's (Whistler, Alabama), James H. Hutchisson, architect, 56, **57**, 58, 77
Church of St. Vincent de Paul (renamed Prince of Peace), James H. Hutchisson, architect, **53-55**, 56, 62, 83, 100
Citronelle Historical Society, 83
City Bank and Trust Building, Andry and Bendernagle, architects, 106
City boundaries, 3, 6, 13, 14, 22, 37, 39, 40, 61, 85, 104
City Directories, 26, 27, 28, 37, 40, 51, 86, 87, 88, 89
City Hospital, 25, 68, 82. *See also* Old City Hospital
Civil Rights Act, 47
Clarke House, Stone Brothers, architects, **111-112**
Classical Revival, 110-111, 148
Coleman House, Hutchisson and Garvin, architects, 128, **129**-130
Collins, John, 25
Colonial Architecture, 5, 6, 7
Colonial Fortifications, 5
Colonial Period, 18
Colonial Revival, 111, 130, 198, 211
Columns, 18-19, 33, 35, 41, 52, 58-59, 67, 70-72, 80, 91-92, 94-96, 98, 104, 109, 111-112, 119, 122-123, 132, 139, 142, 144, 149-151, 157, 164, 172, 177, 179, 184, 199, 213
   capitals:
      Doric, 19, 32, 71-72, 132, 139, 144-145, 149, 151
      Ionic, 119, 122-123, 125-126, 128-129, 132, 149, 151, 163, 164
      Square, 35, 71, 122-125, 127, 141, 144, 153-154, 157, 160, 169, 172, 173, 198
      Tuscan, 41, 109, 157, 160, 179, 214
   shafts:
      fillet, 144, 146
      shaft, 95, 119, 153-154, 198
   types:
      cast iron, 41, 59, 64, 70, 78, 117, 157, 176
      chamfered, 71, 94
      fluted, 72, 80, 125, 128, 146, 164, 179, 200
      plastered, 19, 30, 141, 151, 197
      turned, 17, 20, 28, 71, 78, 81, 91-92, 94-98, 111, 138-139
      twisted, 59
      unfluted, 184, 213-214
Convent of the Visitation, 41, 51, 58, **78-80**, 83
Cottages:
   French Creole style, 7-8, 15, 17, 25, 27-32, 37, 41-42, 60-61, 82-83, 87, 88, 111, 138, 148, 198
   Gulf Coast development, 32, 131, 153, 154, 174
   Victorian cottages, 70-71, 92-98, 104, 148
   worker's cottages, 32, 55, 61, 83, 153, 181, 182
County Poor House and Farm (1915), C. L. Hutchisson, Sr., architect, 107, **161**
Coyle, John, 55
Craftsman, 153, 154
Creagh House, Hutchisson and Denham, architects, **156-158**, 159
Creek Indians, 3, 4, 10-12
Creole Fire Company, station, James H. Hutchisson, architect, 49-51
Creole Fire Hall, 62
Crooks, Burney, 45
Crystal Ice Company, 213
Cullum, Charles, 35
Cumming, David, Jr., architect, 25, 40, 111

D

Dade Cottage, **29-30**
Dakin, Charles, architect, 15, 18, 22, 25
Dannar, Albert C., 85-86
Daughtery, Philip, architect, 40
Deas, James, 34,
Decorative designs:
   Adamesque, 9, 211
   cornice, 101, 119, 153, 193
   Greek Revival
      acanthus, 95
      fret, 142
      rosette, 158
   Italianate
      scroll, 123, 125
      shell, 6, 32, 98
      swag, 119, 120, 211
      wreath, 119
Denham, William, architect, 106, 138, 142, 145
Distyle-in-antis, 145
Dodge and Graham Brothers Building, C. L. Hutchisson, Sr., architect, 165
Door:
   exterior, 17, 19, 23, 29-35, 48-50, 58, 65, 67, 72-73, 76, 80, 94, 96-99, 101, 103, 119-121, 124, 129, 133, 136, 139-140, 144, 146, 149, 151, 153, 156, 158-159, 162, 166, 169, 171-172, 175-178, 183-186, 188-189, 191, 198-200, 201, 202, 208, 211, 212, 214
   types
      arched headed, 101
      bay, 50
      bronze, 183
      batten, 29, 33
      iron, 35, 50, 65, 99, 176
      jib, 198, 199
      paneled, 29, 30, 33, 77, 158, 211
      segmental heading, 67, 202
      semicular headed, 69, 76, 184-185
   interior
      board-and-batten, 111
      folding, 33
      sliding, 124, 133, 159, 208
      square headed, 19
   styles
      Federal, 9, 17, 19, 149, 214
      French, 72, 73, 140, 172, 175-176
      Victorian, 76, 98, 140, 158
Dormer windows, 99, 109, 123, 125, 128, 137, 160, 170, 172, 175, 177, 199-200, 201-202, 214
Downey, Andrew, architect, 106, 183

Doyle, Don, 87
Dudley, Henry, architect, 40, 53, 209,
Dunn, John, 70
Dupree and Company, 135
Durand Mill, 5

E

1893 Chicago World's Fair, 161
Ellicott, Andrew, 3
English Block, Rudolph Benz, architect, 65-66
English Gothic Revival, 209
Eslava, Miguel, 7
Eslava and Dumée, store/residence, and warehouse, James F. Hutchisson, builder, 32-35
Espejo, Anthony, 6
Evans House, C. L. Hutchisson, Jr., architect, 201, **202-204**, 205

F

Factors and Traders Company Building, James H. Hutchisson, architect, 68
Farley, Charles, 68
Federal Housing Authority (FHA), 187, 190, 194, 196-200, 216
Fermier, J., 65
FHA apartment house, C. L. Hutchisson, Jr., architect, **200**
Fidelia Club, 106
Fine Arts Building, Hutchisson and Denham, architects, **160-161**
First Baptist Church of Orion, 56-57
First Christian Church, McCreary and Slater, architects, 107
First Methodist Church (Columbus, Mississippi), 54
First National Bank, Watkins, Hutchisson and Garvin, architects, **118-119**, 120
First Presbyterian Church (Jacksonville, Alabama), 53, **56**
First Presbyterian Church (Wetumpka, Alabama), **56**, 57
First Presbyterian Church (Holly Springs, Mississippi), 54
Flemish bonding, 9, 205
Flo-Claire, subdivision, 105, 150, 152, 155, 172, 190, 197
Forbes, John, 5, 6
Forcheimer Building, James H. Hutchisson, architect, 48, **66-68**
Fort Condé-Charlotte, 6, 14
Fort Gaines, 43, 46
Fort Louis de la Louisiane, 6
Foster, William S., 68
Fowler, John, 24

Frederick-Bender Log House, C. L. Hutchisson, Sr., architect, 174-**175**
Freitag, Joseph Kendall, architect, 89, 115
French Romanesque, 113
Freret, James, architect, 59
Fricke, Charles, 51, 58, 59
Frisco Line, 166

G

Gage, C. P., 47-48
Gale Motor Company, 165
Gallier, James, architect, 15, 18, 22
Gamble, Robert, 75
Garrow, Sam, 17
Gardiner House, C. L. Hutchisson, Sr., architect, **178**-179
Garvin, Joseph, 106, 137
George Hall (Mississippi State University), P. J. Krouse, architect, C. L. Hutchisson, Sr., consulting architect, **109**-110
Glass:
    art, 99, 116, 117, 125
    bevelled, 169
    etched, 94
    leaded, 129, 149, 188-189
    plate, 99,103, 120, 125, 165, 191
    stained, 123
GM&O Railroad Station, Philip Thorton Marye, architect, 106
Goldman House, C. L. Hutchisson, Jr., architect, **200-201**
Goldthwaite family, 148
Goodwin and Haire Maps, 15, 16, 18, 53. *See also* Maps
Gordon, A. W., 16
Gordon House, Hutchisson and Garvin, architects, 96, 126, 128, **129**
Gothic Revival influence and style, 15, 16, 40, 42, 52, 53, 54, 55, 56, 71, 76, 87, 100, 111, 142, 209
Government Street Baptist Church (1906), Rueben Harrison Hunt, architect; Annex, C. L. Hutchisson, Sr., architect, 106, 107
Government Street Hotel, Charles Dakin, architect, 22
Government Street Market, 17
Government Street Presbyterian Annex, C. L. Hutchisson, Sr., architect, 107
Government Street Presbyterian Church, Gallier and Dakin, architects, 15, 18, 22, 25
Grace Episcopal Church (Anniston, Alabama), 53
Graham, Amelia, (Mrs. James Flandin

Hutchisson I, third wife), 26
Grand Hotel, 68
Greek Revival influence and style, 22, 32, 41, 52, 71, 92, 123, 125, 129, 131, 142, 149, 175
Greene and Greene, architects, 153
Griffin, C. C., 99
Griffin, James S., architect, 72
Gropius, Walter, 192, 195
Guesnard House, David Cumming, Jr., architect, 25
Gulf City Oil Company Building, James H. Hutchisson, architect, 68
Gulf Coast Fair, 160
Gulf Coast Produce Company and Exchange, 182
Gulf Coast Ship Building Company, 206, 207

H

Haddon, William, architect, 107
Hale, C. S., 30
    sketch of cottage, **30**
Hall House, Stone Brothers, architects, **112**
Hamilton, Henry, 152
Hammel's Department Store, Stone Brothers, architects, 105
Hanlon Cottage, James H. Hutchisson, architect, 70-**71**
Harriet, 24
Harrod and Andry, architects, 78
Harvard Architecture School, 196
Haviland, John, architect, 41
Herman Shotgun, **90**, 91
Herndon Building. *See* Kirkbride Garage
Heustis, Dr. James F., 82
Hexastyle, 52
Hill, James, 25
Hilliard, George, 31
Historic Alabama Hotels and Resorts (James Sulsby), 83
Historic American Building Survey (HABS), 187
Hobart, Peter House (1776-1828), builder, 3, 5, 7-8, 10, 12, 14, 16-17, 20, 22, 37, 40, 211
    arrival in Mobile from Vermont, 3;
    property holdings, 5;
    marriage to Martha Steele, 5;
    Saucier family, 5-6;
    French and Spanish influence on Mobile, 6-7;
    Creole cottages and log cabins, 8-9;
    War of 1812, United States annexation of Gulf Coast, 10-12;
    elected to first city commission, 13,

reelected in 1815, 13;
fire of 1822, 15;
Bank of Mobile, 16;
T. J. Jarman's sketches of Hobart's courthouse, 16, 19, 20
Mobile County Courthouse, 17-20
Hollinger Bungalow, Hutchisson and Denham, architects, 154
Holmes, Nicholas, Sr., architect, 187
Home Industry Foundry, 68. *See also* Kling Foundry
Homer, Henriette Elkin (Mrs. C. L. Hutchisson, Sr.), 109
Houston, Pat, 52, 55, 60
HUD (Department of Housing and Urban Development), 205
Hulbert, George D., 107, 134
Hunley Building, 68
Hunley, 68
Hunt, Reuben Harrison, architect, 106, 163
Hutchisson, Clarence L., Jr., (1902-1993) architect, 53, 163, 176, 194-200, 202, 205-213, 215-216
Quinlivan House (1940), **194**;
early life and education, 195-196;
Muscatt House, **196**;
FDR's New Deal FHA, 197;
Booksch House, **197**;
Perkinson House's "expansion strip," 197;
FHA houses, 194, 197-200;
Phillips House, **198**;
Martin House, **198**, 199;
Wheeler House, **199**;
FHA apartment building, **200**;
Goldman House, **200-201**;
Evans House, 201, **202-204**, 205;
Neal House (Brewton, Alabama), **205**;
Orange Grove Complex, 205-**206**;
Mobile in World War II, 206-208;
in the Corps of Engineers, 206;
Municipal Airport, Bates Field Hangar, **207-208**;
Trinity Episcopal Church, **209**, 210;
Maryvale School, **210**;
Ogburn House, **211-212**;
portrait of, **212**;
Quinlivan House (1969), **213-216**
Hutchisson, Clarence Lindon, Sr., (1872-1953), architect, 88, 98, 103-115, 117-120, 122-123, 126-136, 138-145, 148-150, 152-156, 158-166, 168-185, 187-193
partnership with George Watkins, 87-88;
Trinty Episcopal Rectory, 98;

Maumanee House, **102**, 103;
early twentieth-century Mobile economy, 103-105;
increase of nonresident architects in Mobile, 105-107;
residential, commercial and religious buildings, 107-108;
designs in Alabama, Mississippi, Wisconsin, South Carolina and Panama, 108;
early life, 108-109;
McAdoo and Worley, 108-109;
P. J. Krouse partnership, moves to Mississippi, 109;
marries Henriette Elkin Homer, Clarence L., Jr., born, 109;
George Hall, **109**;
portrait of, **110**;
Watkins and Hutchisson, 110;
St. John's Episcopal Rectory, **111**;
Leinkauf School, 112-**113**, 114;
Watkins, Hutchisson and Garvin, 114;
Cawthon Hotel, **114-117**;
self-education and library, 115;
First National Bank, **118-119**, 120;
Black Mission Church, and Lily Baptist Church, 120;
Sha'arai Shomayim Temple, **120-121**, 122;
Hutchisson and Garvin, 122;
Lott House, 122-125;
Wilson House, **126**;
Poetz House, **127**;
Metzger House, 127-**128**;
Gordon House, 128-**129**;
Coleman House, 129-130;
Marsh House, **130**;
Walsh House, **130-131**;
Ashland Place development, 130-131;
Partridge House renovations, **131-132**;
Masonic Lodge (Brewton, Alabama), **132-133**, 134;
Knights of Columbus Building, **134-135**;
Mobile Infirmary, **136-137**;
Hutchisson and Chester, 138;
Vincent-Walsh House, **138-139**;
Arnold House, 139-**140**;
Masonic Home (Montgomery, Alabama), 140, **141-142**;
Hutchisson and Denham, 142;
St. John's Episcopal Parish House, 142, **143-144**, 145;
Baptist Church (Bay Minette, Alabama), **144-145**;

Robinson Memorial Parish House, **145-147**, 156, 184;
Rapier-Boone House, **148-149**;
Burke House, **150**, 157;
Ladd House, **150-152**, 177;
bungalows in Ashland Place and Flo-Claire, 152, **153-155**, 156;
Creagh House, **156-158**, 159;
Maddox House, **159-160**, 171;
Fine Arts Building, **160**;
County Poor House and Farm, 107, **161**;
Tanner Williams School, 161, **162**, 210;
Meridian City Hall (Meridian, Mississippi), 162, **163-164**;
Kirkbride Garage, **165-166**;
AT&N Railroad Station (York, Alabama), **166-167**, 168;
St. Charles Apartments, **168-169**, 170;
Warren House, **170-171**;
Christian House, **171-172**;
Christie House, 172-173;
McGowin House, **174**;
Frederick-Bender Log House, **174-175**;
Reaves House, later Casbah Restaurant, 175-**176**;
Long House (Atmore, Alabama), 177-178;
Gardiner House, **178-179**;
Rosen House, **179-180**;
workman's cottage and shotgun, **180-182**;
McGowin Memorial Mausoleum, **182-183**;
Mobile Hall Men's Dormitory (Spring Hill College), **183-184**;
Hutchisson, Holmes and Hutchisson, 184;
Methodist Church (Atmore, Alabama), 184, **185-187**;
Meredith House, **187-188**, 201;
Anderson House, **188-189**, 201;
Partridge House (1931), **190**;
Alabama State Docks Administration Building, **191**;
Chinese Gas Station, **192-193**, 208;
Hutchisson, James Flandin I (1806-1856), builder and architect, 22, 24-37
Mobile's flush cotton era, 22-25;
arrives in Mobile from Long Island, 25-26;
marriage to "Miss Brewster," mother of James Henry Hutchison, 26;
marriage to Ann B. Spenser, 26;

marriage to Amelia Graham, 26;
fire of 1841 and yellow fever epidemics of 1837-1843, 26;
"Ship's Joiner and House Builder," **26-28**;
cornice and roof of the Cathedral of the Immaculate Conception, 27, 36, **37**;
silver pitcher for work on Cathedral, **36**;
Tallapoosa contract, 27-28;
cottage construction during population explosion, 28-32;
commerical construction, 32-36:
    Burns and Riley store/residence, 32-33;
    Eslava and Dumée store/residence, 33-34;
    Eslava and Dumée warehouse, 34-36
Hutchisson, James Flandin II (1856-1926), architect, 52, 85-100, 158
a divided city struggles in the 1890s, 85-87;
Mobile society and Mardi Gras, 87;
finishing the facade of the Cathedral, 87;
field deputy for U. S. marshal, 88;
leaves Mobile for Chicago, 88;
early years and education in Mobile, 89;
designing the shotgun cottages, Victorian and Queen Anne, 90-99;
Scott's two-story house, 98-99;
Boone's house with "hot water and ...gas," 99-100;
St. Emanuel Methodist Episcopal Church, **100-101**
Hutchisson, James Henry (1830-1887), architect, 26, 37, 39-43, 45-66, 68-78, 80-83, 113, 158
son of "Miss Brewster," 26;
comes to Mobile from Long Island, 39;
during Mobile's "Golden Age," 39-40;
architects in Mobile, 40;
working for his father, 41;
advertisement in City Directory, **42-43**;
architectural education and library, 41-43;
in the Civil War, the Battle of Shiloh, and Reconstruction, 43-47;
sketch of the Battle of Shiloh, **45**;
architectural career, 47-51;

chief fireman and designer of Creole Fire Station, **49**, **50**, 51;
reconstruction and economic woes, 51-52;
three important churches:
    (a) Cathedral of the Immaculate Conception, 52;
    (b) St. Vincent de Paul, 53-56;
    (c) St. Bridget's Church, 56, **57**, 58, 77;
Italianate style of the Bernstein House, 59-60;
economic improvement in the 1880s, 60;
commercial buildings in the 1880s, 62-70;
cottages, **70-71**;
residential buildings in the 1880s, 70-76;
religious buildings and Spring Hill College in the 1880s, 76-82;
Hygeia Sanitarium, 82. See also Hygeia Hotel;
architectural accomplishments, 83
Hygeia Hotel, James H. Hutchisson, architect for annex, 82-83

I

Illinois Institute of Technology, 196
Innerarity, James, 8
Italian Renaissance, 58, 110, 111, 119, 160, 164, 170
Italian Revival, 51, 56, 108, 162

J

Jack arch, 50
James, Thomas, 25, 40
Jenny, William Le Baron, 89
Jett Brothers, 114
Jib doors, 198, 199
Johnson, V., architect, 87
Johnstone, Harry Inge, architect, 205
Judson, Lewis, 8, 16, 17
Junger's Drug Store, James H. Hutchisson, architect, **62**-63

K

Karwinski, Thomas, architect, AIA, 99
Kelley, William D., 47
Kenan House, 72, **73**
Kennedy, Joshua, 8
Keyes House (Sheffield, Alabama), James H. Hutchisson, architect, 74, 75, 76
Kilduff House, James Flandin Hutchisson II, architect, 93-95

Kings Wharf, 12
Kirkbride Garage, C. L. Hutchisson, Sr., architect, **165-166**
Kitchen House, 74-75
Kitchen-McMillian Country House, James H. Hutchisson, architect, 74-75
Kling Foundry, James H. Hutchisson, architect, **68**-69
Knights of Columbus, 87, 107
Knights of Columbus Building, Hutchisson and Garvin, architects, **134-135**
Knodel and Thomas, architects, 146
Krouse, P. J., architect, 109-110, 163, 164, 195

L

La Clede Hotel, 51, 118
La Tourrette Map of Mobile (1838), **23**. See also Maps
Ladd House, Hutchisson and Denham, architects, **150-152**, 177
Lancet arch, 100, 101
Lapretre, John, 16
Latin Cross, 144
Latrobe, Henry, architect, 41
Lauber Home and Carriage Shop, James H. Hutchisson, architect, **69**-70
Lavalle House, 7, 8
Lee, Thomas Helm, architect, 41
Lefever, Minard, 42, 73
Leinkauf Bank (1904, now destroyed), Stone Brothers, architects, 106, 119
Leinkauf School, Watkins and Hutchisson, architects, 112-**113**, 161
Lily Baptist Church, C. L. Hutchisson, Sr., architect, 120
Lindon, A. L., 60
Little House, James F. Hutchisson II, architect, **84**, **96-97**
Little, Peter, 72
Little Baptist Church of Orion (Pike County, Alabama), 56-57
Livingston, Aaron, 27
Lockwood, Frank, architect, 106
Long House, C. L. Hutchisson, Sr., architect, **177-178**
Lott House, Hutchisson and Garvin, architects, **122-125**, 126, 127, 207
Lowenstein Bank (1903, now destroyed), Stone Brothers, architects, 68, 106
Lowenstein Investors, 105,
Lyric theater (1906, now destroyed), Stone Brothers, architects, 106

M

McAdoo and Worley, architects, 108-109, 133
McCluskey, John, 49
McCreary and Slater, architects, 107, 133
McDermott, John F., 5
McDonald, March and Company, 53, 55
McDonald Place, 105
McGowin House, C. L. Hutchisson, Sr., architect, 174
McGowin Memorial Mausoleum, C. L. Hutchisson, Sr., architect, **182-183**
MacKenzie, Roderick, 7
McMillan family, 74-75
McNamara, J. T., 138
Maddox, Elmer, 156
Maddox House, Hutchisson and Denham, architects, 159-160, 171
Magnolia Cemetery, 182
Magnolia Sugar Refining Company, 51
Mansion House, 27, 35, **36**
Manucy, Bishop Dominic, 78
Maps:
    Goodwin and Haire Map of Mobile (1824), **15**;
    Gulf of Mexico Campaigns map (1813-1815), **12**;
    La Tourrette Map of Mobile (1838), **23**;
    Map of Mobile (1815), **13**;
    Map of Spanish Mobile (1809), **6**;
    Matzenger Map of Mobile (1888), **60**;
    Pauli 1891 Bird's Eye View of Mobile, **86**;
    Reconstruction of the South (1865-1877), **46**;
    Robertson Map of Mobile (1852), **21**;
    Robertson Map of Mobile (1856), **24**, **40**;
    United States map (1783-1803), **10**;
    United States map (1812-1822), **11**;
    United States Map of Claims and Cessions, **4**;
    Western Theatre of the Civil War (1862), **44**;
    William Johnson Map of Mobile (1905), **104**
March, William, architect, 183, 184, 191, 205
Mardi Gras, 87
Marsh House, Hutchisson and Garvin, architects, 128, **130**
Marshall, John, store, James F. Hutchisson, architect, 32
Marshall-Hixon House, 211
Martin, Clarence H., 89
Martin House, C. L. Hutchisson, Jr., architect, **198**
Marye, Philip Thorton, architect, 106
Maryvale School, Grey and Hutchisson, architects, **210**
Masonic Home (Montgomery, Alabama), Hutchisson and Chester, architects, 140, **141-142**
Masonic Lodge (Brewton, Alabama), Hutchisson and Garvin, architects, 108, **132-133**, 134, 142
Masonic Temple, Stone Brothers, architects, 105, **135**
Mastin, Dr. William, 82
Mather, James, 5
Matzenger Map, **60**. *See also* Maps
Maumanee House, C. L. Hutchisson, Sr., architect, **102**, 103
Maxwell automobile agency, 165
Mennonite Community (Yellow Pine, Alabama), 110
Meredith House, Hutchisson, Holmes and Hutchisson, architects, 187, **188**, 201
Meridian City Hall (Meridian, Mississippi), P. J. Krouse, architect, C. L. Hutchisson, Sr., consulting engineer, **163-164**
Methodist Church (Atmore, Alabama), Hutchisson, Holmes and Hutchisson, architects, 184, **185-187**
Metzger House, Hutchisson and Garvin, architects, **127-128**
Meyer, Ferdinand, architect, 51
Michael, Dr. Jacob, 82
Mills, Robert, architect, 41
"Miss Brewster," (Mrs. James Flandin Hutchisson, first wife, mother of James H. Hutchisson), 26
Mitchell Cottage, **92**
Mobile boundaries. *See* City boundaries
Mobile Commercial Register, 59
Mobile County Courthouse (1828), Peter House Hobart, builder, 16-20
Mobile County Probate Court, 17
Mobile Garden Club, 150
Mobile Hall, Hutchisson, Hutchisson, March, Downey and Roberts, architects, **183**, 184
Mobile Housing Board, 191, 207
Mobile Improvement and Building Company advertisement, **105**
Mobile Infirmary, Hutchisson and Garvin, architects, 107, **136-137**
Mobile Life Insurance Company, James H. Hutchisson, architect, 68
Mobile Register, 87, 88, 99, 101, 103, 107, 111, 112, 114, 117, 121, 122, 126, 134, 135, 137, 161, 168
Mobile Ship Building Company, 180
Mobile Steamboat Company, 24
Mobile Wooden Ware Company, 51
Monin, Louis, architect, 51
Monastery of the Visitation. *See* Convent of the Visitation
Monterey development, 133, 180-181
Morgan County Courthouse, **17**
Mottus, Catalina, 17
Mulligan, R. M., architect, 106
Municipal Airport, Bates Field Hangar, C. L. Hutchisson, Jr., architect, **207-208**
Muscatt House, C. L. Hutchisson, Jr., architect, **196**

N

Neal House (Brewton, Alabama), C. L. Hutchisson, Jr., architect, **205**
Neoclassical style, 18, 56-58, 72, 109, 110, 148, 157, 158, 174, 198
Neutra, Richard, architect, 209
Norrman, G. L., architect, 88, 106
Norton, F. 117
Nutt, Rush, 22

O

Oakdale development, 206
Oakleigh Garden Historic District, 93, 95, 107, 122, 152
O'Conner Cottage, James F. Hutchisson, builder, 31, 32
Odd Fellows, 87
Odd Fellows Lodge. *See* Southern Express Building
Ogburn House, C. L. Hutchisson, Jr., architect, **211-212**
Old City Hospital, James H. Hutchisson, architect for surgical wing, 82
Old Dauphin Way Historic District, 93, 95, 98, 107, 127, 168
Old House Journal, 173
Ollinger-Bruce dry docks, 86
Orange Grove Community, 86, 90, 105
Orange Grove Housing Complex, Johnstone, Hutchisson, Jr., March, and Van Antwerp, architects, 205-

Ordnance Depot, 39, 47, 83
Otts house, Hutchisson and Garvin, architects, 131

Overton, V. G., 91

P

Palladian window. *See* Window
Panton and Leslie Company, 5
Partridge House (1889), Rudolph Benz, architect; 1909 renovations, Hutchisson and Garvin, architects, 131-132
Partridge House (1931), Hutchisson, Holmes and Hutchisson, architects, **190**
Pauli 1891 Bird's Eye View of Mobile, Alabama, **86**. *See also* Maps
Pearson, George, architect, 106
Perkinson House, C. L. Hutchisson, Jr., architect, **197**
Perryman House, James H. Hutchisson, architect, 71, **72**, 73
Phelan and Delamare Company, James H. Hutchisson, architect, 60
Phillips House, C. L. Hutchisson, Jr., architect, **198**
Phoenix Foundry, 51
Pincus Building, Rudolph Benz, architect, 88
Pittfield cottage, James Flandin Hutchisson I, builder, 28-29, 30
Poetz House, Hutchisson and Garvin, architects, **127**
Pond, W. D., architect, 51, 59, 65, 108
Portier, Bishop Michael, 27, 36, 81
Pounsey Bungalow, C. L. Hutchisson, Sr., architect, 154, 155-156
Prairie School and Movement, 170, 173
Price, B. D., architect, 87
Prince of Peace. *See* Church of St. Vincent de Paul
Providence Infirmary, 106
Pugin, A. and Pugin, A. W., architects, 42
Pythian Castle, 107, 112

Q

Queen Anne style, 91-95, 97, 99, 108, 111
Quigley, A. M., 49
Quigley, Ann, 39, 44, 47
Quinlan, Bishop John, 52, 55
Quinlivan House (1940), C. L. Hutchisson, Jr., architect, **194**
Quinlivan House (1967), C. L. Hutchisson, Jr., architect, **213-216**
Quoining, 176, 184, 200

R

Railroads, 22, 47, 85, 107, 166, 191, 216
Raphael Semmes Company, 87
Rapier Cottage, 148
Rapier Tract, 122
Rapier-Boone House, Hutchisson and Denham, architects, **148-149**
Raulston, J. H., cottage, James H. Hutchisson, architect, 60
Reaves House, C. L. Hutchisson, Sr., architect, 175-**176**
Renaissance Revival, 77. *See also* Italian Renaissance and Italian Revival
Ricke, August, 42
Rivers and Harbor Act (1881), 85
Roberts-Staples Cottage, **31**, 32
Robertson Map of Mobile (1852), **21**. *See also* Maps
Robertson Map of Mobile (1856), **24**, 40. *See also* Maps
Robertson Metal Roofing Company, 208
Robinson Memorial Chapter House, Hutchisson and Denham, architects, **145-147**, 156, 184. *See also* Trinity Episcopal Church (1853)
Roche Funeral Home, 59
Rogers, George B., architect, 87, 107, 119
Rogers, Isaiah, architect, 16, 40
Roman Republic influence, 17
Romanesque Revival style, 58, 77; of Italy, 113; of France, 113, 121
Roofs:
 deck, 112, 151, 161, 177
 gable, 71-72, 75-76, 91, 93, 94, 100, 112, 151, 153, 155, 170, 171, 175, 176, 179, 181, 182, 184, 187, 188, 198, 200-201
 gambrel, 170, 171
 hip, 109, 112, 126, 137, 149, 151, 157, 161, 184, 189, 189, 201
 slate, 19, 35, 124
 tile, 137, 150, 193
 tin, 35
Rosalie (Natchez, Mississippi), 72
Rosell Blind Sash and Door Company, 97
Rosen House, C. L. Hutchisson, Sr., architect, **179-180**
Rousso's Restaurant, 69
Rudolph, Paul, architect, 209
Rush, Fonda K., 163

S

Sanborn Fire Insurance Map (1957), 143. *See also* Maps
Sanborn Map (1950), 59. *See also* Maps
Sanborn maps, 59, 99. *See also* Maps
Saucier, François, 5
Saucier, Jean Baptiste, 5
Savary, Marie Gabrielle, 5
Sayner and Allen, 180
Scattergood, B. S., 48
Scheible, P. C., architect, 107
Scott Shotgun, James F. Hutchisson, architect, **90-91**
Scott Two-story House, James F. Hutchisson, architect, 98-**99**
Seifert Company, 151
Seymour, Walter, architect, 106
Sha'arai Shomayim Temple, Watkins, Hutchisson and Garvin, architects, **120-121**, 122
Sherman Plaza, C. L. Hutchisson, Sr., architect, 168
Shotgun cottages, 90-92, 98, 104, 105, 168, 182
Simmons and Young Plumbing Company, 88
Sloan, Samuel, architect, 42, 53, 56, 77
Smith, B. B., architect, 106
Smith, Dr. D. E., 82
Sossaman Brothers, 93, 96
Southern Express Building, James H. Hutchisson, architect, **64-66**, 210
Southern Railway System, 85
Spanish Revival and Mission Style influence, 87, 106, 108, 133, 142, 144, 146, 175, 184
Spencer, Ann B., (Mrs. James Flandin Hutchisson I, second wife), 26
Spotswood Apartments, C. L. Hutchisson, Sr., architect, 168
Spring Hill, 5, 25, 68, 74, 98, 103, 187, 210-213, 216
Spring Hill College, 41, 59, **81**-82, 83, 106, 183-184
St. Bridget's Church, *See* Church of St. Bridget's
St. Charles Apartments, C. L. Hutchisson, Sr., architect, **168-169**, 170
St. Emanuel Methodist Episcopal Church, James Flandin Hutchisson II, architect, **100-101**
St. John's Episcopal Parish House, Hutchisson and Denham, architects, 142, **143-144**, 145
St. John's Episcopal Church Rectory, Watkins and Hutchisson, architects,

111
St. Joseph's Chapel, Downey and Denham, architects, 106
St. Louis Street Baptist Church, 1890 tower by James F. Hutchisson II; 1908 facade by C. L. Hutchisson, Sr., 101
St. Vincent de Paul. *See* Church of St. Vincent de Paul
Stark, Turner, 17
State Capitol at Tuscaloosa, Alabama, William Nichols, architect, **18**
State Street A. M. E. Zion Church, Watkins and Johnson, architects; facàde, James H. Hutchisson, architect, 76, 77, 78
Martha Steele (Mrs. Peter House Hobart), 5
Stephens Steamboat Company, 24
Stone Brothers, architects, 105, 111-112, 119, 134, 135
Storm, Albert J., architect, 136
Sturdivant Hall (Selma, Alabama), Thomas Helm Lee, architect, 41
Sullivan, Louis, architect, 89, 115
Sulsby, James, 82, 83
Swags. *See* Decorative designs
Swasey, A. M., 48

T

Tallapoosa, 27
Tanner Williams School, Hutchisson and Denham, architects, 161-**162**, 210
Tapia, Mr. and Mrs. Mark, 125
Taylor, James Knox, architect, 106
Tensaw, 24
Tetrastyle columniation, 72
Thomas, Mary Martha, 207
Three Mile Creek, 14
Togerson, Gustav, 164
Torrent Fire Company, 37
Townsley, Thomas, 16
Treaty of Ghent, 12
Triennial Book, 78
Triglyphs, 144, 157
Trinity Episcopal Church (1853), Willis and Dudley, architects, 40, 53, 145-147
Trinity Episcopal Church (1945), C. L. Hutchisson, Jr., reconstruction architect, **209**-210
Trinity Episcopalian Rectory, James Flandin Hutchisson II and C. L. Hutchisson, Sr., architects, 98, 108
Tuberculosis Sanitarium, C. L. Hutchisson, Sr., architect, 107
Tudor Revival, 127
Tunstall House, James Flandin Hutchisson II, architect, 98
Turner Building, James H. Hutchisson, architect, **63**, 67
Tuscan Villa, 41
Tuskegee Chapel, Paul Rudolph, architect, 209

U

United States Custom House, Ammi Burnham Young, architect, 40
United States Post Office, James Knox Taylor, architect, 106
Urban Renewal Program, 59

V

Van Antwerp, Cooper, architect, 205
Van der Rohe, Mies, architect, 196
Victorian Gothic Revival, 100
Victorian style, 61, 97-98, 148
Visitation Monastery. *See* Convent of the Visitation
Voussoirs, 55, 101, 116, 201, 214
Vincent-Walsh House, Hutchisson and Chester, architects, **138-139**

W

Wainscoting, 120, 121
Wainwright Building, Louis Sullivan, architect, 115
Walsh, Alabama, 139
Walls:
    exterior
        brick veneer, 33, 185, 198, 213
        concrete block veneer, 133, 191, 207
        granite, 183
        marble veneer, 183
        painted, 117, 198-199
        shingle, 181, 188, 190
        stone, 159, 171
        stucco, 133, 141, 146, 151, 157, 176, 178, 189, 191
        tongue-and-groove, 28, 94, 208
    interior
        plaster, 141, 197
        tapestry, 120
        wainscoting, 120, 121
Ward, John, 16, 17
Warren House, C. L. Hutchisson, Sr., architect, **170**-171
Watkins, George, architect, 61, 87, 110, 112, 122, 195
Watson and Johnson, architects, 76
Webb, Ezekiel, 20
Weeden House (Huntsville, Alabama), 9
Weinecker Apartments, C. L. Hutchisson, Sr., architect, 168
Wheeler House, C. L. Hutchisson, Jr., architect, 199
Wheelright, Edmond March, 114
Where Time Bears Witness to Sound Building, 69, 70
White Shotgun, James F. Hutchisson II, architect, **90-91**
Willis, Frank, architect, 40, 53, 209-210
Wilson, A. C., 27
Wilson, Augusta Evans, 136
Wilson House, **126**, 127
Wilson, L. N., 136
Wilson, Samuel, 5
Windows, 17, 19, 28-29, 32-33, 35, 50, 53-54, 58, 62-65, 67, 70-71, 73, 76, 80, 94-96, 99, 101, 103, 109-110, 113, 116-117, 120-121, 125, 128-131, 133-134, 177, 184-185, 189, 199-200, 202, 211, 214
    bay, 73, 99, 110, 116, 120, 129-130, 133-134, 202
    casement, 129, 155-156, 172, 174, 189, 199
    diamond shaped, 199
    lancet, 53, 54, 56, 101
    Palladian, 112, 123, 125, 126, 214-216
    pedimented, 156
    pointed, 76, 100
    sash, 29, 32, 71, 73, 99, 175
    segmental, 50, 63, 67
    semicircular, 19, 26, 64, 67, 76, 77, 113, 184-185, 186, 198
    showcase, 63, 103, 165
    slide-by, 131
Windsor Hotel, 210
Works Projects Administration (WPA), 187
Workman's cottage and shotgun, 180, **181-182**, C. L. Hutchisson, Sr., architect

Y

York Coleman Cultural Center, 166
Young, Ammi Burnham, architect, 40
Young Brothers, 60

About the Author

Elizabeth Barrett Gould is an Instructor Emeritus at the University of South Alabama where she founded and taught in the Art History Department. She was a major force in the establishment of the Mobile Historic Development Commission, the preservation agency of the City of Mobile. Her thorough training as an architectural historian provided her the tools to do a complete study of buildings in Alabama's port city. Her first work, *From Fort to Port, An Architectural History of Mobile, Alabama, 1711-1918*, was published by the University of Alabama Press in 1988.